PENGUIN BOOKS

The Japanese

Christopher Harding is the author of the widely praised *Japan Story: In Search of a Nation*, described by Neil MacGregor as 'Masterly. How much I admired it, what a lot I learned from it and, above all, how very much I enjoyed it'. Harding teaches at the University of Edinburgh and frequently broadcasts on Radio 3 and Radio 4.

CHRISTOPHER HARDING

The Japanese

A History in Twenty Lives

PENGUIN BOOKS

PENGUIN BOOKS

UK | USA | Canada | Ireland | Australia
India | New Zealand | South Africa

Penguin Books is part of the Penguin Random House group of companies
whose addresses can be found at global.penguinrandomhouse.com.

First published in Great Britain by Allen Lane 2020
First published in Penguin Books 2022
007

Printed and bound in Great Britain by Clays Ltd, Elcograf S.p.A.

The authorized representative in the EEA is Penguin Random House Ireland,
Morrison Chambers, 32 Nassau Street, Dublin D02 YH68

A CIP catalogue record for this book is available from the British Library

ISBN: 978-0-141-99228-0

www.greenpenguin.co.uk

MIX
Paper | Supporting
responsible forestry
FSC
www.fsc.org   FSC® C018179

Penguin Random House is committed to a
sustainable future for our business, our readers
and our planet. This book is made from Forest
Stewardship Council® certified paper.

To Kae, with love.

Contents

PART ONE

From Heaven to Heian: Mythological Time to 1185

PART TWO

From Many to One: 1185–1582

PART THREE

Floating Worlds: 1582–1885

PART FOUR

New Lives: 1868–1941

PART FIVE

'Forward with Culture': 1942 to the Present

List of Maps

List of Illustrations

A Note to the Reader

Japanese names appear in this book in the standard Japanese order of family name followed by given name. Macrons are used to indicate elongated vowel sounds except in the case of place names that are well established in English (e.g. Tokyo).

Introduction

*A beautiful day, like an English June day, but hotter. Though
the Sakura (wild cherry) and its kin, which are the glory of the
Japanese spring, are over, everything is a young, fresh green.
Wooded hills, small picturesque valleys, clear blue wavelets
brightened by the white sails of innumerable fishing-boats.
Streams abound, and villages of wooden houses and temples
with strangely curved roofs. It is all homelike, liveable, and
pretty, the country of an industrious people. Not a weed is to
be seen.*

Isabella Bird, Unbeaten Tracks in Japan *(1880)*

*The serving maid picked up slice after slice from this living
fish, which, although alive, had been already carved. There is
a refinement of barbaric cruelty in this which contrasts
strangely with the geniality and loving nature of the Japanese. The miserable object with lustrous eye looks upon us
while we consume its own body . . .*

Christopher Dresser, Japan: Its Architecture,
Art, and Art Manufactures *(1882)*

Who are the Japanese? To the Victorian-era travellers who launched
and shaped the West's modern love affair with Japan, they appeared
to be a people of polar opposites. The haughty samurai and the obse-
quious peasant inhabiting the same Edenic landscape. The kindly
innkeeper and his fish-torturing staff. The demure and modest geisha
wrapped in layer after layer of luxurious kimono, and the denizens of
mixed-sex bathhouses – naked and shameless, laughing and leering.

There followed a century of Western fascination and puzzlement, as Victorian expectations went largely unrevised. Distant in geography, culture and language, 'the Japanese' tended to be imagined en masse and in the abstract; bound at some level, it was assumed, to a basic consistency in their ideas and values – if only these could be accurately discerned. A mid twentieth-century generation struggled, as a result, to reconcile Japanese aggression in the Asia-Pacific with a culture of peaceful reflection – temples and shrines, gardens and lakes – so precious that Kyoto was passed over for atomic destruction in 1945. Post-war media portrayals of Japan took contrast and contradiction as their keynotes: kimono-clad women riding the futuristic bullet train; grey identikit salarymen wandering through noisy, neon-lit neighbourhoods devoted to fun, fantasy and joyful abandon.

Only with Japan's late twentieth-century emergence as a cultural superpower – manga, anime, film and pop, food, literature and video games – did a more nuanced picture begin to emerge: of diverse regions and neighbourhoods, classes and professions; competing ideologies and rival visions of the future. 'Who are the Japanese?' was steadily revealed as a question asked not only by outsiders, but by the Japanese themselves. In fact, it is the challenge and conundrum at the heart of almost two millennia of recorded history. How do you take a 3,000-kilometre-long archipelago, running from frozen wastelands in the north down to subtropical rainforest in the south, and make it 'Japan'? How do you persuade people who live in very different ways – their languages, loyalties and beliefs – to come together and call that place home? It is a task that has taxed some of the most influential figures in Japanese history: emperors and shoguns, shamans and warlords, poets and revolutionaries, scientists, artists and adventurers.

And it taxes Japan's leaders today, as the country's population ages and shrinks. Ever fewer workers struggle to support an ever larger proportion of the elderly and infirm – financially and physically. The choices are stark: more babies, more robots or more immigration. The third option challenges long-held ideas in Japan about 'the Japanese' as a reasonably homogenous bunch, a social or even spiritual whole. How does such a club adapt to welcome new members?

As the Japanese public and their politicians ponder the question

'Who are the Japanese?' with an anxious eye to the future, this book asks the same question, looking back. One of the best ways to understand a country's history is to explore its questioning of itself. All the more so with a place like Japan, where talk is often held to be cheap – no one who is *kuchi bakari*, 'all mouth', can expect much respect – and where the greatest attention is paid instead to exemplary lives: ideas and ideals not merely thrown idly around, but embodied and tested.

The Japanese delves into twenty such lives: people who either pushed Japan's great self-questioning onwards, building and transforming the nation in the process, or who ended up reflecting in some profound way the changing world around them. Most have since become woven into Japan's national fabric, their accomplishments relived in stories, plays, songs, films and literature. Together, these twenty people and their times offer us an intimate introduction to a vast and compelling history.

We begin in Part One at the beginning, with the world – millions of years in the making – of the first known, named person in Japanese history: the shaman queen Himiko (*c.*170–248). We encounter Prince Shōtoku (573–621), celebrated for his welcoming into Japan of Chinese and Korean culture: writing, poetry and Confucian morality; the austere wonders of Buddhist art and architecture; and the foundations of the imperial court life that is still practised in Japan today. Emperor Kanmu (737–806) was one of Japan's most powerful and creative monarchs. Murasaki Shikibu (*c.*973–unknown) was its first – perhaps the *world*'s first – novelist, fictionalizing in *The Tale of Genji* the colourful Heian (Kyoto) court life that she knew so well.

Part Two takes us from the collapse of courtly Japan, through long years of civil war and regional rivalry, to the country's unification once again. The acclaimed political operator Hōjō Masako (1157–1225) kept a newly powerful class of samurai warriors in line, ensuring that her husband's legacy as Japan's first shogun lived on past his early death. Shinran Shōnin (1173–1262), 'St Shinran', helped to shift the focus of Buddhism in Japan away from the mountain-top exertions of a priestly elite and towards a simple, practical faith for all, with a premium placed on purity of heart. Two contrasting characters move us towards unification: the actor and playwright Zeami Motokiyo (1363–1443) whose Nō plays became central to Japan's self-image as a nation of serious refinement; and Oda Nobunaga (1534–82), who combined strategy, newly imported firearms and a willingness to shed blood on an epic scale to begin knitting Japan's national community back together.

In Part Three, we enter the world of early modern Japan. The global voyages of Hasekura Tsunenaga (1571–1622?) reveal a country whose leaders were determined at first to embrace the world – seafaring Europeans in particular – but who soon decided to take a stricter approach to border control. This helped to foster a thriving popular entertainment culture in the heyday of Japan's Tokugawa shoguns, celebrated and satirized by the literary superstar Ihara Saikaku (1642–93). Sakamoto Ryōma (1835–67), a master swordsman and strategist, was part of a swashbuckling, revolutionary generation that helped Japan to begin making its way in a dangerous, hyper-competitive modern world. Kusumoto Ine (1827–1903) lived and worked through that period of great transition.

Part Four presents contrasting contributions to the raising up of a modern Japan, through to its downfall in 1945. Shibusawa Eiichi (1840–1931), the 'father of Japanese capitalism', helped to fund and steer momentous changes in the lives of the Japanese, while a mixed, confusing upbringing in Japan and the United States made the feminist educator Tsuda Umeko (1864–1929) an astute observer of the results. The pioneering chemist Ikeda Kikunae (1864–1936) tickled modern palates, at home and abroad, with *umami* (MSG), helping in the process to foster a fresh Japanese internationalism in science and commerce. Lastly, through the life of the poet and activist Yosano Akiko (1878–1942) we discover how easily cosmopolitanism can falter, in Japan's case giving way to a rethinking of its place in the world – and in Asia especially – that had devastating consequences.

A generation of Japanese who survived that devastation came to associate gruelling early post-war years with the child star Misora Hibari (1937–89) and her music, characterized by a cheerful optimism mixed with a fear of American entertainment wearing away at the Japanese soul. Part Five of *The Japanese* homes in on the power of culture in shaping Japan and its international image down to the present day. From Hibari we move on to the 'god of manga', Tezuka Osamu (1928–89), whose early, iconic creations coincided with Japan's

4

rebirth across the 1950s and 1960s. Politicians still counted for something, of course, none more so than the 'shadow shogun' Tanaka Kakuei (1918–93) who became synonymous with the stunning yet somewhat shady successes of Japan's Liberal Democratic Party (LDP), which has rarely been out of power since 1955.

We end on an uncertain symbol of a people passing through uncertain times. Owada Masako (1963–) gave up a promising career with Japan's Ministry of Foreign Affairs to marry into the imperial family in the early 1990s, hoping to serve her country as a royal diplomat. Difficult years followed, for Masako as Crown Princess and for Japan as a whole, with a struggling economy, tense relationships in East Asia and a population cultured and comfortable, yet increasingly concerned about what the future might bring. Now, as Empress, Masako seeks to help Japan's oldest institution to do what it always has done, in different ways at different times: serve as a centre of gravity, a source of support, and part of the answer to the perennial question – 'Who are the Japanese?'

N

The Japanese Archipelago and Mainland Asia

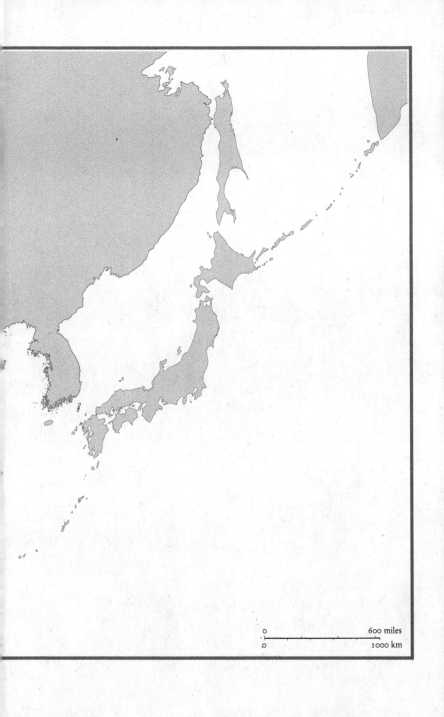

0   600 miles

0   1000 km

PART ONE

From Heaven to Heian:
Mythological Time to 1185

I
Himiko

(卑弥呼)

c.170–248

Shaman Queen

Statue of Queen Himiko in Kanzaki City, Saga Prefecture, Japan.

The people agreed upon a woman for their ruler. Her name was Himiko. There were few who saw her. She had one thousand women as attendants, but only one man. He served her food and drink, and acted as her medium of communication. She resided in a palace surrounded by towers and stockades, with armed guards in a state of constant vigilance.

With these words, a late third-century Chinese chronicle called the *Records of Wei* (*Wei Chih*) gives us the first known, named person in Japanese history: a mysterious queen, ruling from fortified seclusion between around 190 and her death in around 248.

There was as yet no such place as 'Japan', no such people as 'the Japanese'. Instead, the islands of the archipelago were dotted with independent settlements, some of them rice-farming chiefdoms large enough to be called 'countries' by the Chinese. The greatest by far was Queen Himiko's realm of Yamatai. Hegemon over around thirty other chiefdoms, it stationed officials in each whose job it was to keep an eye on people and maintain them in what the Chinese chronicle describes as 'a state of awe and fear'.

Awe and fear of what, exactly, is not clear – but there are clues. The Chinese referred to Himiko's people as the 'Wa', using an ideograph whose meanings include 'dwarf-like' and 'obedient'. The former reflects the basic disdain with which Chinese observers treated all non-Chinese, not just the people of the archipelago. But the latter chimes to a degree with what Chinese writings and the archaeological record reveal of how the Wa lived. Theirs was a world of powerful forces, seen and unseen, amidst which one fared best by knowing one's place. Weapons represented one sort of force, wealth and social status another. A third was an intelligent vitality, coursing through nature and capable of shaping human affairs.

Himiko seems to have enjoyed command of a kind over the first two of these forces, and a shamanic connection with the last. Much about her life is obscure, and will probably always remain so. But her era and its origins offer some first suggestive glimpses of the people who would one day become 'the Japanese'.

*

Himiko's world was 15 million years in the making. It began with the splitting off from the Eurasian continent of an archipelago some 3,000 kilometres in length, consisting eventually of four large islands alongside thousands of smaller ones. At least two land bridges linked across to these islands, including one from Siberia in the north and one from the Korean peninsula in the south. Alternately submerged and revealed, as fluctuating global temperatures caused sea levels to rise and fall, these bridges made of the water between islands and continent at times a sea and at times a vast open lake.

Across these land bridges travelled life of all kinds. The archipelago's richly varied climate – subarctic in the north, down to subtropical in the south – combined with successive phases of worldwide warming and cooling to support, at one time or another, populations of woolly mammoths, elephants, horses and giant deer, brown bears and bison, moose and wolves, monkeys and tigers.

It supported human beings, too, for at least 30,000 years before Himiko's society arose. They lived for the most part on the largest of the islands, today's Honshū, avoiding its thickly forested mountainous spine in favour of the more hospitable coastal plains. There were also populations further south, down to what are now the islands of Okinawa, and to the north in Hokkaidō. These earliest peoples used stone tools, including edge-ground axes, to hunt and forage in the vicinity of the rocky shelters they called home.

From around 14,500 BCE, life began to change. Across more and more parts of the archipelago, people could be found storing and boiling food in clay pots. It proved to be a valuable innovation as large mammals dwindled in number and then disappeared, the result of a warmer environment and more effective hunting techniques – using domesticated dogs alongside bows and arrows. Smaller game helped to keep meat on the menu, and the art of fishing with nets, hooks and harpoons became highly developed. But nuts and berries became more important than ever, along with plant-life so tough that it was only edible as part of a Neolithic stew.

This 'Jōmon' culture, named after the rope patterns found on its pottery, consisted early on of small pots carried around by hunter-gatherers on the move. These gave way to larger vessels as people started to settle down into communities of between five and several dozen simple thatched pit homes, arranged in a horseshoe shape around a central meeting area. Clothes were created from hemp, mulberry bark and animal skin, while rafts and dug-out canoes were developed to help communities trade with one another by sea. Most of these early mariners clung closely to the coastline. But some – adventurous spirits or poor navigators – ended up on the Korean peninsula, around 200 kilometres from the western coast of Kyūshū, the most southerly of the archipelago's four main islands.

It was via links with mainland Asia that two fundamental elements were added to life on the archipelago, preparing the way for societies like Himiko's. The first was rice. Cultivated along China's Yangtze River since 5000 BCE, it entered the archipelago in short-grain form around 500 BCE, quite possibly brought by migrants from the Korean peninsula. Alongside revolutionizing people's diets and requiring of them new, cooperative farming techniques, rice came to serve as a form of wealth and a source of social status: you could accumulate it, store it and live well off the proceeds.

You might, now and again, also have to fight for it. And this was where the archipelago's second great Asian import came in handy: metallurgy, in particular iron and bronze objects, along with the techniques and raw materials required to create them. Far into the future, people on these islands digging deep for evidence of their ancestors would find swords embedded in badly damaged – sometimes decapitated – skeletons. One individual, either spectacularly unlucky or stubbornly unwilling to die, was found with no less than a dozen arrows protruding from what was left of his body.

This new era, beginning around 500 BCE, became known as 'Yayoi' after an area in eastern Japan where examples of its distinctive pottery were later found. It saw a falling population on the archipelago start to rise again, thanks both to rice cultivation and the use of iron, not just for dispensing with enemies, but for fashioning better farming tools. While some communities retreated to high altitudes, possibly in the hope of avoiding aggressive lowland neighbours, successful settlements on the plains grew to hundreds and later thousands of people, protecting their perimeters with moats, embankments of earth and watchtowers.

Himiko's time had come, on an archipelago that now boasted somewhere between half a million and 4 million inhabitants. Her chiefdom of Yamatai, built on warfare and wealth, was a place where the difference between high and low could be immense. A rich man might have four or five wives, dress in silk, live in a large hut with a floor raised some way off the ground, and adorn himself and his home with precious bronze objects – from bracelets to mirrors. Poorer sorts would move to the side of the road to let him pass. They would pay him taxes. And if they had to talk with him, they would do so while squatting or kneeling, both hands pressed to the ground. 'This', concluded a seemingly rather impressed Chinese observer featured in the *Records of Wei*, 'is the way they show respect.'

The Chinese also found the climate sympathetic. Located at the meeting point of several tectonic plates, much of the archipelago was always at risk of earthquakes and volcanic eruptions, to add to a drenching summer monsoon and mighty autumnal typhoons. But all this notwithstanding, residents of the archipelago's mid-section, from northern Kyūshū up into Honshū, enjoyed an annual cycle of four distinct and generally bearable seasons. The Chinese declared Himiko's chiefdom a 'warm and mild' place, where a person could go about barefoot and live off vegetables all year round if they wished – though rice, fish and meat were of course available too, all served on bamboo trays and eaten with the fingers. Men were dressed in spun fabrics that fastened at the side, while women donned simple, single coverlets by slipping their heads through a hole in the centre. There was alcohol aplenty, but little evidence of life getting out of hand. 'Women are not loose in morals, or jealous,' says the *Records of Wei*; 'there is no theft, and litigation is infrequent.'

Most people may simply have been too tired to transgress. Chinese observers found them busy in their fields, cultivating grains, rice and hemp, alongside the mulberry trees required to keep silkworms. They spun, they wove and they hunted. Men went diving for seafood, tattoo-ing their faces and bodies to ward off dangerous or troublesome sea-creatures. Anyone with enough energy left to consider breaking Himiko's 'strict and stern' laws would be mindful of the consequences. A light offence could lose a man his wife and children 'by confiscation'. A more serious infraction would see him, his household and some of his extended family 'exterminated'.

Here was a place tightly governed, and marked by a social hierarchy so vivid and entrenched that, in the words of the *Records of Wei*, 'some men are vassals of others'. When Himiko sent envoys to China in 238, amongst her gifts to the Wei Emperor were ten 'slaves', possibly prison-ers of war: four male and six female. Chinese chroniclers shared with the Wa a low sense of the worth of such people, itemizing them in their records alongside two pieces of cloth, 'each twenty feet in length'.

The woman addressed by the great Wei Emperor as 'friend' and 'Queen of the Wa' was around twenty years old when she came to power, in 190 CE or thereabouts. Himiko had somehow emerged on top after a period of war, but no one knows whether she seized that power or was given it, and whether she ruled directly or preferred to delegate. She seems never to have married, but the *Records of Wei* mentions a younger brother who 'assisted her in ruling the country'. It may be that he dealt with day-to-day affairs while she was left alone and aloof to do what few others could: commune with forces in and beyond nature, for the good of her realm.

Little is known of Himiko's appearance, but her people produced textiles using looms while trading materials, technologies and fashions with communities on the continent. So Himiko may well have worn a one-piece belted tunic and long underskirt similar to those found in parts of the Asian mainland, sometimes swapping them for items that she is mentioned in the *Records of Wei* as receiving from the Wei Emperor: white silk, alongside brocade of blue and crimson.

The Chinese regarded Himiko as a shaman of extraordinary power, helping to deliver Yamatai out of chaos and into peace by using 'magic and sorcery' to 'bewitch' the population. This places her in a long tradition of shamans on the archipelago, stretching back perhaps as far as the middle of the Jōmon era when evidence first emerges that is suggestive of people seeking to reach out to spirits or energies with whom they share the world. Small figurines were crafted in clay, up to 30 centimetres high, with exaggerated eyes, breasts and buttocks, alongside heavy bellies. Known as *dogū*, some were given pride of place atop piles of stones. A number appear to have been deliberately marked or smashed, with pieces buried in separate locations: rituals, possibly, of injury, burial and exhumation that were intended to parallel or even influence cycles of death and rebirth – and with them the fertility of crop and creature. By the late Jōmon era, some human skeletons were being marked with red ochre and reburied in flexed positions, the paint suggesting blood, or a life force, alongside the completion of a life cycle from a baby curled up in sleep to an adult curled up in death.

Women or men who specialized in rituals like these may have been the forebears of the shamans of Himiko's day, one of whose most important roles was to guarantee the food supply. It is thought that they would call down a spirit to inhabit some feature of the natural landscape – a tree, a mountain or a waterfall – thereby giving that spirit a form in which people could worship and placate it, in the hope of avoiding disaster and persuading nature to cooperate. Other rituals were performed at structures used for rice storage. Raised off the ground to protect the crop, these designs came over time to signify sacred space.

Whether out in her chiefdom or within the walls of her palace, Himiko may well have used bronze bells and mirrors in her rituals – possibly hanging them from her belt as a sign of status. Bells have been found from her era whose designs include depictions of shamans in ecstatic states, while the worn backs of excavated bronze mirrors suggest that they were hung about a shaman's person as a sign of their status. Himiko is said to have received one hundred such mirrors as a gift from the Wei Emperor. The people of the archipelago had yet to produce a written account of themselves and their place in the world. But when they eventually did, a few centuries after Himiko, mirrors were revealed as enjoying pride of place, accompanying shamanic rituals involving music and dance.

At some sacred sites from Himiko's time, mirrors and bells have been found grouped alongside bronze weapons – an indication, perhaps, that

Himiko was not unique, but rather was one of the greatest of a powerful caste of people: leaders in whom political and shamanic power was combined, overseeing a culture in which 'obedience' was a matter not just of following human rules but of living in line with the larger order of things.

Alongside Himiko's power, her subjects' behaviour and what they appeared to believe about the world fascinated Chinese observers. When someone died, the Wa would mourn for at least ten days. They would wail and lament; sing, drink and dance. Then, at the end of it all, family members would all take a purifying bath. Purity and pollution seem to have been central elements in Yamatai life in all sorts of ways, from the apparently sacred status of some rivers, springs and waterfalls to the way that lengthy and uncertain sea voyages across the archipelago were planned:

> They select a man who does not comb his hair, does not rid himself of fleas, lets his clothing get as dirty as it will, does not eat meat, and does not lie with women. This man behaves like a mourner and is known as the 'mourning keeper'. When the voyage meets with good fortune, they all lavish on him slaves and other valuables. In case there is disease or mishap, they kill him, saying that he was not scrupulous in observing the taboos.

People also used divination, to seek understanding and to reconcile themselves with the world. This included scapulimancy: the shoulderblade of a deer would be placed in a fire, a person's dilemma described, and then the pattern of fissures formed in the baked remains would be examined for signs of what ought to be done. The choice of deer bone, and the prevalence of deer imagery on Yayoi-era pottery and bronze bells, suggest that this particular animal was regarded as special. This was certainly the case a few centuries later, when some of the archipelago's earliest writings featured stories of rice seeds being planted in deer's blood and miraculously germinating overnight.

*

By whatever combination of earthly and otherworldly power she achieved, Himiko seems to have presided over a long and peaceful interlude in Yamatai's history. After her death, around 248, her people are said to have fallen quickly into conflict once again. 'A king was placed on the throne,' claims the *Records of Wei*, 'but the people would not obey him ... assassination and murder followed.' Order was restored only when Himiko's niece, a girl of thirteen, was made ruler of Yamatai. People may have regarded her as sharing something of Himiko's nature and powers, and thus capable of rescuing their world from chaos once again.

Himiko was an awesome presence in death, as she had been in life: a burial mound some 145 metres in diameter was constructed for her tomb. No evidence has so far been found that human sacrifice was ever practised on the archipelago, so it is probably less a matter of historical fact than a measure of her greatness in Chinese eyes that the *Records of Wei* has the Queen of the Wa being joined on her journey into the next world by no fewer than one hundred of her attendants.

That tomb has not yet been found, and the precise location of Yamatai remains a mystery. Read literally, third-century Chinese directions for getting there would land a person somewhere out in the Pacific Ocean. Read with a little more leeway for distance and detail, two strong contenders emerge – both of them on dry land, and both with implications for the origins of 'Japan' and 'the Japanese'.

The first possibility links Himiko with her people's recent past. If her remains lie at a site on the island of Kyūshū, as some claim, that places Yamatai close to the entry point for the continental imports and expertise that helped to give rise to Yayoi culture. The second possibility links Himiko instead to Honshū, and to the future. From central regions of this largest island in the archipelago were soon to emerge a series of extraordinary achievements in art, architecture, poetry, religion, law and statecraft, for which the people of the islands would become known first in Asia and later around the world.

2
Prince Shōtoku
(聖徳太子)

573–621

Founding Father

Prince Shōtoku, with his two sons.
Woodblock reproduction of an eighth-century painting.

[His mother] was suddenly delivered of him without effort. He was able to speak as soon as he was born, and was so wise when he grew up that he could attend to the [legal] suits of ten men at once and decide them all without error. He knew beforehand what was going to happen . . .

Prince, war leader, statesman. Seer, scholar, patron of the arts. A gentleman, a humanitarian, and an easy birth to boot. The man known to posterity as Prince Shōtoku often appears less as a historical figure than a character in a fairy tale. In many ways that is exactly what he was. His wondrous deeds come down to us for the most part via one of the archipelago's oldest works of literature. And we cannot be entirely sure that he ever existed.

And yet the 'Prince of Holy Virtue' commands our attention because all the stories told about him are, in their essentials, true. They go right to the heart of a remarkable transformation taking place across the sixth and seventh centuries in central Honshū: the coming together of powerful families, disparate gods and ideas from near and far in the fashioning of the archipelago's first recognizable state.

Celebrated as that state's founding father, Prince Shōtoku didn't so much create it as find himself created *by* it, becoming a hook on which it hung its most precious claims about itself. Above all, where this new state owed an enormous debt to Chinese and Korean civilization – for its politics and poetry, its laws and religion, its food, clothing and architecture – the Prince is recalled as a cultural diplomat of rare judgement and vision. He is the archipelago's first great integrator-in-chief. His life takes us from settlements and chiefdoms to the very cusp of 'Japan'.

*

Prince Shōtoku's origins lie in Queen Himiko's demise. In the decades following her death around 248 CE, burial mounds of the kind in which she was interred began to multiply. These *kofun* ('ancient graves') were built to house great leaders' wooden or stone coffins, alongside the tools and treasures – swords, shoes, mirrors, jewellery – that marked their status in this life and may have been thought useful in the next. *Kofun* became progressively grander over time until one appeared around the middle of the 400s that was nearly 500 metres long, 300 metres wide, and rose thirty-five metres above the surrounding landscape. Known as the Daisen Kofun, from the air this awesome structure looks like a keyhole – a circle atop a triangle – set amidst lush greenery and surrounded by three broad moats. It may be the final resting place of 'Nintoku', one of the greatest leaders of a chiefdom in the Yamato basin, in south-central Honshū, which across the fourth and fifth centuries was expanding and steadily consolidating its status as regional hegemon.

Tall figurines called *haniwa*, crafted from reddish-brown clay and arrayed along the external slopes of burial mounds – perhaps as a form of spiritual protection – give us a flavour of how this power was accrued. Farmers brandish hoes. Women carry water vessels on their heads. Whether this up-and-coming Yamato chiefdom was an outgrowth of Himiko's Yamatai or a geographically distant realm that rose as hers receded, it relied on the extraordinary wealth that came from controlling richly fertile tracts of rice land. Horses saddled for journeys, and men helmeted and armoured for war, reveal the serious military capability purchased with the proceeds. Other *haniwa* suggest a regime that prospered by honouring the spirits and making alliances, often intermarrying with smaller but strategically important chiefdoms. We find female shamans with ritual headdresses and mirrors; musicians and wrestlers.

By the turn of the sixth century, these Yamato chiefs had taken to calling themselves 'Great Sovereigns' (*ōkimi*), binding their allies ever closer by bestowing upon them lucrative – and hereditary – roles and titles in their own administration. In this way, wealth and power began to depend more upon family, or 'clan', than territory. And what started out as a confederation of chiefdoms, with Yamato at its head, steadily morphed into a single polity stretching all the way from Kyūshū in the south-west up into central Honshū.

Never before had so much of the archipelago come under the control, however tentative, of a single leadership. Yet life at the royal court, moving from place to place around the Yamato heartland, was fragile and fractious. The 'Great Sovereigns' were rarely so great that they didn't have to worry about intrigue, murder and violent uprising at the hands of the influential cluster of rival clans now gathered close around them. How, then, to keep the show on the road? How to govern on this scale? How to gain and maintain legitimacy amongst people up and down the archipelago, and even beyond?

Finding solutions to these problems proved to be the work of two long and frequently bloody centuries, culminating in two great creative acts in the early 700s. The first was the building of a capital city in 710, at a place called Nara. The second was the finalizing, under official auspices, of two chronicles: the *Record of Ancient Matters* (*Kojiki*) in 712 and the *Chronicles of Japan* (*Nihon Shoki*) in 720. The oldest surviving pieces of writing to come out of the archipelago, neither offered a straightforward chronology of the Yamato chiefdom's rise. They were both less and much more than that. Combining myth, history and high ideals, they furnished the people of the archipelago with some of their earliest exemplars, their founding heroes and heroines, while striving above all to answer that profound, perennial question – 'Who are we?'

The groundwork had been laid in the centuries since Himiko, as some of the mysterious, impersonal forces with which she communed steadily acquired names, functions and favoured features of the landscape – often great rocks or trees – which they were thought to inhabit on a seasonal or a more or less permanent basis. Clan heads linked themselves with local spirits, or *kami*, taking personal responsibility for the rituals that ensured adequate rainfall and good harvests. Some went as far as 'adopting' particular *kami* as ancestors, with the Yamato clan choosing a female solar deity called Amaterasu. She was worshipped at Ise on the eastern coast of south-central Honshū, at a site facing towards the rising sun.

The Yamato clan then went one very significant step further. They took a rich oral tradition of *kami* stories from around the archipelago and wove them into a single fabric, producing in effect a family history, running from the moment of creation down through generations of *kami*, including Amaterasu, into their own times. This became the substance both of the *Record of Ancient Matters*, which bursts with poetry, song and saucy anecdote, and the *Chronicles of Japan*, with its attempt at a more sober ordering of time – closer to the Chinese chronicles in which Queen Himiko had featured.

The 'Great Sovereigns' now began to style themselves as 'Heavenly Sovereign': *tennō*, usually rendered in English as 'emperor'. The *Chronicles of Japan* read this new self-designation right back into the distant past. It described an Age of the Gods giving way to a line of divine emperors of Japan, beginning with the mythical Emperor Jimmu in the seventh century BCE. From 201 CE to 269, an Empress Jingū was said to have ruled the land, following the death of her husband Chūai, the fourteenth emperor. The compilers of the *Chronicles of Japan* equated Jingū with the 'Queen of the Wa' mentioned in the *Records of Wei*, sidestepping potential complications by avoiding any use of the name Himiko. By the 500s and 600s, rulers begin to appear in the chronicle for whom there is strong historical evidence.

Allied clans of the Yamato were worked into this grand mythohistorical mix. Their place in the earthly pecking order found itself mirrored in the position of their adopted clan *kami*, within a hierarchical pantheon that featured Amaterasu at its apex. There was always the risk in such a strategy that allies – both human and divine – might feel underrated or under threat. For all that the *Record of Ancient Matters* and the *Chronicles of Japan* treated Yamato rule as a cosmic inevitability, they also hinted at serious bumps along the road as the new state coalesced. It is at just such a moment of crisis that we first encounter Prince Shōtoku, working his diplomatic magic.

As told in the *Chronicles of Japan*, the trouble began in 552, when an envoy from the Korean kingdom of Paekche arrived at the Yamato court bearing an impressive gold and copper statue of the Buddha, along with a collection of scriptures.

A thousand years had passed, by this point, since the historical Buddha, Siddhartha Gautama, was said to have laid out his 'Four Noble Truths' at a deer park near Varanasi: namely, that human existence is a mass of suffering and frustration; that our appetites and attachments make it so; we can end this situation; and the means of doing so is the Noble Eightfold Path. Centuries of contact with other Indian and Chinese ideas had helped to transform these insights into an enormously rich and varied set of cosmologies, rituals and art forms. But aside from perhaps a few pockets of practice here and there, Buddhism was unknown on the archipelago. And it was controversial from the start. The *Chronicles of Japan* reports that opinion amongst powerful families at court was divided, in 552, over whether or not to welcome the newcomer. The Mononobe clan feared the wrath of the native gods, the *kami*, while the rival Soga clan argued – successfully – that Buddhism should be adopted on a trial basis. Members of their clan would perform rituals in front of this new statue, and see what happened.

What happened was a disastrous epidemic, allowing the Soga's opponents to claim that the *kami* were indeed offended by this interloper. The statue was duly thrown into a canal and a newly built pagoda was burned to the ground. A second attempt at adoption in 584 again met with natural disaster. This time a Buddhist image, a pagoda and a temple were all set on fire, while three Buddhist nuns were stripped and flogged.

There was politics at play here. The Mononobe's influence at court rested on their specialist ritual role worshipping the *kami*. The Soga clan, for their part, seem to have been descended from some of the many Korean migrants who brought with them to Yamato valuable expertise in everything from metallurgy and medicine to irrigation and administration. The Soga perhaps saw in Buddhism another element of the advanced culture of the peninsula, to be welcomed like the rest. For the Mononobe, here was an immigrant god, sponsored by an immigrant clan – and both were quite possibly after their jobs.

In the *Chronicles of Japan*'s version of events, it is just as hostility between the Soga and Mononobe descends into bloodshed in 587 that Prince Shōtoku appears, quite literally riding to the rescue. He is said to have been born in 573, to parents with both Yamato and Soga blood running through their veins: the great sovereign Yōmei (reigned 585–7) and his consort Princess Anahobe no Hashihito. The *Chronicles of Japan* refers to Prince Shōtoku as 'Prince Umayado', a nickname of sorts relating to the story that his mother's effortless delivery of him occurred near to a stable door (*umayado*). The teenage Prince is depicted now taking to the battlefield on horseback, fighting for the Soga in a short but epoch-making conflict. As enemy arrows rain down, and the Soga are pushed back for a third time, the young Prince thrusts himself forward. 'Will we be beaten?' he cries. 'Let us make a vow!' With that, he cuts down a tree, whittles tiny images of four Buddhist gods known as the Heavenly Kings, places them in his top-knot, and proceeds to pray:

> If we are now made to gain the victory over the enemy, I promise faith-
> fully to honour the Four Heavenly Kings, guardians of the world, by
> erecting to them a temple with a pagoda.

The tide of battle abruptly turns. The Soga forces win out. The prom-ised temple is built, and the Prince now begins to emerge as the leading light in a period of Buddhist-inspired enlightenment across the Yamato kingdom.

The puzzle of how closely Prince Shōtoku's legend fits a real historical figure, who achieved some or all of the things with which he is credited, may never be solved. But the Soga clan do indeed seem to have enjoyed ascendancy after 587, capable in 593 of placing their favoured candi-date on the throne. The *Chronicles of Japan* refers to her as 'Empress Suiko', although the title of *tennō* ('Heavenly Sovereign') was prob-ably not in regular use at this point. According to the *Chronicles of Japan*, Prince Shōtoku was her nephew, appointed as regent by her in 594 and granted 'general control of the Government . . . entrusted with all the details of administration'.

The Prince's battlefield vow in 587 proved that by bringing in new, Buddhist gods Yamato was not risking its divine protection, but rather reinforcing it. Where rulers like Himiko had interceded with forces or *kami* for the protection and prosperity of their realms, the role of Yamato sovereigns was now expanded to include the worship of Buddhist deities to the very same ends. In practice, much of this work was delegated to Buddhist monks and nuns, who recited sutras at the temples that began to spring up around the country. Some forty or more were commissioned during Prince Shōtoku's lifetime alone, the most famous being Hōryū-ji. Said to have been completed under the auspices of the Prince himself in 607, it later burned down and was rebuilt in the late 600s or early 700s. Hōryū-ji went on to become a centre for the veneration of Prince Shōtoku, celebrated in modern times as the world's oldest wooden building.

Cosmic protection was to remain the primary role of Buddhism for many years to come. It would be a while before it evolved into a religion of the people. But the impact of the new temple complexes on people's imaginations was nevertheless enormous. With a network of shrines to the *kami* yet to develop, these were some of the first permanent structures in the archipelago to be dedicated to ritual worship. A typical temple complex consisted of several heavy wooden structures, each topped with a cascade of tiles, situated within a walled enclosure. One of these buildings would be a multistorey pagoda, housing sacred relics and tall enough to dominate the surrounding landscape.

These complexes, including colourful, awe-inspiring temple interiors, were based on Korean and Chinese designs. Many were actually built by Korean hands, with Buddhist monks doubling as carpenters and wood-carvers, roof-tile makers, sculptors and wall-painting artists. Builders, buildings and the rituals that went on within – the wearing of robes, the use of incense and chanting – combined to make a deep impression, putting down permanent cultural roots.

Prince Shōtoku is credited with making all of this possible by replacing ad hoc continental contacts up to this point with something far more systematic, establishing relations around the year 600 with a newly reunified China under the Sui dynasty. Alongside priestly and practical expertise, the Prince drew deeply and thoughtfully on Chinese and Korean scholarship – in Buddhism, classical Chinese philosophy, history, law and administration. According to the *Chronicles of Japan* and the cult that grew up around his memory, Prince Shōtoku was one of very few people in Yamato to see beyond Buddhism's ritual potential and appreciate its philosophical depths. He delivered lectures on Buddhism at the Empress's request – one talk apparently lasted for three days – and composed sutra commentaries that were later sent to China as part of diplomatic missions.

One of the most celebrated products of all this learning was the archipelago's first constitution, credited to the Prince in 604, though thought in fact to have been the work of a later generation. Consisting of seventeen articles, it was less a legal document than a series of principles on which an ideal state should be based. They included harmony and good faith, the acceptance of differing views and the recognition of merit. Feuding and gluttony were to be strenuously avoided, as were flattery, covetous desire, sycophancy and anger. Government officials were enjoined to place the greatest value on hard work, public-spiritedness, 'decorous behaviour' and open debate. Above all, people were encouraged to show reverence for Buddhism and for imperial commands.

These were more than mere airy ideals. Power in Yamato depended upon family, spanning blood ties and claims of godly descent. Prince Shōtoku was suggesting something revolutionary: that leadership and privilege should henceforth be conferred on the basis of merit and moral conduct instead. He instituted, for court officials, a Chinese-style system of 'cap-ranks' similar to one that was in use in Korean kingdoms at this time. There were twelve in all, each named after a Confucian principle – virtue, benevolence, propriety, sincerity, justice, and knowledge – and each distinguished from the others by the design of the silk cap worn by a person of that rank.

Anyone aspiring to rise through the new ranks would require, on top of the personal qualities laid out by Prince Shōtoku, a familiarity with Chinese. The lingua franca of East Asian Buddhism, it was also essential to continental statecraft and diplomacy. From the Prince's time onwards Yamato saw a rapid increase in Chinese literacy amongst the courtly elite, making possible the compilation of the *Chronicles of Japan* (in literary Chinese) and the *Record of Ancient Matters* (in a more experimental linguistic blend of Chinese mixed with an early attempt to render spoken Japanese in Chinese script).

Renewed contact with China had all sorts of other impacts besides. Courtiers began to adopt Chinese clothing: for women, a tunic emphasizing a flowing, plaited skirt beneath; for men, a loose, longer tunic with a stand-up collar, atop a pair of trousers tied with a sash. Imported Chinese dress codes meant that, as with the administrative caps, certain colours could be worn only by people of a certain status. Early in the 700s, a new 'clothing code' required that all robes be fastened left over right, according to Chinese practice – the origins, some have argued, of what would one day become the kimono.

The archipelago now embarked on a long-term love affair with Chinese styles of poetry. A highlight of diplomatic banquets, the composition of short lines capturing a moment or a mood became a source of cultured competition at court. A few decades after the *Record of Ancient Matters* and the *Chronicles of Japan* were completed, the first poetry anthology appeared: *The Ten Thousand Leaves* (*Man'yōshū*), featuring more than 4,000 poems composed between the mid-600s and mid-700s and taking for their subject matter the lives of courtiers and the coarser-born alike. The islands, of course, had their own pre-existing poetic traditions. But as in ritual and statecraft, so in the worlds of fashion and literary pursuits the great theme of this era was the integration of the foreign and the domestic.

This was also the case for music and dance. Native traditions included *kami* songs, folk songs and drinking songs, alongside singing competitions that would end in carnal revelry. Accompaniment was provided by varying combinations of flutes, drums, bells and rattles. To these domestic traditions was added – probably as early as the 400s, but gathering pace during and immediately after Prince Shōtoku's era – a range of new instruments, songs and dances from mainland Asia. Within the Prince's lifetime the most important newcomer, from Paekche, was *gigaku*. Taught at Buddhist temples and performed at court and elsewhere, this was dance-drama using brightly coloured masks of animals, including lions and horses, alongside famous historical figures and caricatures of barbarians and kings. Later on came a form of dance called *bugaku*, with more of a narrative focus, accompanied by the koto, a horizontal stringed instrument that was laid on the floor and plucked.

The Prince is said to have made a modest musical contribution of his own, burnishing in the process his Chinese-style credentials as a man of virtue and filial values. One day in 613 he was walking along when he noticed a starving man lying in the road. He stopped and gave him food and drink. Taking off his own robe and covering the man with it, he wished him peace and composed for him a song of lament:

> Alas! for
> The wayfarer lying
> Hungered for rice . . .
> Art thou become
> Parentless?
> Hast thou no lord
> Flourishing as a bamboo?
> Alas! for
> The wayfarer lying
> Hungered for rice.

When the man died not long afterwards, Prince Shōtoku had a burial mound built for him. Suspecting that this had been no ordinary human being, the Prince sent one of his attendants back to check the mound. The tomb was found to be empty, with only the Prince's robe remaining. Writers in later years linked this story to those of Jesus Christ and the Buddhist monk Bodhidharma, both of whom left empty tombs and appeared to people after their deaths. Some went further, wondering whether the Prince's many talents might have extended to helping bring the dead back to life.

As if to counter any impression that Prince Shōtoku was responsible for too slavish an approach to continental culture, his legend extends to one final celebrated act. The Chinese at this point still regarded their neighbours across the water – the 'Wa', using the same demeaning ideograph as always – as a vassal people. Given all that the Yamato kingdom was achieving, this would clearly no longer do. So around 608 the Prince drafted a letter for Empress Suiko to send to her counterpart in China. It began with the words: 'The Child of Heaven [tenshi] of the land where the sun rises sends a letter to the Child of Heaven of the land where the sun sets.' Other sources credit the Prince with conjuring the term later chosen by the Yamato sovereigns to refer to themselves – 'Heavenly Sovereign' (*tennō*) – and with trying it out for size on the Chinese around this time.

The Yamato kingdom had not yet formally adopted the name 'Nihon' ('root of the sun'), the appellation which, passing through various Asian and European languages, eventually gave the world 'Japan'. And given the vantage point of mainland Asia, the 'land where the sun rises' could be interpreted as no more than a geographical observation. But there were already connotations here of cosmic importance – of a newcomer destined to outshine an old-timer and, above all, the audacious assumption of parity between the two sovereigns. The Chinese Emperor appears to have understood. 'This letter from the barbarians', he is said to have complained to one of his staff, 'contains improprieties. Do not call it to my attention again.'

*

What some refer to as the broad 'Yamato period', beginning around the mid-200s with grand burial mounds suggestive of up-and-coming chiefdoms, gave way in 710 to the 'Nara period', named after the location of an impressive new imperial capital established that year. Laid out on a Chinese-style grid pattern and featuring buildings with stone bases and tiled roofs, the archipelago's first great capital city became home to 100,000 people – out of a national population of around 6 million. When the *Chronicles of Japan* was completed ten years later, in 720, it confirmed Prince Shōtoku as the person who had laid the city's cultural and political foundations.

Nara became the focal point of the sort of centralized and professionally managed bureaucratic state, based on Chinese-inspired criminal and administrative codes, that the Prince had envisaged. Government was split into two branches. The Great Council of State (Dajōkan) featured a Chancellor, Ministers of the Left and the Right (each responsible for various specific ministries) and four senior counsellors. The Office of Deities (Jingi-kan) managed rituals and shrines for the *kami*. A parallel network of Buddhist temples was meanwhile emerging, home to monks and nuns who were regarded essentially as state bureaucrats to be trained, regulated and charged with reciting sutras for the good of the realm.

The realm, encompassing the southern two-thirds of Honshū and most of Kyūshū, was divided up into around sixty provinces, and from there into districts and villages. Villagers paid taxes in kind: a combination of rice and vegetables, raw materials, labour and military service – all of which helped to fund and secure a courtly culture in Nara that was ever more firmly rooted in the Chinese imports facilitated by the Prince. People across the land were encouraged to keep a careful eye on their neighbours as a way of promoting virtuous behaviour: a cheap and effective means of surveillance.

Not everything turned out as the Prince might have liked. His hoped-for meritocracy was conspicuously absent. Family feuding remained intense, with the Soga clan overthrown in the mid-600s and many more violent comings and goings thereafter. When career-minded young men went to study the Confucian classics at Nara's State Academy (Daigaku-ryō), they did so knowing that districts and villages were controlled largely by influential local families, while provincial governorships were handed out to major clan allies – the country's emerging aristocracy. Talented individuals of lowly stock might work their way up temple hierarchies as Buddhist monks or nuns, but otherwise birth trumped graft every time.

The impact upon the imperial institution of this heavy focus on family would be profound over the centuries to come. The Yamato sovereigns had achieved something remarkable in remaking themselves as divine emperors, establishing in the sixth and seventh centuries an imperial line that is still going strong in the twenty-first. But the feeling in the realm never went away that they were really just one elite family amongst others. When their earthly fortunes faltered, other families would be quick to muscle in.

For now, however, the emperors enjoyed considerable authority, advertising their divine descent ever more forcefully. Imperial edicts were not personal missives, they were drafted and promulgated by the Great Council of State. But from the reign of Emperor Tenmu (673–86) onwards they opened with the words: 'Hear ye the edict of an emperor who is a manifest *kami*'. Emperors also boasted their own armed forces. Clan chiefs had been successfully turned into imperial military commanders, with each province required to raise and maintain a unit of at least 1,000 men and the realm's roads shored up to accommodate swift and easy troop movements.

The *Chronicles of Japan*, completed at the beginning of this golden era of Sinicized, centralized imperial governance, made clear in its treatment of Prince Shōtoku's passing the immense debt owed by the new state to the great diplomatic and integrating feats that he had come to represent:

Spring, 2nd month, 5th day [621]

In the middle of the night the Imperial Prince died in the Palace of Ikaruga. At this time all the Princes ... as well as the people of the Empire [mourned him]. The old, as if they had lost a dear child, had no taste for salt and vinegar in their mouths. The young, as if they had lost a beloved parent, filled the ways with the sound of their lamenting. The farmer ceased from his plough, and the pounding woman laid down her pestle.

They all said: 'The sun and moon have lost their brightness; Heaven and Earth have crumbled to ruin: henceforward, in whom shall we put our trust?'

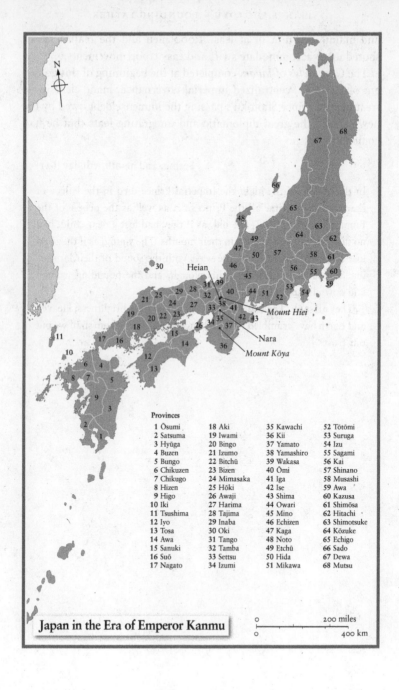

N

30

Heian

Mount Hiei

Nara

Mount Kōya

Provinces

1 Ōsumi	18 Aki	35 Kawachi	52 Tōtōmi
2 Satsuma	19 Iwami	36 Kii	53 Suruga
3 Hyūga	20 Bingo	37 Yamato	54 Izu
4 Buzen	21 Izumo	38 Yamashiro	55 Sagami
5 Bungo	22 Bitchū	39 Wakasa	56 Kai
6 Chikuzen	23 Bizen	40 Ōmi	57 Shinano
7 Chikugo	24 Mimasaka	41 Iga	58 Musashi
8 Hizen	25 Hōki	42 Ise	59 Awa
9 Higo	26 Awaji	43 Shima	60 Kazusa
10 Iki	27 Harima	44 Owari	61 Shimōsa
11 Tsushima	28 Tajima	45 Mino	62 Hitachi
12 Iyo	29 Inaba	46 Echizen	63 Shimotsuke
13 Tosa	30 Oki	47 Kaga	64 Kōzuke
14 Awa	31 Tango	48 Noto	65 Echigo
15 Sanuki	32 Tamba	49 Etchū	66 Sado
16 Suō	33 Settsu	50 Hida	67 Dewa
17 Nagato	34 Izumi	51 Mikawa	68 Mutsu

Japan in the Era of Emperor Kanmu

0   200 miles
0   400 km

3
Emperor Kanmu
(桓武天皇)

737–806

Boundary Pusher

Portrait of Emperor Kanmu (painted *c.* sixteenth century),
held in Enryaku-ji Temple, Shiga Prefecture, Japan.

To advance not at all, and then to dismiss the troops – what kind of reasoning is there in this plan of Our generals? We know that it is because Our generals fear the ferocious rebels that they remain in garrison. They cleverly employ words to avoid facing their crimes. Nothing can surpass this in disloyalty.

Such was the verdict of Emperor Kanmu on a notorious military debacle in 789, suffered at one of the far frontiers of his realm, in north-eastern Honshū. From an imperial force claimed by court chroniclers to have numbered in excess of 50,000 men, a number of detachments had been sent across the Koromo River to attack the home territory of a 'barbarian' leader by the name of Aterui. The soldiers set about their task enthusiastically, managing to burn down some 800 homes spread across fourteen villages. But then things started to unravel.

Based on a Chinese model, the imperial army was organized to fight mostly on foot. They used wooden shields for protection and deployed against their enemy a combination of bows and arrows, spears, and catapult-like devices built on top of mobile platforms. Aterui's forces, by contrast, consisted of skilled archers mounted on horseback, capable of launching volleys of arrows before galloping away out of reach. They now counter-attacked, harassing Kanmu's men into a hasty and disorganized retreat back across the river. Nearly 300 imperial soldiers were killed or wounded in the fighting, while more than 1,000 drowned. Another 1,250 ended up fleeing the scene half-naked, having survived in the water only by letting go of their weapons and wrestling their armour from their bodies.

The whole thing was a disgrace, as far as the Emperor was concerned. Born in 737, Kanmu had ascended the throne in 781, becoming Japan's fiftieth emperor according to the traditional line of succession going back to the mythical Emperor Jimmu. Japanese emperors tended to have a number of official consorts. It was a useful way of maintaining alliances with important clans, but a source of endless conflict over which of an emperor's children – by which wife – would be named heir. Kanmu's half-brother had initially been designated Crown Prince instead of him. Kanmu's Korean ancestry on his mother's side perhaps held him back; only later was the succession altered in his favour.

Kanmu proved to be an excellent monarch. As a former Head of the State Academy – Nara's training centre for future officials – he was well placed to operate the levers of a centralized imperial system of government whose inspiration the *Chronicles of Japan* credited to the great Prince Shōtoku. And where that system was not to his liking, Kanmu found ways of working around it. With the Dajōkan, or Great Council of State, threatening to become the means by which elite clans like the Fujiwara could compromise imperial power, Kanmu dealt with vacancies there, when they arose, either by installing members of his own family or by leaving the posts empty.

This keeping of the clans at bay helped Kanmu to become one of the most powerful emperors in the archipelago's history, a worthy contemporary of Charlemagne at the other end of the Eurasian continent. He epitomized the kind of forceful imperial leadership, seen on and off between the late 600s and mid-800s, which was capable of pushing important boundaries in a country by this time referred to in official correspondence as 'Nihon' (Japan). Kanmu expanded and shored up his country's frontiers. He advanced its religious and artistic imagination, and he corralled its wealth and manpower into the establishment of its greatest city.

*

Alongside Kanmu's unprecedented political and military authority ran what his chroniclers recalled as a powerful dislike of 'literary floweriness'. Here was a man not to be failed, and certainly not to be plied with unlikely excuses or poetic protestations. Kanmu's military commanders discovered all this to their cost in the wake of the humiliation at the Koromo River:

Government losses are nearly 3,000! What is there to be joyous about? You say, 'Wherever the heavenly troops were sent, there were no strong enemies before them. In their homes in the caves along the sea and bays, no more will there be human smoke; in their nests and holes in the mountains and valleys only ghost fires can be seen.' These are only floating words; they far exceed reality.

As to the sending of victory reports to court, these should be made <u>after</u> the rebels have been levelled and merit made to stand. Without advancing into the depths of their territory, you boast that you have destroyed their villages and rush to proclaim your joy. Is this not too shameful?

Had Kanmu's commanders taken their leader's preference for straight talking and forensic analysis more seriously, they might have tried a different tack in their reports – admitting failure and blaming it on the raw materials they were given to work with. Theirs was, after all, merely a conscript army. Four years in the military – one served in the capital, three on one of the frontiers – was part of the price that a man paid for the honour of being an imperial subject. The rest of the time he would farm his state-allocated plot of rice, labour on public works projects when required (up to sixty days a year), pay his taxes and behave himself.

It didn't always make for an easy life. Population pressure on the land could be heavy. Outbreaks of famine and disease were not unknown. And conscription tended to compound economic hardship. Little of the military equipment lining the bottom of the Koromo River after 789 had been paid for out of courtly coffers. A conscript was expected to feed, clothe and equip himself on the basis of an official kit-list – including a bow, bow-strings, arrows, quiver, two swords, leggings and boots – whose proper fulfilment could easily bankrupt a family.

When it all became too much, some farmers chose to flee to the north-east of Honshū in an attempt to escape imperial reach. Others journeyed in the same direction as official colonists: they were sent by the state during the 700s as part of a boundary-pushing exercise in which new forts were established – a combination of garrison, granary and administrative centre – and farmers were required to break and till the land around them.

Both sorts of migrant ended up in conflict with the older inhabitants of this part of the archipelago. They were a mix of hunter-gatherer and agriculturalist clans, lumped together as 'barbarians' and 'savages' by a Japanese state whose approach to outsiders was yet another of its cultural borrowings from China. In the words of the *Chronicles of Japan*:

> Amongst these savages the Emishi are the most powerful. Their men and women live together promiscuously, there is no distinction of father and child. In winter they dwell in holes, in summer they live in nests. Their clothing consists of furs, and they drink blood. Brothers are suspicious of one another. In ascending mountains they are like flying birds; in going through the grass they are like fleet wolves.
>
> When they receive a favour, they forget it, but if an injury is done them they never fail to revenge it. Therefore they keep arrows in their top-knots and carry swords within their clothing . . . If attacked, they conceal themselves in the herbage; if pursued, they flee into the mountains. Therefore ever since antiquity they have not been steeped in the kingly civilizing influences.

The present trouble with these 'Emishi' had begun in 774, when the old policy of slow and steady colonization, combined with some judicious alliance-making, was brought to an end by an imperial order to 'strike down the barbarians'. Emperor Kanmu inherited the resulting conflict, its painfully slow progress and even more painful costs becoming the bane of his early reign.

A small victory was won in 801–2, when a new military commander by the name of Sakanoue no Tamuramaro managed to put sufficient pressure on Aterui to persuade him and another prominent Emishi leader to negotiate their surrender. But where Emishi prisoners taken in this way were usually dispersed across Japan, serving as slaves of the nobility or living in their own segregated communities, these two high-profile prisoners ended up losing their heads. Kanmu and his advisers had had enough of the north.

A few years later, Kanmu ended the Emishi campaigns altogether, reluctantly allowing parts of north-eastern Honshū to remain beyond his reach. The fighting had become one of two great 'sources of suffering in the realm', as one of his advisers put it. The other was the new capital city growing up around them.

Almost immediately upon ascending the throne in 781, Kanmu had decided to transfer his court to a new location. In the past, emperors had moved around for a variety of reasons. Some thought that a new era should begin in a new place, and ideally in a more impressive palace than their predecessor: this was a matter not merely of self-regard, but of advertising one's role as the 'sacred centre' of the realm. Others found themselves facing a famine or epidemic, and sought to escape this combination of physical threat and spiritual contagion by upping sticks − literally, in terms of valuable timber structures, which could be taken down and reassembled elsewhere. Semi-regular uprisings by armed rivals offered a third compelling rationale for a hasty relocation.

Kanmu, in the end, found himself having to move home not once but twice. He first transferred his court from Nara to an area called Nagaoka, in 784. But it was quickly beset by political assassination, suicide, famine, flood and disease, persuading Kanmu to seek out a more auspicious location. This he did on horseback in 793, under cover of a 'hunting trip' on which he was joined by his royal diviners.

They found what they were looking for around fifty kilometres north of Nara. The topography ticked all the boxes. There were mountains to the north, west and east, offering excellent defensive potential. Chinese geomantic requirements for pleasing the gods of the four quadrants were also met: a mountainous north, a roadway to the west, a river to the east, and a large area of water to the south. The inauspicious north-east, from which it was said demons might invade, was guarded by the formidable Mount Hiei. Added to all this was rich, naturally irrigated rice-growing soil, timber aplenty in the hills, good access via river to the Inland Sea (separating the islands of Honshū, Shikoku and Kyūshū), and a generally flat central area on which to build without too much preparatory work required.

If there was a catch, it was the climate. The site was located in a basin, meaning that summers and winters would not be much fun for residents: alternating intolerably hot and humid weather with bitter cold. Kanmu endured his own first winter there in 794. From the confines of a palace that was still under construction, he issued a grand edict announcing the new location for the imperial capital alongside his choice of official name. It was to be called Heian-kyō: 'Capital of

Peace and Tranquillity'. Most Japanese would one day know it simply as 'Capital City' – in Japanese, 'Kyoto'.

A city destined to be home to Japan's emperors for more than a thousand years started life on a relatively modest scale. A rectangular-shaped grid ran for five and a half kilometres from north to south, and nearly five kilometres from east to west. Wide avenues ran along both axes, paralleled by narrower lanes in between. Most buildings were limited to a single storey, meaning that residents suffering with the climate could at least claim the consolation of fantastic views – lush, forested mountains, whose seasonal changes of colour became a favourite theme for the writers who soon flourished in Kanmu's new capital.

And this really was Kanmu's capital. The north end of Heian-kyō was dominated by a 'Greater Imperial Palace' that sprawled across nearly 7 per cent of the city's total land area, and whose construction, alongside that of associated princely residences, accounted for up to three-fifths of central government expenditure during Kanmu's reign. Provincial workers, here to pay their imperial labour tax, were kept busy erecting around 200 buildings, towers and corridors – including fourteen separate gateways, of which the most important was the Suzakumon: the 'Gate of the Vermilion Sparrow'.

This was both the Emperor's home and his place of business. A residential compound was located at the north end of the palace complex, while government offices and meeting areas, including the three buildings that comprised the Great Council of State, were laid out to the south. A large area of greenery, the 'Park of the Divine Spring', was maintained nearby for imperial banquets, entertainment and the occasional spot of hunting and fishing.

Southwards from the palace, all the way through the city, ran Suzaku Ōji. Possibly the broadest boulevard in the world at the time at around ninety metres wide, and terminating in the famous Rashōmon gate (two storeys high and painted red and white with a green roof), it was lauded in song for its beautiful willow trees:

> Light green they shine,
> Dark green they shine,
> Stretching into the distance as far as the eye can see,

They glitter like jewels.
Oh, how they glitter – those low-hanging boughs
Of the willows on Suzaku Ōji!

In the centre of the city lay two shopping areas, where business was based mostly on barter and items for sale included everything from rice and fruit to writing brushes, medicinal herbs and suits of armour. Fine accommodation was created for visiting foreign dignitaries, in the hope of striking favourable trade deals, while aristocratic residents settled into expansive villas whose exquisitely kept gardens and ponds were fed from the city's waterways – so numerous that Heian-kyō quickly became home to hundreds of bridges. Most of the population, estimated at around 100,000 people in the city's early years, lived rather more modestly and were involved, directly or indirectly, in some kind of service to the state and the aristocratic class: from keeping accounts and guarding prisoners to brewing *sake*, weaving silk and reviving heat-stricken humans or their pets.

Heian-kyō had no perimeter wall worthy of the name, because Kanmu had no earthly enemies worthy of the name. Concerned instead with cosmic vulnerability and defence, he was quick to send tributes to the Upper and Lower Kamo Shrines, situated in the feared north-easterly direction, in order to seek the protection of the *kami* enshrined there. This offering of tributes soon morphed into an annual night-time ceremony in which priests called out to the gods in darkness, bidding them to come down into specially created structures of sand and pine logs. From there, the *kami* were transferred into small *sakaki* trees, to be carried into the main sanctuary of the shrines. This accomplished, the shrines were illuminated and public festivities were held for the *kami*'s amusement.

These festivities grew in scale, year on year, until the Kamo Festival became the major event in Heian-kyō's social calendar. A Grand Imperial Emissary and a specially selected imperial princess would travel to the two shrines, the former to present tributes including dances and horses, and the latter to worship there – just as a member of the imperial family worshipped at Amaterasu's Ise Shrine, to whose level the Kamo Shrines were now elevated. Both the emissary and the princess travelled with glamorous retinues. Senior courtiers rode on horseback or rumbled along inside ox-drawn carriages lavishly adorned with hollyhock flowers, accompanied on their journey by musicians and dancers. The whole city turned out to watch the spectacle, with vantage points varying according to the decorum demanded by one's status. The higher-born sent someone ahead to save a good parking spot for their carriages. Humbler sorts roamed rooftops and the branches of tall trees.

Solicitous of the *kami*, Kanmu was rather more sceptical about the role that Buddhism might play in the welfare of his city and his country. One of the reasons for leaving Nara behind after he became Emperor had been its powerful, even overbearing Buddhist institutional presence: from great temples, grown wealthy and excessively independent of imperial and clan patronage, to a population of monks so large that Kanmu's father had striven to weed out any who were living in the capital illegally and have them returned to the provinces whence they came. If rival clans were one perpetual threat to imperial power, Buddhism had come to represent a second. And Kanmu was determined to do something about it.

One of Buddhism's most powerful backers after Prince Shōtoku had been Emperor Shōmu (reigned 724–49). A mixture of personal devotion and desperate pragmatism, in the midst of a devastating smallpox outbreak in 735–7, had led him to establish a protective nationwide network of temples and nunneries: one of each, in every province. The awesome Tōdai-ji in Nara was built to serve as the central temple for this network and as home to an enormous sixteen-metre gilded bronze statue of the celestial Buddha Vairocana. Its casting, said to have required 338 tons of copper and 16 tons of gold, nearly drove the nation into bankruptcy. The statue's dedication in 752, during which its eyes were ceremonially opened, had been one of the events of the era, attended by no fewer than 7,000 courtiers and 10,000 monks.

Alongside keeping the country safe and furnishing some of its great early aesthetic achievements, Buddhism also became a way for talented individuals born into families of modest means to acquire education and enter public service. Some outstandingly wise and compassionate figures emerged in this way, amongst them a monk by the name of Gyōki (668–749) who was celebrated for his preaching and his practical aid to poor farmers – notably a number of precious irrigation projects – alongside his work as an imperial adviser.

Yet some clergy seemed to treat Japan's legal restrictions on monastic behaviour – from taking wives to lending money and holding private property – less as a series of prohibitions and more as a to-do list. Temples loaned money to farmers, then took their land when they defaulted on repayments. One temple was said to be operating as a pawnbroker, charging an annual interest rate of 180 per cent. The biggest fear was of monks playing politics, potentially giving rise to an anti-imperial perfect storm of eloquent preaching, deeply impressive ideas and vestments and rituals, hostile clan backing and popular discontent about the direction in which the world was heading. This had yet to happen, but in the 760s a mercurial monk called Dōkyō had managed to persuade Emperor Shōmu's daughter and successor to grant him progressively greater influence in government. Amidst rumours of intimacy with the Empress, he eventually sought the throne itself, thwarted in the end only by vehement courtly opposition and by the Empress's death.

Kanmu fought back against all this on several fronts. He banned the establishment of 'private temples', a practice that was often less about devotion than tax-avoidance: institutions claiming to conduct rituals for the good of the realm were exempt from contributing to its coffers. And he banned existing temples from receiving donations without permission. At the same time he opened up temple property to provincial audits (and possible confiscation), and set the maximum interest rate for a temple loan at a comparatively reasonable 10 per cent. Kanmu clamped down, too, on clergy fathering children, claiming to be able to work miracles and engaging in 'black magic in the mountains with the aim of harming their enemies'. All the while, he tried to raise the bar for people wishing to become monks or nuns. Character and learning were given renewed importance, the latter tested via rigorous examination.

But Kanmu's most consequential move was the one he made against the supremacy of the Buddhist establishment in Nara, which was made up of six major sects. In this he was helped by a monk called Saichō. Born in 767 and ordained at Tōdai-ji in 785, Saichō swapped what he saw as the corruption of contemporary Buddhism for an austere life on Mount Hiei – a rare move in his day. When Kanmu moved his capital to the area in 794, he came to hear of Saichō's life on Hiei and his study of Tiantai Buddhism. Struck by the potential of the latter as an alternative to the squabbling Nara sects, Kanmu allowed Saichō to travel to China to learn more.

Saichō arrived in China in 804, returning to Japan the next year having studied these and many other Buddhist teachings besides. The result, within a few short years, was a new 'Tendai' sect, established on Mount Hiei and taking its name from 'Tiantai' while in fact being very much more. It incorporated elements from Zen, from a set of advanced moral codes called the Bodhisattva Precepts and from esoteric Buddhism. Tiantai by itself was already an attempt to work Buddhism's various sects and scriptures into an ambitious hierarchical whole, with the Lotus Sutra at the apex. Tendai ended up so comprehensive – across ritual, contemplation, faith and morality – that Saichō saw no need for any other sect in Japan.

Saichō dubbed his teachings 'Buddhahood for all'. The basic idea was very much in tune with the Mahayana branch of Buddhism. Coalescing in India by around 200 CE and mixing with Chinese philosophical and religious traditions across the centuries since, the Mahayana ('Great Vehicle') had helped to broaden Buddhism from being the preserve primarily of monastics to a 'vehicle' for the salvation of laypeople too. Devotional possibilities expanded with the idea that the Buddha takes on three different forms or 'bodies': a cosmic, all-embracing form, akin to the Absolute; a celestial form, appearing as various gods inhabiting the realms that make up the cosmos; and more limited forms manifesting in ordinary time and space – the most famous being Siddhartha Gautama. There was great emphasis, too, on the figure of the 'bodhisattva': beings on the path to Buddhahood across many lives, who out of compassion seek to release all other sentient beings from suffering along the way.

For Saichō, 'Buddhahood for all' meant that traditional distinctions between clergy and laypeople, and between men and women, did not matter. What mattered was that the Buddha in his cosmic form resided in the depths of every person, as their 'Buddha nature'. Enlightenment was, as a result, not something to be striven for across many lifetimes via monastic vows, complex rituals and unending austerity. It was already here, already the truth of things, needing only to be apprehended via a simple faith nourished in contemplation and everyday life – if, that is, a person really wanted it. As Saichō himself cautioned his followers: 'There is room for food and clothing within an aspiration for enlightenment, but there is no room for an aspiration for enlightenment within the quest for food and clothing.'

In one respect, Saichō was developing here a characteristically East Asian take on Buddhism. In India, the idea of reincarnation was so deeply entrenched that moral effort across many lifetimes seemed an entirely natural proposition. In China and Japan, by contrast, where reincarnation was just one amongst many possible posthumous outcomes, Buddhism came to have a greater focus on the here-and-now; on the possibility that people, even inanimate objects, possess the Buddha nature; and on the religious practices and artistic ways of looking at the world that flow from that.

But the politics of Tendai were distinctive and clear from the start. Saichō regarded Prince Shōtoku as a great statesman and his 'spiritual grandfather'. Where the Prince was credited with helping to establish 'Nihon' as his country's name, Saichō was amongst those to use the powerful expression *dainipponkoku*: 'the great country of Japan'. The cosmic protection of this great country, he claimed, and its freedom from chaos, was one of Japanese Buddhism's most weighty responsibilities.

If Saichō was Kanmu's ideal Buddhist – scholarly, moral, highly patriotic – he nevertheless had a rival in a second Buddhist monk arriving in China in 804 as part of the same diplomatic mission. His name was Kūkai, and just like Saichō he returned to Japan to establish a brand new Buddhist sect. Where Tendai was broad in its philosophy and ritual, Kūkai's new sect – Shingon ('True Word'), which came to be based on Mount Kōya – focused more closely on esoteric Buddhism. Monks studied mudras (ritual gestures, mostly using the hands), mandalas (visual representations of sacred realms), mantras (sacred phrases) and mental concentration.

Saichō and Kūkai became two of the most influential Japanese Buddhists who ever lived. Their rise might not have been good news for women, who thrived as nuns in the existing system but were, early on at least, barred from Mounts Hiei and Kōya for fear of compromising the efficacy of the rituals performed there. But where Buddhism in Japan had, in the past, relied heavily on foreign scholarship, Saichō and Kūkai were its first great Japanese innovators.

Japan's native gods, meanwhile, remained very much in the picture. At its own request, via an oracle, the *kami* Hachiman had been moved from Kyūshū to Nara, so that it could pay homage to the great Buddha at Tōdai-ji. Now, the Tendai and Shingon sects turned to the *kami* of Mounts Hiei and Kōya respectively to help secure themselves in their new homes. Buddhism and the *kami* would continue to interweave – philosophically and ritually – for a millennium to come, so that eventually few Japanese would recognize them as two separable traditions.

*

Emperor Kanmu did not live to see the full fruits of his boundary-pushing efforts, which contributed so much to Japan's Heian era, beginning with the establishment of the new capital and ending in 1185. Already unwell by the time Saichō returned from China in 805, Kanmu died the following year, after an esoteric Buddhist ritual intended to revive him failed to achieve its end. But in the decades following his death, Buddhism's boundaries were steadily and radically redrawn thanks to his support for Saichō and Kūkai: from an urban system in which six sects mixed and mingled, to a mountain tradition, firmly rooted in Mahayana Buddhism, where differing sects maintained their own temples, lineages, interests and eventually even armies.

More broadly, Kanmu had helped to usher in an era of remarkable cultural confidence in Japan. He left his country on the cusp of a classical era in which contacts with China fell away and instead fashion, art, architecture, music, poetry and prose all took on distinctively Japanese forms. Tendai and Shingon had an important part to play here. The idea that Buddha nature resides in everyone and everything made possible a shift from the relative austerity of the Nara schools to a broad and enthusiastic embrace of aesthetics as yet another means of accessing the Absolute. Kūkai became famous not just as a Buddhist pioneer but also as a poet, painter and calligrapher. For centuries to come, some of Japan's greatest artists would also be Buddhist priests.

Kanmu's new capital at Heian-kyō became synonymous with these celebrated cultural achievements. The city was also the governmental and administrative heart of a centralized imperial realm that encompassed most of the islands of Kyūshū and Shikoku, along with southern and central areas of Honshū. Its population stood at around 6 or 7 million people in Kanmu's lifetime. Thanks to his political achievements and his siring of three strong sons – whose combined reigns continued until 833 – Kanmu's legacy in all these areas was given time to develop before enemies crowded in.

But crowd in they would. Clan power had been dampened down, not defeated. Before too long, successors to the imperial throne would look back on Kanmu's era less as a practical example and more as a glorious and utterly irretrievable past.

4
Murasaki Shikibu

(紫式部)

c.973–unknown

Court Reporter

Murasaki Shikibu, at her writing desk.
By the painter Miyagawa Chōshun (1602–1752).

As autumn advances, the Tsuchimikado mansion looks unutterably beautiful. Every branch on every tree by the lake and each tuft of grass on the banks of the stream takes on its own particular colour, which is then intensified by the evening light.

The year is 1008, and an aristocratic diarist and lady-in-waiting by the name of Murasaki Shikibu is settling in for what promises to be a long night. From her room in the east wing of the Tsuchimikado mansion she can hear Shingon priests embarking on a vigil of sutra recitation. 'In the slowly cooling breeze', she notes, 'it is difficult to distinguish them from the endless murmur of the stream.'

As dawn approaches, the tone of the chanting changes:

The Ritual of the Five Great Mystic Kings begins. The voice of each priest as he tries to best his neighbour can be heard near and far, solemn and awe-inspiring. Then, the ritual over, the Archbishop of the Kannon'in leads twenty acolytes in procession from the east wing over to the main building to cast magic spells; as they cross the bridge, their thundering feet sound strange and unfamiliar.

Since the death of Emperor Kanmu, some 200 years before, esoteric Buddhist prayers like these, for protection and healing, have become popular amongst the elite of Heian-kyō as a means of warding off the evil spirits believed to cause illness and misfortune of all kinds. Worship of the native gods is linked for the most part to institutional affairs. The Kamo Shrines protect Heian-kyō, as the *kami* of Mounts Hiei and Kōya do the temple complexes of Tendai and Shingon. Amaterasu, the Sun Goddess and ancestor of the imperial family, is enshrined at Ise, while each of the major clans have deities and great shrines of their own. Buddhist prayers, by contrast, are often now personal: requested by individuals or families in times of danger and distress. They are well suited to an occasion like this.

Empress Shōshi, whom Murasaki serves, is due to give birth – and it is starting to look as though this most consequential of labours may not end well.

These are momentous minutes not just for Shōshi herself but for Heian Japan as a whole and for the head of the Tsuchimikado household in particular: Fujiwara no Michinaga. The supreme political operator of his day, Michinaga is the Empress's father, and has managed to plot her rise from the ranks of Emperor Ichijō's consorts to hold the coveted position of Empress. Now, if she can successfully bear a male child into the world, an heir to the imperial throne, Michinaga's own ascent to power will be complete.

Had all this been taking place in an earlier era, we might know about it only from a few simple lines in an official chronicle. A child was born, or wasn't. The Empress lived, or didn't. Instead, we follow a struggling, anxious Shōshi – just nineteen years old – as she is moved to a dais surrounded by curtains of pure, ritual white. We find the priestly presence around her become larger and more diverse. 'Everyone worthy of the name exorcist' has been called down from nearby mountain temples to cast noisy spells as her pain begins to build. 'You could imagine every Buddha in the universe flying down to respond ...' There are 'Ying-Yang' diviners here too, alongside female shamans, each one shielded by a screen as they call out to their spiritual contacts. Courtiers crowd around, jostling for position outside the dais curtains. Inside, rice is thrown to ward off evil spirits while attendants hurry Shōshi through Buddhist vows (cutting off a symbolic lock of hair in the process), in case she doesn't make it.

We owe this rich, dramatic snapshot of Heian life both to Murasaki herself and more broadly to a trend of the time for reflecting, in writing, on aristocratic existence: in diaries, miscellanies, poems and stories – all of them handwritten, with copies made by calligraphers. Some of the best of these works earn their authors celebrity status of a sort. For a while, Shōshi was in the odd position of sharing the title of Empress with her cousin and rival, Empress Teishi. And because Teishi boasted Sei Shōnagon as part of her entourage – a writer already feted for the mischievous, merciless wit of *The Pillow Book*

(*Makura no sōshi*, c.1001) – Michinaga had been determined to sprinkle a little literary stardust on his own daughter's inner circle. For this he turned to Murasaki Shikibu, the author of an intriguing, accomplished piece of prose that was beginning to circulate around the court. It may not be much comfort to Empress Shōshi as she lies there in scarcely imaginable pain and distress. But one of those fretting over her fate, while carefully noting the manner in which others do the same, is the woman credited with creating the world's first novel and Japan's towering literary masterpiece, *The Tale of Genji* (*Genji monogatari*).

That work preserves in amber this heyday of Heian-kyō's aristocracy: a small, insular world of peace and prosperity, with poetry and open-air parties, gleeful gossip, carefully calibrated fashion and, of course, grand romance. It will strike later generations as almost impossibly sophisticated, with Chinese high culture reworked into distinctively Japanese forms of refinement. Some of those who are part of this brief moment, immortalized in the writings of Murasaki Shikibu, are perhaps aware of how fleeting it must inevitably be. In fact, it is already passing away. The sometimes violent contests over provincial land wealth that impinge upon many aristocrats' lives merely as news from the far-off countryside will one day overtake them. But not just yet.

*

Murasaki Shikibu's real name is unknown. She was born around 973, at a time when it was considered poor form to record – or even use, in public – an aristocratic woman's personal name. Instead, women might be referred to by some combination of family name, place and the post held by their father or brother. 'Shikibu' probably came from Shikibu no Daijō, 'Senior Secretary in the Ministry of Ceremonies', a post held for some time by Murasaki's father, Tametoki. The origins of 'Murasaki' may well lie with the character who goes by that name in *The Tale of Genji*: a beautiful young girl, whom Genji ends up marrying. Someone at court is said to have applied it in jest to the book's author as a nickname – hinting at some resemblance between character and creator – and it stuck.

The other, more circuitous, explanation for 'Murasaki' involves the meaning of the word itself: 'purple'. Purple is the colour of wisteria, and the word for wisteria in Japanese is *fuji*. Murasaki's immediate family may have been of little social account, with her father never rising to great professional heights, but both her father and her mother, the latter passing away when Murasaki was young, were descended from a junior branch of what was by this time the country's most important clan by far – the Fujiwara ('wisteria field').

Something of Emperor Kanmu's authority had lingered through the reigns of the three sons and one grandson who succeeded him. But in 850, Fujiwara efforts to ensure that women from their clan dominated the market for imperial brides at last paid off. An emperor, Montoku, ascended the throne whose mother and main consorts were all Fujiwara. From that point on, for around two centuries, the Fujiwara family – and its Northern House in particular (this was a large and competitive clan) – effectively ruled the realm. They influenced the choice of each new imperial heir, ensuring that it was always someone with some Fujiwara blood. They guided his policies as emperor, installing a Fujiwara grandee as his regent and later as his 'spokesman'. And, lest they became less pliable with age, each emperor was persuaded to abdicate around the age of thirty. The Fujiwara controlled major government appointments too, both in Heian-kyō and out in the provinces, bringing them yet further influence and funds.

As imperial authority dwindled and the compilation of imperial histories ceased (the last of the six national histories *(Rikkokushi)* which began with the *Chronicles of Japan*, was completed in 901), power in Heian-kyō shifted from Emperor Kanmu's beloved palace complex in the north – which burned down in the mid-900s, taking with it countless precious books and works of art – to the mansions of the nobility, many of them concentrated in the north-east of the city. Such homes were usually built in a style called *shinden*: rectangular wooden buildings, one storey high, connected by covered walkways. Various measures were employed to help cope with the hot and humid summers for which Heian-kyō was so well known, from overhanging roofs of bark to create shady verandas through to the use of wooden pillars rather than solid walls for structural support, allowing buildings to be lined with removable screens. Most structures were raised a foot or so off the ground on stilts, to allow cooling air to flow underneath, while inside the floors were of cool bare wood and furnishings were kept few and simple: blinds, screens and curtains for privacy; cushions and straw mats; cabinets and tables alongside a brazier in winter, struggling valiantly against all the heat-releasing features of the home.

One of the most important areas of any mansion complex was its garden, situated south of its main buildings. Designed to echo in miniature the landscape surrounding Heian-kyō, these gardens often included an artificial pond featuring an arrangement of rocks and small islands dotted with pine trees. Seasonal flowers were planted, including cherry, plums and chrysanthemums, while one or more streams flowed languidly through the garden – sometimes used to send a small cup of *sake* bobbing precariously along from pourer to drinker. The grass itself might be sprinkled with a little white sand, causing it to glitter in the moonlight. Around the outside of the whole compound ran a gated stone wall.

Growing up amidst what must have been rather more modest surrounds, Murasaki didn't so much receive an education as overhear one. Her brother Nobunori spent much of his time at home being prepared for his future studies and career. That meant studying, sometimes in the company of his father, Chinese classics of history and literature, alongside major Buddhist texts and Japanese works like the *Chronicles of Japan*. A popular method was to read out loud – thus allowing a curious sister to listen in.

Murasaki's father seems to have realized that his daughter was smarter than his son. Murasaki later recalled him saying one day: 'Just my luck! What a pity she was not born a man!' But while men for the most part read and wrote in Chinese, linked as that language was with their professional duties, aristocratic women were the true literary pioneers of their day. Their work was more imaginative in scope, and was written in something called *hiragana*.

Up until this point, the Japanese language had been rendered in script using Chinese characters deployed in one of two ways. A character's meaning could be borrowed, so that it was read using the Japanese word that corresponded with that meaning. Alternatively, the Chinese pronunciations were borrowed, used to sound out the syllables of Japanese words. *Hiragana* was different. It was a straight-forward phonetic system whose constituent parts were drawn from simplified cursive forms of Chinese characters: one for each sound. In its early days, *hiragana* was so heavily associated with women writers, Murasaki included, that it was known as *onnade* – 'women's hand'.

Through a combination of eavesdropping and reading for herself, Murasaki became familiar with a broad canon of Japanese literature whose earliest elements stretched back nearly three centuries to the 700s: to the *Record of Ancient Matters* and the *Chronicles of Japan*, alongside the first poetry anthology, *The Ten Thousand Leaves,* and the more recent *Collection of Poems Ancient and Modern* (*Kokinshū, c.*905). Beyond its courtly and diplomatic uses, poetry – especially in the style known as *waka*: thirty-one syllables spread across five lines in a 5-7-5-7-7 pattern – was also a means by which a keen sense of beauty, delicacy and transience was passed on from one generation to the next. Much Japanese poetry turned on the connections between nature – changing seasons, splendid vistas, some fine detail of flora or fauna – and shifting human emotions and relationships. Allusion and restraint were highly prized. To be able to recognize, and produce, good poetry marked a person out not merely as clever or well-read but as decent, sensitive and worthy – including, perhaps, as a marriage partner: many an aristocratic courtship began with a testing of the waters via the exchange of a few short lines of poetry.

Alongside all this, in shaping Murasaki's upbringing and writing, ran two new literary forms that emerged in the 900s. The first was the 'poem-tale': a series of poems, interspersed with a small amount of prose, telling a short story about aristocratic life. One of the best-known collections was *The Tales of Ise* (*Ise monogatari*), inspired by the life and poetry of the courtier and romantic adventurer Ariwara no Narihira (825–80) and coming together in its final arrangement around 980. The second new form was the literary diary, some akin to travelogues while others focused on life in high society. Outstanding amongst the latter was *The Gossamer Years* (*Kagerō nikki, c.*974). Written by an aristocratic woman known to posterity only as the 'mother of Michitsuna', it features near the beginning an account of a poetic advance poetically rebuffed. The author is sent a note by a princely suitor, containing a short line of verse: 'Sad am I, 'mid talk about the warbler; may not I too hear its voice?' The author regards the paper used for the note as 'unbecoming', and the man's handwriting as 'astonishingly bad'. She replies accordingly. 'Let no bird waste its song in a wilderness where it finds no answer.'

Murasaki discovered romance of her own relatively late for her times. She was already in her mid-twenties when in 998 or 999 she married a man by the name of Nobutaka. He was a Fujiwara too, a reasonably successful government official whose career included the governorship of several provinces. He was also said to be a good dancer, selected to perform at the Kamo Festival in 988. On the downside, he was nearly as old as her father, already married to several other women and given to seeing concubines on the side.

This wasn't, in fact, especially villainous conduct for his times. Men often took a number of 'wives' (a complicated concept in this era) the first of whom enjoyed a degree of prominence over the others: she would be around her husband's age, he would usually live in her family home and their children would probably do the best socially and professionally. Women, by contrast, were permitted only one husband, and they rarely took a second if their marriage ended in divorce or the death of their husband. A woman's primary security lay in her ability to inherit property within her own natal family (the great Tsuchimikado mansion originally belonged to Michinaga's wife, not to him). She would retain her family's name after marriage, and be buried with them when she died.

Murasaki's marriage to Nobutaka lasted only a few short years. She gave birth to a daughter, Kenshi (also known as Kataiko), in 999. But then in 1001 Nobutaka passed away during an epidemic. Murasaki seems to have grieved at the time, both for Nobutaka and for herself. Seized by the fear that her life from then on would be one of drab loneliness, she later recalled 'feeling depressed and confused':

> [I] existed from day to day in listless fashion, taking note of the flowers, the birds in song, the way the skies change from season to season, the moon, the frost and snow, doing little more than registering the passage of time . . . The thought of my continuing loneliness was unbearable.

Murasaki's fears were well grounded. Women of her high station tended to spend most of their time at home engaged in calligraphy, reading, music and the care of children, mostly away from centres of activity like the court, noble mansions or the city's markets. Pilgrimages and family visits might be the extent of their travel. A story from this era, perhaps rooted in reality, tells of a girl of Murasaki's class who became completely lost in the streets of Heian-kyō, having no idea where her home was located.

But in Murasaki's case, life was just getting started. Sometime between 1001 and 1005, and possibly earlier, she settled down at her inkstone and began to write the first lines of what became *The Tale of Genji*. She drew on much that Japan's literary culture was capable of offering by this point, from Chinese and Japanese poetry to *The Tales of Ise*. For the celebrated complexity of her characters, she relied more than anything else on the intimate diaries written by court ladies.

In the end, *Genji* became something very much more than the sum of these parts. It departed from the limited and sometimes fanciful tone of the poem-tales to become instead a historical epic and a deep psychological study, awesome in length and scope. Spanning nearly three-quarters of a century, coming close to Murasaki's own day, the story follows the life of a man named Hikaru Genji ('Shining Genji') from the richness and romance of his early years as the son of an emperor to a more mixed and contemplative existence in later life. We follow him to his death before moving into the lives of others, across further chapters that some argue may not have been written by Murasaki. The work is thought to have been completed sometime between 1005 and 1013.

It may have been the early chapters of *Genji*, passed by Murasaki to friends for comment and then copied and circulated more widely at court, that provided her entry ticket into high society – or at least smoothed her path once she got there. Michinaga certainly thought well of the work, offering high-quality brushes, ink and paper to the scribes involved in producing new copies. Whatever the circumstances, in 1005 or 1006 Murasaki was called into Empress Shōshi's service as a lady-in-waiting. And her adventure at court began.

*

Empress Shōshi's ordeal, in the autumn of 1008, must have been all the more unbearable for knowing that her rival Teishi had died in childbirth just a few years before. Nor can the behaviour of nearby men have helped, some of them trying to peek over the curtains at the Empress in labour, surrounded by her ladies. 'Somehow one expected this kind of behaviour from [Michinaga's] sons,' commented Murasaki in her diary, adding that she was sorry to see it in some of the others. But this was no time to fret over appearances and etiquette:

> We lost all sense of shame being seen in such a state, our eyes swollen with weeping . . . We must have presented a sorry sight, rice falling on our heads like snow and our clothes all crumpled and creased.

Then, right at the height of everyone's despair, with the young Empress being led with anxious urgency through her Buddhist vows, her child – a son – was at last safely born. The chaos continued a little while longer, through new priestly chants and prostrations alongside 'wails of anguish . . . from the [defeated] evil spirits'. One priest was thrown to the ground as the spirits departed, and a colleague had to rush to his aid with fresh spells. Finally, the gathered throng recovered themselves and began to rejoice in the birth of the future Emperor Go-Ichijō.

There followed a long round of official celebrations and gift-giving, beginning with the first of many ritual baths for the newborn baby. He was carried along by his proud grandfather, Michinaga, as a richly accoutred female attendant walked out in front bearing a ceremonial sword:

> [Her] train was decorated with autumn grasses, butterflies and birds sketched in glittering silver. We were none of us free to do exactly as we pleased because of the rules about the use of [different sorts of] silk. . .

Murasaki filled her diary with descriptions like these: this was an era when a great deal turned on a person's sense of taste and choice of clothing. For high-born women, white-powdered skin with rouged cheeks and red lips, alongside painted eyebrows and blackened teeth, was simply standard. A person seeking to stand out had to look to how she wore her hair and coordinated her outfit, always paying attention to what was appropriate for her age and present company, while remaining within strict rules that dictated the materials and colours that a person of a given status might wear.

The sheer complexity of women's formal attire offered endless options here. On top of a simple undershirt and trouser-skirt was worn a set of robes which, depending on the nature of the occasion, might extend to five separate layers. On top of these in turn came a gown, a train and finally a jacket. Most of these garments were created from different types of silk, including damask and brocade, carefully dyed, stencilled and stitched to achieve the desired results.

The court's menfolk laboured under lesser but related presentational pressures. With the meritocracy dreamed of by Prince Shōtoku having failed to materialize, and the State Academy once headed by Emperor Kanmu now gone to ruin, how a man dressed, how he spoke and how he behaved mattered more than ever to his career. Some of the rules on personal behaviour dated back to the famous seventeen-article constitution credited to the Prince. Others were newer, bound up with legal codes and with the religious works that formed part of the Japanese literary canon. Alongside both ran a man's looks, bearing and repartee. On these, together with rather more prosaic struggles over power, his prospects – and those of his family – might rise or fall.

If literary sources are any indication, Heian-kyō's elite men had plenty of fun nonetheless. While those of slightly lesser birth (including Murasaki's father) were out running the country, courtiers enjoyed excursions on horseback to the countryside around Heian-kyō, boating and blossom-viewing, composing poetry and hunting with falcons. They pursued music, archery and games like *sugoroku* (backgammon) and *kemari*, a sort of communal keepy-uppy, played by a team of eight men using a deerskin ball (Murasaki found the game distastefully inelegant). They watched bigger men wrestle. They drank and they gambled on archery (the latter vice also meeting with Murasaki's disapproval). They engaged in extensive personal grooming, from face powder to carefully prepared varieties of perfume. They wept freely when moved by nature or culture. They dispensed witticisms where they could. And, of course, they pursued women.

Murasaki seems to have ended up on the receiving end of this last activity courtesy of no less a figure than Michinaga himself, who veers in her diary from the responsible patriarch to the drunken lecher. On one occasion in 1010, by which time Michinaga had seen his daughter produce not one but two imperial heirs – with the associated fanfare taking up much of Murasaki's diary space – we find him approaching Murasaki and the Empress. The latter has a part of *The Tale of Genji* with her, and Michinaga begins to comment on the work before seizing a piece of paper used to hold some plums and writing on it a short poem – intended for Murasaki:

> She is known for her tartness
> So I am sure that no one seeing her
> Could pass without a taste[.]

Murasaki replies that she is 'shocked', but Michinaga is not dissuaded. That night there comes a tapping at Murasaki's door. She remains still and quiet, waiting for the sound to cease. Then in the morning she receives a new piece of poetry:

> How sad for him who stands the whole night long
> Knocking on your cedar door
> Tap-tap-tap like the cry of the *kuina* bird.

Murasaki is unmoved, and writes back:

> Sadder for her who had answered the *kuina's* tap,
> For it was no innocent bird who stood there knocking on the door.

*

Murasaki's diary ends not long after Michinaga's thwarted advance, and we know little of what happened to her afterwards. Claims were made from the fourteenth century onwards that she and Michinaga had indeed been lovers – and that it was this relationship, rather than her *Genji* chapters, that gained Murasaki access to the court. There may be something to it. For all Michinaga's occasional boorishness, Murasaki does seem to have had a soft spot for him. She once watched him pluck a flower in the garden, finding him 'magnificent' in the act.

As to Murasaki's fate more generally, some suggest that she remained in court service until the 1020s, relinquishing her diary-writing when she did because her daughter – for whom it was perhaps intended as an instructional manual on court service – had no further need of new advice. Kenshi was twelve years old at this point, and on the verge of her own successful career as a lady-in-waiting. Others say that Murasaki may have died as early as 1014.

We do know that despite a busy calendar of ceremonies and festivities during her time at court – including New Year, the Kamo Festival, the Festival of the Dead, the Great Moon Viewing and the Gosechi Dances (linked to the rice harvest) – Murasaki sometimes found life at court rather boring and lonely. 'People traipse in and out day and night and there is little mystery,' she wrote, so that even 'ordinary conversation' started to sound intriguing. On the other hand, Murasaki seems to have had elements in her character that suited her poorly for life at court. She was relatively prudish for her era, and may have felt uncomfortable with much of what went on. And she was almost too accomplished a critic, of poetry and people alike, regarding Sei Shōnagon as 'dreadfully conceited' and believing her writings to leave 'a great deal to be desired'. Perhaps too much criticism of the unsolicited kind contributed to the loneliness that Murasaki talked about in her diary.

Murasaki could be just as hard on herself. She claimed not to have 'achieved anything of note', regarding herself as a poor player of the koto who was neglectful of the necessary practice. She felt both distanced from and hemmed in by her servants, who gossiped about her; and far removed, too, from the ladies at court, whom she found petty, 'full of themselves' and intent upon composing laundry lists of criticisms of others. Murasaki had a vivid sense of what they must surely be saying about her: that she was 'pretentious, awkward, difficult to approach, prickly, too fond of her tales, haughty, prone to versifying, disdainful, cantankerous and scornful'. Her familiarity with literature composed in Chinese, a language considered unbecoming for a woman, certainly landed her in trouble. People called her 'Lady Chronicle' when they found out that she had read the *Chronicles of Japan*. When Murasaki started reading Chinese classics with the Empress, at the latter's request, the two of them had to keep the affair secret so as to avoid criticism. 'Ah,' sighed Murasaki in her diary, 'what a prattling, tiresome world it is!'

There is no telling how far Murasaki's melancholy and self-reproach were spontaneous, and how much they were part of her art, in an era when being attuned to transience and loss was highly prized in both aesthetic and moral terms. Perhaps she could not have answered that question herself. But towards the end of her diary we find this unparalleled chronicler of an extraordinary moment in Japanese history offering up a combined verdict on her times and on herself, which, but for some of the details, seems to cut a distance of more than a thousand years down to nothing at all:

Each one of us is quite different. Some are confident, open and forthcoming. Others are born pessimists, amused by nothing, the kind who search through old letters, carry out penances, intone sutras without end, and clack their beads, all of which makes one feel uncomfortable. So I hesitate to do even those things I should be able to do quite freely, only too aware of my servants' prying eyes. How much more so at court, where I have many things I would like to say ... but people would never understand ... So all they see of me is a façade.

PART TWO

From Many to One:
1185–1582

5
Hōjō Masako

(北条政子)

1157–1225

The Nun Shogun

Statue of Hōjō Masako, Izunokuni City, Shizuoka Prefecture, Japan.

Two centuries after early chapters of *The Tale of Genji* circulated at the Heian court, a brand new sort of literature was doing the rounds in Japan. Its delight in the intimate repartee that passes between a woman and a man would have been familiar to someone of Murasaki Shikibu's time and temperament. And yet when a warrior woman called Tomoe Gozen chides a man named Uchida on his bad manners, we find the couple's exchange taking place not via scented letter, nor in the moonlit garden of some magnificent mansion. They are on the battlefield, locked in hand-to-hand combat. And Uchida has Tomoe by the hair:

'What is wrong with my manners?'

Tomoe answered: 'Does a man good enough to close with a woman draw his dagger as they fight and let her see it? Uchida, you know nothing of the old ways.'

Then she clenched her fist and struck him hard in the elbow of his dagger arm. The blow was so powerful that the dagger fell out of his hand. 'See . . . ' she cried, 'I am from a mountain village in Kiso, acknowledged the best in the land. I am the combat instructor you need!' And she stretched out her left hand, seized Uchida's faceplate, and forced his head down on to the pommel of her saddle; then she slipped her hand under the faceplate, drew her own dagger, wrenched the head round and struck it off.

Something had clearly changed since Murasaki's day.

A major point of reference for this new culture was a civil war, subsequent dramatizations of which credited a woman called Tomoe Gozen with playing an important part. She was lauded as a 'warrior worth a thousand, ready to confront a demon or god, mounted or on foot'. Raging on and off between 1180 and 1185, across a country whose territory by now extended to the northernmost tip of Honshū, the war ended with authority shifting from Heian-kyō to a military government in Kamakura. At the heart of this momentous change was Hōjō Masako, the wife of the first Kamakura shogun.

From a minor landowning family in eastern Japan, Masako rose to the pinnacle of power in the new regime. Later generations of Japanese would remember her as someone who had been quicker than many others to understand and respond to its novel combination of landed wealth, military strength, individual character and obligation, canny deal-making and family ties. Confucian virtues of filial piety and respect for ancestors now became fused more deeply than ever with Japan's older clan mentality. Grasping all this, and making the most of it, Masako helped the new regime to survive – very much on her own terms, and those of the Hōjō family. What might, under other circumstances, have been a short-lived new political arrangement amidst turbulent times instead became an institution central to Japan's history and sense of itself as a country and culture: *bakufu*, or military government.

*

Heian-kyō's founder would barely have recognized his city in 1157, the year of Hōjō Masako's birth. Emperor Kanmu's palace complex had burned down and been rebuilt several times since the mid-900s, and the site was soon to be abandoned altogether. What was once the secular and sacred centre of an imperial state would end its days as a vegetable patch, its turnips said to be especially good. The nearby Park of the Divine Spring meanwhile embarked on a sad trajectory of its own, from Edenic recreational spot to dumping ground for rubbish and corpses. The city's great southern gate, Rashōmon, was already no more than a memory. It had turned out to be less sturdy than it looked, and after succumbing twice to strong winds it had not been re-erected.

Some of Heian-kyō's airy avenues and lanes, especially in its western half and around the periphery, were clogged these days by pedlars and prostitutes, beggars and gamblers. There were no-go areas, derelict houses and thieves so brazen that when it wasn't on fire the Imperial Palace was at constant risk of being broken into. Just beyond the city lay danger of another kind. Kanmu had gazed upon the awesome mountains arrayed around his capital, and felt protected. Later emperors felt hemmed in. Those mountains had become home to wealthy and independently minded Buddhist sects, Tendai being the greatest amongst them, whose activities now ran to the recruitment and training of warrior monks or *sōhei*. They would muster up in the mountains, Buddhist robes bulging over the armour beneath, before descending into the 'Capital of Peace and Tranquillity' in their hundreds – sometimes thousands – to intimidate and attack religious rivals and political enemies.

Kanmu would have wept for his successors every bit as much as for his city. Imperial authority never recovered from the two centuries of Fujiwara clan rule beginning in 850. Change of a sort came in 1068, when Emperor Go-Sanjō ascended the throne. He was the first emperor in 170 years whose mother was not a Fujiwara. The result was a certain independence of spirit: Go-Sanjō retired to a Buddhist monastery in 1073, seeking to influence events at court from there. He died a few months later, leaving his son and successor Shirakawa to develop the novel trend for 'cloistered rule' (*insei*) that Go-Sanjō had inspired. Shirakawa was emperor for just fourteen years before retiring in 1086 while still in his mid-thirties. With the burden of his ritual role lifted, he spent the next forty years scheming behind the scenes to influence preferment for important official posts, shoring up his family's finances, checking his rivals' power and ensuring that his favoured candidates were well placed in the line of succession. The major disadvantage to all this was an ever more fractured politics. Parental interference in imperial rule effectively doubled, with an emperor now forced to contend both with his mother's side of the family – frequently, still, the Fujiwara – and his father's side, which might include one or more retired emperors with more time on their hands and more experience of government.

Out in the provinces, too – home to the vast majority of the population – the old ideal of a unified imperial state was falling away across the 1000s and 1100s. People still, in theory, leased their land from the state, paying taxes in return for permission to farm it. But an old imperial practice of relinquishing rights over small portions of land as a means of supporting religious institutions and paying government officials had morphed into a system whereby wealthy and well-connected temples and families accrued vast private holdings by having others sign over their lands to them – in return for political, financial or physical security. Everyone still recognized the legal authority of the Heian court, and sought charters to confirm the land they claimed. But real power in the provinces now lay in these large estates, known as *shōen*, often comprising holdings scattered across the country. Semi-autonomous provincial governors controlled tracts that remained nominally in the state's hands, amounting to less than 50 per cent of the land in most provinces by the late 1100s.

Hōjō Masako was born into one of the many rural landowning families that emerged as beneficiaries within this system. Based in Izu Province on Japan's east coast, the Hōjō were relatively minor players. They were not especially wealthy, and Masako's father Tokimasa boasted little influence beyond the immediate locale. So when Masako's mother died in childbirth, and it fell to a teenage Masako to take care of her family, that might well have been it for her: a difficult life destined to go unrecorded, with history happening elsewhere. Except that when Masako was three years old, a boy called Yoritomo, ten years her senior, had moved into the area. Brought up in Heian-kyō, he had relocated to the peninsula not for its inspiring scenery and fresh sea air: he was a political exile, a casualty of violent conflicts racking the country in recent years, which were far from over.

As the court's authority waned and the *shōen* system developed, landowners had found that protecting their gains occasionally required the use of force. And with Kanmu's conscript army rarely covering itself in glory, his successors had increasingly turned to smaller groups of seasoned fighters instead, some of whom had picked up tips from the 'barbarian' Emishi of the north-east, including an expertise in mounted archery. Warrior work emerged as a heritable profession in the 900s and 1000s, associated with two great families in particular: the Taira and the Minamoto.

Tracing their origins back to attempts from the ninth century onwards at downsizing the imperial family, by giving surplus members their own surnames (most often 'Taira' or 'Minamoto'), these two warrior houses saw their power grow along with demand for their services. Landowners and provincial governors sought help with defence; the court, less cavalier about the countryside than the aristocratic literature of the era tended to imply, employed them to put down rebellions. And many a nobleman in Heian-kyō, anxious about rivals or the possibility of yet another monkish militia invading the capital, found that he slept more easily if men with blood on their hands stood vigil outside his door. In return for some combination of money, land and prestigious official positions, such men were willing to 'serve' or 'attend' – *saburau*. People started calling them 'saburai', later 'samurai', and the more successful of them gathered large bands of followers: hungry, in the early days, for the personal rewards of private military service, but willing in later generations to fight for the same master as their fathers before them.

Hōjō Masako's family claimed 'Taira' descent, but they were only distantly related, if at all, to the most powerful lineage bearing that name, which dominated central and south-western Japan, enjoyed lucrative trade with China and under Taira no Kiyomori was called in to help settle a dispute over the imperial succession in the 1150s. The Taira ended up on the opposite side from the most powerful of the Minamoto families, and the two warrior houses shed one another's blood on the streets of the capital before Kiyomori came out on top. By rewarding allies and making excellent marriages for his daughters into the imperial and Fujiwara families, he dominated the court during the late 1160s and into the 1170s, marking the moment when samurai exchanged service for rule.

And yet Kiyomori had made a mistake. He had his rival general Minamoto no Yoshitomo executed, along with his two eldest sons. But he let Yoshitomo's two younger sons live. One, Yoshitsune, a baby at the time, was sent off into the care of Buddhist monks. The other, Yoritomo, was banished to Izu into the guardianship of a Taira ally whose hospitality he rewarded by getting his daughter pregnant. The guardian was forced to kill his own grandchild in order to prevent trouble with the Taira, while Yoritomo was hurriedly moved into the care of another Taira ally, one Hōjō Tokimasa.

*

While Tokimasa was away serving guard duty in Heian-kyō in the mid-1170s, Masako and Yoritomo began an affair. Tokimasa was furious when he found out, and hurriedly arranged an alternative match for Masako. But she was twenty years old by this point, and through some combination of maturity, independence, love for Yoritomo and anger at her father for recently getting married to a woman of around her own age, Masako resolved to resist. She and Yoritomo ran away together to a temple in the mountains, hiding out there until Tokimasa relented and agreed to take the biggest gamble of his life – allowing a Minamoto into the family fold.

It quickly began to look like a bad bet. There were those at court who had always felt that, despite his great victory, Taira no Kiyomori, born of a rustic father who had danced well enough but whose poetry had been terrible, did not belong in their elevated company. Kiyomori had forgotten his place and was now very much outstaying his welcome. A plot was hatched in 1180, calling on Minamoto warriors to rise up and assist in putting things right. With Japan now on the brink of civil war, Tokimasa threw in his lot with his son-in-law Yoritomo, who was beginning to gather together allies old and new from across eastern Japan.

Yoritomo went about this in a bold, even groundbreaking way. Where land rights and official posts were traditionally only granted by the imperial court, Yoritomo started to hand them out on his own authority. He was declaring independence of a sort, tying warriors and landowners to himself personally and taking as his alternative seat of government a small village called Kamakura, on the eastern coast of central Honshū.

Masako, meanwhile, was forced to seek refuge for herself and the couple's daughter Ōhime in a mountain temple friendly to the Minamoto side, whose warrior monks would protect her. When it became safe for her to join her husband in Kamakura, she found she was no longer the daughter of a small provincial landowner. She was aristocracy: the wife of a powerful, up-and-coming leader – no matter that the war had only just begun and there was no telling yet where it would go. People started to address Masako as 'Her Ladyship', and according to a chronicle of the period called Mirror of the East (Azuma Kagami), compiled by members of the Hōjō family, her chambers were guarded at night by the best Minamoto archers. When her second child, Yoriie, was born around 1181, he was treated like a prince by Yoritomo's supporters, who were by now hurrying to build homes in Kamakura. Ceremonies were held, gifts made of swords and horses, and several high-ranking wet-nurse (*menoto*) families were brought in to look after the boy during his early years.

All was not domestic bliss, however. Not long after Yoriie's birth, Masako heard a rumour from her stepmother Lady Maki that while she was pregnant Yoritomo had been taking time off from plotting a war and planning a brand new system of administration to visit an old flame, Lady Kame. He had even set her up with a house in Kamakura. Someone else in Masako's position might have concluded that such was the price a newly minted aristocratic wife must pay for her status. Instead, Masako had her stepmother's brother, a man named Munechika, take a small band of warriors over to the place where Lady Kame was staying and set fire to the building. Lady Kame just managed to escape with her life.

There was precedent here. Aristocratic diaries of the era contained tales of *uwanari-uchi* or 'acts of revenge against the next wife'. These were commissioned or even personally carried out by noblewomen against a husband's new lover, and could include violent attacks on the person, property or family of the offending individual. Readers in later centuries would thrill to stories of such acts, sometimes with a supernatural flavour: for example, spurned wives transforming themselves into demons, the better to wreak their revenge.

But Masako may also have been setting down a marker early in her married life with Yoritomo – and with some success. Such was her influence over him, and the need he had of her father's war support, that Yoritomo did not punish Masako for what she had done. Instead, the *Mirror of the East* has him inviting Munechika on an outing, and taking the opportunity to demand an explanation. With Munechika prostrating himself in apology, Yoritomo subjects him to a severe humiliation, cutting off his topknot. He concedes that 'it was most praiseworthy of you to have carried out Her Ladyship's orders', but says that Munechika should at least have informed him first. Munechika flees the scene in tears.

Masako's marriage survived her vengeance against Yoritomo's lover. But it soon came under severe strain once again. With Taira no Kiyomori suffering serious reverses almost from the outset of the war, dying in 1181 having lost everything, Yoritomo's prospects looked increasingly bright. Yet this was a complicated conflict. Known to later generations as the Genpei War – from a combination of 'Genji' and 'Heishi', using the Chinese readings of the first characters of 'Minamoto' and 'Taira', respectively – was not in fact simply a straight fight between families bearing those names. Forces claiming Taira and Minamoto connections fought on both sides in a series of uprisings that could only later and loosely be described as a 'war'. The greatest worry for Yoritomo by 1184 was whether or not he could trust his own cousin, Kiso no Yoshinaka, who had himself taken up arms against the Taira in Heian-kyō.

Yoshinaka succeeded in forcing the Taira out of Heian-kyō, with the young emperor – Kiyomori's grandson – in tow. And it soon became clear that Yoshinaka intended to set himself up in power. In 1184, Yoritomo had to send in his own army, under his brother Yoshitsune, putting Yoshinaka and his men to the sword and persuading the court to acknowledge Yoritomo's rightful efforts at bringing peace to an unruly land.

All of this made life very difficult for Masako and her five-year-old daughter Ōhime. Yoshinaka had sent his eleven-year-old son Yoshitaka to stay with Yoritomo's family as a sign of his good intentions. Masako and Ōhime had taken a great liking to the boy, and both seem to have expected that Ōhime and Yoshitaka would one day marry. Now that Yoshinaka was a traitor, and had died for it, Masako and Ōhime feared that Yoritomo would not allow Yoshitaka to live. So either mother or daughter – perhaps both, working together – persuaded Yoshitaka to dress up as one of Masako's female attendants as a way of smuggling him away to safety. One of Yoshitaka's men stayed behind, buying time for the escape by impersonating his master.

But the scheme was discovered, and five days later Yoshitaka was captured and killed. Once again Masako raged at her husband, accusing him of plunging their daughter Ōhime into serious illness with his cruelty against someone she had loved. And once again, Masako proved she could make an impact. There was no bringing Yoshitaka back, but Yoritomo was sufficiently chastened that he had the man who had murdered Yoshitaka executed in turn.

*

The Genpei War finally came to an end in 1185, when Yoshitsune caught up with what remained of the Taira forces and destroyed them in a major sea battle at Dannoura, off the southern coast of Honshū. The rival fleets engaged one another first with long-range archery and later at close quarters with swords and daggers, before Minamoto archers picked off Taira rowers and helmsmen, leaving their boats adrift. Some of the Taira forces switched sides during the fighting, while others took their own lives once they saw how it was all going to end.

This victory and other feats turned Yoshitsune into an early star of Japan's new literary genre: the war epic. *The Tale of the Heike* (*Heike monogatari*) was one of its first and greatest instalments, based on tales told by travelling storytellers and first compiled as a single text around 1240. It focused primarily on the 'Heike' ('Taira family'), but offered an enthralling, if heavily romanticized, account of the civil war in general. It was here that the famous, and at least semi-fictitious, female samurai Tomoe Gozen made one of her first appearances in literature: as the traitorous Yoshinaka's foster-sister, and one of seven samurai retainers left defending him when Yoshitsune arrives to punish him in 1184, at what became known as the Battle of Awazu. Yoshinaka orders Tomoe to leave and save herself, and soon afterwards he is killed. With all now clearly lost, one of Yoshinaka's last and most loyal retainers taunts his attackers – 'Take a look, easterners! This is how the bravest man in Japan commits suicide!' – before positioning the tip of his sword in his mouth and jumping head-first from his horse.

The *Tale of the Heike* later turns to the Battle of Dannoura, focusing on the fate of Taira no Kiyomori's widow. Grandmother to the young emperor, and a Buddhist nun, she is lauded for her handling of the war's tragic denouement:

> The Nun of Second [court] Rank took the Emperor in her arms and walked to the side of the ship. The Emperor had turned eight that year, but seemed very grown up for his age. His face was radiantly beautiful, and his abundant black hair reached below his waist. 'Where are you taking me, Grandmother?' he asked, with a puzzled look.
>
> She turned her face to the young sovereign, holding back her tears. 'Don't you understand? An evil karma holds you fast in its toils. Your

good fortune has come to an end. Turn to the east and say goodbye to the Grand Shrine of Ise [where the Sun Goddess Amaterasu is enshrined], then turn to the west and repeat the sacred name of Amida Buddha, so that he and his host may come to escort you to the Pure Land. This country is a land of sorrow; I am taking you to a happy realm called Paradise.'

With tears swimming in his eyes, [the Emperor] joined his tiny hands, knelt towards the east, and bade farewell to the Grand Shrine. Then he turned towards the west and recited the sacred name of Amida. The Nun snatched him up, said in a comforting voice, 'There is a capital under the waves, too,' and they both entered the boundless depths.

*

With the fighting over in 1185, Yoritomo and Masako moved to take control. Japan's Heian era had ended, and its Kamakura era had begun. Yoritomo appointed samurai estate-managers (*jitō*) to look after landholdings across the country, gathering to himself in Kamakura administrative and judicial power that had previously been in the gift of the imperial court alone. He later sent out a warrior-constable (*shugo*) to each province to keep the peace. Yoritomo's dominant role in maintaining law and order across Japan was formalized in 1192 with the granting by the imperial court of the title *Sei-i-Taishōgun* or 'Commander-in-Chief of the Expeditionary Forces against the Barbarians'. The title of shogun had earlier been used in Kanmu's era for a military leader tasked with securing the country's northern border against the Emishi. Now it was bestowed upon a man with far more power: the head of Japan's first military government (*bakufu*).

The court perhaps didn't expect this new state of affairs to last very long. And indeed the years after 1185 turned out to be anything but plain sailing for Yoritomo and Masako. The first to begin squabbling over the great prize that had been won was Yoritomo's own brother, Yoshitsune. The hero of Dannoura and countless other campaigns tried to turn his military reputation into civil power in Heian-kyō. Those dreams ended with his severed head being transported back to Kamakura in 1189, marinating in sweet *sake* to preserve it for identification by Yoritomo's men. Next, the couple's hopes of marrying their daughter Ōhime to an emperor were dashed through double-crossing at court and Ōhime's death in 1197.

Two years later, Yoritomo died. Never really the swashbuckling samurai, Yoritomo met an ignominious end after falling off his horse on the way back from the ceremonial opening of a bridge. Such was Masako's reputation as a jealous wife in later centuries that legends emerged suggesting that she must have killed her husband. Other stories about Yoritomo's demise attributed it to the wreaking of ghoulish posthumous revenge by Yoshitsune or the drowned boy-emperor – anything, perhaps, to avoid the awkwardness of having a military government founded by a man who couldn't ride a horse.

Like many a noble spouse, including the wife of Taira no Kiyomori, Masako took Buddhist vows after her husband's death. For her, it served as a way of signalling an intention to forego remarriage in favour of exercising authority in her deceased husband's name. Japan had only recently acquired its first fully fledged shogun. Now people began to talk of the *ama shōgun* – the 'Nun Shogun'– who at moments of crisis stepped in to remind everyone of what Yoritomo had stood for and achieved in his life, and what they all owed him now after his death.

The Nun Shogun's political gifts were called upon almost immediately. Yoritomo's seventeen-year-old son Yoriie had been set to succeed his father ever since a ceremony at the age of six at which he had been presented with armour, bow and sword, and led around the garden on horseback. When the time came, however, Yoriie seemed to have romance rather than rule on his mind. He sent one of his vassals, Adachi Kagemori, away from Kamakura to take care of some bandits, who he claimed had been causing trouble. When Kagemori returned to Kamakura, having failed to locate any bandits, he found that Yoriie had set him up: getting him out of the way while he kidnapped one of his concubines and had her brought to his palace.

Masako may not have felt especially close to Yoriie at the best of times. He was raised away from her household, with wet-nurse families. And when he killed his first deer at the age of eleven, at the foot of Mount Fuji, this seminal moment in a young warrior's life passed almost without comment from his mother. The *Azuma Kagami (Mirror of the East)* portrays Masako as sometimes indulging Yoriie, while also being driven to despair by his lack of interest or ability as shogun. But she did manage to make him listen to her, when he would rarely listen to anyone else. With Yoriie threatening a pre-emptive attack on the home of his wronged vassal, Masako went to stay in the house to protect its occupants. She cautioned her son in a letter that if he planned to kill people there, then 'aim your first arrow at me'.

Yoriie was forced into a climbdown, and Kagemori's concubine was duly returned. But Yoriie soon switched his sources of entertainment to drinking and the ball game *kemari*. Masako put a stop to one particular fixture, which Yoriie was due to play sooner than was decent after the death of one of his more important vassals. But she sometimes watched him play, perhaps realizing the potential of sports diplomacy. *Kemari* was associated with the imperial court and proved to be a useful means of maintaining relations with the capital after a difficult few years following the failure of Masako's and Yoritomo's attempted matchmaking for Ōhime. Retired Emperor Go-Toba even recommended an instructor for Yoriie.

Intolerable to Masako, however, was the way that her son increasingly allied himself with one of his old wet-nurses' families: the Hiki, headed by Hiki Yoshikazu, under whose care he had chiefly grown up. Yoriie married one of the Hiki daughters, Lady Wakasa, and they had a son called Ichiman. When Yoriie fell seriously ill in 1203, he and Yoshikazu appear to have plotted the destruction of Masako's family, the Hōjō, so that Ichiman could become shogun after him – without having to compete for power with Yoriie's younger brother, Sanetomo.

In the *Mirror of the East* account, which perhaps unsurprisingly favours the Hōjō family as regents in Kamakura over their scheming enemies, Masako is credited with overhearing – through a set of paper doors – Yoriie and Yoshikazu hatching their plan. She raises the alarm and a series of clashes ensue between Hiki and Hōjō forces. Hiki Yoshikazu, Lady Wakasa and Ichiman are all killed, while Yoriie is exiled and Sanetomo becomes shogun.

Further plotting two years later forced Masako and her brother Yoshitoki to send their own father into exile. A decade of effective joint rule by Masako and Yoshitoki followed in Kamakura, until in 1219 Sanetomo was assassinated and the direct Minamoto line of shoguns came to an end. When Masako and Yoshitoki found themselves forced to install a distant relative of Yoritomo's (still a baby at this point) as Kamakura's fourth shogun, Retired Emperor Go-Toba spotted his opportunity to restore imperial authority in Japan.

Go-Toba had been quietly recruiting new fighters to his personal guard for a while by this point, most of them from central and western Japan, where the Kamakura *bakufu* had few close friends. He continued to do so, offering patronage in return – much as Yoritomo had once done – until by 1221 he had an army. Declaring Yoshitoki to be a rebel, Go-Toba issued an imperial order for warriors around the country to attack him. Yoshitoki urged senior Kamakura vassals to be cautious in their response, and many agreed: it would be a terrible thing to take up arms against an emperor, retired or not. But in a celebrated speech credited to her in the *Mirror of the East*, Masako reminded these vassals of their late lord, their duty to him and also their own basic interests:

> Since the days when Yoritomo ... put down the court's enemies and founded the [Kamakura] regime, the obligations you have incurred for offices, ranks, emoluments and stipends have in their sum become higher than mountains and deeper than the sea. You must, I am sure, be eager to repay them. Because of the slanders of traitors, an unrighteous imperial order has now been issued. Those of you who value your reputations will wish [to fight] to secure the patrimony of the three generations of shoguns. If any of you wish to join the ex-emperor, speak out.

At this, the vassals were 'choked with tears . . . determined to repay their debts with their lives'. They were soon riding for Heian-kyō, recruiting more men along the way until they were so numerous that – in words attributed by the *Mirror of the East* to an apprehensive imperial ally – 'they resemble clouds and mist. Only divine intervention can save us from disaster.'

No such intervention was forthcoming, and in the intense fighting of what became known as the 'Jōkyū Incident', Go-Toba's forces were quickly routed. Remnants were pursued through their home provinces, where 'heads rolled constantly', 'naked blades were wiped over and over' and 'in their tilled fields not a sprout remained'.

As the *bakufu* army settled down in the capital, Go-Toba, his two sons and various of their allies separately embarked on long journeys into remote exile. A new emperor and retired emperor were found to serve as puppets for the Kamakura regime: the old imperial order would have its uses for many centuries yet. Property across the country totalling around 3,000 pieces of land was confiscated from the court and those who had sided with it, to be redistributed amongst the victorious warriors of eastern Japan. Having received a divine revelation of this great victory in a dream, Masako duly presented new lands to the Grand Shrine at Ise: she and the *bakufu* wished to be enemies only of 'unrighteousness', never of the court itself or its divine ancestors.

Meanwhile, Retired Emperor Go-Toba, not the last monarch to harbour impossible dreams of restoring imperial power, finally arrived at his lonely place of exile in the Oki Islands, out in the chilly Sea of Japan – there, as far as the *Mirror of the East* was concerned, to enjoy his just deserts:

> No tidings were borne to him by wild geese or blue birds from across the silent, cloud-rimmed sea, in whose vast expanse north and south seemed one, nor could he discern [the passing of time] as he gazed at the mist-shrouded waves, in whose boundless tracks east merged with west. He thought of nothing but the misery of life.

*

The Nun Shogun faced one final test when her brother Yoshitoki died in 1224. His may have been that seemingly rare form of death in this era – the result of natural causes. But there were rumours that in yet another attempt to wrest power from the Hōjō, Yoshitoki was in fact poisoned by his second wife's family. Masako is said to have seen off an incipient takeover bid for the *bakufu* both quickly and peacefully, remonstrating in person with the would-be plotters. With Yoshitoki's son Yasutoki safely installed as the new regent for the young shogun, the continuing dominance of the *bakufu* by Masako's family was assured. Yasutoki would go on to establish Kamakura's reputation for solid rule: creating a new, broader council as its main organ of governance, issuing legal codes – previously the prerogative of the imperial court – and sharpening the *bakufu*'s administration of impartial justice in the many suits over land that became a feature of the period.

By the time Masako died in 1225, at the age of sixty-eight, she had outlived many of the most powerful men of the era: her husband, her father, her brother and her two sons. She had seen off a retired emperor and his army. She had proven herself one of the first great players of Japan's new warrior politics, acknowledged as such in Heian-kyō with the rare award to a lay nun of official court rank. And against all the odds she had helped to secure a fresh form of government at Kamakura, under the regency of her own family, which would stand for another century and provide a model of warrior rule for another 500 years after that. This history would make profound and enduring contributions to the self-image of the Japanese in literature, theatre and film, in art and fashion, in politics and technology, in spirituality and that great warrior concern – self-cultivation.

6

Shinran

(親鸞)

1173–1262

Power to the People

The elderly Shinran, pictured with rosary and a walking
stick with a fur-covered handle. Portrait, 14th century.
Nara National Museum.

At the dawn of the thirteenth century, as Hōjō Masako battled to keep the new Kamakura *bakufu* on course, up on a mountain overlooking Heian-kyō a monk was in the throes of an existential crisis. Shinran had been born down in the city below in 1173. At the age of nine he had left his family – the wealthy Arinori, perhaps distantly related to the Fujiwara – to join the Tendai order. He spent the next twenty years living and working on Mount Hiei, sharing in the scriptural and ritual life of the place and doing his best to get used to the demands of monasticism.

By 1201, it had become clear that he couldn't do it. The rigours of monasticism were simply not for him. Some would later speculate that he had also struggled with celibacy and with the tainting of life on Hiei by the politics of the secular world. So precarious had Tendai's existence been in the years after its founder Saichō had died in 822, that there was talk of the 'foodless monks of Hiei'. Now, from the sprawling headquarters of the Enryaku-ji temple complex, Tendai dominated the Buddhist landscape in Japan. It was the closest thing the country had to a national church, its priestly ranks mirroring those of the court – occupied, at the higher end, by much the same class of people. It was a major player in Japan's *shōen* system of private estates, and its armies of warrior monks, based on Mount Hiei and at temples across the country, had recently seen action during the Genpei War.

Whatever the combination of factors, political and personal, that fuelled Shinran's despondency about his vocation, life now looked very bleak indeed. He was painfully aware of his own deep inadequacy and certain that he could not remain a priest any longer. Yet to turn his back on the priesthood would surely, he believed, disqualify him from any hope of salvation. The conclusion seemed inescapable: hell awaited.

*

A priest who gives a sermon should be handsome. After all, you're most aware of the profundity of his teaching if you're gazing at his face as he speaks. If your eyes drift elsewhere, you tend to forget what you've just heard, so an unattractive face has the effect of making you feel quite sinful.

The literature of the Heian era's heyday had at times suggested a society impervious to anguished reflections on life, death and salvation. Sei Shōnagon's classic of social commentary, *The Pillow Book*, depicted an aristocratic elite living quite contentedly at a knowing, ironic remove from such concerns. They seemed to regard matters of religion, like the affairs of government, as ultimately reducible to human relationships – with all their attendant foibles and delicious missteps:

I must say, from my own sinful point of view, it seems quite uncalled-for to go around as some do, vaunting their religious piety and rushing to be the first to be seated wherever a sermon is being preached . . . [Some] talk and nod and launch into interesting stories, spreading out their fans and putting them to their mouths when they laugh, groping at their ornately decorated rosaries and fiddling with them while they talk, craning to look here and there, criticizing the carriages, discussing how other priests do things this way or that in other Lotus Discourses and sutra dedication services they've been to, and so on and so forth . . .

And yet, for all its brilliant self-confidence, Heian life was marked by a sense of the world as profoundly strange and often hostile: full of ghosts and goblins, demons and evil spirits, malevolent spell-casting foxes, and taboos on where and when a person might safely travel.

Underlying everything was an awareness that nothing in the world is forever. An element of poetic posturing might sometimes be at play, when a person mused on the all-too-brief blossoming of a cherry tree or the melancholy evidence offered by their mirror as the years went by. Still, there were moments when the abyss really did seem to beckon.

One of the most striking products of just such a juncture in life was

Hōjō-ji, a temple founded in 1019, on the banks of the Kamo River, by the great Fujiwara patriarch Michinaga.

Laid out across more than five hectares, with a garden and lake at the centre, Hōjō-ji was a fabulous architectural achievement. A contemporary recalled sand that 'glittered like crystal' and a lake on which artificial lotus blossoms floated, each holding a buddha, 'its image mirrored in the water'. Jewelled boats glided along under the boughs of trees over which jewelled nets were draped. On an island in the middle of the lake, artificial peacocks and parrots were at play.

Splendid though it was, Hōjō-ji was no mere vanity project, dreamed up by the realm's de facto ruler keen to broadcast his status and power. It was the work of a dying man. Designed on the basis of vivid descriptions found in Buddhist scriptures, Hōjō-ji was intended to be a representation on Earth of the 'Pure Land' into which Michinaga hoped to be reborn.

A powerful influence on this aspiration was a Tendai monk by the name of Genshin. He produced a book in 985 entitled *Anthology on Rebirth in the Pure Land* (*Ōjō Yōshū*), in which he recalled the conventional division of Buddhist time into three periods, dating from the death of the historical Buddha. In the first period, Buddhist ideas and practices flourish. Later, they begin to lose their vitality. The third and final period, spanning 10,000 years, is known as *mappō*, the age of the 'Latter-Day of the Law'. Genshin claimed that the world was about to enter this final stage of cosmic time, in which the conventional Buddhist practices required for salvation – meditation, ritual, sutra recitation – would become all but impossible for people to perform.

This did not mean that all was lost for humanity. It meant that humanity needed help – in the form of the celestial Buddha Amida, a prominent figure in the Mahayana Buddhist pantheon. Amida was said to have vowed that anyone who called faithfully on his name would be reborn, after death, into his Pure Land: a paradise that would be ideal for working towards one's final freedom from the cycle of birth and rebirth. Popularizing the Amida tradition, Genshin counselled people seeking Amida's aid to recite the *nembutsu*: '*Namu Amida Butsu*' or 'I take refuge in the Buddha Amida'; and to visualize

Amida's 'welcoming descent' (*raigō*), as he swept down from the sky on a puff of cloud, attended by his bodhisattvas, to whisk a dying believer away to his Pure Land.

Michinaga ended up living longer than he had expected. But when his time came, in 1027, his chronicler recalled him dying the ideal death of his era. He lay down in Amida Hall, part of the Hōjō-ji complex, surrounded by *raigō* paintings and nine giant statues of Amida, each three metres high and made from gilded wood. His head positioned towards the north and his face turned westwards, in the direction of Amida's Pure Land, Michinaga repeated the words of the *nembutsu*. As he did so, he clutched at silken cords connecting him to the nine statues, so that Amida might draw his spirit from his body and take him away to his new home.

Over the next two centuries, as political uncertainties mounted and parts of Japan were racked by disorder and armed conflict, Amida Halls became an increasingly common feature of the architectural landscape. Their design, mirroring the *shinden* style of aristocratic mansions, together with the heavy use in Heian-era Buddhist art of sumptuous and expensive materials like gold, silver, silk and mother-of pearl, appeared to reflect the expectation that the primary objects of Amida's mercy were ailing aristocrats. An especially wealthy or anxious noble could even pay to have Buddhist monks dress up in imitation of bodhisattvas – complete with golden masks and jewelled crowns – and 'welcome' him or her into the Pure Land.

But the sense of human powerlessness on which the Amida teachings rested ended up gaining far broader appeal across the eleventh and twelfth centuries. While Japan's wealthy turned to Amida when their bodies failed them, others lower down the social scale did so when the world failed them – or when they thought they had failed themselves. People whose daily activities sat uneasily alongside Buddhist precepts, such as fighting and fishing, or who were otherwise caught up in living less than saintly lives, proved receptive to stories of Amida and his Pure Land when wandering monks passed by, offering dire warnings and making great promises. Collections of short biographies began to circulate in the twelfth century, telling of people who had done the most terrible things — including a monk who first fathered a daughter and then 'turned [her] into his wife' — and yet had been saved through Amida's mercy.

The *nembutsu* became central to all this, revolutionary in its simplicity and egalitarianism. You didn't have to build a temple, commission expensive artwork, study the sutras or fork out to have monks gather around your deathbed impersonating bodhisattvas. The *nembutsu* required no money, no learning and not even very much time — farmers recited it while working away in the fields. Others sang and danced it in the streets. Buddhism in Japan was moving towards a new and highly consequential stage on its journey: from protecting the state, through looking after the elite, to touching and shaping the inner lives of ordinary Japanese as never before.

*

Critics found these *nembutsu* teachings rather too easy. The idea that salvation had nothing to do with status, money, time, effort, intellect or personal worthiness was not just very unlikely, it also ran counter to the deepest instincts of people who possessed and valued some or all of these things. That might help to explain why Shinran passed twenty years on Mount Hiei, where the Amida teachings were part of his training, without seeing in them a way that he might be saved. Instead, by 1201, failure had forced him into misery and despair. Convinced that his time as a Tendai monk was drawing to a close, Shinran embarked on a hundred-day retreat at the Rokkakudō temple in Heian-kyō. There — according to one account — he received, at dawn on the ninety-fifth day, a visionary message from none other than Prince Shōtoku himself: founding father of the nation, spiritual grandfather to Saichō and now the bearer of instructions about what Shinran should do next.

Shinran did as he was told. He left the Rokkakudō and set out for a place called Yoshimizu. There he found a man by the name of Hōnen, a fellow Tendai monk who had left Mount Hiei a quarter of a century before and who had since established an eclectic and enthusiastic band of followers including fishermen, former samurai, robbers and prostitutes. His message was simple. Nothing in the world matters, he said, except for the *nembutsu*. Priestly robes and rituals achieve nothing. Illiteracy, sexual incontinence and all manner of roguish behaviour endanger nothing. One need only call sincerely on Amida's name, and one will be saved.

Thanks to some combination of this stark message and its embodiment in Hōnen, Shinran came alive at this point to the Amida teachings. He found himself overwhelmed by a sense of a compassionate power active in the world, immeasurably beyond his own strivings and accomplishing on his behalf all that he knew he could not do for himself. It proved to be the great turning point in his life. He became one of Hōnen's disciples and worked with him for the next six years, propagating what became known as the 'exclusive *nembutsu*' teaching.

It did not endear them to all. Alongside opposition from Japan's various religious hierarchies, which did not take kindly to news of their obsolescence, worries emerged about law and order. Some amongst Hōnen's followers interpreted Amida's compassionate generosity in the next life as a licence to misbehave in this one. Lobbying of the imperial court by the Buddhist establishment finally resulted, in 1207, in a ban on preachers of the exclusive *nembutsu*. Hōnen and some of his followers, Shinran included, were ejected from the clerical class and banished to different parts of the country. Shinran would never see Hōnen again.

*

Exiled to Echigo, in north-central Honshū, Shinran spent the years that followed raising a family with his wife Eshinni – whom he may have married while still a monk, thereby compounding his errors in the eyes of his critics – and engaging in studies in support of his new-found ideals. In 1211, the ban on the exclusive *nembutsu* teaching was at last lifted. But Heian-kyō remained a hostile place. Fresh edicts were occasionally issued, and a few years after Hōnen died in 1212 monks from Mount Hiei tried to smash up his tomb and remove his body. Rather than risk going back to the capital, Shinran moved his family to eastern Japan. A later account of his life would claim that his vision in 1201 had included images of multitudes in that part of the country crying out for his help.

A village called Inada, in Hitachi Province, became Shinran's base for the next twenty years. There he began to preach and to gather around him a small but growing band of 'fellow practitioners, honoured friends', as he called them, drawn from a mixture of lower-ranking warriors, merchants, artisans, farmers and people working in industries like timber and mining. Shinran did not believe in having disciples, regarding himself as having nothing of his own to offer. He was, as he put it, 'neither monk nor layman'; just '*Gutoku*', the 'foolish, bald-headed one'. Everything of value came from Amida, in gratitude for which Shinran sought to inspire awareness and faith in others.

Faith – or 'true entrusting' (*shinjin*) – became Shinran's great contribution to the *nembutsu* movement, developed through his major work *The True Teaching, Practice and Realization of the Pure Land Way* (*Kyōgyōshinshō*) and in poems, hymns and letters. So profound did Shinran believe human weakness to be, and so inauspicious the times, that he saw people as simply unable to contribute anything towards their own salvation. That included reciting the *nembutsu*, if they tried to do it under their own steam – relying on what was called *jiriki* or 'self-power'. A person must instead entrust themselves completely to the 'other-power' (*tariki*) of Amida, so that when the *nembutsu* was said it was really Amida doing the willing and the talking in some deep and fundamental part of that individual. Such a person became 'grasped' by Amida, as Shinran put it, 'never to be abandoned'.

The laying aside of one's own ideas and efforts, intrinsic as these were to a person's identity, proved for many a difficult and daunting prospect. People were naturally tempted to calculate and to conceptualize rather than diving right in. But Shinran insisted, time and again, that 'the *nembutsu* is beyond description, explanation and conception'. Only an encounter with Amida could move a person's knowledge on, not in terms of furnishing them with new propositions, but via a changed awareness of the world and a renewed sense of themselves, less bound up than before with words and with past deeds. This new sort of knowing did not displace ordinary reasoning. It ran alongside it, illuminating its limitations – just as a follower of Shinran could expect to gain insight into his or her faults and foibles without actually being relieved of them.

Interpreters of Shinran down the centuries would disagree about what all this meant for whether, and in what sense, Amida and his Pure Land existed. There were those for whom both were real in a fairly straightforward sense: one could expect to be reborn after death in something resembling Michinaga's temple garden, with its soothing waters and gossamer-like lotus blossoms. For others, Amida and the Pure Land were the products of infinite light and compassion acting in a limited human heart and upon a limited human imagination. In this sense, they were *more* real than something 'out there', since the very notion of 'out there' was part of a flawed human apprehension of the world to begin with, from which true entrusting could release a person.

With the salvific heavy-lifting left to Amida, one of the things required of a believer was to engage in unflinching reflection on themselves and their lives. The awareness of ignorance and weakness thereby generated would aid them in their abandonment to Amida's embrace – like a child who needs to discover for himself that a given task is beyond his capacities before he surrenders it to a parent. Believers struggling with this task, or clinging to a sense of their own basic worthiness or level-headedness, could find in Shinran's thought an idea that was encouraging and profoundly shocking in equal measure. Where conventional morality assumed that good people had a better claim on divine favour, Shinran insisted that the 'evil person', the constitutionally incapable person, was the focus of Amida's mercy and compassion.

From the 1230s onwards, Shinran's growing band of followers in eastern Japan – soon numbering in the thousands, perhaps the tens of thousands – formed themselves into close, supportive and self-funding congregations, meeting around once per month to chant the *nembutsu* together. They found their new movement dogged not just by misunderstandings on the part of insiders, but misrepresentations by outsiders too. The most compelling of these, put forward by religious rivals and secular authorities alike, was the so-called 'licensed evil' charge. Some of these fledgling congregations, it was alleged – and indeed the allegations were sometimes true – harboured people who thought that they could do whatever they wanted to, on the basis that the *nembutsu* would make everything all right again. Some were drinking and gambling; others were insulting one another and subjecting *kami* and Buddhist deities to ridicule.

Shinran responded as best he could. Possession of the antidote, he argued, is not a good reason to drink poison. And, in any case, a true appreciation of Amida's gift will inspire gratitude, and gratitude is an unfailing wellspring of ethical behaviour. Japan's various *kami* and deities, Amida aside, might indeed be irrelevant to a person's salvation. They might even become a source of distraction and confusion. But to show them outright disrespect was hardly the product of gratitude, and it risked providing fresh ammunition to opponents of an already marginalized movement.

Shinran's pastoral letters, together with a work called the *Notes Lamenting Deviations* (*Tannishō*), compiled decades after his death, reveal other problems amongst his followers. Congregations were vulnerable to falling back into the standard moralities of the day, running the related risk of the pride that comes from self-conscious simplicity and an embattled state. They are warned against affectation, against the insistence that 'knowledge is essential for the religious life' or that 'only good people should say the *nembutsu*', and against what appears to have been a trend for banning undesirables from congregations' meeting places, or *dōjō*. Such people, says the *Notes Lamenting Deviations*, 'show outwardly how wise, virtuous, and diligent they are, while inwardly cherishing vanity and falsehood'.

Sometime in the mid-1230s, when he was around sixty years old, Shinran returned to his birthplace of Heian-kyō. The move may have been prompted by a fresh ban on radical preachers of the *nembutsu*, issued by the *bakufu* for the city of Kamakura and its surrounds. Shinran's village of Inada wasn't far away, and he was sufficiently well known to represent an obvious target.

Shinran spent the last years of his long life in Heian-kyō, gifts from his followers back east allowing him to lead a reasonably comfortable existence. One portrait, from 1255, shows him dressed in a black robe, with catskin slippers for his feet and a walking stick decorated with fur. This was no quiet retirement, however. Alongside composing the bulk of his written output during these years, Shinran found himself encountering a problem with which Hōjō Masako had been all too familiar: the imperilling of a revolutionary new initiative by a family member determined to commandeer it for their own benefit.

The trouble started in the mid-1250s when Shinran asked his son Zenran to deal with some difficulties amongst *nembutsu* followers in eastern Japan. These included the by-now-familiar 'licensed evil' problem. Matters had escalated to the point where some of Shinran's senior followers had been summoned to Kamakura to explain themselves. Zenran's response to the crisis was to involve the local authorities against the troublemakers, and to try to establish a more unified community under his own personal leadership, by claiming to have received secret new doctrines from his father. Nothing could have been further from Shinran's conception of himself and the non-hierarchical nature of the movement. Struggling to piece things together at a distance, with deep reluctance he reached the conclusion that he could no longer fully trust Zenran. In the end, the price of clarity in communicating deceptively simple teachings to an audience beset by all the usual human flaws was for Shinran publicly, and painfully, to disown his son.

*

In 1262, just a few years after the Zenran scandal erupted, Shinran passed away. Ninety years of age, he died facing west towards the Pure Land, with the *nembutsu* on his lips. His daughter Kakushinni, who had cared for him in his last years, now took responsibility for interring Shinran's ashes in Heian-kyō. This grave site, known as the Ōtani memorial, later became a focus for religious services and acts of devotion. It was the beginning of unexpected shifts in Shinran's movement that might have dismayed the man himself, but which, given his clear-eyed view of humanity's needs and frailties, would probably not have surprised him.

Where Shinran had refused the mantle of doctrinal or ecclesiastical authority, his movement developed an influential leadership, established not along the master–disciple lines of other Buddhist organizations but via a family lineage consisting of Shinran's own descendants. While he had called himself the 'foolish, bald-headed one', one of those descendants, his great-grandson Kakunyo (1270–1351), encouraged people to revere Shinran as an incarnation of Amida. Kakunyo meanwhile worked to develop the Ōtani memorial into the movement's first temple: the Hongan-ji or 'Temple of the Primal Vow'.

The idea began to gain currency that only descendants of Shinran could accurately interpret his teachings for new times. These descendants headed the Hongan-ji, as patriarchs and leaders of what gradually became the most important branch of Shinran's movement. Instrumental in this transformation was the Patriarch Rennyo (1415–99), who brought into the Hongan-ji fold many formerly independent congregations whose leadership successions had been based on teaching rather than blood. Rennyo won large numbers of new rural converts across the country. And through a series of pastoral letters he clarified the basic doctrines of a new Buddhist sect, based on Shinran's teachings: Jōdo Shinshū or the 'True Essence of the Pure Land Teaching'. By this time, the movement had spread westwards, moving towards and then beyond Heian-kyō, securing lucrative support along the way from the country's merchant class. Sure proof of Jōdo Shinshū's success came in 1465, when warrior monks descended Mount Hiei and burned the Hongan-ji to a crisp. It was not the last that Japan would hear of Jōdo Shinshū.

For all that his successors changed the game, people remembered 'saint' Shinran, as they came to call him, for his uncompromising radicalism. He had overturned conventional morality and shown unusual, insightful concern for the spiritual lives of the middling and lower classes, risking the wrath of the authorities all the while. Many, both in Japan and further afield, would one day spot parallels here with Martin Luther. Both were idealized as lone men of conscience who turned their backs on the wealth, corruption, complacency and ritual complexity of the religious establishments of their day, taking refuge instead in a faith rooted in grace, which was less dependent on the ministrations of an elite priesthood. Both penned hymns in the vulgar idiom (in Shinran's case, Japanese rather than Chinese), the better to reach ordinary women and men with their message. Both movements gave rise to meeting places that were funded and controlled by the laity, and which for spiritual reasons remained aesthetically sparse – early *dōjō* were sometimes just a room in a person's home, with an inscription bearing Amida's name hung over a simple altar. And both leaders launched a revolution in clerical marriage, although Jōdo Shinshū's permitting of its monks to marry spread eventually to rival Buddhist sects while the Catholic Church continued to resist the idea.

The comparison with Luther was apt in one last way: like Luther, Shinran was part of a broader movement of religious reformation in his era. He and Hōnen were not the only ones to become disaffected with Tendai, turning their backs on their temples to seek out a more direct and authentic path to truth. Three more monks left the order during the late twelfth and early thirteenth centuries, going on to initiate new religious movements on the basis of personal trials and insights. Alongside Hōnen's and Shinran's communities, these would become so successful that they would end up eclipsing Tendai, Shingon and the earlier Nara sects, effectively replacing them as Japan's Buddhist mainstream and reshaping the way the Japanese thought about themselves and the world.

Eisai (1141–1215) travelled to Song China, bringing back what was by that time the dominant form of Buddhism there: Chan, or 'Zen' in Japanese. Its primary focus was a direct intuiting of the Absolute, achieved via a combination of practices including meditation and the use of *kōan*, riddles designed to push a person beyond words and logic and towards enlightenment. Sponsorship from the Kamakura *bakufu* (including Hōjō Masako) and Eisai's embrace of the broader Buddhist tradition helped his Rinzai sect to gain rapid acceptance in high society. Dōgen (1200–1253) made the same journey to China. He returned with a stricter focus on meditation alone that left his Sōtō sect a relatively marginal player in its early generations, though it became a major force in Japanese Buddhism across later centuries.

Finally, Nichiren (1222–82) emerged from twenty years of studying Japan's major Buddhist sects with a disdain for them all. He launched fearsome attacks on the Pure Land sects in particular, and counselled his followers to rely instead on a simple recitation – 'I take refuge in the Lotus Sutra' – alongside an eclectic series of principles for practical everyday living that he had distilled from across Japan's philosophical spectrum. These, he claimed, would bring about the salvation of each person individually and the good of the nation as a whole. Nichiren's interest in politics, and his criticism of the Kamakura *bakufu*, earned him exile to Izu in 1261 and later to Sado Island. But Buddhist sects bearing his name went on to flourish nonetheless.

Japan's religious old guard did what they could to engage with the ideas and practices championed by the new sects of what became known as 'Kamakura Buddhism'. Tendai and Shingon were in any case too strong, widespread and well-funded for their immediate futures to be at risk from upstarts. But the strength of these upstarts lay not just in their fresh approaches to the deep problems of life. They were actively supported by up-and-coming sections of the population. For Japan's aristocracy, interest in Amida had come as their leadership role in the country's culture and politics was waning. For the lower-ranking warriors, merchants and farmers who flocked to mass movements like Shinran's, the *dōjō* community and the high standards of conduct associated with it formed an important part of their identity as their fortunes rose. At death, these people would claim a place in the Pure Land – but first they would inherit the Earth.

7
Zeami

(世阿弥)

1363–1443

Master of Arts

Scene from the play *The Well-Cradle (Izutsu)*.
Woodblock print by Tsukioka Kōgyo (1926).

A monk arrives at a well in the grounds of the Ariwara temple. A woman comes to draw water and to offer prayers at a grave-mound nearby. Intrigued, the monk asks her name. The woman demurs, telling him instead about the grave. This may be the resting place, she says, of a courtier from centuries before, whose famous name the monk knows well: Ariwara no Narihira. He grew up around here and was friends with the daughter of Ki no Aritsune:

> There lived in this province, long ago,
> two families, house by house
> and, at their gates, a well.
> To the well-cradle their two children came
> fondly to talk and to watch each other
> in the mirroring water,
> cheek to cheek and sleeve on sleeve.

Narihira and the girl used to measure their heights against this 'well-cradle' (a wooden frame built over a well), says the woman. Later they fell in love and were married. He was unfaithful. But she, the one people call the Well-Cradle Lady, remained true to him always.

As the woman continues her tale, it gradually becomes clear that *she* is the Well-Cradle Lady, from all those years ago. Sleeping that night on a bed of moss under the moon, the monk finds the Lady appearing to him in a dream. Dressed in the head-piece and robe once worn by Narihira, she dances by the well before parting the grasses that surround it and gazing down into its waters:

> Cradle, well-cradle,
> well-cradle that told

who was the taller,
I've grown up, love . . .
I've grown old . . .

I see myself, yet still I love him!
Departed lover in phantom form,
a flower withered, all colour gone,
but fragrant yet, Ariwara.

Written by Zeami Motokiyo, *The Well-Cradle* (*Izutsu*) came to be regarded as a classic of Nō theatre, and its author as the genre's pioneering figure. Nō's signature feature is its radical economy of form. Plays are performed, traditionally by men alone, on an open stage of polished cypress wood with a pine tree painted on a panel at the rear. There are few props save for a fan, its design linked symbolically to the theme of the play. Audiences focus their attention instead on the main actor and his mastery of *monomane*, literally 'imitating things', not by mimicking outward appearances but by capturing and expressing what Zeami called their 'fundamental essence' – in a slow and spacious blend of prose and poetry, dance and song, which has been likened to living sculpture.

The main actor wears a mask, a revered object finely crafted from wood – cypress, camphor or paulownia. Its fixed expression is brought to life by the play of light and by the actor's movements as he glides across the floor in white *tabi* socks; sometimes seeming almost still, at other times performing sudden, unexpected jumps, turns and stamps. A second actor – in *The Well-Cradle*, the monk – plays a minor, unmasked role, as 'witness'. Off to one side of the stage sits a chorus of around eight people, their chanting backed by a small ensemble of bamboo flute and drums of varying sizes, from the small *kotsuzumi*, tapped with the right hand, up to the thunderous *taiko*, resting on a stand and struck with two large drumsticks. The drummers cry out at key moments, building the atmosphere.

Much is required of the audience. Most Nō plays draw their stories and a great deal of their text from classical Japanese literature. *The Well-Cradle* is based on episodes from the tenth-century *Tales of*

Ise, inspired by the life of Ariwara no Narihira. By weaving new elements into old and, like his poetic predecessors, using the rhythms and textures of the natural world to suggest the subtle play of human emotions – a breeze passing through grass; the moon rising over the still waters of a well – playwrights like Zeami could elicit powerful, complex forms of recognition and response from the suitably prepared.

Although Nō ended up as the epitome of high culture – beautiful, lavish, demanding – playwrights and performers like Zeami and his father Kan'ami were regarded by many members of polite society in their day as *majiwaranu hito*, 'those with whom one does not mix'. It was a telling turn of phrase. Once upon a time, in the era of Murasaki Shikibu's *Tale of Genji*, Japan had been a relatively segregated society. Nobles had their villas, Buddhists their mountain temples, merchants their marketplaces, warriors their provincial playgrounds, and performers – dancers, singers and actors – the open road: they travelled between the shrines, temples and villages where they plied their trade. But the rise of warrior influence in Japan from the 1100s onwards helped to change the game. By Zeami's time, 'mixing' was very much the order of the day. In Kyoto (Heian-kyō) especially, warrior culture and aristocratic culture were coming together, taking connoisseurship and entertainment in brand new directions.

Zeami lived and worked at the heart of all this change. Exposed to the cultural ferment of the capital from a young age, he drew on many of its most highly valued arts and attitudes in shaping Nō and creating some of its finest plays. Zeami was also one of the first to reflect, in writing, on the importance of theatre for actors and for audiences of all kinds. 'The origin of the art of Nō', he claimed, 'is to soothe the minds of the people, and to move the sensibilities of the high and the low equally. This is the very basis for a long life, happiness, and prosperity.'

Close attention of this kind to how art, philosophy and a person's development intersect became a celebrated feature of Japanese culture in the Muromachi period (1336–1573) and remained so ever after. When in later centuries the question 'Who are the Japanese?' arose, many people both inside and outside the country would look

to the accomplishments of this era – in poetry and painting, the tea
ceremony, gardens and theatre – in seeking their answer.

*

Zeami's world had roots of a kind in a piece of prose rather less
refined and allusive than his own:

> We, the Great Mongolian Empire, have . . . become the master of the
> universe. Therefore, innumerable states in far-off lands have longed to
> form ties with us . . . However, this has not happened [with Japan].
> This must be because you are not fully informed. Therefore, I hereby
> send you a special envoy to inform you of our desire. From now on, let
> us enter into friendly relations with each other. Nobody would wish to
> resort to arms.

Fights over power and lucrative land rights had already begun to
weaken the Kamakura *bakufu*'s hold on law and order when in 1268,
around forty years after Hōjō Masako's death and six years after
Shinran's, this odd and distinctly unwelcome piece of correspondence
arrived from abroad. The sender was one Kublai Khan, grandson of
Genghis Khan and heir to a loose-knit empire whose reach by this
point extended from Poland to the Korean peninsula. Kublai was
presently engaged in putting an end to China's Song dynasty, and would
shortly proclaim himself the first in a new Chinese imperial line – the
Yuan – with his capital at Dadu, modern-day Beijing.

The *bakufu* – still controlled by the Hōjō family as regents – passed
the missive on to the imperial court in Kyoto, where the *bakufu*'s
inclination to ignore it was upheld. Several further overtures went
unanswered while the *bakufu* hurriedly prepared Japan's west coast
for a possible invasion. It came in November 1274. A Mongol force of
around 20,000 soldiers landed at Hakata Bay, in northern Kyūshū,
and set about schooling the samurai in a brand new form of combat.
Japanese warriors still favoured one-to-one clashes from horseback,
as they had done during the Genpei War a century before: calling on
an opponent by name, and inviting them to do battle. But there were
few speakers of Japanese in an invasion force that comprised Mongol and Korean fighters. In any case their preference was to attack en

masse. Forming up in great phalanxes, they sent thickets of poison-tipped and gunpowder-propelled arrows arcing high through the air, while their catapults lobbed exploding iron balls whose deafening, blinding effects were profoundly disorienting for samurai and steed alike.

Japan's defenders were forced to pull back. But the invading forces suffered losses of their own and ended up reboarding their 900 vessels. What was intended as a temporary retreat by Kublai's men turned into one of history's most famous defeats. Legend has it that a great storm blew up, ripping through the Mongol fleet and forcing what remained of it to return home. Around a third of the army never made it back.

Members of a new Mongol diplomatic mission the next year were treated to a trip out to the seaside suburbs of Kamakura – and executed. The inevitable new invasion, far larger than the first, followed in 1281. This too was reputedly thwarted by the weather, and relieved Japanese began to speak of salvation – twice – at the hands of a 'divine wind' or *kami-kaze*. Unfortunately for the Hōjō, the gods declined to help with their domestic difficulties. Further decades of bloody factional strife and worsening banditry on land and sea eventually inspired a fresh attempt, this time by Emperor Go-Daigo, at restoring imperial sovereignty in Japan. The Hōjō responded by exiling him to the Oki Islands in 1331, and then, when he escaped, sending an army against him, led by Ashikaga Takauji. Descended from the same imperial family line as Minamoto no Yoritomo, Takauji was secretly unhappy about the comparatively lowly and Taira-related Hōjō enjoying such influence. He defected to Emperor Go-Daigo in 1333, helping to destroy the Kamakura *bakufu* and returning effective power in Japan to the Emperor. And then in 1336 he double-crossed Go-Daigo and established his own shogunate. This brief, three-year period of imperial rule, later known as the 'Kenmu Restoration', would prove to be the last in Japan for more than 500 years.

The Ashikaga shoguns who succeeded Takauji emulated their Kamakura predecessors to a significant extent, but with two important differences. First, lacking the nationwide influence that the Kamakura shoguns had once enjoyed, they were forced to allow regional warrior-constables (*shugo*) more autonomy than would one day turn out to have been wise. Second, while the Kamakura shoguns had developed a distant, uneasy relationship with the imperial court in Kyoto, the Ashikaga shoguns chose to base themselves in the capital, in a suburb called Muromachi, giving this new era of Japanese history its name.

While Emperor Go-Daigo fled to the mountains south of the city, Takauji installed a biddable imperial prince in his place and set about insinuating himself into courtly life. The result was a line of shoguns who felt at home in Kyoto and at ease with aristocratic tastes – no one more so than Takauji's grandson Yoshimitsu, who became the third Ashikaga shogun in 1368. Yoshimitsu was smart, he was cultured, and when one day in 1374 a theatre troupe from Yamato Province led by a man called Kan'ami performed for him, the seventeen-year-old shogun decided that he very much liked what he saw.

Precisely what Kan'ami's troupe performed that day, we do not know. But Kan'ami had made a name for himself by this time as a great innovator within Japan's centuries-old performing arts tradition. One of its most important sources was shamanic ritual, dating back perhaps as far as the ancient Jōmon period, but first appearing in Japanese literature in the eighth-century *Record of Ancient Matters* and the *Chronicles of Japan*. In both, a story is told of the Sun Goddess Amaterasu hiding herself away in a cave, thus plunging the world into darkness. She is lured out only after Ame no Uzume, Goddess of Mirth and the Dawn, jumps on to an upturned tub, stamps her feet, enters a state of divine possession and begins to strip. The gathered *kami* burst into laughter, and Amaterasu peeks out of her cave to see what is going on. Startled by the sight of herself in a mirror that one of the *kami* has left strategically suspended from a tree, she pauses for a moment – and is promptly hauled all the way out of her cave, restoring light to the world.

Ame no Uzume's cave-mouth gambit is most likely a projection into myth of ritual dances performed by shrine priestesses in the eighth century to ensure the health of emperor, community and crops, and at other times to pacify restless and potentially dangerous spirits. These ritual dances seem to have been part of a progression, taking place across centuries, from a dancer becoming a *kami*, to being taken over by a *kami*, and finally to 'performing' possession in a carefully choreographed series of steps. In this way, a connection was established between possession and role play which, carried through as ritual performance, evolved into genres of dance and theatre geared more obviously towards entertainment – though the distinction was a fine one and not always made. These genres retained much else besides of their forebears' cosmic character: a deep respect for the stage as a sacred place, sparse musical accompaniment, a trance-like pace and even specific dance movements – including Ame no Uzume's spirit-pacifying stamp, enhanced for Nō audiences by the placement under the stage of giant pots to amplify the sound.

Chinese and Korean entertainment became influential in Japan from the 600s onwards. Early animal-mask dances (*gigaku*) were superseded by the stately storytelling style known as *bugaku* – eventually taken up in Nō drama to evoke China for Japanese audiences. *Shōmyō* Buddhist chanting, originally from India, became the basis of the Nō chorus. And circus-like diversions, including acrobatics, puppetry, juggling with balls and knives, fire-eating and magic, found favour both at the Heian-era court and out in the provinces, where theatre troupes incorporated them into their programmes.

For Kan'ami, the art form that mattered most was *dengaku* (field music). Originally a combination of *kami*-worship and light relief amidst the toil of planting rice, it had since morphed into a storytelling genre incorporating rich costumes and a musical accompaniment of drums and rattles. Some of Kan'ami's plays were reworkings of *dengaku* dramas. Others were new pieces that drew on a store of popular tales shared by performers of all stripes. Favourite subjects for Kan'ami included the deeds of Buddhist priests and madness and conflict of all kinds. Bearing his rural audiences closely in mind, he offered pacey plots, realistic acting and colloquial dialogue.

It was Kan'ami's rising reputation that earned his troupe the chance to put on a show for the shogun in 1374. But it was his eleven-year-old son Zeami, growing up training and performing with his father, who particularly caught Yoshimitsu's eye. Like many powerful men of his era, Yoshimitsu enjoyed the company of beautiful, graceful boys – there was even a genre of literature devoted to this sort of affection: *chigo monogatari* or 'tales of young boys'. Kan'ami and Zeami together seem to have so impressed Yoshimitsu that he offered

Kan'ami's theatre troupe, the Yūzaki-za, his patronage, and Zeami an intimate, life-changing relationship.

It became a turning point for Japanese theatre. Kan'ami's work was already more sophisticated than the name of his genre might suggest – *sarugaku*, literally 'monkey-music'. His troupe combined exclusive contracts at particular religious sites with participation in 'subscription events' arranged by temples seeking restoration funds: spectators donated small amounts – 'specks of dust accumulat[ing] to form a mountain', in the words of one such religious appeal – and performers received a cut of the takings. But with the shogun's patronage, the Yūzaki-za now based themselves in the capital and geared their work to a mixed aristocratic and warrior audience. The content and tone of their *sarugaku* began to shift accordingly: from popular rural fare towards something slower and more ethereal, steeped in classical culture.

The transition was largely Zeami's achievement. While his father always retained strong connections with the countryside, Zeami was soon sitting at Yoshimitsu's side in his new Palace of Flowers in Muromachi. Completed in 1381, the *shinden*-style complex covered twice the area of the Imperial Palace, in a part of Kyoto associated since the time of Murasaki Shikibu with Japan's aristocratic elite. It looked – and sounded – exquisite. Water from the Kamo River was channelled around large, luscious gardens landscaped to resemble an idealized mountain scene, feeding a great pond along the way, flowing serenely over carefully placed rocks and even passing with a soothing babble underneath the raised corridors that connected the palace's various rooms. One of those rooms was a music chamber, from where the strains of classical court music would be joined, on special occasions, to the sounds of the water and of wind passing through pine trees.

At the palace, Zeami watched some of the great artists of the day perform and listened to Yoshimitsu share his critiques of them. He encountered some of the leading intellectuals and poets of the age, too, including Nijō Yoshimoto, an elderly courtier and master of the art of *renga*, a 'linked verse' style of poetry in which several poets contributed their own lines to a single chain-like final product. Yoshimoto praised the young Zeami for his poetry, his skill at the ball game *kemari* and much else besides:

I quite lost my heart. A boy like this is rare . . . Such a charming manner and such poise! I don't know where such a marvellous boy can have come from.

In *The Tale of Genji*, Lady Murasaki is described as 'adorable with her misty, yet-unplucked eyebrows', and this boy is just as entrancing. I should compare him to a profusion of cherry or pear blossoms in the haze of a spring dawn; this is how he captivates . . .

When he dances, the movements of his limbs and the flutter of his sleeves are, in truth, more graceful than a willow swaying in the gentle breeze of the second month, more beautiful than all the flowers of the seven autumn grasses soaked with the evening dew . . . It's no surprise that the shogun is so taken with this boy.

Not everyone welcomed Zeami's rapid rise through the social ranks. An aristocratic diarist by the name of Go-oshikōji Kintada was scandalized when he spotted Zeami and Yoshimitsu sharing an observation platform at Kyoto's annual Gion Festival in 1378:

The shogun has shown an extraordinary fondness for him . . . He sat with the boy and shared drinks with him. Sarugaku like this is the occupation of beggars, and such favour for a sarugaku player indicates disorder in the nation. Those who give things to this boy find favour with the shogun, so the regional lords all compete with one another in making him presents, and they spend prodigious amounts.

Go-oshikōji was perhaps also in mourning for a time when not only a 'beggar' but also a military man would have known his place. But those days were long gone, and were not coming back. The streets of Kyoto were now full of samurai. Some settled into urban life by way of conspicuous consumption, drinking, womanizing and wagering large sums at tea gatherings and *renga* meetings – where the competitive element lay, respectively, in identifying a tea's region of origin and improvising a witty response to an opponent's poetical challenge. Others, more conscious of the lingering distaste in which they were held by the likes of Go-oshikōji, were in search of the finer things: culture, connoisseurship, personal development and a renewed sense of identity.

Many found these things in the company of monks from the Rinzai Zen sect, which was now becoming a new Buddhist establishment of sorts. It held great tracts of land out in the provinces, while wielding significant cultural influence in the capital, to whose architecture it contributed its main temple, Nanzen-ji, alongside five major temples known as the *Gozan* ('Five Mountains'). Where Shinran's successors preached humble gratitude for Amida's free gift of salvation, samurai found that Zen offered them struggle, achievement and the attractive immediacy and austerity of meditation and *kōan* study. In addition, as well as being famously tough and terse, many Zen masters had either studied in China or with Chinese monks living in Japan. This gave them sought-after expertise in Chinese philosophy and the high arts of poetry, porcelain, painting and calligraphy. Some temples ended up doubling as salons, prompting the *bakufu* to issue edicts requiring warriors and Zen monks alike to behave themselves: warriors must stop throwing away their money on expensive art; monks should get back to their meditation cushions.

Such was the milieu in which Yoshimitsu and now Zeami grew up, shaping profoundly the latter's writing and thinking about theatre. Of his early, formative years in the capital, Zeami left little personal record. But in a later work he divided an actor's life into seven distinct phases, and many have read this as semi-autobiographical. In phase one, from the age of seven, an actor learns the 'chanting, movement and dance' that form the basis of Nō theatre. In phase two, from twelve or thirteen, he enjoys a natural grace and a voice that carries well – something that both Yoshimitsu and Yoshimoto clearly saw in Zeami. Then, in phase three, from seventeen or eighteen years of age, the challenges begin. An actor finds that his child-like grace has deserted him, and he is at risk of giving up if practice feels burdensome or audience responses are muted.

In Zeami's case, one of the greatest challenges in the third phase of his life was staying on the right side of the shogun. Zeami's son later wrote delicately of his father's struggles to remain 'sensitive to the workings of the human heart' when dealing with Yoshimitsu. One of the shogun's consorts apparently managed him well, knowing 'when to offer him wine and when not to'. Her life 'was a success' as a result. Zeami, too, seems to have done well for a while, receiving from Yoshimitsu a warm, even nurturing directive about how he should pronounce the characters of his professional name – as 'Zeami'

ZEAMI – MASTER OF ARTS

rather than 'Seami'. But Yoshimitsu went much further with a rival actor called Inuō, from Ōmi Province, bestowing upon him a brand new name, 'Dōami', based on the first character of Yoshimitsu's own religious name of Dōgi.

Zeami also had to cope with the death of his father during these years. Kan'ami passed away in 1384, while performing out in the countryside. Bereft, Zeami seems to have taken some time away from his work at this point, for study and reflection at the Sōtō Zen temple Fugan-ji, Yamato Province. He always thereafter recalled his father in the highest possible terms: a big man who nevertheless possessed extraordinary grace; Nō's great innovator, whose ideas Zeami himself was merely codifying and passing on; and someone with an unparalleled gift for knowing and catering to the 'customs and morals' of particular audiences. A true professional, Zeami insisted, 'can perform without criticism at aristocratic venues, mountain temples, the countryside, the far-off provinces, and at the festivals of every kind of shrine'.

An actor who makes it through this tough period can, according to Zeami's scheme, look forward to happier times in the fourth and fifth phases of life. From twenty-four or twenty-five years of age, he is in his 'prime' and must work to avoid conceit. From thirty-four or thirty-five, he reaches the height of his professional powers, 'acknowledged by the public, and secure in his reputation'. In Zeami's case, this period saw him taking up the reins of his father's troupe. They performed for Yoshimitsu and his court on several occasions during the later 1380s and 1390s, including in the course of a grand shogunal pilgrimage to the Kasuga Shrine in Nara.

Yoshimitsu, meanwhile, was enjoying good years of his own. The mountain refuge to which Emperor Go-Daigo had fled back in the 1330s had developed, for a time, into a 'Southern Court', while Kyoto had become known as the 'Northern Court'. Both had enjoyed warrior backing, meaning that the early decades of the Ashikaga shogunate passed in intermittent civil warfare. Yoshimitsu negotiated an end to that rivalry in 1392, and two years later he combined his title of shogun with the highest official role that the imperial court had to offer: great minister of the Council of State. In 1401, he established diplomatic and trading relations with China's new Ming dynasty.

One of the true highlights of Yoshimitsu's life came a few years later, in 1408. Having hosted one emperor at the Palace of Flowers back in 1381 – the first ever imperial progress to a warrior leader's private residence – Yoshimitsu hosted another at a second luxurious property of his, the Kitayama Villa, incorporating the magnificent Kinkaku-ji (Golden Pavilion) in its famous 'mirror pond' setting. The Emperor's stay lasted three full weeks and included the enjoyment of *sarugaku* plays. Zeami's name is not mentioned in the records (whereas Dōami's is), but his troupe may have been amongst the performers. If so, it would have been one of the last times that the shogun saw his old favourite on stage. Just weeks after the Emperor's visit, Yoshimitsu fell ill and died. Zeami had lost two of the biggest influences on his life: his father and Yoshimitsu. But as a playwright and as Nō's great philosopher, he was just getting started.

*

Zeami was now forty-five years old, and entering the sixth phase of life. At this point, an actor finds his beauty and physical strength starting to desert him. He should no longer 'be seen [on stage] without a mask'. He is also duty-bound to begin counselling younger actors, which Zeami undertook by way of treatises including *The Transmission of Style and the Flower (Fūshikaden)*, in which he laid out the phases of life and much else besides.

Zeami was also hard at work during these years producing some of the greatest plays in the Nō repertoire. It is impossible to say how many plays he wrote: Nō plays were usually neither signed nor dated, attracting as a result a great deal of detective and guesswork down the centuries. Amongst the thirty or forty plays that are reasonably certain to have been Zeami's the two most innovative types were his 'warrior plays' and 'woman plays'.

The warrior plays are a vivid testament to the arts and audiences of Zeami's day. Drawing their subject matter mostly from *The Tale of the Heike*, many feature an ordinary-looking protagonist who turns out to be the ghost of a famous warrior – appearing in a revelation scene impressively costumed in samurai armour. His spirit is unsettled not because of some terrible act of gratuitous violence – Zeami's audience would hardly have approved – but because he possesses, as many amongst Kyoto's nouveau riche warrior class wanted to believe of themselves, a cultured and sensitive soul.

Tadanori tells the story of a Taira-clan warrior by that name who was killed during the Genpei War and whose spirit cannot settle because he still desires recognition as a poet. The eponymous hero of *Atsumori* is another Taira warrior, cut down in his youthful prime during the same conflict. Atsumori's Minamoto assailant is filled with remorse after he finds a flute inside a brocade bag tied around the boy's waist – a sign of Atsumori's innocence and commitment to the peaceful over the martial arts. Victim reappears to killer in ghostly form, and the two are reconciled, in a scene that idealizes the coming together of warrior and aristocratic culture in Zeami's day: what might look superficially like a clash or competition is, deeper down, a meeting of spirits, in which the best is drawn out of both.

As with his warrior plays, many of Zeami's woman plays, including *The Well-Cradle*, are *mugen nō* ('apparition Nō'): the main actor is a ghost, while the minor actor shares the audience's here-and-now, creating a tension on stage between the two realms. The influence of Buddhist ideas about life, death and the hereafter can be found everywhere: from karmic come-uppances to the kind of tragic, romantic attachment to this world suffered by the Well-Cradle Lady. Amida and his grace feature heavily too, both in the plays themselves and in the professional names chosen by the likes of Zeami and his father Kan'ami – the 'ami' (阿弥) being short for 'Amida'.

The subtleties of his subject matter and the demands of his audience – some of whom enjoyed practising the chants and dances of Nō at home – forced Zeami to think hard about how his hoped-for effects could be achieved. Structure was important: a rhythm of *jo-ha-kyū* – a 'beginning', followed by a 'breakdown', followed by a 'quickening' – should be applied, he thought, both to phases within a play and to the sequence of plays making up a programme. (A Nō programme in Zeami's day typically featured three Nō plays and two Kyōgen plays – the latter being short, down-to-earth comic sketches that included improvised dialogue and often featured a Buddhist monk as the butt of the joke.) But much of the onus, inevitably, fell upon Zeami's actors, to whose development and craft he devoted much of his time in the later years of his life.

A basic requirement was to 'remain within the sensibilities of the aristocratic element of the audience'. This was not merely about flattering one's patrons. A key concept in Nō was 'the flower': a transcendent effect arising unbidden in an audience in response to an actor's performance, perhaps at some small moment of enchantment or the unexpected. Beauty expressed fused with beauty beheld – but only if the alchemy of actor and audience was right.

Actors must also do their research, seeking out and reproducing the essentials of their subject. You can't play an old man simply by adopting a stoop, Zeami insisted. You need grace and purpose, which only an actor of advanced experience and talent can manage. In the same way, madness should not be milked for entertainment – which it frequently was in Zeami's day. It is evidence of inner torment, so an actor must study the particular spirit that is possessing his character: god, buddha, demon or spirit of the dead. To really get this right, an actor must ultimately become deranged in his own mind.

The ultimate ideal was to raise all this to the level of *yūgen*. The word meant 'profound sublimity', and had its origins in Buddhist hermeneutics and Japanese literary criticism, though it was flexible enough in practice that it could be used to describe a stand-out moment in *kemari*. Zeami learned about *yūgen* in theatre from his *Ōmi sarugaku* rivals, before going on to make the concept his own. An actor should begin with the technical basics learned in the earliest phase of life: posture, movement and dance. He then gets a first feel for *yūgen* by observing the speech and deportment of nobles. After that, it becomes a matter of deeper, personal accomplishment: one moves beyond conventional standards of refinement and beauty, conveying instead some mysterious, dimly perceived truth, simultaneously sad and uplifting. This cannot be forced. An actor can only focus on getting the form right by being diligent over the course of a lifetime. *Yūgen* may then emerge of its own accord.

Zeami frequently favoured Zen terminology in setting out these most difficult elements of an actor's craft. He was influenced here by the company he kept, but also by his own commitment to Sōtō Zen, in which he seems to have taken vows in 1422. The keyword, in Zen, is *mushin*, 'no-mind'. 'The actor himself becomes the [subject] at his very foundation,' Zeami wrote. 'He should have no thoughts of imitating him.'

*

Yoshimitsu's son, Yoshimochi, turned out to prefer *dengaku* (field music) to Nō. He also harboured resentment towards his late father that extended to Yoshimitsu's favourites. Zeami nevertheless survived and thrived for a while under the new shogun, but worse was to come. In 1428, Yoshimochi died and was succeeded by his brother, Yoshinori, who was adamant that leadership of Zeami's troupe should pass to his own favourite, Zeami's nephew On'ami. Zeami had sought that honour for one of his own sons, Motomasa, and so he resisted. Relationships turned sour, and Zeami and Motomasa soon suffered two professional setbacks. They were banned, after 1429, from performing at the Retired Emperor's palace. And the next year they lost the musical directorship at the Kiyotaki Shrine. In both cases On'ami, with the new shogun's backing, benefited in their place.

Nor was that the end of it. In 1430, Zeami's son Motoyoshi quit Nō for the priesthood. Two years later, Motomasa died suddenly, possibly murdered. Zeami was forced to pass his writings on to someone from another troupe: his son-in-law, Zenchiku, who went on to become a celebrated Nō performer and playwright. Treatises like *The Transmission of Style and the Flower* were not, after all, intended for general public consumption. In the highly competitive world of theatre, and in common with other areas of Japanese cultural and religious life, they were to be passed down in secret to trusted and suitably qualified successors. On'ami meanwhile gained the leadership of Zeami's troupe after all. His descendants went on to enjoy a monopoly on official support all the way down to the mid-nineteenth century.

Finally, in 1434, Zeami found himself banished altogether from the cultured surrounds of Kyoto which had nurtured and shaped him since boyhood. Perhaps in punishment for his obstinacy over On'ami, he was exiled to Sado Island, off the western coast of northern Honshū. He seems to have remained in good spirits, despite everything, living in Shōhō-ji temple and carrying on with his writing almost right up to his death in 1443, at the age of eighty. He was buried in the grounds of Fugan-ji temple, Yamato Province, where he had once stayed and studied after his father's death. His wife Juchin, of whom we know very little, died not long after Zeami and was buried nearby.

Banishment to Sado Island perhaps brought to mind for Zeami his rural childhood spent touring, his father's gifts and guidance, and a play – written by Kan'ami, adapted by Zeami and said to have held a special place in the latter's heart – that was steeped in exile and longing.

The play's title and main character is *Matsukaze*, meaning 'Wind Through the Pines' but also carrying the sense of a waiting, lingering wind; depending on the ideograph used to write it, *matsu* can mean either 'pine' or 'wait'. The play begins, as *The Well-Cradle* does, with a wandering monk intrigued by an act of remembrance. This time it is not a grave mound but a single pine, planted on the shore at Suma, in Settsu Province. It stands, the monk is told, in memory of two sisters, salt-makers from many years ago. He chants a sutra and calls upon Amida in their name, before setting off to beg for shelter overnight at a nearby salt-house.

Two women – salt-makers – live in the house. We encounter them first out at work with their brine wagon, lamenting an existence that they cannot escape:

> The sorry world's labours claim us,
> And wholly wretched the sea-folk's craft
> That makes no way through life, a dream
> Where, bubbles of froth, we barely live,
> Our wagon affording us no safe haven:
> We of the sea, whose grieving hearts
> Never leave these sleeves dry!
>
> Withdrawing tides leave behind stranded pools,
> And I, how long will I linger on?
> Dew agleam on meadow grasses

Soon must vanish in the sun,
Yet on this stony shore
Where salt-makers rake seaweed in,
Trailing fronds they leave behind,
These sleeves can only wilt away . . .

The two women return home to find the monk waiting for them. They are soon, of course, revealed as the unsettled spirits of those ancient sisters in whose memory the pine tree now stands. They were once the lovers of an exiled courtier, Yukihira, who named them for nature and the seasons – Matsukaze (Wind Through the Pines) and Murasame (Autumn Rain) – but later returned to the capital and died.

As ever with Zeami's art, the plot is not the point. Instead, from everything that life in the capital had to offer – *The Tale of Genji* and *The Tales of Ise*, shamanic power and Buddhist vision, old poetry anthologies and the newly minted sensibilities of a warrior audience acclimatizing to an aristocrat's city – he weaves an intricate allusive fabric, hinting at what it might be like to lose yourself in someone and then to lose them, left in the end with no more than fragments of either.

Yukihira left Matsukaze his robe, but it brings her no joy. She picks it up, then throws it down. She cannot part with it. She begs the monk to bring her peace. Eventually she puts the robe on – and sees her lover on the shore, though her sister sees only the pine tree. Yukihira has kept his promise, Matsukaze insists: to return if only they wait long enough for him. Suddenly, Murasame sees him too . . .

Whatever the sisters see, whoever they are or were – these things Zeami intended the actor and audience to conjure and know between them, as Matsukaze dances her last dance and the wind and rain together rise and at last recede:

Waves fall silent
Along Suma shore,
A breeze sweeps down from off the hills.
On the pass, the cocks are crowing.
The dream is gone, without a shadow

Night opens into dawn.
It was autumn rain you heard,
But this morning see:
Wind through the pines alone lingers on
Wind through the pines alone lingers on.

8

Oda Nobunaga

(織田信長)

1534–1582

Unity or Else

Oda Nobunaga, painted by Kanō Motohide soon after Oda's death, Chōkō-ji temple, Aichi Prefecture, Japan.

September 1571. Temples and towns around the lower reaches of Mount Hiei begin to empty out as their many thousands of inhabitants – Tendai monks alongside ordinary men, women and children – set out together on the hard climb towards the summit. They are desperately seeking refuge from what lurks at the bottom of their mountain: a series of encampments containing around 30,000 heavily armed, battle-hardened men.

Those men have been offered 300 pieces of gold and 450 pieces of silver to go away and leave everyone in peace. But their leader isn't in this for money. This is about punishment, for siding with his enemies.

On the morning of 30 September his force begins its ascent, quickly dispensing with the mountain's warrior-monk defenders and proceeding to murder thousands of people in cold blood. Some are hacked to death. Others are picked off by arquebus snipers as they cower in whatever hiding places they can find. Women and children plead with the leader of these men that they cannot possibly be his enemies. He disagrees, and they are all beheaded.

The Enryaku-ji temple and its numerous sub-temples around the mountain – some 3,000 buildings in total – are looted and set alight, giving birth to a swirling, engulfing firestorm. In the space of a few days Mount Hiei goes from being a byword for wealth, political influence, erudition and artistic achievement spanning seven centuries to a barren landscape, carpeted in ash, across which it is said only badgers and foxes now move.

The man who ordered all this is in his late thirties, described as tall and lean, with 'an extremely sonorous voice'. He is said to be just, compassionate and a master strategist – but also arrogant, secretive, unaccustomed to taking advice and disdainful of all, high and low alike. He believes in no god, no immortality of the soul and no life after death. In this world he takes no chances, surrounded always by a bodyguard of 2,000 men.

This is Oda Nobunaga, a warlord who spent a quarter of a century in almost constant military campaigning across central Japan, the economically most developed and politically most important part of the country. Had he merely been an unusually ruthless man in already ruthless times, Nobunaga would not merit a prominent place in history. But he had a favourite phrase: *tenka no tame, Nobunaga no tame*, 'For the sake of the realm, for the sake of Nobunaga'. To this he added a motto, proposed to him by a Zen priest: *tenka fubu*, 'Rule the realm by force'.

Regarding himself as the personification of a realm which, as yet, existed only in his head, Nobunaga poured his strategic abilities and ever-expanding armies into a grand, historic process: the unification of a fragmented Japan under one leader and one law. In a country where power had long been divided between an imperial court and aristocratic class, shoguns and their vassals, and Buddhist sects with their militant monks and loyal adherents throughout the land, it took someone with no special regard for any of these people or institutions to transcend them – in his vision for Japan and in the uncompromising way he went about trying to fulfil it.

Nobunaga did not accomplish this alone. He is remembered as the first in a line of three unifiers, succeeded by two men with whom he worked in his lifetime. The son of a farmer and sometime soldier, Toyotomi Hideyoshi started out carrying Nobunaga's sandals and ended up carrying his plans to near-final fruition. Tokugawa Ieyasu, from a warlord family in eastern Japan, was an early ally of Nobunaga and became the ultimate beneficiary of all that he set in train. The laws and institutions that Ieyasu put in place, building on the innovations of his predecessors, eventually brought peace, prosperity and effective governance to Japan. His descendants would still be in power when American steamships came cruising up the country's coast in the 1850s, heralds of a new and uncertain world.

This legendary triumvirate of Nobunaga, Hideyoshi and Ieyasu, operating from the 1550s through to the early 1600s, has been celebrated in Japanese culture down the centuries as central to the

country's later achievements. Many a schoolchild learns of their combined efforts by way of a simple saying:

> Nobunaga pounded the rice.
> Hideyoshi baked the cake.
> And Ieyasu ate it.

A second saying speaks more to each man's character. Less palatable,
perhaps, for younger audiences, it nonetheless seems true to Nobunaga's status as a transitional figure in Japanese history, a man very
much of the violent, unstable late-medieval era into which he was
born, and yet who paved the way towards a peaceful and high-achieving
early modern age. 'What to do', the saying goes, 'with a cuckoo that
refuses to sing?' Hideyoshi, clever and charismatic, would find some
way to persuade it. Ieyasu, canny and wise, would watch and wait while
it found its voice. And what of Nobunaga? The bird, naturally, would
have to die.

*

If Zeami returned, as some suspect, from exile on Sado Island to live
out his last days back at home in Kyoto, he may have been in the city
in the summer of 1441 as news began to circulate of an unusually
dramatic Nō performance unfolding within its walls. On 14 July,
Zeami's nemesis Yoshinori was invited to the residence of one of his
shugo (provincial warrior-constables), a man by the name of Akamatsu Mitsusuke. It was the shogun's forty-seventh birthday and, to
celebrate, Akamatsu had laid on a banquet and a Nō performance
starring Yoshinori's favourite actor, On'ami. But Akamatsu had made
other arrangements besides. The real source of entertainment that
night ended up being Yoshinori himself. Midway through the festivities, the shogun was attacked – and decapitated.

It was a shocking, unprecedented offence whose consequences
came in the form of a *bakufu* army pursuing Akamatsu back to his
home province of Harima and forcing him to perform ritual suicide.
According to legend, Akamatsu prayed first to Amaterasu in the east
and then to Amida in the west, before 'ending his sixty-one years by

ripping open his stomach'. Sixty-nine of his retainers followed him into death, 'likewise expiring with their swords in their bellies'.

Justice had been served, but the writing was on the wall for the Ashikaga shoguns. The *shugo* system had started out as the *bakufu*'s means of controlling the provinces. As time passed, however, the *shugo* had come to use their responsibilities and powers to secure their own positions. The raising of troops for guard duty in the capital and Kamakura morphed into the gathering of armed men around them as personal vassals. The collection of taxes, the punishment of criminals and the redistribution of valuable land were also deployed to help build loyal local bases. Provinces into which many *shugo* had initially been parachuted with no social connections whatsoever ended up in effect as their families' fiefs.

By 1441 it had become, at least for Akamatsu, an intolerable liberty for a shogun to meddle in matters of succession within a *shugo* house. Yoshinori's attempt to do just that earned him his bloody birthday entertainment. And when the *bakufu* demanded retribution, it was both slow in coming – Akamatsu died weeks rather than hours or days after his deed – and reliant upon the help of another *shugo* family, the Yamana, whose price was the inheriting of Akamatsu's lands.

The Ashikaga shoguns now found themselves ever more under the control of powerful *shugo* families, two of which – the Yamana and the Hosokawa – took up arms against one another in 1467 in a dispute over the shogunal succession. The resulting Ōnin War dragged on for eleven long years, drew in most of the country's other *shugo*, and was fought in and around Kyoto. More than half of the city disappeared in flames, including around 30,000 homes, amongst them the shogun's residence in Muromachi. Thereafter it was primarily the Hosokawa family pulling the shoguns' strings, while the *bakufu*'s writ barely extended beyond the confines of their ruined capital.

Power now passed decisively to the countryside. The *shugo* returned there at the war's end in 1477, some to rule while others discovered that their deputies had effectively usurped them when they were away, steadily carving out for themselves domains that were generally smaller than the old provinces but more firmly under their control.

This new breed of domain lord (*daimyō*) began to do away with the old *shōen* system of private estates owned from afar, seizing land for themselves and their vassals, and in time issuing their own legal codes. They took no orders from the capital and they sent nothing back, save when the bestowal of some kindness on a shogun or emperor – patching up a palace, rebuilding a shrine – garnered them in return some reputation-enhancing official bauble from either of those two impotent institutions.

A few sources of revenue remained to the shoguns: taxes on local trade and gratuities received in exchange for court or temple appointments. But the glory days were over, symbolized by the failure even to complete the shogun Yoshimasa's Higashiyama retirement villa, later known as Ginkaku-ji (the Silver Pavilion). Work on it began in the early 1480s, but plans to cover the temple in silver foil, echoing the splendour of Yoshimitsu's Kinkaku-ji (Golden Pavilion) and setting the building aglow in the moonlight, were delayed and eventually abandoned. It became known, instead, for its withered wooden aesthetic: an achievement in its own right, but not what Yoshimasa had been aiming for.

Meanwhile, courtier families accustomed for centuries to regular income from the provinces were forced to venture out into those provinces, often for the very first time, and fend for themselves. Some found their estates mercifully intact and managed to live off them directly. Others sought to ingratiate themselves with local samurai, drawing on their knowledge of poetry, *kemari* and other courtly arts to pursue an ignominious cash-for-culture existence. The imperial family entered upon such straitened times that one emperor was apparently forced to sell his own calligraphy to make ends meet, while another went unburied for a time, for want of funeral funds.

Japan was entering a period of almost constant conflict that later generations would know as *Sengoku jidai*: 'the Era of Warring States'. The *daimyō* spent the late 1400s and much of the 1500s striving to secure and expand their domains against local rivals, by way of agreements, intermarriage, neatly timed betrayals and pitched battles. One small part of this patchwork was a warrior by the name of Oda Nobuhide, who sought to increase the power and raise the profile of his branch of the Oda family within the central Japanese province of Owari. When he died suddenly from illness in 1551, it fell to his seventeen-year-old son Nobunaga to take up the task. Some around him doubted the young man's fitness for it, such was his reputation for eccentricity, in dress and behaviour alike:

> He wore a short-sleeved shirt and a bag of flints hung from his waist. His hair was done in the *chasen* style, tied up with red and green cords, and a long sword in a lacquered sheath hung from his belt. He strode around town laden with chestnuts, persimmons and melons, and with his mouth stuffed with rice cakes.

Nobunaga was later rumoured to have had the Buddhist priests who prayed unsuccessfully for his ailing father locked in a temple, surrounded by retainers wielding arquebuses, and shot to death. At his father's funeral, he is said to have turned up armed and unkempt, hurling a handful of incense powder at the altar before storming out again.

But Nobunaga's nicknames from these early years – 'Great Fool', 'Idiot' – fell away once he took to the battlefield. By the end of the 1550s he had vanquished his family rivals and united Owari Province under his own command. In 1560 he won an important victory at the Battle of Okehazama, using a surprise attack in heavy rain to defeat a much larger enemy force belonging to the *daimyō* Imagawa Yoshimoto, who had entered Owari on his way to try to take Kyoto. The night before the fighting, Nobunaga is said to have performed some dance steps from Zeami's play *Atsumori*, while singing a few of its lines:

> When we consider man's fifty years in this world,
> They are like a passing dream.
> We have life but once . . .
> How perishable we are.

Victory at Okehazama led to an alliance in 1561 with Matsudaira Ieyasu – the future Tokugawa Ieyasu – based in next-door Mikawa Province, immediately to the east of Owari. The two allies now stood back to back: Ieyasu faced eastwards and fought battles in that direction, while Nobunaga faced north and west, continuing his early run of conquests in 1567 with the capture of the large province of Mino, to Owari's north. It was a huge achievement. Japan was divided into around 120 warlord domains at this point, with only fifteen or so the size of a province. To control two full provinces marked the young Nobunaga out as a man on the up.

Possession of Mino came with more than a mere reputational boost: tens of thousands of fighters were now added to Nobunaga's ranks. Many were foot soldiers, or *ashigaru* ('light feet'). Peasants fighting in exchange for loot, *ashigaru* had once been considered sufficiently dispensable that they were given no protection to wear in battle. Now they were becoming so central to an army's success – both as fighters and as carriers of equipment, from basic supplies to the bells, conch-shell trumpets and marching drums used on the battlefield – that many wore good armour of lacquered iron scales, bound with leather and bearing their *daimyō*'s badge, or *mon*.

Samurai bore that same mark on a flag, attached to a wooden pole and secured to the back of their armour. Where *ashigaru* made do with a conical hat, samurai enjoyed the protection and status of a sometimes elaborate iron helmet. Both elements in an army, low and high, would be ordered into the fray by a commander wielding a drastically repurposed Heian-era accessory. Once employed in the ostentatious shielding of an aristocratic giggle, a fan abruptly lowered was now a signal to attack, its angle an indication of which way the troops should go.

A large army was no use if you couldn't get it to the right place at the right time. Nobunaga soon became known for his adeptness in widening roads and making effective use of galley-ships and floating pontoon bridges. He and other leading warlords of the time also experimented with organizing and training their men in specialized corps of spearmen (wielding weapons sometimes more than five metres in length), archers and above all arquebusiers. Proficiency with a Portuguese-style arquebus, versions of which were produced in Japan from the mid-1500s onwards, came far quicker than skill with a bow and arrow. Once mounted samurai had been persuaded to allow lowly *ashigaru* to the forefront of the fighting – a place usually reserved for those of elite station – the arquebus proved devastatingly effective, especially when troops were organized into ranks, firing volleys in rotation. A suit of armour bearing a certain kind of dent became a much-valued piece of kit, its ability to take a bullet a matter of battlefield proof rather than a blacksmith's promise.

Famous though he became for his disciplined use of *ashigaru*, Nobunaga always relied on his horse guards, mostly from Owari Province, for the core of his fighting force. These were his best and most loyal men. Their duties included protecting Nobunaga himself, and their rewards reputedly ran to some distinctly bloodthirsty entertainment, including the presentation at a New Year's banquet of platters bearing the skulls of three enemy warlords. Lacquered and gilded, they were admired by all while *sake* was drunk and a celebratory song was sung for Nobunaga.

By the autumn of 1568, Nobunaga was ready to do what many *daimyō* in this era dreamed of doing – march on Kyoto, and claim it for himself. A man called Yoshiaki, the great-great-grandson of the murdered Yoshinori, had appealed to Nobunaga to help him gain the shogunate for himself and Nobunaga was resolved to install him as his puppet. Potential opposition to the plan, in territories through which Nobunaga would need to pass in reaching the capital, was dealt with through a combination of a strategic marriage involving his younger sister, Oichi, and the deployment of around 50,000 soldiers. Nobunaga entered Kyoto in triumph in October 1568, and Yoshiaki was invested as shogun the next month.

Nobunaga accepted no official title from Yoshiaki. Many at the time were surprised, but such was Nobunaga's vision for the *tenka*, the 'realm'. This was an old word with multiple meanings. One of them, for Nobunaga, was a new nationwide polity centred on Kyoto, transcending emperors and shoguns and featuring Nobunaga as its beating heart – *tenka no tame, Nobunaga no tame*: 'For the sake of the realm, for the sake of Nobunaga'.

Step one in making a reality of this plan was to secure the shogun, literally: responding to an attack on Yoshiaki's temporary home in January 1569, Nobunaga built him a castle in the Muromachi district where Yoshiaki's Ashikaga ancestors had lived. Some 25,000 labourers, operating under the no doubt terrifying personal command of Nobunaga – himself wielding hoe and bamboo cane as symbols of getting personally stuck in – completed in just seventy days a project that one observer thought should have taken four or five years.

The construction of the shogun's castle, complete with inner and outer moats, strong stone walls and adornments liberated from a nearby temple, was turned by Nobunaga into a powerful symbol of his status. He commanded warriors and even *daimyō* to come to Kyoto as part of the building process and its associated festivities, and then told them when they could go home again. Such was Nobunaga's reputation now that few dared to disobey. Even when he took to wearing a tigerskin around his waist, visitors rushed to copy this odd affectation, lest entering his presence in smarter attire be taken as an affront.

Step two for Nobunaga was to work out a system of joint rule with Yoshiaki. This proved more difficult than step one. Yoshiaki tried to build his own base of support by contacting potential allies and making grants of land. He was, as far as Nobunaga was concerned, missing the point of *tenka*. Across a series of three official documents produced between 1569 and 1572, Nobunaga steadily trampled on the hopes and dreams of his new associate. He made it clear that the affairs of the *tenka* were his to deal with, noting with menace in his final missive that people had taken to calling Yoshiaki 'evil lord' – the very same epithet, all concerned would have known, that was applied to Yoshinori prior to his assassination in 1441.

Yoshiaki now had little choice but to part company with his overbearing ally, contributing to dangerous months for Nobunaga in 1572–3. The list of Nobunaga's conquests was impressive: he controlled Owari and Mino Provinces, along with the capital and its surrounds. And yet his success had the effect of creating and motivating an equally impressive array of enemies across the central and eastern provinces. Most forbidding amongst them were Azai Nagamasa in Ōmi Province, Asakura Yoshikage in Echizen Province and Takeda Shingen in the province of Kai.

The first to move against Nobunaga was Takeda. His army defeated troops under the command of Nobunaga's ally Ieyasu in January 1573, and by March he had made it into Mikawa Province, bordering Nobunaga's home territory of Owari. Yoshiaki now seized his chance to come out against Nobunaga. He fortified his castle and mobilized his relatively small personal force of 5,000 retainers, hoping all the while that Nobunaga's enemies would keep him occupied and well away from the capital.

But Nobunaga got lucky. In April, Takeda fell fatally ill – some said of pneumonia, others blamed a wound inflicted by a sniper. His troops began returning to Kai, allowing Nobunaga to turn his attention back to Kyoto and Yoshiaki. He began by demanding exorbitant military tributes from the citizenry of Kyoto. When they refused to pay, he proceeded to burn down much of the north of the city, including thousands of homes, and to raze around ninety nearby villages. While residents in southern parts of the capital rushed to empty their pockets, saving themselves from a similar fate, Yoshiaki reluctantly made peace. In August, Nobunaga forced him from the city, bringing the Ashikaga shogunate to an end and launching Yoshiaki on a life so humiliating that he became known as the 'Beggar Shogun'. The next month, Azai and Asakura succumbed to Nobunaga's forces too. Theirs were two of the lacquered and gilded skulls said to have been brought out as part of the New Year's festivities (1574) – the third had belonged to Azai's father.

Only one major player in the shifting anti-Nobunaga alliance now survived: a Buddhist organization of legendary reach and military potential. Not Tendai: the monks of Mount Hiei had sided with Nobunaga's enemies in 1570, and had paid the devastating price a year later. This other Buddhist organization had started out as small groups of people meeting to recite the *nembutsu* as Shinran suggested, acknowledging their helpless gratitude to Amida. Now they boasted wealth, arms, a heavily fortified headquarters on central Honshū's southern coast, and a rural network comprising tens of thousands of willing would-be soldiers.

*

Wars like those waged by Nobunaga could quickly make life unbearable for Japan's farmers, who made up by far the greatest proportion of the population. Improvements in agricultural productivity in recent centuries had helped to make some of them wealthy, producing enough to sell directly at markets. But many others dressed in simple hemp, lived in shelters of mud and wood, and cultivated rice while being unable to afford to eat it themselves – subsisting instead on millet or wild grasses, along with whatever they could fish or hunt. More than most other Japanese, they lived during these years at the mercy of two kinds of climate, natural and political.

Only so much could be done about nature, but more and more villages sought to insulate themselves from the country's fragmenting politics by asserting new sorts of autonomy. They negotiated as a community with outside authorities while regulating the lives of their own members, from what they farmed to how they behaved. Some communities even took up arms and built defensive moats and embankments around their villages. A second trend in rural self-defence was the banding together of villagers, warriors or both to form *ikki*: temporary confederations dedicated to the pursuit of a particular objective, political or economic. They promoted their interests by way of written remonstrations, strike action and violence. Nobunaga called them a 'curse on the nation'.

Japan's towns, too, threatened trouble for an aspiring national leader. The country was now home to enough towns – located principally around the capital and along the coasts – that most people could make a day-trip to their nearest one. With populations ranging from 5,000 people up to 30,000 or more, they served as hubs for a thriving inter-provincial trade that was carried mostly by water but which used overland routes when required, individual horse-and-carts sharing the roadways with well-protected merchant caravans.

The whole system was lubricated by imported Chinese coins, now accepted as payment right across the country, and the successful taxation of trade helped the *daimyō* to replenish their war chests. Many of the busiest and most affluent of Japan's towns had grown up around pilgrimage sites, and Buddhist temples especially, while some had actually developed from within the grounds of temples and were as a consequence firmly under their control – commercial profits included.

The Hongan-ji branch of Jōdo Shinshū, still led by Shinran's descendants, owned and profited handsomely from one of the greatest of these temple-towns. It had developed around a small retirement temple built for the Patriarch Rennyo in 1496 by the Inland Sea, south-west of Kyoto. It took its name from the 'long slope' on which it was located: 'Ō-zaka', or 'Osaka'. When the Hongan-ji headquarters in Kyoto was destroyed in 1532, a casualty of the era's complex and violent politics, the sect moved its operation to Osaka instead, developing there the Ishiyama Hongan-ji and securing it with more than fifty fortified outposts.

For Nobunaga, all this was the stuff of nightmares. The urban wealth and rural loyalty that the Hongan-ji Patriarch had at his command effectively made him a *daimyō*. But whereas the power of most *daimyō* was geographically concentrated and could be tackled on those terms, the Hongan-ji Patriarch was able to call upon tens of thousands of followers spread out across the land. Mainly merchants, artisans and farmers, these followers were well organized by way of local parishes, they were generous in donating to Hongan-ji coffers and they looked to the Patriarch for temporal as well as spiritual leadership. Their powerful shared rallying point, a faithful devotion to Amida, led them to be called *ikkō* ('single-directed') and their confederations *ikkō ikki*.

The Patriarch exercised no formal military command over these people. Some ignored his messages, others fought amongst themselves; and in general they lacked training or strong, experienced leadership. But when enough followers chose to answer a call to arms, it could be as though a fighting force had appeared out of nowhere: a pop-up army, with thousands of members who fed, clothed and armed themselves, and for whom the promise of rebirth in the Pure Land relieved them, at least in part, of an otherwise distracting and demotivating fear of death. Some followers were said to go into battle with pieces of paper bearing the words of the *nembutsu*. When their object was accomplished, they could disappear, frustrating any attempt at punishment or revenge.

By 1570 the Patriarch Kennyo, deeply concerned about Nobunaga's intentions, had allied himself with anti-Nobunaga forces. In a letter sent to his followers across Japan that year, he declared Nobunaga 'an enemy of the Buddhist law' and asked for their help in dealing with him – adding that 'anyone who does not respond will not be a sect member'.

The resulting conflict lasted, on and off, for a decade. Nobunaga's forces were ruthless in their punishment of *ikkō ikki* uprisings. A 1574 siege against the sect's Nagashima fortresses in the central province of Ise ended with the estimated deaths of 40,000 people, from starvation and from fires started by Nobunaga's troops. A similar number are said to have been executed in Echizen Province the following year, though reliable figures do not exist for most of the conflicts of this era. Nobunaga was briefly distracted from the Hongan-ji by a last hurrah from one of his secular enemies – a resurgent Takeda family under Shingen's son Katsuyori. But having seen them off at the Battle of Nagashino in June 1575, with the help of Ieyasu and the pitiless use of arquebusiers to take down cavalry, Nobunaga proudly claimed to have only one enemy left in the world: the Ishiyama Hongan-ji at Osaka, bereft now of big *daimyō* allies and with much of its rural network in pieces.

Nobunaga had roads widened, bridges built and supplies and men gathered. In the spring of 1576, his troops began systematically destroying crops in the area around the Hongan-ji. Two outright assaults ended in failure and a bullet in the leg for Nobunaga. But by July the Hongan-ji was running low on supplies. Kennyo appealed to Mōri Terumoto, a powerful western Honshū warlord, and to groups of Inland Sea pirates – somewhat akin to maritime *daimyō* – to supply him by water. Some 800 ships duly destroyed Nobunaga's smaller naval force, which was similarly reliant on deals struck with pirates. The siege was broken – for now. Two years later, Nobunaga was back, this time with a force including seven ships built by his maritime allies on a revolutionary design: thirty metres long and more than ten metres wide, loaded up with heavy cannon and their wooden frames clad with metal plates. These may have been the world's first iron-clad warships. They were certainly beyond anything Mōri's side could muster. Their navy was defeated, and the slow starvation of the Hongan-ji resumed.

Kennyo continued to call for uprisings by his followers, hoping to sap Nobunaga's energies elsewhere in central Japan. But Nobunaga now had 60,000 troops committed to his task. In April 1580, Kennyo finally put his name to a formal peace proposal – said to have been signed by Nobunaga in his own blood – which included the vacation of the Ishiyama Hongan-ji. Kennyo left the next month and his son Kyōnyo followed suit in August, having briefly held out as leader of a hard-line Hongan-ji faction opposed to surrender. Then, just as Nobunaga was preparing to embark on a personal tour of one of his most difficult, drawn-out conquests, smoke and flames became visible on the horizon. Kyōnyo's followers had set light to their own fortress, burning it to the ground rather than see Nobunaga set foot in it.

Still, Nobunaga had achieved something of historic significance with his defeat of the Hongan-ji. A thousand years on from Buddhism's introduction into Japan, and its rise to power via state, aristocratic and then popular patronage, Buddhist military and political power had been all but eliminated. And by resisting the urge to visit upon the inhabitants of the Ishiyama Hongan-ji the sort of catastrophic retributive bloodshed he had meted out on Mount Hiei – as well as to Hongan-ji followers across central Japan – Nobunaga managed to avoid the endless round of fresh uprisings that he would surely have otherwise incurred. Instead, he was free now, as never before, to develop his grand plans for the 'realm'.

*

On a mountain looming a hundred metres high over Lake Biwa stood a castle featuring a towering seven-storey donjon: fortified with sloping stone at its base, dazzling white towards the top and capped with gold. Inside were tatami-mat floors, lacquered and gold-leaf pillars, and rooms decorated with golden wall-paintings featuring Chinese monarchs and sages, tigers and hawks, demons and dragons. There were gardens, too, and an aviary; there was space for a temple, the tea ceremony and sumo tournaments. One room, even grander than the rest, was dedicated to receiving the Emperor.

'Rule the realm by force' was Nobunaga's motto. And it had served him well by the middle of 1580. But he was a creative leader, not merely a destructive one. Azuchi Castle, shiny and new in the summer sun while the Ishiyama Hongan-ji lay blackened and charred, was not just a new and fitting home for the supreme warlord of the age; it was a symbol of Nobunaga's plans to develop the *tenka* far beyond mere force of arms.

An important part of those plans was the imperial court. Emperor Ōgimachi had been wooing Nobunaga since his early victories in the 1560s, seeking his help in recovering lost imperial land and making repairs to the Imperial Palace. Nobunaga obliged on both counts, going on during the 1570s to lavish gifts on the imperial family: from land to gold dust, expensive wood to dried persimmons, and a special tax, levied twice in Kyoto, whose proceeds were paid to the imperial court.

In return, once the shogun was out of the way Nobunaga was awarded high court rank and a number of prestigious, if practically meaningless official appointments, culminating in Minister of the Right in 1577. Nobles put on a demonstration game of *kemari* for him in 1575 and the next year staged a musical performance – with the Emperor and Crown Prince Sanehito amongst the musicians – to pray for Nobunaga's success against the Hongan-ji. The imperial family were also there to be deployed when Nobunaga wanted to make peace. One of the best ways to stop a conflict while saving face in this era was to appeal to the Emperor to demand that an opponent seek terms, and then to use imperial envoys in smoothing the process.

For the imperial family, treating Nobunaga in this way helped not just their finances but their public image too. Rather than cowering before a dictator, they were seen willing him on for the good of the country. Meanwhile, Nobunaga well understood, as the Fujiwara dynasty and later the Kamakura and Ashikaga shoguns had, that in a world where history and family are the basis of legitimacy the imperial court was an institution to be worked with rather than against.

The first of April 1581 saw this mutually beneficial relationship rise to new heights. Nobunaga staged an enormous military parade near the Imperial Palace in Kyoto in celebration of the vanquishing at last of the Hongan-ji. The Emperor looked on as an estimated 130,000 men, on foot and on horseback, passed by. Nobunaga had ordered his vassals to spend vast sums on their attire, and still no one managed to upstage the man himself: seated in a sedan chair of crimson velvet and wearing 'clothes and decorations as bright as the sun'. Having two years previously adopted Emperor Ōgimachi's son, Prince Sanehito, Nobunaga was looking forward in time to becoming the father-in-law of an emperor. In fact, he was soon seeking to speed that moment along, putting pressure on Emperor Ōgimachi to abdicate.

While the *tenka* was taking promising shape in Kyoto, Nobunaga also busied himself with Japan's towns and villages. A town grew up around Azuchi Castle, as Nobunaga required his vassals to build homes there. He offered tax exemptions for merchants and artisans willing to set up shop in this and other towns under his control. He worked to do away with transport tolls and with the exclusivity of the old guilds – especially in goods and trades that supported his war efforts: guns and ammunition, swordsmiths and stone-cutters. And he tightened the rules on criminality and debt, as a further encouragement of commerce. Azuchi became a model for what came to be called 'castle towns', where economic activity gathered at the gates of a *daimyō*'s home.

In rural Japan, where the old *shōen* system was in tatters but not yet officially at an end, Nobunaga made the first small moves towards establishing a new order. *Daimyō* and their vassals would no longer be farmers' tormentors, tearing up their land in battle or taxing it to the hilt. They would be their rightful rulers and chosen champions – while also, of course, collecting fair taxes and levying reasonable military contributions. As part of this new pact with the peasantry, Nobunaga became, in 1580, one of the first warlords to commission detailed land surveys. He tried to find out who was who in each village, what they farmed (as landholders or tenants), and what they owed as a result in tax and labour. Here, as in a great many other areas, Hideyoshi and then Ieyasu would one day build on Nobunaga's foundations.

*

Nobunaga was not, of course, satisfied with controlling central Honshū alone. Next on his list, in 1582, were enemies on the island of Shikoku and in western Japan. The former were expected to offer such an easy ride that Nobunaga parcelled out the island's four provinces to retainers far in advance of their conquest. The Mōri of western Japan would be harder, but more interesting. He would go there himself. He was, after all, still only forty-eight years of age, and with the Mōri's eight provinces conquered Nobunaga would be master of the whole of western Honshū. Ignoring for now imperial appeals for him to accept the role of Chancellor, great minister of the Council of State, even shogun, he set off to do battle once more.

Nobunaga stopped off, on his way, in Kyoto. There he lodged at a temple called Honnō-ji, suitably fortified with great walls, moats and watchtowers. One of his vassals, Akechi Mitsuhide, was meanwhile marching 13,000 men into the capital, where they were told they would be inspected by Nobunaga himself. When they arrived at Honnō-ji at dawn on 21 June 1582, they found themselves instead ordered by Mitsuhide to surround the place. And then to open fire.

Nobunaga and his men at first thought that some trouble must be breaking out between a few locals. When they realized what was actually going on, Nobunaga yelled 'Treason!' and grabbed his bow. His men gave it everything, but to no avail. As the attackers closed in, Nobunaga switched to his spear before finally sustaining a serious wound. The man who might have been lord of all Japan withdrew to a back room to take his own life, as all around him a scene familiar to so many of those he had called his enemies was played out: a temple, turned inferno, from which there could be no escape.

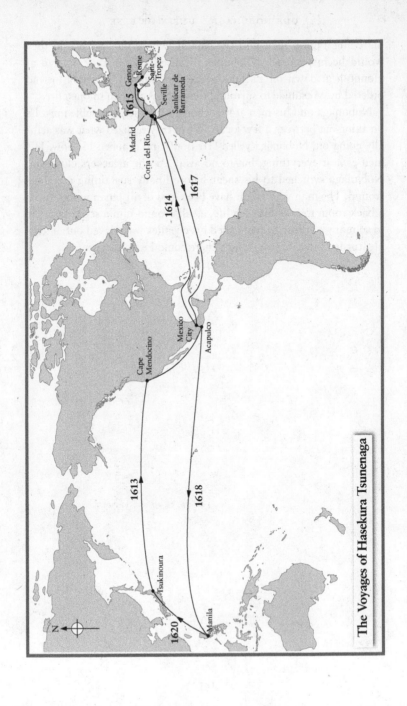

The Voyages of Hasekura Tsunenaga

PART THREE

Floating Worlds: 1582–1885

9
Hasekura Tsunenaga

（支倉常長）

1571–1622?

Voyager

Portrait of Hasekura Tsunenaga (*c*.1615) by the
French painter Claude Deruet.

December 1613. A samurai retainer from northern Japan stands on the deck of his ship as it clips along, sails billowing in the wind. For centuries, craft of all kinds have ferried passengers, troops and trade goods around the Japanese archipelago. But the *Date Maru* is different. At 500 tons, it is enormous by the standards of most earlier vessels, requiring thousands of labourers to construct it. And where other ships cling to the coast, seeking out Japan's great trading entrepôts, this one is way out in the mid-Pacific. Hasekura Tsunenaga is heading not for Osaka or Nagasaki – but for Acapulco, in the Spanish Empire.

From there, Hasekura will journey overland through the Empire's Viceroyalty of New Spain, stopping off in Mexico City before departing from Veracruz to sail the Atlantic. This is the first official Japanese embassy ever to be sent to Europe. Its purpose is to establish relations between Hasekura's lord – the *daimyō* of Sendai, Date Masamune – and two of the great global leaders of the day: King Philip III of Spain and Pope Paul V.

Lingering for a thousand years on one another's imaginative peripheries – in myth, legend and rumour – East Asia and Western Europe have become far better acquainted in recent decades. The first known Europeans to set foot in Japan did so in 1543 – by mistake: a small group of Portuguese were forced to make landfall on the island of Tanegashima, just off the southern main island of Kyūshū, when their Chinese junk encountered stormy weather. Portuguese-style firearms, duly nicknamed *tanegashima*, were soon raising the volume and the body-count on Japanese battlefields. Oda Nobunaga was amongst the earliest and most effective adopters. European maritime technology has also made its way into Japan. The *Date Maru* was built on the design of a Spanish galleon, with Spanish assistance. It even bears an alternative Spanish name: the *San Juan Bautista* (*St John the Baptist*).

That name hints at a third European import, possessing the potential to strike far deeper than guns or ships into how a nation thinks about itself, organizes its affairs and deals with its neighbours. The responses of Japan's leaders to the dilemmas posed by Christianity, across three decades from Nobunaga's death to the launching of the *Date Maru*, are set to tax Hasekura's talents as a diplomat throughout his epic seven-year journey. Trouble is already brewing below deck, where around 140 Japanese merchants and samurai are packed together unhappily with forty Europeans, mostly Spaniards. Hasekura perhaps takes these tensions as a sign of what awaits him: encounters with Europeans that are coloured by recent history and by conflicting ambitions. What do the Japanese aboard the *Date Maru* want from Europe? And what might Europeans want from Japan?

*

In the hours and days following Oda Nobunaga's death, very little retribution came the way of his assailants. Akechi Mitsuhide's forces proceeded unimpeded from Kyoto to Azuchi, where they looted Nobunaga's splendid castle. Soon afterwards it burned to the ground, following its owner into oblivion. But then Toyotomi Hideyoshi's men, pursuing Nobunaga's planned campaign against the Mōri in western Japan, captured an Akechi emissary and learned of their overlord's fate. Hideyoshi moved swiftly to claim his inheritance. He persuaded the Mōri to make a truce with Nobunaga, neglecting to mention that the latter was dead. And then he marched his men towards Kyoto, destroying Mitsuhide's forces not far from the city in early July. The man Nobunaga called 'that bald rat' carried the traitor Mitsuhide's head back to Honnō-ji, where he presented it to the spirit of his former master.

Justice done, coalition-building began. Hideyoshi made terms with Tokugawa Ieyasu. He began awarding fiefs to key allies. And he had himself adopted by a Kyoto courtier, so that he could accept the post of Imperial Regent. Hideyoshi then set out to extend his hegemony across the rest of the country, beginning in the south. Free of Honshū's costly conflicts in recent centuries, many of Kyūshū's leading families could trace their roots all the way back to service as warrior-constables and samurai estate-managers in the Kamakura era. The Shimazu clan was currently the paramount power, pushing for control over the whole island. Hideyoshi responded in late 1586 by moving an enormous force – around a quarter of a million men – from Honshū to Kyūshū, where they made short work of the Shimazu.

By 1590, Hideyoshi's last remaining enemy was the Hōjō clan in eastern Japan. After their leader, Ujimasa, refused calls to submit peacefully, Hideyoshi launched one of history's least hurried sieges, of the Hōjō stronghold at Odawara Castle. Starting in May, he invited concubines, musicians, dancers, merchants and tea ceremony specialists to provide entertainment for himself and the troops, while the enemy slowly starved. The castle finally surrendered in August, at which point Ujimasa was ordered to perform ritual suicide and his family's vast holdings were confiscated.

Hideyoshi took the opportunity of the Odawara siege to require the *daimyō* of northern Japan to demonstrate their loyalty, backing him in teaching the Hōjō a lesson. The region had seen its fair share of intrigue and fighting since the authority of the Ashikaga *bakufu* broke down and Japan broke apart in the late 1400s. But its remoteness from self-consciously 'civilized' central parts of the country – notably Kyoto – had long garnered it a rather unfair reputation for equal parts barbarity and banality: of little political or cultural consequence, save as the wild natural setting for folk tales and travel poetry. Northern warlords had become accustomed to the role of semi-detached observers of events down south.

No longer. Amongst those who travelled to Odawara in 1590 to offer their submission to Hideyoshi was Date Masamune, a much-feared *daimyō* in the southern part of Mutsu Province, known as the 'One-Eyed Dragon' after losing his right eye to smallpox as a child. Confirmed in his fief by Hideyoshi, two years later Date found himself leading an army of retainers all the way down to Kyūshū. One of them was a teenage Hasekura Tsunenaga. Born around 1571 to a northern samurai family, Hasekura served Date as a valued spy, emissary and information-gatherer.

Date, Hasekura and the rest of their northern army joined around 160,000 warriors and supporting personnel mustering at a giant, purpose-built fortress on the north-western coast of Kyūshū. Hideyoshi had made himself master of all Japan. But his ambitions did not end at his own borders. It was time to carve out a place in the wider world for what he called the 'Land of the Gods'. China would fall, and then India. The first stop along the way would be the peninsula just across the water from Kyūshū. Date and Hasekura were about to take part in a full-scale invasion of Korea.

The East Asian order that Hideyoshi was setting out to overturn had long been shaped by the Chinese concept of *tianxia* ('all under heaven'): a physical and moral universe in which China was in every respect central. Successive Chinese dynasties established official tributary relationships with peripheral 'barbaric' peoples across East and South East Asia, India, the east coast of Africa and the Persian Gulf. Networks of Chinese traders and pirates played an important ancillary role, spreading Chinese culture far and wide. The Japanese understood themselves as part of this tributary system while at the same time forming the centre-point of their own *tianxia*. Kanmu's old northern foes the Emishi were amongst those cast in the role of barbarian outsiders.

Japan's original place in the European imagination was more impressive: it was Paradise. Working with the Book of Genesis and alighting on the line 'Now the Lord God planted a garden in the east, in Eden', writers and map-makers had begun in the early 600s to adapt conventional divisions of the world into the territories of Europe, Africa and Asia by marking out 'Paradise' at a location remarkably close to that of the Japanese archipelago. The country's fall from grace began a few centuries later, with the Venetian traveller Marco Polo (1254–1324). Living at the court of Kublai Khan not long after the latter's failed invasion of the Japanese islands in 1274, Polo claimed that 'Cipangu' was rich in red pearls and gold and that its people were 'good-looking and courteous'. But they were also given to 'outlandish and diabolical exploits', including the killing, cooking and eating of prisoners, whose flesh they considered 'the finest food in existence'.

The first European actually to set eyes on Cipangu was Christopher Columbus – or so he thought at the time. In fact, his search in 1492 for a lucrative westward sea-route from Europe to spice-rich

Asia had led him to Cuba. It was one of a series of unexpected discoveries that persuaded Europeans to rethink their picture of the world and to begin dividing it up between them. The Treaty of Tordesillas (1494) drew a line down the Atlantic, approximately halfway between the Cape Verde Islands off the west coast of Africa and the lands discovered by Columbus. The Spanish took everything to the west: much of the Atlantic, all of the Americas, a new ocean beyond – christened 'the Pacific' in 1520, for its preternaturally calm waters – and finally the Philippines, claimed and named for King Philip II. The Portuguese travelled in the opposite direction, employing a combination of deal-making and war-making to build a network of trading outposts as they went: the southern Indian port of Calicut (1500), Mozambique Island (1505), Goa (1510), Malacca (1511), Hormuz (1514), Colombo (1518), Bombay (1534) and finally Macau in southern China (1557).

Japanese met European visions of the world in 1543, with the forced landing of a small group of Portuguese at Tanegashima. Japan, for the Portuguese, was the 'far east'; less rich in resources than many parts of their empire, but promising nonetheless. The chaos of the Sengoku (Warring States) era, and associated problems with piracy, had brought trading relations between China and Japan almost to a halt. Portuguese merchants were able to step in, carrying raw Chinese silk to Kyūshū – where it fetched up to ten times its value in China – and shipping Japanese silver and other goods back in the opposite direction.

The Japanese regarded the Portuguese, in turn, as 'southern barbarians' (nanban), since they sailed to Japan from the south-west. They were associated with trade and soon with Christian missionaries, the first of whom arrived in 1549: three Spanish Jesuits, Francis Xavier amongst them, reached the southern tip of Kyūshū in a Chinese pirate ship. Buddhist clergy were fascinated. The missionaries claimed to have come from India (blurring origins and way-points) and they talked about their God as 'Dainichi': the celestial Buddha central to Shingon Buddhism. It followed that they must be offering a new interpretation of the Buddha's teachings. The missionaries soon realized their mistake, switching to the word 'Deus' and dismissing Dainichi as 'an invention of the Devil'. Their disillusioned Buddhist interlocutors gave as good as they got, pronouncing Deus as *'dai uso'*, 'great lie'.

The Jesuits had better luck with the *daimyō*, especially in Kyūshū, where enthusiasm for the missionaries' message combined with interest in the influence they appeared to enjoy over Portuguese merchants' choices of ports and business partners. By the time Hideyoshi arrived in Kyūshū in 1586, a striking new phenomenon was sweeping the island: Christian *daimyō*, some of whom were capable of compelling large numbers of their vassals to convert in turn.

A man so concerned with his image that he inked his scalp to approximate the hair that he didn't have, Hideyoshi was an enthusiast for Kyūshū's hybrid *nanban* fashions: Portuguese-style cloaks, worn over armour; helmets based on exotic hat designs; baggy breeches; rosaries, reliquaries and crosses, designed to be hung about the body. Hideyoshi was keen, too, on trade and the wealth it generated. Nor was he philosophically opposed to Christianity. But surveying the scene in Kyūshū, he was reminded of a phenomenon against which he and Oda Nobunaga had struggled hard just a few years before: the coming together of commercial with religious and political power in a way that threatened the project for a single, secular, unified rule in Japan.

Nagasaki provided the clearest, most egregious example of the problem. A small fishing village on Kyūshū's western coast had gained favour with the Portuguese for its sheltered natural harbour. Beginning in the early 1570s, a 'Great Ship' had begun arriving there most years from the Portuguese base at Macau. The Jesuits helped to facilitate this trade, ploughing their share of its enormous profits into missionary work that soon included schools and a printing press. Then, in May 1580, something truly shocking transpired: the Christian *daimyō* in control of the area *gave* Nagasaki to the Jesuits. He ceded them control of its land, administration and trade. Barely a fortnight after Nobunaga had forced the Buddhist Patriarch Kennyo out of the Ishiyama Hongan-ji at Osaka, another religious domain had started to take shape in Japan, complete with influential warlord allies and its own burgeoning fortifications.

Elsewhere on Kyūshū, Hideyoshi heard of shrines and temples being attacked by Christian converts. One temple was repurposed as a boys' prep school, while others had their precious artefacts sold off, thrown into rivers or used for firewood. There were rumours that some foreigners, quite possibly Portuguese, were involved in trafficking Japanese people to China and elsewhere as slaves. To top it all off, a missionary approached Hideyoshi in advance of his Kyūshū campaign, offering to intercede on his behalf with the island's Christian *daimyō* – as if their loyalties lay within the Jesuits' gift.

Here was sacrilege on so many levels, evidence of a changing world order over which Hideyoshi resolved to exercise some serious influence. He began in July 1587. In a rage apparently enhanced by imbibing a generous quantity of Portuguese wine, he produced an edict condemning the 'pernicious doctrine' of Christianity and giving the Jesuits twenty days to leave the country. He seized Nagasaki from their grasp the following year, taking over its trade directly. In the end, Hideyoshi let the Jesuits stay: their merchant allies were too important to Kyūshū's economy. But European influence in Japan had been curbed and Christians put on notice.

Hideyoshi followed up with a flurry of inflammatory missives sent to foreign powers near and far. In 1590, he wrote to the King of Korea explaining that he had been invested by heaven with a unique will to rule in the region: he was the 'Sun Child', conceived when his mother dreamed that the sun had entered her womb. On this basis, he expected the king, as his vassal and ally, to assist him in subjugating China. The following year, Hideyoshi wrote to the Philippines, demanding that the (Spanish) *nanban* there likewise accept his suzerainty. He promised otherwise to attack and destroy their walled enclave at Manila. Similar messages went out to the Ryūkyū Islands, to Japan's far south, to Taiwan and even to Goa.

Amongst the few to respond to Hideyoshi was the King of Korea, making it clear in 1592 that he would not let Hideyoshi treat his peninsula as China's driveway. Hideyoshi duly sent his 160,000 men – Date and Hasekura included – into action. The invasion of Korea became one of the most vivid signs of the unprecedented global mixing and mingling taking place in the sixteenth century. A Japanese force crossed the sea to Korea, aboard ships built with European merchant help, and led by *daimyō* with names like Dom Agostinho Konishi, Dom Sancho Ōmura and Dom Protasio Arima.

Landing at Pusan under their Christian commanders, Hideyoshi's troops chased the Korean king steadily northwards, out of Seoul and later out of Pyongyang. For a few short months, almost the entire peninsula was in Hideyoshi's hands. Then the Korean navy, Korean guerrillas and Chinese troops belatedly sent south across the Yalu River began to push his men much of the way back. By early 1593, nearly a third of the Japanese force had been wiped out and the war was at a stalemate. Hideyoshi had remained in Japan all the while – in contrast with Nobunaga, he rarely led from the front. There he moved from planning the precise format of ceremonies for when the Japanese emperor relocated to China to commencing years of humiliating talks on the terms of a truce.

Relationships with Spain and the Philippines went little better. The Spanish hoped to temper Hideyoshi's bellicosity, establishing friendly trading relations instead. But in 1596 a Spanish galleon called the *San Felipe*, in service on the Manila–Acapulco route, was wrecked on the Japanese coast. When Hideyoshi proved reluctant to return the cargo, the ship's pilot intervened, foolishly harping on Spain's imperial designs for Japan. Brandishing an up-to-date world map to illustrate Spanish in relation to Japanese power, he claimed that missionaries in Japan were spying for the Spanish and that the Christianization of the country – home to around 300,000 believers by this point – was part of a grand colonial plan.

Hideyoshi was at first so angry that he ordered every Christian in Kyoto to be killed. He was persuaded by the governor of that city to limit himself to just twenty-six. Six Franciscans (four Spaniards, one Portuguese and one Mexican), three Japanese Jesuits and seventeen Japanese Franciscan tertiaries were rounded up. Their ears were cropped – a sign of criminal status – and they were taken to Nagasaki, paraded along the way through Osaka. On 5 February 1597 they were led up a hill overlooking the former Christian stronghold of Nagasaki, and crucified.

Hideyoshi died the next year in his lavishly appointed Kyoto home of Fushimi-Momoyama Castle, his planned conquest of Asia stalled in Korea. Discovering in the course of negotiations with the Chinese that they still – after everything that he had achieved – regarded the Japanese as a tributary people, he had launched a fresh invasion of Korea in 1597, this one even more brutal than the first. Hopes of a smooth succession went similarly awry. Hideyoshi's plan had been for a board of five regents to keep his seat warm until his young son Hideyori came of age. Instead, one of those regents, Tokugawa Ieyasu, began dealing with the other *daimyō* as though he were now in charge.

Two factions quickly formed amongst Japan's warlords: one in the east, supportive of Ieyasu, and another in central and western Japan, protecting Hideyori's claim. The two sides met in battle at Sekigahara in October 1600 and Ieyasu won an epoch-making victory. He bolstered his position by taking the title of shogun, in 1603, and by launching the largest redistribution of land in Japanese history. Eighty-seven enemy *daimyō* were deprived of their holdings. Others were moved around, in some cases to weaken their support base. Allies were meanwhile rewarded via the creation of brand new domains. One of the great beneficiaries was Date Masamune, receiving the large north-eastern domain of Sendai.

While Kyoto remained Japan's capital, real power now shifted to the Tokugawa castle town of Edo on the east coast. There, a new *bakufu* (military government) was established. Ieyasu stepped down as shogun in 1605, determined to achieve the intra-familial transfer of power – to his son Hidetada – which he had so conspicuously deprived Hideyoshi. But he remained very much in charge, seeking to address the legacy of Hideyoshi's disastrous foreign policy. Ieyasu made peace with Korea in 1605 and limited trade was resumed. In 1609, the recently established Dutch United East India Company (VOC) was granted permission to set itself up at the port of Hirado, near Nagasaki. Agreement was reached with the English East India Company in 1613.

Ieyasu negotiated with the Spanish, too, hoping to increase trade with Manila and to enlist the help of mining experts from New Spain in maximizing profits from Japan's silver mines – over which Ieyasu exercised personal control. A Spanish explorer by the name of Sebastián Vizcaíno was appointed as New Spain's first ambassador to Japan, arriving in 1611. Two years later, the privilege of ferrying him back across the Pacific was claimed by Date Masamune, who successfully applied to the *bakufu* for permission to build a ship. The new vessel would do double-duty: as ambassadorial transport and as the means for Japan's first official diplomatic embassy to Europe – sorely needed in the aftermath of Hideyoshi's provocations – to complete the initial leg of a pioneering voyage.

*

Hasekura Tsunenaga led a reasonably quiet life for a few years after the Korean war. Receiving a commendation from Date for his service in the conflict, he returned home to raise a young family and continue in the service of his lord. Life changed in 1612 when Hasekura's birth-father was required to perform ritual suicide after charges of fraud were brought against him. Such were the standards of the day – linking suicide with atonement and father with son – that Hasekura should have been ordered to do the same.

But Hasekura was too valuable. Instead of putting him to death, Date put him to work, leading a maritime mission so risky that Hasekura would either disappear along the way or return suitably chastened. In addition to helping his country's international relationships recover, Date had personal plans for the voyage. No more northern 'backwater': he would turn Sendai into a global trading hub, bypassing Nagasaki and Manila. To that end, Hasekura was charged with opening up trade negotiations with Spain and the Viceroyalty of New Spain. He was also to ask King Philip III and Pope Paul V to send Christian missionaries to northern Japan – a diplomatic sweetener for convert-hungry Europeans, and also a source of the kind of cosmopolitan culture that had marked Nagasaki out as special.

Hasekura's guide and interpreter on the trip was the Spanish Franciscan missionary Luis Sotelo – and he too had his own agenda. There was at present just a single Catholic diocese for the whole of Japan, based at Nagasaki, under the control of the Franciscans' Jesuit rivals. Sotelo hoped to turn Date's domain into the centre of a new Japanese diocese. He even hoped one day to become Archbishop of Japan.

What became known as the 'Keichō Embassy', after the name of the current era in Japan, departed from Tsukinoura harbour aboard the *Date Maru* on 23 October 1613. They made it safely across the Pacific to Cape Mendocino on the west coast of North America, while the first English colonists were settling in on the continent's far eastern fringe. From Cape Mendocino, the *Date Maru* tracked the coastline down to a port near Acapulco, docking there in late January 1614. An advance party proceeded north overland towards Mexico City, where a Nahua annalist known by the Christian name of Don Domingo de San Antón recorded their grand entrance:

> The 4th of the month of March of the year 1614 . . . there arrived here and entered inside the city of Mexico these Japanese nobles. They came in on horseback at 12 o'clock noon. Their vassals came ahead of them, just coming on foot, holding high something like little long narrow black poles . . . perhaps that signifies royal leadership there in Japan. They came attired in the same way they go about and are attired back home: they wear something like a tunic, tied in the back, and they tie their hair at the backs of their necks.

Conspicuous by their absence from the annalist's account were the incomers' weapons. And for good reason. Tensions between Japanese and Spanish passengers during the Pacific crossing erupted into violence shortly after they landed near Acapulco, ostensibly over who had responsibility for looking after gifts brought from Japan – including a number of folding screens commissioned by Ieyasu. The New Spain ambassador Sebastián Vizcaíno was beaten and stabbed, prompting the Viceroy of New Spain to demand that, with the exception of Hasekura and a handful of others, the Japanese surrender their weapons. It made for an unfortunate first impression.

Hasekura arrived in Mexico City some three weeks after the advance party. He had taken a scenic route through the hills of New Spain, stopping off at a number of Franciscan monasteries along the way, including one at Cuernavaca. Making it to the city in late March, he handed the Viceroy a letter from Date Masamune. Luis Sotelo passed over a separate letter from Ieyasu and Hidetada. Meetings were held with the Franciscan Order, aimed at having missionaries sent to Japan. And over the course of the next month, around sixty of Hasekura's retainers were baptized and confirmed, with Franciscan friars for their sponsors. Hasekura himself was persuaded to hold off. Baptism would be a diplomatic act as well as a religious one. Better, therefore, to wait until he reached Europe.

In May, Hasekura split his embassy into two groups. One stayed in Mexico City to trade, while the other went with Hasekura to Veracruz. From there, they sailed via Cuba across a stormy Atlantic, arriving at the south-western Spanish port of Sanlúcar de Barrameda in early October and cruising up the Guadalquivir River to the town of Coria del Río. Changing into more formal attire, they continued their journey by road to Seville: Luis Sotelo's home and, more importantly, the only town in Spain permitted to trade beyond Europe.

The mayor and senior dignitaries crowded on to the Triana Bridge to greet Hasekura's party as they arrived. Locals found Hasekura 'calm', 'humble' and 'reasonable'. The archbishop was impressed by the manner and dress of his men, who brought to mind for him the biblical Three Wise Men.

At a special meeting of the Seville Senate, Hasekura presented gifts from Date Masamune, including a sword and a dagger sheathed in silk. Then, unrolling a calligraphic scroll adorned with gold, with Sotelo's help he presented and elaborated on a message from his lord to the leaders of Seville:

> I have learned of the afterlife, after hearing the teachings of Deus. Owing to unavoidable reasons, I cannot yet accept these teachings for myself. But in order to spread the word in my land, I have asked Friar Sotelo for his assistance, and am sending a samurai by the name of Hasekura. I hope for the safe arrival of these two at the feet of the King and the Pope, and the passing on of my wishes. It is my intent, by asserting the viability of maritime travel between Japan and Seville, to begin annual sea voyages.

Such grand requests required ratification at a higher level. So, according to a plan worked out well in advance by Sotelo, Hasekura's embassy headed north for Madrid. Their caravan of carriages, sedan chairs, guards, guides, patissiers and chefs made for such a spectacular sight that people crowded around them in villages and towns all along the way, slowing their progress and causing them to arrive in the Spanish capital nearly a month behind schedule, on a snowy late December day in 1614.

And there the trouble began. King Philip III's chamberlain and chaplain came to meet them, assuring Hasekura of the King's help and encouraging him to make the most of the Christmas season in Madrid. But two weeks went by and still an invitation to meet the King at his home in the Royal Alcázar of Madrid was not forthcoming. The Spanish were beginning to think twice about their guests.

European impressions of the Japanese had come to be dominated, in recent decades, by Jesuit accounts, coloured by their hopes that the conversion of Japan would make up for the Catholic Church's losses in Reformation Europe. Francis Xavier described the Japanese as 'the best who have yet been discovered'. They were well-mannered, honourable, educated and proud. They rarely gambled, swore or stole, and they didn't eat animals – preferring a diet of fish, rice and grain for which Xavier personally had little appetite but which hardly constituted a vice. They were open to having their understanding of the world challenged, and they seemed interested in Christianity and the West. Other Jesuits found the Japanese naturally given to interiority – a compliment, given the Jesuits' own deep interest in the inner life – and more encouraging of women's literacy and freedom than was generally the case in Europe.

Shortcomings were relatively few by comparison. Some Japanese held their own country in such high regard that they tended to disdain foreigners as a matter of course. The men seemed overly fond of weaponry – and of one another. Widespread male homosexuality, the missionaries concluded, was the result of Buddhist influence and years of civil war: twin evils that also accounted for the inhumanity of ritual suicide and summary execution, heavy drinking and a tendency to dissemble when questioned. Such difficulties were not insurmountable, and in 1582 the Jesuit 'Visitador' to India and the Far East, Alessandro Valignano, had decided to show Europeans at first hand just what a promising place Japan was. He sent four young Christian nobles from Kyūshū on a mini-European tour between 1584 and 1586, where they met, amongst others, King Philip II – the present King's father – and for a time generated quite a stir.

But then news of the twenty-six 'martyrs' of 1597 reached European ears, seeming to confirm some of the more negative Jesuit commentary on Japan. Accounts doing the rounds in Portuguese Macau that year told of Japanese onlookers throwing stones at the men as they made their way to Nagasaki, calling them beasts and stuffing weeds into their mouths. A procession was held in their honour in Macau in December, accompanied by paintings of the grisly events, copies of which were sent to New Spain, Spain and Rome. A sermon was preached in Mexico City the same month – one of the dead, Felipe de Jesús, was a son of the city and New Spain's first martyr.

The Franciscan missionary Marcelo de Ribadeneira, present in Nagasaki at the time of the crucifixions, published a highly romanticized account of the events and accompanied the remains of the six dead Franciscan friars to Mexico City in December 1598, later travelling to Rome to seek their beatification. His writings eventually became the source for a series of large murals commissioned by the Franciscan Order for the nave walls of the very monastery at Cuernavaca through which Hasekura had recently passed. Cuernavaca was one of the places where Spanish missionaries to Asia would stop on their way to the western coast of New Spain, so here perhaps was a reminder for them of how much they were risking – and why. Hasekura's men may even have played a part in the creation of the murals, whose detail suggests either that Japanese physiques were used as models or that a Japanese painter did some of the work.

By the time Hasekura arrived in Madrid, King Philip III had thrown his weight behind the martyrs' claim to sainthood. He had also received disturbing updates about Japan and the Hasekura embassy from the Viceroy of New Spain and from the Council of the Indies, the latter administering the Spanish Empire from within the Royal Alcázar. Hasekura's embassy, it turned out, originated not with Japan's national ruler but with a mere regional lord. And though they professed a desire for missionaries, their main aim was trade. Meanwhile, Christianity in Japan was in serious difficulty, returning, it seemed, to the dark days of Hideyoshi.

Unfortunately for Hasekura, Spanish intelligence on this last point was entirely accurate. Ieyasu had initially tolerated Christianity for the same economic reasons as Hideyoshi. But it soon started to seem more trouble than it was worth. Spanish Franciscan missionaries and the Jesuits were constantly at each other's throats, while Japanese Christians were rumoured to have responded to the execution of some of their number in 1612 by saying prayers, singing hymns and collecting relics of the dead. Here was a religious community, Ieyasu concluded, whose worship centred on a criminal lawfully executed on a cross many centuries ago, and which appeared to treat present-day criminals with similar reverence.

It was an intolerable challenge to the *bakufu*'s still-fragile authority. So in December 1613, while Hasekura was sailing the Pacific, Christians in Kyoto and Edo were forced to renounce their faith. Churches were destroyed and some of Ieyasu's own Christian retainers were sent into exile. On 27 January 1614, two days after Hasekura arrived in New Spain, Ieyasu ordered the drafting of a document banning Christianity and expelling all missionaries. It was disseminated across Japan in February, so that while Hasekura was seeking new missionaries in Mexico City, Seville and Madrid, those already in Japan were either leaving or going into hiding.

Aware of much of this by the time Hasekura turned up requesting an audience, King Philip first made him wait and then treated him coolly when he finally granted the audience on 30 January 1615. Hasekura entered the audience room to find the King standing near his throne, leaning casually on a table, surrounded by ministers and nobles. He refused to be greeted in the traditional way, with a kiss on his hand, and instead ordered his guests rather curtly to state their purpose. Luis Sotelo, mindful of his own mission, did what he could to soften the King up. He offered a creative interpretation of Date's wishes, adding to the latter's request for missionaries and trade the laying at King Philip's feet of his vast lands in Sendai, his title and his unstinting service.

This bought the embassy a little warmth. Hasekura's wish for baptism was granted, at a ceremony conducted in the presence of the King and other members of the royal family, to the strains of a choir singing *Laudate Dominum*. Hasekura received 'Felipe Francisco' for his Christian name, and the powerful Duke of Lerma for his god-father, a man said to have amassed a personal fortune of some

3 million ducats while ruling the realm on behalf of his less-than-conscientious king. Hasekura told Philip how moved he was to be born afresh with the King's own name. Philip gave him a hug and wrote a letter in support of his request for an audience with the Pope. Philip's advisers argued that now was not the time for such a meeting. The King countered that now was precisely the time, if matters in Japan were to improve.

The final leg of Hasekura's European voyage took place that autumn, passing through Barcelona and Saint-Tropez. The latter – unplanned – stop marked the dawn of Franco-Japanese relations. Townspeople marvelled at samurai solemnly attending Mass, eating with the aid not of cutlery but of 'two sticks' and blowing their noses into small pieces of paper which they then discarded on the ground – and which the curious of Saint-Tropez proceeded to pick up and claim as souvenirs.

Genoa and the port of Civitavecchia followed, before Hasekura's party arrived on the outskirts of Rome, to be met once again by European emissaries expressing suspicions about Japanese intentions towards Christianity. Luckily, Hasekura had three things in his favour. One of Europe's most powerful monarchs had written him a reference. His long journey from Japan was taken as evidence of Date Masamune's sincerity. And, perhaps most important of all, the Pope had personal need of him.

Paul V, born Camillo Borghese and elected to the papacy in 1605, was acquiring a reputation both for looking after his own – the Borghese family was now far advanced on its journey from Siena elite to Italian aristocracy – and for seeking to promote the Catholic Church's claims to global universalism. He beatified Ignatius of Loyola in 1609 and would do the same with the one-time Japanese resident Francis Xavier: two of the principal founders of a religious Order, the Jesuits, that was responsible for leading mission work beyond Europe – learning new languages, exploring new cultures and testing the limits of pragmatic accommodation with non-Christian ideas and ways of life. The Pope lent his support, too, to the case for sainthood of the Nagasaki martyrs: heroic advocates for a faith whose progress in the world, from the time of Peter and Paul onwards, had often been marked by tragedy and pain.

The city of Rome would gain a great artistic symbol of this global Church in 1651: Bernini's Fountain of the Four Rivers, representing the Danube (Europe), the Nile (Africa), the Río de la Plata (the Americas) and the Ganges (Asia). Well in advance of that, Pope Paul V was pioneering the use of diplomatic pageantry and art to stake his own claim to centrality in a Catholic *tianxia*. He had already welcomed embassies from the Kongo (in 1608) and Persia (1609). Now it was the turn of the Japanese to play their part.

So it was that, after a brief informal audience with the Pope at the Quirinal Palace on 25 October, Hasekura was awarded the accolade of a formal entry into Rome. It began at 3 p.m. on 29 October at the Porta Angelica. Wearing a kimono of white silk threaded with gold and silver motifs of flowers, birds and animals, Hasekura set out in a carriage while his men rode in front of him on finely caparisoned horses provided by the Pope. They were joined by ambassadors and aristocrats from Rome, Spain and France, alongside Swiss guardsmen and cavalry. The sound of trumpets and drums resounded around the streets as the embassy passed through, briefly drowned out by welcoming cannon-fire in St Peter's Square and then the Castel Sant'Angelo. The procession ended at the Capitoline Hill, where Hasekura descended from his carriage and was welcomed to his accommodation by the Pope's chamberlain.

For all its splendour, this was the economy version of a papal welcome. Senior cardinals and papal aides stayed away, according to rules under which only an embassy sent by a Christian head of state had a claim on their presence. A few days later, Hasekura dressed in his best for his second audience with the Pope, only to find the Holy Father dressing down in simple red, and greeting him in the relatively low-status Sala Clementina, within the Apostolic Palace. It was an impressive occasion nonetheless, for the visitors: the Pope sat on his red-velvet throne, a golden canopy overhead, surrounded by cardinals, archbishops, bishops and secretaries.

Hasekura entered, knelt once in the middle of the room and then again three times at the Pope's feet, kissing them before he arose. Greeting the Pope in Japanese, with Sotelo interpreting, he took Date Masamune's letter – written in Japanese and Latin – from a silk bag and presented it to the Pope. He then knelt again, but the Pope motioned him to stand as an aide read the Latin portion of the missive. Date was asking for Franciscan missionaries, pledging to build churches and protect priests. He hoped, too, for a bishop, whom he promised to maintain in appropriate comfort. The Pope's aide responded by expressing pre-scripted delight that the mission had come from so far away, adding that he hoped for Date's baptism soon.

In keeping with the best traditions of diplomacy, what each side really wanted could not be included in official correspondence, nor articulated in public. The Pope's hopes for the visit were made manifest in art a few years after the visit. The Sala Regia, a large audience chamber at the Quirinal Palace, was redecorated, turning the upper parts of the room's walls into an imagined spectators' gallery. There, looking down on the Pope's visitors, was a Japanese samurai dressed in an embroidered kimono of white silk: Hasekura Tsunenaga, freeze-framed in a fresco. Joining him in the image were four of his retainers, along with Luis Sotelo, gesturing downwards as though explaining to the Japanese the meaning of events taking place below. Further along the walls, likewise surveying the scene, were groups of Persians and Kongolese, alongside Armenians and Nestorian Christians from central Asia – all of them based on embassies received by the Pope, and all of it an implied rebuke of Protestant parochialism.

The discerning of Hasekura's hidden motives required a careful reading of the letter from Date. It contained a rather strange and nebulous line: 'For all the rest I thoroughly rely on [Sotelo and Hasekura], and I shall ratify anything they may conclude and ratify in my name.' The Venetian ambassador to Rome suspected that he knew what this meant. He reported back to his Senate that Hasekura had quietly put an additional request to the Pope: 'to receive under his protection as a sovereign prince his king, Masamune, who is on the way to become Emperor of Japan'.

Bearing in mind European uncertainty around this time over the roles of emperors versus shoguns, the Venetian ambassador seemed to be saying that Date's real aim in sending the Hasekura mission to Rome was to forge foreign friendships that would help him declare his independence from Ieyasu and Hidetada, and perhaps go after the latter's job. This was early days for the Tokugawa *bakufu*, and with

Hideyori still alive there was everything to play for. Date perhaps hoped that by bringing the Pope onside he could leverage the latter's authority and exploit to his advantage Japanese Christian concern over Ieyasu's hostility towards them.

Whatever the truth behind the Venetian ambassador's claims, the Pope showed little interest in forming an alliance – or, indeed, in agreeing to anything that Hasekura asked for. He made clear that his jurisdiction did not cover the trade policy of European powers. Nor did he show any willingness to create a new bishopric or support the sending of missionaries, shifting responsibility for the latter back to King Philip. Everything else Hasekura received during his stay in Rome – from honorary citizenship to a papal gift of a thousand gold ducats – represented consolation prizes at best.

Hasekura left Rome in early January 1616, beginning a long and dispiriting journey home. He found himself unwelcome in Spain: King Philip had secretly written to the Pope advising him to refuse all Japanese requests, while the Council of the Indies now barred Hasekura from Madrid and bade him return directly home instead. Hasekura ended up back in Seville for a few months, deploying his newly minted European contacts to the best effect he could. The Duke of Lerma, Pope Paul V and the Senate of Seville all received requests for help in meeting Date's demands, with Hasekura now claiming that the fate of Japan's Christians depended on them.

It was all to no avail, and in the summer of 1617 Hasekura was effectively deported: forced to sail back down the Guadalquivir River and to recross the Atlantic to New Spain. From there, his embassy reboarded the *Date Maru*, arriving in Manila in August 1618. The ship soon ended up in the hands of the Spanish navy, either commandeered by the Governor-General of the Philippines for service in an ongoing war with the English and the Dutch or donated by Luis Sotelo for that purpose. While the *Date Maru* was refitted for war, Hasekura, Sotelo and the others waited for an alternative ride home.

*

Hasekura and Sotelo may well have welcomed the delay in their return to Japan; Sotelo perhaps even engineered it, by making a gift of the *Date Maru*. One reason was the failure of their mission, another the Tokugawa turn against Christianity. Sotelo finally made it back in 1622 disguised as a merchant, only to be discovered, arrested and then burned at the stake with other Christians in 1624. All were tied loosely in the pyre, so that their writhing bodies would impress upon people the pain in store for those who broke the law. Setting out to lead the Christian community in Japan, Sotelo had ended as a martyr. He would be beatified in 1867, the final full year of Tokugawa rule.

Hasekura returned to Japan two years before Sotelo, reaching Sendai in September 1620 with presents for Date Masamune that included a portrait of the Pope and one of himself kneeling at prayer. The one thing he couldn't give his lord was good news. Having maintained his support for Christianity throughout the period of Hasekura's voyage, angering the shogun in the process, Date now turned his back. He banned Christianity in his domain and ordered the missionaries out.

No one knows for sure what became of Hasekura after this. Some say that he renounced his Christian faith, others that he died for it, along with his wife, children and servants. The most interesting afterlife afforded Hasekura insists that his 'death' in 1622 was faked by his family: a ruse to allow him to escape into the mountains. There he lived on for another thirty years as a recluse, finally passing away in 1654, at the age of eighty-four or thereabouts.

By this time the waters of Bernini's Fountain of the Four Rivers were flowing in Rome, while in Japan the Tokugawa *bakufu* had finished mopping up their enemies and were firmly in control of the country's affairs. Ieyasu and Hidetada had defeated Hideyoshi's son Hideyori and almost 100,000 of his supporters in 1614–15, besieging them at Osaka Castle and forcing Hideyori and his mother into suicide. Ieyasu had passed away the next year, leaving his successors to continue the arrest and execution of Christians all the way into the 1630s. A final armed stand took place in 1637–8 on the Shimabara peninsula near Nagasaki. Tens of thousands of disaffected samurai and Christian peasants battled the *bakufu*, but eventually went the way of Hideyori and his loyalists: besieged in a castle, and then wiped out.

If Hasekura was indeed still around in the early 1640s, he would have seen a century of Japanese contact with Europe – beginning with the first shipwrecked Portuguese in 1543 – come almost full circle. Alongside missionaries, Portuguese traders were banned from Japan. Only Nagasaki was open to foreign ships, and soon the only Europeans with whom the *bakufu* would do business were the Dutch. Japanese were meanwhile forbidden from leaving the country, on pain of execution when they returned. Issued across the 1630s, these rules were known collectively as the *sakoku* – 'closed country' – edicts.

Across the decades that followed, the ban on Christianity was enforced with the help of Japan's Buddhists, recovered from bloody setbacks under Oda Nobunaga and once again hand-in-glove with the state. Shinran's sect in particular was so powerful that in 1602 Ieyasu had decided to turn an internal split into a permanent separation of an Eastern (*Higashi*) Hongan-ji from a Western (*Nishi*) Hongan-ji. Buddhist temples now ran a nationwide system of compulsory registration, so that the country's leaders knew who was who and where they lived. And they administered a method of anti-Christian surveillance known as *fumi-e* (picture-treading). People suspected of harbouring Christian sympathies were required, once a year, to tread on an image of Jesus Christ or the Virgin Mary, many of them wrought in copper by apostates, working from the heart and taking as their model the kind of art that Hasekura had found everywhere during his travels in Europe.

For that deeply divided continent, long years of bloody religious conflict lay ahead. Japan, by contrast, had brought its own to a close. Its global relationships had also been settled, according to a vision – a Tokugawa *tianxia* – that prioritized domestic unity and *bakufu* control over foreign ambitions or friendships. It may have been less than Hideyoshi hoped for the Land of the Gods, but Japan was at last entering an era of remarkable peace and prosperity.

10

Ihara Saikaku

(井原西鶴)

1642–1693

Amorous Man

浪
華
西
鶴
公
羽

芳
一
晶
寫

Ihara Saikaku, painted by his friend Haga Isshō.

The waitress, taking off her linen robe and dainty underwear, threw them upon the fence and slipped into the tub. She was quite sure that no one was about. If there should be any sound at all, it could be nothing but the sigh of evening breezes among the nearby pines.

So thinking, at any rate, she started to rub herself vigorously with rice-bran soap and a towel. The water was pleasantly hot. Tomorrow would be the Iris Festival, and she needed a thorough cleaning of her plump warm torso. She took particular relish in removing the dirt from the lower parts of her body.

Suddenly, as though by instinct, she looked up. And there, on the tiled roof of the Azumaya teahouse next door, she saw the crouching figure of the boy Yonosuke levelling a long spyglass at her.

Yonosuke's name means 'man of the world'. Like Hasekura Tsunenaga, he is a voyager. But where Hasekura's journeys took him to Europe and the New World, Yonosuke moves through a universe of sensual enjoyment, into which his mother is said to have inducted him as a child: 'fondling him on her lap, hand tapping hand, hand tapping lips, she mumbled sweet nothings and the child gurgled gleefully'. During a life spent criss-crossing the country in search of amorous adventure, Yonosuke meets courtesans, innkeepers and actors, monks, and nuns, and country girls down on their luck. Of stampeding samurai armies he sees very little. He finds no castles under siege, no villages destroyed, no roadways or waterways clogged with bodies. He is a pleasure-seeker in a time of peace.

Both Yonosuke and his creator, Ihara Saikaku, were very much products of that peace, which saw Japan's economy and population alike grow apace during the first century of Tokugawa rule – from around 15 million people in 1600 to 30 million in 1700. More and more Japanese made their homes in towns and cities, where a world of urban recreation emerged – comprising art and theatre, books and bathing, tea parties and the company of courtesans – which people came to call the 'floating world' (*ukiyo*). Originally a Buddhist term denoting the fleeting quality of existence, full of sadness and pathos, it referred now to a world of pleasure, immortalized in woodblock prints and stage-plays as Pax Tokugawa's golden age: politically sound, socially stable and bearing its first and best cultural fruit.

Born into a merchant family in Osaka, Ihara was to capture this world in prose, helping to kick-start a brand-new literary genre called *ukiyo-zōshi*: 'books of the floating world'. His first and most influential work was *The Life of an Amorous Man* (*Kōshoku ichidai otoko*, 1682). The story followed Yonosuke's erotic escapades, devoting one chapter to each of his fifty-four eventful years of life.

Like Murasaki Shikibu before him, Ihara was an observer at heart, full of warmth and feeling for the people whose lives inspired his characters. He was a satirist too, holding nothing about his world in true reverence and delighting in upsetting his readers' expectations. Together with Yonosuke he is the ultimate tour guide around a culture defined by commerce, conspicuous consumption and enormous creativity, which the *bakufu* helped to build in two contrasting ways: by sustaining an unprecedented military peace, and by imposing a social one so disciplined and constraining that it drove people into the arms of fantasy, pleasure and play.

*

The Tokugawa *bakufu*'s radically restrictive approach to international relations by the end of the 1630s had more to do with control than with religion or philosophy or xenophobia. The same was true at home, where the Tokugawa shoguns built an impressive political and social settlement on foundations laid by Oda Nobunaga and Toyotomi Hideyoshi – the latter had been a diplomatic disaster, but a smart and capable leader at home.

At the apex of Japan's new social and political system, in formal terms at least, stood the imperial institution. Between them, Nobu-naga and Hideyoshi had helped Japan's emperors to replace decades of aristocratic uncertainty and embarrassing wooing of warlords with something resembling normal court life. Ieyasu and his successors followed up by ensuring that this life was confined to scholarship, ceremony and the arts. Stationing retainers in a newly built Nijō Castle in Kyoto, they kept an eye out for emperors or nobles tempted to scheme a return to the political frontline.

One rung below the ceremonial power of the Emperor and the real power of the shogun were the *daimyō*, around 250 in all, from the Shimazu in southern Kyūshū up to the Matsumae clan on the southern tip of Ezo (later known as Hokkaidō). They enjoyed control over everyday affairs in their domains, including commerce, tax collection and the administration of justice. In exchange, they pledged personal allegiance to the shogun and agreed to abide by a 'Code for the Military Houses'. First issued in 1615, and regularly updated, this banned them from harbouring criminals and traitors, required them to notify the shogun of suspicious activity in surrounding domains and forced them to seek the shogun's permission before making marriage arrangements.

The great guarantee and public sign of this new covenant was a hostage system first used by Hideyoshi and then formalized during the 1600s as *sankin kōtai*: 'alternate attendance'. *Daimyō* lived every other year in Edo, leaving members of their family behind in the *bakufu* capital during the year they spent back in their own domains. In this way, around half of Japan's *daimyō* were in Edo at any one time, comprising the *fudai* ('hereditary') *daimyō* who had joined Ieyasu before the Battle of Sekigahara in 1600 alongside *tozama* ('outside') *daimyō* who submitted only afterwards and were treated as a result with a healthy degree of suspicion.

For innkeepers, brothel-owners, restaurateurs and other service providers situated in Edo and along Japan's major roads – especially the Tōkaidō (Eastern Sea Route) between Kyoto and Edo – *sankin kōtai* was a blessing. For the *daimyō*, it was a financial curse, requiring regular journeying with a grand retinue, gifts to the shogun upon arrival in Edo and the suitably lavish upkeep of not one but two residences. On top of this, they were required to contribute men and materials to an enormous wave of construction, repairing imperial and noble residences in Kyoto, improving shogunal properties across the realm and generally restoring the country's war-torn infrastructure. Draining *daimyō* coffers was one way the *bakufu* forestalled resistance to its rule. Another was forbidding them from shoring up their own defences. Each lord was limited to just one castle in his domain, though not everyone complied.

The rest of Japan's population was divided into a carefully articulated four-fold class system. At the top were the samurai, making up around 8 per cent of the population and steadily exchanging warrior work for office work. Many became tax collectors, paying routine, sometimes intimidatory visits to the country's 63,000 villages. The samurai no longer possessed any land of their own. Increasingly they survived instead on stipends paid by their lords in bales of rice, and resided for the most part in domain capitals, or castle towns, such as Nagoya and Hiroshima, which were rapidly becoming bustling centres of commerce, culture and administrative activity.

Below the samurai came the farmers. One of Hideyoshi's great achievements had been to complete the land surveys that Nobunaga began. His emissaries estimated the productivity of every piece of land and set tax at two-thirds of that amount, to be paid in rice. 'Two to the lord, one to the farmer,' as a saying of the time had it. Two other sayings perhaps captured the grim reality better: 'farmers should be kept suspended between life and death', and – pithier still – 'squeeze them like seeds'.

Here, as elsewhere, while Nobunaga and Hideyoshi sketched out the fundamentals, the Tokugawa shoguns filled in the details, issuing regulations on everything from conduct to couture. Samurai were permitted swords, surnames, silk kimono – of varying grades, depending on status – and the top-knot hairstyle: tied in a small queue at the back or on top of the head, while the pate was shaved. Farmers, by contrast, were forbidden from carrying weapons, had to make do with a given name only (at least in public) and were confined to clothes of simple hemp or cotton (cultivation of which began in Japan in the 1600s). Regulations issued in 1649 commanded them to work hard in the fields from dawn to dusk, switching in the evenings to the making of rope and sacks. Tea, *sake* and rice were off limits; coarse grains were to be eaten instead. If wives idled away too much time visiting temples, their flightiness was to be rewarded with divorce.

Not every farmer's lot was the same. Some owned their own land, enjoying rising agricultural yields – thanks to higher-quality seeds and fertilizer – while supplementing that income with side ventures including silk, cotton and tea cultivation. As time went on, full-blown rural industries began to emerge. Other farmers lived and died as tenants, with very narrow margins for error where the vicissitudes of the climate were concerned, and with little expectation that life could change. Relocating to a new village or to a town was forbidden, although domain authorities were often so desperate to avoid leaving land uncultivated – a hungry castle town might rapidly become a lawless one – that farmers who absconded were treated relatively leniently as long as they had not tried to cross over into someone else's domain.

Even the lowliest farmer was at least producing something. According to the Neo-Confucian values that underpinned Tokugawa society – community, family, frugality, hierarchy, obedience and mutual obligation – this fact alone placed them in moral terms above the *chōnin*, or 'townspeople': artisans, ranked third in the system, and merchants, ranked last on the basis that all they did was deal in the produce of others.

Where you lived, and how you lived, said a lot about your worth in Tokugawa society. The centres of most towns and cities were marked by the stacked towers of the *daimyō*'s castle. Radiating out from there, in roughly concentric circles, came first the homes of senior vassals, followed by humbler merchant dwellings – a matter of convenience for samurai shoppers since merchants lived and worked out of the same building, with a public-facing business room to the front and living space towards the rear.

As wealthier merchants sought to emulate samurai lifestyles, their homes gained tatami-mat flooring, *shōji* partitions of waxed translucent paper glued over a wooden grid and richly decorated sliding screen-doors called *fusama*. In good weather, *shōji* and *fusama* alike could be removed, letting a breeze blow through the house and affording a view – in the case of especially well-appointed homes – of an internal garden. Further out from the town centre, after the merchant dwellings, were the homes of lesser vassals, with temples – many of them rebuilt during the early years of peace – situated on the outer perimeter.

Neo-Confucian pieties aside, merchant activity was – as Nobunaga, Hideyoshi and Ieyasu all well appreciated – a vital element in the building of a unified and prosperous Japan. Nowhere was the truth of this more obvious than in Ihara Saikaku's home town of Osaka. Rebuilt under Hideyoshi, after the destruction of the Ishiyama Hongan-ji in 1580, the city's population was approaching 400,000 in Ihara's time. That made it Japan's second-largest city behind Edo, whose population was set to rise to almost a million by 1700 (becoming perhaps the largest city on Earth), and ahead of Kyoto, home to around 350,000 people.

A hub for overland and waterborne trade, Osaka was amongst those parts of the country considered important enough to be retained by the Tokugawa shoguns under their direct control, along with other major urban and trading centres including Kyoto, Edo and Nagasaki, large swathes of fertile rice fields and Japan's major copper, silver and gold mines. The port and its many waterways, lined with warehouses, welcomed vessels from across Japan each autumn, laden with *daimyō* tax rice sent for conversion into cash of various kinds. A new national currency, making use of precious metals, now ran alongside paper currencies issued by and circulating in each domain. Osaka was rapidly becoming synonymous with the sorts of financial services required to make this complex system work: rice-brokers, money-changers and money-lenders, along with issuers of advance payments against future rice deliveries. The city was known, too, as 'Japan's kitchen' for its awesome culinary range, and as a producer of sought-after textiles.

Ihara Saikaku was thoroughly immersed in Osaka's commercial culture from a young age, growing up in a merchant family and from the age of fourteen using *haikai* poetry to document life around him. Like the 'linked verse' (*renga*) tradition out of which it developed, *haikai* was rooted in collaborative composition: one person's verse picked up where the previous person left off. But it did away with many of the old rules and restrictions on form and content, becoming in the process a medium for the masses, associated above all with Matsuo Bashō, a contemporary of Ihara who became famous for his standalone starting verses known as *hokku*, later *haiku*.

One of Ihara's major influences was the Danrin School of *haikai*, which drew much of its language and inspiration from everyday commoner lives. This made him controversial in some quarters and he was dubbed *Oranda Saikaku*, 'Dutch Saikaku', by his critics. A few decades into the *bakufu*'s closed-country policy, words like 'Dutch', 'padre' and 'red-haired' had become bywords for weirdness and eccentricity.

Ihara was certainly unconventional. One day in 1675, working by himself, he composed a record-breaking 1,000 *haikai* in a period of around twelve hours. They were published that year as *A Thousand Haikai Alone in a Single Day* (*Haikai dokugin ichinichi senku*). The book's preface, addressed by Ihara to his young wife, reveals the roots of his feat in the defining tragedy of his life:

> While you lived, we mourned others. Now you have gone. I could not stop you . . . A crane leaving her crying children, you died on the night of the third of the fourth month. Just then I heard a nightingale's tear-thick call, and a *hokku* [opening verse] came. Alone, between dawn and sunset today, I made a thousand haikai for you, while a single calligrapher recorded them. Please accept these, my farewell offering.
>
> Saikaku

The verses began with Ihara checking his wife for signs of life:

> Nightingale,
> fold your now
> pulseless hands.

Ihara – or perhaps his calligrapher – chose for 'nightingale' a set of characters meaning 'bird of impermanence', connecting its cry with his wife's departing soul. From here, Ihara moved back to his wife's last moments, reciting the *nembutsu*, and then forward to her funeral preparations:

Breaths shorter,
Ten night Buddha names.

Body washed
Third day, fourth month
By monks.

Two years after his wife's death, Ihara handed over his business affairs to an assistant and took the Buddhist tonsure. It was a sign of grief, and also of a person retiring from the world to devote themselves to art. He began to compete with rivals in the 'poetry marathon' form that he had established with *A Thousand Haikai*. On one occasion, Ihara managed 23,500 verses in twenty-four hours: an average of one verse every three and a half seconds. He travelled widely, too, becoming a keen observer of the world that the early Tokugawa shoguns had helped create.

Poetry and travel alike soon found their way into the activity that made Ihara's name: the turning of prose fiction from a not especially well-respected genre into an enormously popular vehicle for social commentary and satire. *The Life of an Amorous Man* was published in 1682, its debt to *haikai* clear from its economy of style, episodic structure and earthy language. Yonosuke's odyssey of romance, gallantry and misadventure was fantastical in all sorts of ways – there were surely not many in the Edo era who could claim to have slept with 3,742 women and 725 men. But he moved through a world that Ihara had seen for himself and was vividly recognizable to his readers.

Yonosuke was born into a Kyoto merchant family, and his future course becomes clear one night at the age of seven when he attempts to seduce his maid:

'Blow out the light,' the little boy commanded ... 'Don't you know that love is made in the dark ... ?'

What sounds like a proposition, comical on the lips of one so young, is in fact precociousness of a different kind. It is an allusion to Tanabata, Japan's summertime Star Festival, and to its origins in a romantic Chinese folk tale, about a weaver girl and a cowherd who can only meet once a year when a flock of magpies arrives to form a bridge to unite the lovers. Ihara was flattering his merchant readership here, offering them a hero who is more than a mere sexual dynamo. Yonosuke is clever and cultured. He survives life's ups and downs on his wits, his entrepreneurial spirit and his knowledge of what makes a city tick.

If readers spotted a parallel between Murasaki Shikibu's Genji and Ihara's Yonosuke – the ideal types for an aristocratic and a mercantile age – then so much the better, as far as Ihara was concerned. He playfully modelled the structure of his story on Murasaki's masterpiece, even emulating some of its scenes. Yonosuke ogling his maid as she bathes was inspired by Genji stealing a glance at his lover through some curtains.

But Yonosuke's lust for life takes him in directions of which Murasaki Shikibu would not have approved. Ordered by his father to check on a part of the family business in Edo, Yonosuke stops off at a seaside inn. He enjoys some fine seafood, and is engrossed in counting his money before bed when he hears someone out on the road singing a mournful song. He asks the cook about it and discovers that this particular song is associated with two beautiful sisters who work nearby as entertainers. Wakasa and Wakamatsu are wildly popular, but famously coy about the company they keep. Confident that he is up to the challenge, Yonosuke decides to put his dreary business trip on hold:

> With his winning, cajoling ways, he encountered little difficulty in making the sisters' acquaintance. For the next few days, he enjoyed their amorous company, earning for himself the enviable title of lady's man once attributed to an ancient courtier named Narihira. He decided to take the girls back with him to Kyoto. They were willing enough, and he prevailed upon the proprietor of the inn to accept his promissory note as the price for their release.
>
> On the long road back, however, Yonosuke's travel money, with expenses trebling at the inns where they tarried fondly, became exhausted. They went their separate ways. The girls started a wayside noodle shop, hoping to attract passers-by with their charming songs. Later it was said that the sisters, failing in business, entered a temple at the foot of Mount Hanazono, where they shaved their heads – the fate of all misplaced confidences.

Yonosuke meanwhile resumed his journey to Edo. But hot blood now surged in his veins. He tarried at every inn on the way, writing more promissory notes, making new conquests, discarding old flames. Months later, in a pitiful state of dissipation, he reached the family branch shop in Edo.

Money, women and the open road. Love, life and the free market. Here, a young merchant reader's governing concerns were folded into a single episode, with a mention of Narihira – the aristocratic subject and putative author of *The Tales of Ise* – thrown in as a nod to his classical education.

Yonosuke proceeds to wear his parents' patience and finances sufficiently thin that his father disowns him. Up until now, Yonosuke has seen poverty and insecurity only from the perspective of the moneyed. He has watched Kyoto noblemen enter a pleasure district in the 'poorly managed disguise' of white turbans, there to 'pluck forbidden flowers among the plebeians'. He has found a girl of 'startling beauty' doing favours in a tumbledown shack to earn money to send back to struggling parents in the countryside. He has met Buddhist nuns offering their bodies in return for 'alms', and a samurai so poor that he owns only a broken fan and a tea-kettle, which he heats by burning dried leaves. And he has listened to a lengthy disquisition on the happy vulnerability to sexual predation of freshly widowed women:

> 'Dead leaves pile up in her garden. She forgets to have her house re-roofed. On stormy nights the roof leaks, the thunder rolls, and she remembers how in her fear she used to nestle close to her husband . . .'

There's a fine art to cashing in, Yonosuke is told. One keeps an ear out for funerals, introduces oneself there as a childhood friend of the deceased and then prays for a fire in the neighbourhood – readying oneself to rush to the rescue.

Tasting poverty, now, for himself, Yonosuke is forced to take refuge in a life of Buddhist asceticism. Boredom and religious doubt quickly set in, and he casts around for the funds required to resume his 'life of sin'. He sells his rosary beads and finds work as a pimp for a group of male prostitutes working under the guise – as they often did at this time – of itinerant sellers of incense and perfume. Later, he performs Nō chants for scraps and sells salted salmon door-to-door in snowbound villages, whose frostbitten inhabitants believe it to have medicinal properties. He even spends a few months in a lice- and flea-infested prison, avoiding the mandatory newcomer's beating by charming his fellow inmates with song and dance.

Eventually, Yonosuke's luck returns. His father dies and his mother showers him with gold. Overwhelmed with gratitude, Yono-suke vows to dedicate this money to liberating 'the lovely courtesans of this country' from bondage. 'At last, I shall have all the famous beauties at my command!' His mission takes him through some of the best-known pleasure quarters of the day: Shimabara in Kyoto, Shinmachi in Osaka and Yoshiwara near Edo, around six kilome-tres out from the city centre. First established with the approval of the authorities during the first half of the 1600s as a way of concen-trating a city's iniquities (fleshly ones, at any rate) in one area, they were places where stifling social rules could be broken or overlooked. The stresses and strains of everyday life could be relieved through lively conversation, tea, music, dance, a meal by candlelight, a dip and a chat in the public bath, and of course a little private time with a courtesan.

Though noblemen and samurai visited these areas, the latter required to leave their swords at the gates, the pleasure quarters really belonged to a merchant class in the process of creating a culture of its own. His-tory was repeating itself here. Three hundred years before, in the early days of the Ashikaga shogunate, warriors had been the social interlopers, seeking to spend and bluff their way towards something approaching the high culture of Kyoto's courtiers. Warrior and aris-tocratic life came together – helped along by fresh inspiration from China – and gave Japan the tea ceremony and Nō theatre, flower-arranging and new forms of poetry. Now, a new class of social climbers was using its money and energy to push Japanese culture onwards, drawing as the warriors once had on what had come before. The evi-dence was everywhere, from kimono designs inspired by *The Tale of Genji* up to the building of Nō stages in the homes of the ultra-rich.

Merchants new to Zeami's art could buy themselves a rapid and inexpensive initiation via that classic symbol of social and cultural

THE JAPANESE

aspiration: the guidebook. Here was a reminder that the 'floating world' was a technological as well as a commercial and cultural accomplishment. Where Genji's adventures had first been copied out by hand and passed around discerning circles at the Heian court, thanks to woodblock printing Yonosuke's were quickly available all over Osaka. Calligraphers and artists produced their work on thin sheets of paper, each of which was pasted to a block of cherry wood, to be carved so that the words and images stood out in relief. The blocks were then washed and inked, and printing paper was applied. Hundreds of prints could be made from a single set of blocks, after which they were planed and recarved with some new creation.

Large towns and cities were soon bursting with bookshops, itinerant book-pedlars and lending libraries offering dictionaries and dance manuals, maps and medical books. There were cookbooks of all kinds, along with travel guides listing and rating everything from religious sites and tourist spots to shops, restaurants and brothels. A booklist published in Edo in 1696 ran to 7,800 available titles – and that was excluding poetry books and theatre scripts.

One of the reasons for preferring woodblock over movable type was the complexity of the Japanese script, with its mixture of Chinese characters and the phonetic syllabary known as *hiragana*. Another reason was the importance of images appearing alongside words in many Edo-era books. Early editions of *The Life of an Amorous Man* featured illustrations created by Ihara himself, including one of the young Yonosuke training his telescope on his naked maid. And where Ihara's work was suggestive rather than explicit, people who wanted someone else to do their imagining for them sought out *shunga* ('spring pictures'), a genre of erotica that ranged from conventional intimacies rendered in close anatomical detail, down to the last brittle hair and fleshy protrusion, through to fantastical encounters in which not being human was no bar to participation.

Alongside books went the single woodblock print. For the price of a snack, you could take home your very own picture of a famous courtesan, a warrior of yesteryear, some terrible ghoul from Japanese folklore or perhaps one of the heroes of a great theatrical innovation of the early 1600s – 'kabuki'. The word came from *katamuki*, 'slanted', suggesting unusual or eccentric behaviour, and managed to attach itself to the work of a woman called Okuni, possibly a shrine attendant earlier in her life, who in 1603 began performing an unconventional outdoor dance routine, imitating a man visiting a brothel. As word spread, and Okuni was called to perform at Edo Castle in 1607, entre-preneurial brothel-owners in Kyoto began setting up open-air stages along the bank of the Kamo River, where women and men in their employ would perform variations on Okuni's basic theme as a way of advertising their wares. It was not, at least according to one Confucian commentator, an especially elevated art form:

> The men wear women's clothing; the women wear men's clothing . . .
> They sing base songs and dance vulgar dances; their lewd voices are
> clamorous, like the buzzing of flies and the crying of cicadas. This is
> the kabuki of today.

But samurai liked what they saw, enough to begin fighting over the actors, forcing the authorities to ban women from kabuki. Similar fights promptly broke out over the boys who replaced them, leading to their participation being banned as well after 1652. It returned in a new form during Ihara's lifetime. Only men could now take to the stage: they were ranked in guidebooks, pictured in prints and widely gossiped about around town – perhaps none more so than Ichikawa Danjūrō I (1660–1704). One of Japan's first celebrities, he was famed for his *aragoto* ('tough stuff') acting style and his pioneering smear-ing of black and red stripes on his face to complete the tense, intimidating effect. Other actors, known as *onnagata*, used stylized gestures and vocal techniques to play women. What began as a sim-ple skit was developing into a full-blown dramatic art, performed in purpose-built theatres and featuring plots, narration, dialogue, song and dance.

What Bashō was to *haikai* in this era, and Ihara to prose fiction, Chikamatsu Monzaemon (1653–1724) was to theatre. He wrote both for kabuki and for bunraku (puppet theatre), a spectacle involving high-quality mechanical puppets, some of them up to two-thirds the size of human beings, with movable eyes, eyebrows, mouths and fin-gers. Chikamatsu's *sewamono* ('domestic pieces') became classics of Japanese theatre. Some were inspired by current affairs and rushed into production before the early modern news cycle moved on. Many ploughed the rich Tokugawa-era furrow of people caught tragically between the demands of the heart and of heavy social responsibility: *ninjō* (personal feelings) versus *giri* (duty). With marriage in this era taking the form of a contract between two families, a married man could more easily give free rein to his appetites in the pleasure quarters (as long as he was reasonably discreet about it) than he could seek a divorce in the name of love for someone else. Women were even more constrained, by familial and social expectations.

There emerged as a result the drastic romantic act of *shinjū*, or 'double suicide', in which two people who could not be together in this world – hailing from different walks of life, or the victims of otherwise impossible circumstances – would die together in the hope of being reborn by one another's sides. *Shinjū* plays were so powerful that the *bakufu* took steps in the early 1700s to ban suicide, both in real life and on stage.

Playwrights had to be similarly careful about politics, many preferring to make the most of their audiences' historical literacy to project contemporary concerns and criticisms back into the past. This gave extra bite to a *jidaimono*, or 'period piece', genre that was already a great deal of fun: high emotions and vivid action scenes (for which puppets were especially useful), with larger-than-life characters and gasp-inducing denouements.

Hideyoshi would have loved it. In his time, he had commissioned Nō plays celebrating his achievements and then assumed the lead role when they were staged (performing on one occasion for the Emperor, to reviews that could best be described as diplomatic). Now, he was a box office hit. Where Nobunaga was usually presented as a despot deserving of his fiery death, Hideyoshi was cheered to the rafters as the peasant who rose to rule a realm.

For all the romance of the 'floating world', Ihara was alive to its darker sides. The class logic of the era combined with a highly refined commercialism to produce a grading system for the attractions of the pleasure quarters that could be disturbing to behold. At one end were an elite cadre of women known as *tayū*. Often of samurai birth, they were highly proficient in singing, dancing, poetry composition, the tea ceremony and shamisen (a three-stringed banjo-like instrument, plucked with a plectrum). They dressed lavishly, travelled to their appointments in palanquins, accompanied by maids, and were groomed to behave like nobility. At the other extreme were the uncultured, unkempt daughters of desperate farmers, struggling pathetically to approximate a high-culture fantasy for which they lacked the resources and their clientele the sophistication.

At one point in *The Life of an Amorous Man*, Yonosuke reluctantly agrees to show some new-found friends around Shibaya-machi, the pleasure quarters of the port town of Ōtsu:

> What they saw was a strange and ugly vista. Prostitutes exposed themselves to view in front of their apartments, speaking in loud shrill voices. Heavy coatings of liquid powder made their faces look repulsively ghastly. Some of them were twanging the shamisen in all stages of jarring unproficiency, singing with heads held high without regard for their ugliness. Those walking the street waddled hurriedly on large ungainly feet.
>
> Worse, the men who came to gloat at them were a rough and quarrelsome lot. It was they who, more than the prostitutes themselves, gave a notorious character to the street. Pack-horse leaders, boatmen from nearby Lake Biwa, fishermen, wrestlers, playboy sons of rice-cake dealers, wayward clerks of fancy-goods shops – they were tough men of all ages, utterly without sentiment or modesty.
>
> Furtive male eyes sought out rivals approaching. Before long they began to taunt, abuse and insult each other. Sleeves were rolled up, hoods removed from shaggy heads. Quick hands fished out hidden weapons from hip sashes. Sharp blades flashed in the sunlight. Suddenly the street became a bedlam of little groups here, there and everywhere, cursing, knocking, kicking, slashing . . . A horrible street indeed. No one who valued his life, thought Yonosuke, would venture to enter it at night.

While the fortunes of Yonosuke and the people he met tended to ebb and flow in a world that was peaceful but not predictable, Ihara's rose rapidly as *The Life of an Amorous Man* enthralled readers across Osaka and later in Edo, where a pirated version of his book began doing the rounds. Ihara's publisher made sure that later works appeared simultaneously in both cities. They included an unsuccessful attempt at writing for bunraku before Ihara returned to safer territory, with *Five Women Who Chose Love* (*Kōshoku gonin onna*) and *The Life of an Amorous Woman* (*Kōshoku ichidai onna*). Both books were published in 1686, tracking the descent into depravity and dishonour of women who, much like Yonosuke, allowed passionate and exploratory natures to take them where they would.

Hoping to consolidate his urban audience of townsmen and samurai across all 'three capitals' (*santo*) of Osaka, Kyoto and Edo, in 1687 Ihara published a book of forty short stories called *The Great Mirror of Male Love* (*Nanshoku ōkagami*). Romantic relationships between men and adolescent boys, in which the former served as models and allies in the boys' lives, were a long-established feature of Japanese culture by this point. Yoshimitsu's relationship with Zeami in the 1300s had been a scandal not so much because they were both male but rather on account of the vast difference in status between them.

Where *Life of an Amorous Man* drew on the *Tale of Genji* for its inspiration, this new book took its forty-chapter structure from another Heian-era masterpiece – *Great Mirror* (*Ōkagami*), which told the story of Fujiwara Michinaga. The purpose of a literary 'mirror', both in Michinaga's time and Ihara's, was to 'reflect' with useful expository clarity some person or event or idea. Ihara's intention with *The Great Mirror of Male Love*, whose stories focused on samurai and kabuki actors, was to complement his earlier exploration of what the connoisseurs called *nyodō* ('the way of loving women') with attention to *wakashudō*, 'the way of loving boys'. In characteristically mischievous spirit, Ihara opened his book with twenty-three scenarios, purporting to prove the superiority of boys over women:

Which is to be preferred . . .

Lying rejected next to a courtesan, or conversing intimately with a kabuki boy who is suffering from haemorrhoids?

Caring for a wife with tuberculosis, or keeping a youth who constantly demands spending money?

Marrying the master's daughter and going to bed early every evening until you gradually waste away, or falling in love with the master's son and seeing his face only in the daytime?

The mouth of a woman as she blackens her teeth, or the hand of a youth as he plucks his whiskers?

*

Towards the end of his life, Ihara explored samurai and merchant existences beyond the bedroom. *The Eternal Storehouse of Japan* (*Nippon eitaigura*), published in 1688, featured stories about the making and losing of fortunes, in the course of which Ihara offered his own business management advice – memorably branded as the 'millionaire pill'.

He became less prolific after this, and the tone of his work more serious. His daughter died in 1692, and Ihara himself passed away the following year. He was fifty-two by Japanese reckoning, according to which a person is 'one' when they are born. This put him a couple beyond 'man's fifty years in this world', as Zeami's play *Atsumori* had it. Ihara's final *haikai* suggests that he was anxious to move on:

> I have gazed at it now
> For two years too long –
> The Moon of the Floating World.

Much like his creator, Yonosuke eventually feels the years pressing in upon him. He gives much of his money away: to temples and shrines, homeless actors and courtesans in need of rescue from their contracts. He travels south to Nagasaki and the pleasure quarters at Maruyama. There he finds some old faces: courtesans from Kyoto who are so pleased to see him that they stage Nō plays for his pleasure, Zeami's *Wind Through the Pines* (*Matsukaze*) amongst them. Yonosuke eats with them, chats with them and lays out his personal collection of forty-four bunraku puppets for their viewing pleasure.

At last, it is time to go. Yonosuke is tired, grey, thin. He needs a walking stick now, and his hearing is slowly going. He gathers together six similarly ailing friends and does something that you're not supposed to do any more. He builds a ship. For a sail, he uses an old lover's silken inner garments; for the rigging, lengths of braided hair, given to him as mementos by other women he has known and loved. He stocks up on food, stimulants and painkillers, *The Tales of Ise* and some erotic prints, clove oil, pepper and several thousand sex toys of various types and manufacture. Then he and his friends head for the open sea. We are off, he tells them, to an island inhabited solely by women, god-like in their appetites and strength. Old we may be, but the night is yet young.

11

Sakamoto Ryōma

(坂本龍馬)

1835–1867

Revolutionary

Sakamoto Ryōma, photograph dated *c.*1866, Kochi Prefectural
Museum of History.

I must say that it's beyond me the way things work out in a man's life. Some fellows have such bad luck that they bang their privates on getting out of a bath tub and die as a result. When you compare my luck with that, it's really remarkable ... I really thought I was going to [die], and instead I am to live. Now I have become the disciple of the greatest man in Japan ... I'm giving everything I have for the province and the country.

Vivid imagery aside, Sakamoto Otome must have been relieved to hear from her little brother in the summer of 1863. The near-death experience to which he alluded had nothing to do with the risky business of bath-time and everything to do with his politics, which in recent years had been on a trajectory from enthusiastic to single-minded to sanguinary. What was more, Otome herself had provided him with a weapon: a sword, dormant down the generations in the Sakamoto family, but now, in these times of crisis, all too likely to see some action.

Ihara Saikaku had witnessed, towards the end of his life, the first glimmerings of that later crisis. Entrepreneurial talent alone seemed less and less likely to carry a man forward. Concentrations of wealth passed down within merchant houses mattered more: this was a society, as he saw it, where 'only silver can produce more silver'. At the same time, people seemed to be adhering ever more selectively to easily satirized yet nevertheless precious ideals of family, duty and compassion.

Ihara passed away on the cusp of a century – the 1700s – that came to be marked by Pax Tokugawa's gradual decline. Peace persisted and standards of living continued to rise. But as the size and shape of the country's economy changed, with unexpected social consequences, the *bakufu* struggled to respond effectively. Attempts at reform, often couched in the language of a return to the resolution of the Ieyasu years, rarely achieved more than temporary respite. The shoguns' aura of legitimacy began to wear away.

Born in 1835, Sakamoto Ryōma grew up at a time when these troubles, bubbling away for generations, were beginning to boil over. These were anxious years for Japan, but for Sakamoto it was an exciting time to be alive. He became one of a large number of lower-ranking samurai to turn their backs on day-to-day domain duties and to roam the land instead, in pursuit of what they regarded as a national calling. They dubbed themselves *shishi*, 'men of high purpose', in contrast to the many men of low or no particular purpose whom they saw as dominating domain and *bakufu* politics.

Swords like the one Sakamoto received from his sister were central to this sense of urgent, noble purpose. They symbolized a warrior caste that needed to recover its old steel. They represented sharpness of intent, a cutting to the chase. They could also be used to kill people. Such had been Sakamoto's firm intention in December 1862, arriving at the home of a quisling government official whose violent death he was sure would invigorate his cause.

But this official managed to convince Sakamoto that violence was not – yet – the answer, guiding him from a narrow, hot-headed take on Japan's problems towards a more expansive vision of the country's future. Sakamoto began to help knit a new sense of national purpose to replace a worn-out Pax Tokugawa. It was the beginning of the end for samurai rule in Japan, a clearing of the decks for something new.

*

Japan in the 1700s was one of the most highly urbanized societies on Earth. Up to 10 per cent of the population lived in towns and cities, while an urban culture of books, entertainment and commerce came increasingly to be shared with the country's larger villages. The challenge for the shoguns was to keep Ieyasu's system ticking over, in a world that he could never have imagined. They worked to steward the *bakufu*'s finances and the country's sense of purpose alike, while avoiding extremes of wealth or poverty that might threaten the class system and undermine public peace.

Two of the most celebrated reforming shoguns were great-grandsons of Ieyasu: Tsunayoshi, shogun from 1680 to 1709; and Yoshimune, shogun between 1716 and 1745.

Tsunayoshi was remembered for trying to promote talented people rather than merely well-connected ones, for tackling embezzlement amongst local officials, and for sponsoring Buddhist and Chinese scholarship and values – ordering the erection of public signs around the country reminding people of key Confucian virtues. He particularly emphasized benevolence towards animals. People were not to hurt them, abandon the sick, or sell tortoises or birds for food. Anyone found to have killed a dog could themselves face the death penalty – an injunction that led Tsunayoshi to be remembered by posterity, with a mixture of fondness and mockery, as 'the dog shogun'.

Yoshimune shared little of his second cousin's warm feeling towards the animal kingdom. He loved hunting with falcons and was rumoured to celebrate the capture of a bird by ripping its head off and drinking its blood. Japan's commoners might have spotted a metaphor there. Yoshimune was happy to consult samurai on *bakufu* reform, instituting a suggestion box and, like Tsunayoshi, working to raise capable men within his administration. But he had little time for the lower orders. He raised rural taxes and created new penalties for anyone seeking to flee their land and its associated tax burden. He placed restrictions on money-lenders and herded merchants into guilds, where their activities would be easier to police. And he required people to settle their commercial disputes privately, including through the use of mediation, rather than eating up *bakufu* resources.

Like many reformers of the 1700s and early 1800s, Yoshimune combined practical measures with moral exhortation. Concerned that the excessive wealth and power of some merchants posed a threat to Pax Tokugawa, he urged Japan's overly keen consumers to return to the frugality of the past – setting a personal example by limiting himself to two meals per day and requiring his staff to do the same. And yet no amount of hectoring could change the fact that the *bakufu* had been built on shaky foundations: a coalition of semi-independent *daimyō*, controlling their own economic affairs while possessing varying degrees of enthusiasm about their Tokugawa overlords; and a class system that in 1600 had seemed little more than a formalization of the facts – so powerfully had the samurai shaped recent history – but which increasingly relied on mere convention to keep it going. Japan developed a national economy across the 1600s and 1700s, with goods and money flowing across domain borders, but it lacked a national government to regulate it.

Each new generation of *bakufu* reformers discovered this to their cost: any intervention risked offending either *daimyō* autonomy or some element of the class system. Squeeze farmers too hard, and the result was protest, absconding and even infanticide, leading to a smaller population, untilled fields and a reduced rice income. Apply pressure instead to merchants and money-lenders, by regulating them more heavily or cancelling samurai debt, and credit suddenly became more expensive or was cut off altogether. Rice prices could be fixed by fiat, but low rates angered farmers and samurai (whose stipends were paid that way), while high ones risked the rage of the urban poor. Interfere with the money supply, and you risked inflation or recession. Even the attempt to recruit reliable administrators could backfire: Tsunayoshi was accused – not entirely unfairly – of cronyism.

Problems and attempted solutions alike began to erode the Tokugawa social covenant during the 1700s and early 1800s. A hierarchical society seemed natural and defensible when the respect and obedience offered by a junior party – within the class system, or within a home – was met by justice and benevolence travelling the other way. Using hierarchy as a means of passing on economic pain was another matter altogether. Hard-pressed *daimyō* damaged the system when they levied arbitrary taxes on farmers – including, in one instance, a tax on girls who reached a particular age – or put their hands in their samurai retainers' pockets, reducing their stipends or 'borrowing' against future payments. Samurai striving to maintain a lifestyle appropriate to their place in an increasingly theoretical class system wrought damage of their own when they pressured villagers over their tax payments.

Rural Japanese sufficiently endowed with land and capital could afford to be leaned on a little. Those living more precarious everyday lives, whether in the countryside or in the cities, found that tax hikes, price fluctuations or periods of crop failure could tip them into starvation. Japan suffered three major famines in this era: in the 1730s, the 1780s and finally the 1830s. The last, known as the Tenpō famine, led to rocketing rice prices, reports of infanticide and cannibalism, and the deaths of hundreds of thousands of people. Town and country alike were hit by severe unrest. Large parts of Osaka went up in flames in 1837, and there were calls in the city for merchants – accused of callously hoarding precious resources – to be executed.

Such violence was rare: protesters generally sought fairness rather than revolution, and most of the thousands of economic disputes that erupted in the 1700s and early 1800s were resolved via peaceful petition. But a time was coming when no amount of negotiation in the villages or tinkering from Edo could keep Pax Tokugawa afloat. As long-running domestic woes combined with fresh foreign crisis, the strain would prove too much.

For those in Japan who felt nostalgic for the purpose and clarity of the early Tokugawa years – encountered in books, schools and stories passed down from one generation to the next – one of the more worrying developments of the 1700s was the erosion of the old class distinctions. While wealthy merchants lived it up, regarding fines for decorating their homes or dressing too lavishly as simply the price of the good life, struggling samurai cast around for part-time jobs, set themselves up producing ribbons and umbrellas, and even sold off their daughters in an effort to make ends meet.

Not everyone was sympathetic to their plight. The samurai of the history books and kabuki plays were heroes, selfless and courageous. Today's bunch appeared less impressive by contrast: a combination of idle bureaucrat and incorrigible shopaholic, some willing to accumulate vast amounts of debt in order to afford the latest trinkets. More ignominious still was the spectacle of samurai offering up their heritage for sale. Individuals hawked their armour while Morioka domain, in northern Japan, produced a detailed official price list, running from the right to wear a sword up to the deluxe option of full warrior status.

There were plenty of takers for opportunities like these. One of them was Sakamoto Ryōma's grandfather, a *sake* brewer from rugged, mountainous Tosa domain in southern Shikoku, who in 1771 purchased the relatively lowly samurai rank of *gōshi* ('country samurai') for himself and his descendants. Rather than take up rural residence and its associated duties, the family remained in Tosa's castle town of Kōchi, continuing on with the lucrative business of producing alcohol in a famously hard-drinking part of the country.

So it was in Kōchi, in 1835, that Sakamoto Ryōma was born, the fifth of five children. He had one brother, Gompei, set to inherit their father's business, and three sisters, the youngest of whom was Otome – his correspondent and confidante throughout much of his life. Where Gompei was the ideal heir, smart and capable, Ryōma came to be known as a man of more modest intellect, possessed of a rough, easy-going charm. Otome encountered it first at home and later in letters, where her brother delighted in offering unsolicited and largely useless life advice – what to do if attacked by robbers; how to make it as a nun – while comparing his mounting achievements around the country with her pointless existence lounging about at home ('spend[ing] your time in stupid ways like an idiot').

In 1846, Sakamoto's parents enrolled him, perhaps without especially high expectations, in a private academy near Kōchi Castle. Institutional learning was by this point a feature of many young lives in Japan. Samurai since Ieyasu's time had been encouraged to cultivate the literary as well as the military arts, while commoners had been quick to see the personal and professional value of education. By the time Sakamoto went to school, 40 per cent of boys and 10 per cent of girls were receiving a formal education – some of the highest rates in the world at this time.

A choice of schools was on offer. Samurai boys could attend institutions set up by their domains, while private academies were open to all. Some of the latter offered specialized tuition, rooted in the expertise – and, if students were lucky, the charisma – of an independent scholar. The most popular type of school was the *terakoya*, often meeting in a temple and focusing on basic literacy and ethics alongside practical skills geared to the backgrounds and needs of its attendees. All this was rarely free of charge, but competition helped to keep fees low. Japan was home, in the early 1800s, to around 300 private academies and 3,000 *terakoya*.

In some of these schools, teachers and students could be found arguing over the state of the nation. While *bakufu* reformers sought technical fixes for Pax Tokugawa, the country's intellectuals had long been asking bigger, broader questions. The Confucian philosopher Ogyū Sorai (1666–1728) suggested that the samurai should restore their old sense of purpose by returning to the countryside and immersing themselves in the earliest Confucian texts, where they would find practical examples of human genius in action. Urban merchants would also benefit from the frugality forced upon them by a loss of samurai custom.

Others counselled a fresh look, not at China's ancient culture, but Japan's. The influential *kokugaku* ('national learning') scholar Motoori Norinaga (1730–1801) claimed that the *Record of Ancient Matters* and *The Tale of Genji* revealed an emotional sensitivity and range that distinguished the Japanese from the rationalistic and moralizing Chinese. He believed in a 'pure Japanese heart' (*yamato-gokoro*) that was essentially feminine, defined by what he called *mono no aware*: a capacity to be moved by the world, allowing one's response to beauty to be heightened by the knowledge that it was here only fleetingly. The *kami* of the *Record of Ancient Matters*, in whom Motoori possessed a fervent and literal belief, lived this way, he thought, as did the aristocrats of Murasaki Shikibu's classic work.

Hirata Atsutane (1776–1843) developed Motoori's thought in more explicitly political directions. He offered a worldview that blended *kami*-worship – his own private academy doubled as a shrine – with a renewed respect for the Emperor as a living (or 'manifest') god: the point of earthly connection between the *kami* and the people of Japan, in his person and through his performance of ritual.

Hirata was amongst those, in the early 1800s, to suggest tackling Japan's problems by restoring the Emperor to a political as well as a ceremonial role. The Confucian scholar Aizawa Seishisai (1782–1863) made a similar case, adapting Motoori's and Hirata's nationalistic and anti-Chinese themes for deployment against the West. As word of creeping European colonialism in Asia reached Japanese ears, Aizawa argued in *New Theses* (*Shinron*, 1825) that Japan must return to the ancient way of the *kokutai*, the 'national body', with the Emperor at its head.

Had he stayed at his private academy in Kōchi, Sakamoto might never have come into contact with ideas like these. But his parents quickly noticed that he was handier and happier with a sword than with a writing brush. So they withdrew him, sending him instead to a fencing academy in Kōchi and then in 1853 to the elite Kyōbashi fencing school in Edo, run by the sword master Chiba Sadakichi. There Sakamoto came into contact with other low-ranking samurai from around Japan, some of whom were starting to commit themselves to a pro-imperial vision of the country's future, inspired by *kokugaku* thought and taking Aizawa's *New Theses* as their bible.

For waverers, of whom Sakamoto was one, July 1853 became a turning point. Four American ships, led by Commodore Matthew C. Perry, arrived in Edo Bay seeking diplomatic relations. Having recently wrested control of California from Mexico, the United States was on its way to becoming a Pacific power. As President Millard Fillmore noted in a letter to the Emperor which he had commissioned Perry to deliver, the US and Japan were now separated by a comparatively brief eighteen-day cruise. Friendship, plus a little trade, was surely in order.

Japanese officials were sufficiently aware of their own history to understand that foreign trade carried the significant risk of political interference. The *sakoku* ('closed country') edicts had been issued for a reason. And while President Fillmore expressed his desire not to 'disturb the tranquillity of your imperial majesty's dominions', a separate letter from Perry himself noted with menace that more of his nation's ships stood ready to head this way if required – and that those presently in Edo Bay, each of them at least six times the size of anything in Japan, were 'four of the smaller ones'. The manner in which these two letters were delivered was similarly threatening. Perry stepped ashore accompanied by 100 sailors, 100 Marines, two military bands and a white handkerchief. This last, he explained, was for use in the unhappy event of war: the Japanese should wave it when they were ready to surrender.

As news spread of the foreign ships' arrival, Sakamoto joined thousands of samurai pouring out of domain residences in Edo to take up positions along the coast. Some were sent to hillsides overlooking Edo Bay, where they became witnesses to Perry's beachfront pageantry. Looking up at them, the Commodore was unimpressed. They struck him as small, effeminate, ill-disciplined and poorly equipped (some were carrying Sengoku-era muskets). They would be no match for his own well-armed, well-drilled men.

Promising – threatening – to return the following year for a response to his President's letter, Perry went back to his ship and led his flotilla back out to sea. Samurai from Tosa domain, Sakamoto included, were put to work shoring up coastal defences near Edo. 'I think there will be a war soon,' Sakamoto wrote to his father in October. 'If it comes to that, you can be sure I will cut off a foreign head before coming home.'

*

The *bakufu*'s response to Perry's arrival was highly unusual. An institution charged with national defence – the 'shogun' was, after all, the Emperor's 'barbarian-crushing generalissimo' – started casting around for ideas about how to do its job. *Daimyō* across the land were furnished with translations of the Americans' letters and asked for their thoughts. The result was an unhelpful blend of conflicting recommendations, albeit tending towards a consensus on avoiding war for the moment. To that end, a Treaty of Peace and Amity was signed with Perry on his return in the spring of 1854. Two Japanese ports were opened up: Shimoda, at the mouth of Edo Bay, and Hakodate, up north in Ezo.

Arriving in August 1856 to take up the role of American consul, the New York merchant Townsend Harris began pushing immediately for a full commercial treaty. He made the most of news, filtering through to Japan via traders at Nagasaki, of Britain's humiliating treatment of China in defence of its opium interests. Japan, claimed Harris, stood in desperate need of an ally.

The *bakufu* eventually agreed, signing a Treaty of Amity and Commerce in July 1858 that included an unprecedented programme of staggered port openings. Edo, Osaka, Nagasaki, Kanagawa (later known as Yokohama), Hyōgo (Kobe) and Niigata were all to be made available to American merchants. They would have the right not only to trade there, using a tariff regime that strongly favoured the US, but to live there under American rather than Japanese criminal jurisdiction. Treaties with similarly far-reaching and unpopular terms were soon signed with the British, the Russians, the French and the Dutch.

Japan was abuzz. Everywhere – in the *bakufu,* at the imperial court, amongst the *daimyō,* on city streets and out in the countryside – people began to argue over the country's future direction. At one extreme, it was said that China's woes were the result of a badly outdated idea of its central place in the world. Having arrogantly ignored barbarian affairs, it had now been overtaken by them. Japan should do things differently: engage in international trade and relations (Japan sent its first embassy to the United States in 1860), build up some wealth, and then use it to close the vast technology gap – most worryingly in weapons – that seemed to have opened up since Hideyoshi's day. Taking the time required to achieve all this, working with the occasional Westerner along the way, was not cowardice; it was a matter of playing nice while preparing to play dirty, should the need arise.

Opponents of this *kaikoku* ('open the country') approach argued for a return to the old policy of limiting foreign trade to approved merchants at Nagasaki and chasing away all other foreign ships. This *jōi* – 'expel the barbarian' – tendency could soon claim a singularly powerful backer. The imperial court in Kyoto initially supported the Harris treaty, but it later reneged, urging the *bakufu* to remain faithful to 'sound laws handed down from the time of Ieyasu'.

For most Japanese, the emperors remained the remote figures that they had always been. But the politics and print culture of the Tokugawa era had helped to wear away at this. The *bakufu* had long funded both the *kami*-worshipping ceremonial life of the imperial court and the upkeep of major shrines like Ise, where the Sun Goddess Amaterasu was understood to reside. Shoguns, including Tsunayoshi, requested prayers to be said at Ise, for the health of the shogun or the broader good of the realm. Scholars such as the Confucian Hayashi Razan (1583–1657) meanwhile had worked to clarify the nature of the *kami* and their links with Confucian principles, Buddhist deities and national governance – popularizing along the way the use of the term Shintō: 'way of the Gods'.

Pilgrimages to great sites like Ise became popular during the Tokugawa era. Many went in search of healing, via priestly prayers and the charms that could be purchased at shrines and temples, to be carried around in everyday life for protection. Others were tourists pure and simple, escaping the daily grind to see a new place and enjoy some regional delicacies. Motivations were not straightforwardly divisible into the sacred and the sacrilegious. As the ancient story of Amaterasu lured out of her cave by a bawdy dance showed, prayer and play could be two sides of the same coin in Japan. *Kami* were not primarily concerned with monitoring behaviour or listening to people drone on about their troubles and transgressions; one could enjoy a *kami*'s company – and vice versa – through 'playing' with it (*asobi*).

Guidebooks helped to grease the wheels, offering shrine lists, potted histories and information on particular *kami* – the Edo era saw a boom in the worship of Inari, a fox deity – alongside simplified vernacular versions of ancient *kami* classics like the *Record of Ancient Matters* and the *Chronicles of Japan*. In this way, people began to move from a focus on individual *kami* with connections to their part of Japan to a sense of Shintō as a national system, closely connected with the imperial family and with good and legitimate governance.

The result by the 1850s was the emergence of a broad and powerful basis, from political theory to pilgrimage, for connecting – or, rather, reconnecting – *kami*, court, self-cultivation and the national interest. Keen to exploit all this were the *shishi*, the 'men of high purpose'. Dressed in simple rags, they clopped around sockless in wooden clogs, allowing their hair to grow, their stubble to thicken and their bodies to smell. They borrowed or stole to stay alive. Vowing to protect this 'sacred land' against its enemies, they adopted an ancient slogan recently popularized by Aizawa: *sonnō jōi*, 'Revere the Emperor, expel the barbarian!'

The *shishi* claimed their first high-profile scalp in March 1860, when eighteen of them attacked and beheaded Ii Naosuke, the senior *bakufu* official who had signed the Harris treaty in 1858. In June 1861, a group of around fifteen *shishi* attacked the British Legation in Edo, killing two guards and wounding ten others. Violence against foreigners began to gather pace in the treaty ports, with many starting to carry guns around town in response, even sleeping with one under their pillows.

In the years after Perry's arrival, Sakamoto came steadily under the influence of men like these, both at home in Kōchi and amongst his swordsmen comrades in Edo, culminating in a radical – and thoroughly illegal – decision in April 1862 to leave his domain behind and join their ranks. Ignoring his brother's pleas, and taking with him some money borrowed from a relative and a sword given to him by Otome, he left Tosa via a secret mountain route. From there, he travelled through some of the country's emerging political hot-spots: Chōshū domain on the south-western tip of Honshū; down into Kyūshū; back up north to Kyoto; and finally eastwards across to Edo, arriving there in December.

Sakamoto intended to make his murderous debut later that month, with the killing of Katsu Rintarō, a *bakufu* official who was deeply involved with the foreigners. Katsu had studied naval technology with the Dutch at Nagasaki, joined the embassy to the United States in 1860 and had since been serving as the *bakufu*'s naval commissioner, working to build a modern Japanese navy. He also, much to Sakamoto's surprise, seemed to know something about his would-be assassin. 'Have you come to kill me?' he asked, when Sakamoto and an accomplice crept up on him at home. 'If so, you should wait until we've had a chance to talk.'

And talk they did, Katsu explaining that from what he had seen in the United States it was clear that Japan could not risk a war until it had had time to replicate foreign technology. With modern ships of its own, it might be able to gather allies in Asia – including Korea and China – to help roll back the Western presence here. To this end, Katsu was planning to establish a training institute and shipyard in Hyōgo, a little way westwards along the coast from Osaka. He invited his assailant to become his assistant.

Sakamoto agreed, receiving through Katsu's auspices a pardon for deserting his domain and heading to Hyōgo in early 1863 to start work. One of his jobs was to help Katsu recruit other former *shishi*. Another was to travel around Japan in search of domain contributions to the project, in the course of which he discovered people beginning to think the unthinkable: rather than fiddle around with Ieyasu's system, perhaps the time had at last come to replace it. The shogun could relinquish his title, retain the vast ancestral Tokugawa lands and become a prominent player in a new national government – perhaps a bicameral system along Western lines, featuring *daimyō* on one council and court nobles on the other.

A revolution was in the offing, and Sakamoto planned to be at the centre of the action. Though technically he now worked for the *bakufu*, his letters to Otome made clear that the pro-imperial *shishi* spirit had not deserted him. 'It is my firm desire to clean up Japan,' he told her. 'It's just a shame there aren't more like me.' There was humour mixed in with the conceit here, but Sakamoto really did find it hard to understand people who saw their country suffering, yet sat back and did nothing. Writing in 1863 to the parents of a friend of his who had recently escaped from Tosa to join *shishi* in Kyoto, Sakamoto was scathing about those who choose safety or family over duty:

> Loyalty to what is called the divine country seems to have no influence [on them]; these men do not understand the idea of returning His Majesty to a position of power, yet still that is the thing that has to be done. What are we men of low rank going to do to ease His Majesty's mind? Surely you realize that one ought to put the Imperial Court before his own province, and ahead of his parents.

Sakamoto's grand plans were dealt a sudden blow in 1864, when conservatives in the *bakufu* managed to have Katsu removed as naval commissioner. Katsu had too many suspicious characters like Sakamoto under his wing for their liking, at a time when all-out civil war now seemed to be on the horizon.

The *bakufu* had tried to heal the split with the imperial court over the Harris treaty by using marriage to effect a 'Union of Court and [Military] Camp'. The young shogun Iemochi was married to Princess Kazu, the sister of Emperor Kōmei, in 1862. But much depended on what Japan's *daimyō* decided to do with the opportunity that the foreign threat presented. *Daimyō* dynasties that had long been close to the Tokugawa family continued to back the *bakufu*. But the *tozama* ('outside') *daimyō*, whose ancestors had made peace with Ieyasu only after the Battle of Sekigahara in 1600, were weighing their options with care.

Two of the most important *tozama* domains, alongside Sakamoto's home of Tosa, were Satsuma in southern Kyūshū, controlled for centuries by the Shimazu clan, and Chōshū in south-western Honshū, run by the same Mōri family who had once helped the Hongan-ji to break Oda Nobunaga's naval blockade. Long histories meant long memories. In Satsuma, the anniversary of Sekigahara was marked by warriors each year with a temple visit, in full armour, to reflect on that epoch-making defeat. Chōshū mothers put their children to bed with feet facing towards Edo, in a gesture of deliberate disrespect, and admonished them never to forget Sekigahara. When the cock crowed at the dawn of each New Year, senior Chōshū vassals would voice a single ritual question before their lord: 'Has the time come to begin the subjugation of the *bakufu*?'

The ritual response to that question was a cautionary one: 'It is still too soon.' But while the *daimyō* of Satsuma and Chōshū supported the *bakufu*'s efforts to strengthen ties with the court in the early 1860s, plenty of *shishi* in both domains were vehemently and impatiently opposed – spurred on by news of the reluctance with which the Emperor and his sister were said to have agreed to the match. Kōmei was well known for his anti-foreign feelings, having called for shrine and temple prayers to be said to help cast the intruders from his realm.

Sakamoto discovered during a visit to Chōshū that *shishi* there were prepared to rise up against their own leaders if they failed to oppose the *bakufu* and transfer their loyalties to the court alone. In 1863, they began to force the pace, commandeering Chōshū shore batteries and using them to shell an American ship as it passed through the Shimonoseki Straits, a stretch of water separating Honshū from northern Kyūshū, used by foreign shipping heading for the Inland Sea. Dutch and French ships were later fired on from a similar position, prompting retaliatory strikes in 1863 and 1864 by the British, French and Dutch – the Americans were too consumed with civil war to play a substantial role. Chōshū forces ended up surrendering, and the domain was forced to pay a large ransom.

Shishi in Kyoto were meanwhile plotting with allies at the imperial court, resulting in two attempts – in 1863 and 1864 – to liberate the Emperor from *bakufu* control and take him as their figurehead in marching against Tokugawa forces. Both attempts were thwarted, but tens of thousands of Kyoto homes were destroyed in fighting and fires. Chōshū samurai loomed large enough in these plots to persuade the *bakufu* and its *daimyō* allies to mass 150,000 troops on Chōshū's borders in 1864, threatening unpleasant consequences if senior figures known to have supported the latest coup were not punished and *sonnō jōi* extremists not dealt with immediately. Assailed first by foreigners and now by the *bakufu*, an exhausted and divided Chōshū leadership backed down.

Having lost his mentor and protector to these febrile political times, Sakamoto realized that he was now in serious danger. He changed his name and fled south to Satsuma, offering his naval know-how in exchange for shelter from the *bakufu*. He was appointed as head of a new private organization initially known as Shachū ('The Company'), whose role was to trade in secret on Satsuma's behalf with foreign merchants in *bakufu*-controlled Nagasaki. In the autumn of 1865 this facility was extended to a handful of anti-*bakufu* samurai from Chōshū, who after a short civil war in their domain had at last toppled the old leadership.

With Sakamoto's help, two of these Chōshū samurai, Itō Hirobumi and Inoue Kaoru, found themselves sitting down in the Satsuma residence at Nagasaki with a Scottish merchant by the name of Thomas B. Glover. Glover knew them well. A couple of years previously, he had helped to spirit them out of Japan and all the way to Britain, where they studied for a few months at University College London. Having helped educate them, he was now arming them: with 7,300 rifles and later a steamship.

With Itō and his fellow imperial loyalists seizing control in Chōshū, while similarly minded young men – including Saigō Takamori and Ōkubo Toshimichi – began a peaceful ascendancy in Satsuma, an alliance was on the cards between Japan's two most formidable anti-*bakufu* powers. That prospect had long been held back by rivalry between them. But arms deals brokered by Sakamoto went a long way to bringing them closer, as did an arrangement he negotiated to supply Satsuma forces with grain from Chōshū.

In March 1866, Sakamoto persuaded leaders from both sides to meet for talks in Kyoto, pushing them onwards when progress stalled and succeeding eventually in creating what became known as the Sat-Chō Alliance. Should Chōshū face military action from the *bakufu* – busy modernizing its military with French help, while threatening another punishment expedition against Chōshū – then Satsuma would intercede for Chōshū at the imperial court. If necessary, it would intervene on the battlefield.

Sakamoto was now a marked man, and in late March 1866 his luck finally seemed to have run out. He and a friend, Miyoshi Shinzō, were about to turn in for the night at the Teradaya Inn in Fushimi, near Kyoto – one of Sakamoto's favourite hostelries and reasonably safe thanks to its proximity to the Satsuma residence in the town – when a maid came rushing in, warning that men with spears were on their way up the stairs.

Sakamoto and Miyoshi grabbed their weapons just as twenty armed men, sent by the authorities, burst into the room. Sakamoto briefly tried to talk his way out of trouble. He failed, and suddenly all hell broke loose – spears and charcoal braziers flying, Sakamoto firing his pistol, the room's wood and paper partitions first punctured and then ripped to shreds. A number of Sakamoto's assailants were soon crawling around on the floor, half-dead. But Sakamoto was down to his last bullet. Resting his gun on Miyoshi's shoulder, he fired at the chest of one of the men and then quickly tried to reload. An injury to his hand made him drop the gun and he lost it in the chaos and semi-darkness of the room.

Sakamoto and Miyoshi decided to make a run for it, hurrying down a ladder at the back of the inn, breaking into a nearby house and then hacking and kicking their way through its walls until they arrived back out on to the street, some distance from the inn. They ran, Sakamoto feeling sick and out of breath, until they found a place where he could hide while Miyoshi went off to seek assistance from Satsuma forces. They spent the next few days in the Satsuma residence until an agreement with the forces of an ailing *bakufu* gained them safe passage out of town.

Travelling south with Sakamoto back to Satsuma was the maid

who had raised the alarm at the inn. Oryō had saved his life, so he gave her in return the most precious gift he could think of: himself, as a husband. They honeymooned at one of Kyūshū's hot-spring resorts, while back in Honshū the *bakufu* continued its fight for survival. Economic problems were piling on top of military and political ones, as Japan's forced entry into global markets took its toll. Merchants in tea and silk thread had done well out of the trade deals signed with foreign powers: these two commodities topped the list of Japanese exports, which as a whole quadrupled between 1860 and 1865. The downside was a rapid increase in the cost of raw silk at home, threatening the livelihoods of producers of finished garments, along with soaring rice prices as more and more land was given over to producing tea and silk. Crop failures in 1866 compounded the misery, as did *bakufu* tax rises, resulting in violent unrest in the countryside and in cities like Osaka and Edo.

Amidst all of this, the *bakufu* had been forced to delay its second expedition against Chōshū. It was finally launched in June 1866, with thirty domains taking part in an assault by land and sea. Honeymoon over, Sakamoto joined the fight. He sailed the ship bought by Chōshū from Thomas Glover towards the Shimonoseki Straits, with a samurai force aboard.

Tokugawa power was fading now. *Bakufu* officials found some *daimyō* reluctant to send men against Chōshū, merchants wary of providing finance and the campaign itself bitterly disappointing: out-of-date weapons wielded by Tokugawa forces were no match for Chōshū's well-equipped men. When the shogun Iemochi died suddenly in August 1866, they retreated back to Edo.

All that now stood between the *bakufu* and the abyss was the French. In the wake of the August retreat, the French Consul General in Japan, Léon Roches, promised the *bakufu* the weapons, uniforms, blankets and loan money required to put 25,000 infantry, 500 cavalry and 1,250 artillerymen into the field – enough for the *bakufu* to curtail *daimyō* independence and put itself on a secure footing. Iemochi's successor, Yoshinobu, agreed. The new shogun cut a sufficiently impressive figure that leaders in Satsuma and Chōshū decided, with allies in Tosa and at the imperial court, that matters must be brought to a head before the *bakufu* had time to make good on its plans. They met in Kyoto in June and July 1867 to plot their next moves. Sakamoto travelled there by sea from Nagasaki, drafting along the way, with the help of his secretary Nagaoka Kenkichi, an Eight-Point Plan:

1. Political power in the entire country should be returned to the imperial court, and all decrees should come from the court.
2. Two legislative bodies, an upper and a lower house, should be established, and all government measures should be decided on the basis of general opinion.
3. Men of ability amongst the lords, nobles and people at large should be employed as councillors, and traditional offices of the past which have lost their purpose should be abolished.
4. Foreign affairs should be carried on according to appropriate regulations worked out on the basis of general opinion.
5. The legislation and regulations of earlier times should be set aside and a new and adequate code should be selected.
6. The navy should be enlarged.
7. An imperial guard should be set up to defend the capital.
8. The value of goods and silver should be brought into line with that of foreign lands.

Sakamoto's plan became the basis of a memorial addressed to Yoshinobu by Tosa domain in October 1867, seeking his peaceful resignation. He would become, they promised, the first amongst equals on a council of *daimyō* serving the country's new teenage Emperor, who had ascended the throne earlier that year following the death of his father, Emperor Kōmei. On 8 November, a reluctant but realistic Yoshinobu told a gathering of *daimyō* at Nijō Castle in Kyoto that he accepted the proposal. The next day, 9 November, he petitioned the Emperor to allow him to hand back the powers of his office. The Tokugawa shogunate was over.

Satsuma and Chōshū were in too strong a position to let that be the end of it. The same day, having conspired with allies at the imperial court, they secured the Emperor's seal on an order to attack the *bakufu*. While they prepared their troops, branding them now an 'imperial army', Sakamoto set about refining his thinking on Japan's future. Based in Kyoto, sleeping in the back room of a house belonging to a soy sauce merchant, he wrote to his brother to tell him that he was 'working day and night for our country'. The result was exhaustion – and carelessness. Catching a cold in early December, Sakamoto moved to a front room in the house, finding it more convenient even though it lacked the escape route for which the back room had initially been chosen.

On the evening of 10 December, Sakamoto was in his room, chatting by lamplight to his friend Nakaoka Shintarō. There was a knock at the main door, which Sakamoto's servant Tōkichi answered. The man handed over his visitor's card, and Tōkichi took it up the stairs to show Sakamoto. As he did so, three men – pro-*bakufu* assassins – barged through the doorway and attacked him from behind, killing him. Racing up the stairs, two of them set upon Sakamoto and Nakaoka with their swords. This time, Sakamoto did not even have the chance to pick up a weapon.

*

On 3 January 1868, a few weeks after the murder of Sakamoto and Nakaoka, forces under Satsuma command took control of Kyoto. The 'Restoration of Imperial Rule' was proclaimed, and Yoshinobu was ordered to surrender not just his powers but most of his lands as well. This was more than Yoshinobu and his allies could accept and Japan was plunged into a civil war that pitted 'imperial' forces from Satsuma, Chōshū, Tosa, Hizen and Echizen against a large pro-*bakufu* army. Over the course of what became known as the Boshin War, the army was driven steadily north-eastwards until Edo was surrounded in May. The city and its castle were surrendered peacefully by the man whose life Sakamoto had spared six years before: Katsu Rintarō, who had worked his way back into *bakufu* favour, only to become army minister at the least auspicious moment. The imperial push continued northwards from Edo, all the way up to Japan's northernmost main island of Ezo. There the pro-*bakufu* remnants established a short-lived republic, before imperial forces finished them off in the summer of 1869.

In April 1868, while war continued to rage, the Emperor gathered around 400 officials to his Imperial Palace in Kyoto to hear a 'Charter Oath' read out: a series of short pledges plotting the country's future course. Had Sakamoto been there, in amongst the gathered throng, he would have smiled at what he heard:

1. Deliberative assemblies shall be widely established and all matters decided by public discussion.
2. All classes, high and low, shall be united in vigorously carrying out the administration of affairs of state.
3. The common people, no less than the civil and military officials, shall all be allowed to pursue their own calling so that there may be no discontent.
4. Evil customs of the past shall be broken off and everything based upon the just laws of nature.
5. Knowledge shall be sought throughout the world so as to strengthen the foundation of imperial rule.

'I don't expect I'm the sort that's going to be around very long,' Sakamoto once wrote to his sister, Otome. 'I don't expect to die like an average man, either.' He turned out to be correct on both counts – and also on a third: 'I don't expect I'll be quite worthless,' he assured her. Sakamoto's journey had come to an early end, but not before a burst of revolutionary energy had seen him help set his country on a brand new path.

It would fall to fellow rebels like Itō Hirobumi of Chōshū and Ōkubo Toshimichi of Satsuma to take Sakamoto's Eight-Point Plan, transformed now into an imperial oath, and make of it something that could secure Japan's position in a very rough global neighbourhood. Sakamoto meanwhile, like Ieyasu before him, would live on in the era that he had helped to bring forth – as a revered point of reference, and as someone whose spirit could be invoked when times became tough and a little charm, a little swagger, was called for to get people moving again. Plenty such moments lay ahead.

12

Kusumoto Ine

(楠本イネ)

1827–1903

Building the Body

Kusumoto Ine, by an unknown photographer.

Eighteen sixty-eight was Year One. For centuries, the era name in Japan had changed whenever the imperial court decided to respond to some happy or unhappy event in the world by declaring a new national phase. Sakamoto Ryōma's rebel allies resolved to do things differently. The era name would now change only when a new emperor took the throne. Known in life as *tennō*, 'Heavenly Sovereign', he would bear that era name in death. The young Emperor's reign was proclaimed as 'Meiji': 'enlightened rule'. And so 1868 became 'Meiji 1'.

April's Charter Oath, and the events of the months that followed, gave compelling substance to this sense of a radical reset. In September, Edo was renamed 'Tokyo', or 'Eastern Capital', based on its geographical position in relation to Kyoto. The Emperor left Kyoto in a grand procession a few weeks later, arriving in Tokyo to take up residence in the Tokugawa shoguns' castle. Emperor Kanmu's beloved city had served as the country's official capital for more than a millennium, including periods when real power was exercised from elsewhere. No more. After some wrangling with advocates of Kyoto and Osaka, Tokyo was eventually announced as Japan's one and only capital city.

This particular decision aside, Kanmu would doubtless have approved of the general direction of travel in Year One. The rebels revived, as their instrument of administrative control, an ancient institution with which he had been very familiar – the Dajōkan, or Great Council of State. Representatives were sent fanning out across the country, visiting its nearly 280 domains to lay the groundwork for an epoch-making event in 1869: the return to the Emperor, by the *daimyō*, of their enfeoffment registers. Hereditary rights surrendered, the *daimyō* would rule now as 'imperial governors'.

History seemed to be moving forwards and backwards at the same time. For the small clique now in charge of the country, this was very much the intended effect. From Chōshū domain, there were the University of London students Itō Hirobumi and Inoue Kaoru, alongside Kido Takayoshi and the imperial army commander Yamagata Aritomo. From Satsuma, there was another military commander, Saigō Takamori, together with Ōkubo Toshimichi and Mori Arinori. Joining them at the top table were Ōkuma Shigenobu from Hizen domain, Itagaki Taisuke from Tosa and Iwakura Tomomi of the imperial court. One day, these men would be revered as founding fathers. In 1868, most people had never heard of them. They lacked legitimacy, and they lacked an agreed plan for Japan beyond securing its survival as an independent country – via, as a popular slogan of the time had it, 'enrich the country, strengthen the military' (*fukoku kyōhei*).

These men found a solution to their collective problem in the imperial institution. Opposition to the ailing *bakufu* had coalesced around the idea of restoring the Emperor to power. And what other way was there of persuading people long accustomed to thinking in terms of village, town or domain to instead imagine and strive for a 'national' good? Through the Emperor, as the head of the *kokutai* or 'national body', an ancient concept popularized by the nationalist thinker Aizawa Seishisai, the strong, centralized rule of which Tokugawa-era reformers had only been able to dream might at last become possible. The Emperor would supply, too, an aura of continuity and purpose while Japan entered upon the decades of experimentation required to turn a moment of revolution into an era of national renewal.

Much was duly made of the Emperor's journey from Kyoto to Edo. A fifth of the national budget for 1868 was spent on organizing and advertising the procession, ensuring that crowds of people would crouch in hushed respect by the roadside as he passed by in his palanquin. In many other ways besides, the Meiji-era leaders would demonstrate an important talent for reshaping tradition in the pursuit of modern goals. The new Japan would be built on bequests from the old: long years of peace and stability, highly developed commerce, a culture of education and self-cultivation, a premium placed on duty and conduct. And where the Charter Oath pledged the seeking of 'knowledge throughout the world', Japan's leaders would rely, early on, on a cadre of experts – scientists and medics, for the most part – who had been doing just that since the 1700s. Barred from leaving the country, generations of *rangakusha*, 'scholars of Dutch studies' ('*ran*' from *Oranda*: 'Holland') had instead flocked to Nagasaki in search of whatever books and artefacts incoming Dutch traders had brought with them.

One of the last of the *rangakusha* was Kusumoto Ine. A woman with a strong claim to be Japan's first female doctor trained in Western medicine, she was one of many Japanese in whose lives Year One wrought unexpected changes. The promise, in the Charter Oath, to allow people to 'pursue their calling' was soon subordinated to another element of that important but artfully vague manifesto: the unity of all in 'vigorously carrying out the affairs of state'.

The late 1800s was the 'high noon' of European imperialism. It was a world in which a nation had to bring to bear its every resource, including every human resource, in securing its position. The rebels of 1868 understood this well, making of the 'national body' a powerful metaphor for channelling the population's collective energies into building a state that could hold its own in turbulent, predatory times. Living through this transition, this time of great experiments, Kusumoto watched it radically reshape her professional prospects and her family life alike.

*

From the 1640s through to the 1850s, personnel of the Dutch United East India Company (VOC) were the only Europeans with whom the Japanese would do business. And even they were tolerated rather than warmly welcomed – confined to a fan-shaped artificial island just off the coast of Nagasaki, linked to the mainland by a stone bridge that was guarded around the clock. 'Dejima' was only around 180 metres wide and no more than 60 metres from top to bottom, with room for just two streets lined with warehouses and living quarters, along with a little space for growing vegetables and keeping some livestock.

The Dutch were charged rent, and had to fork out separately for their water supply – piped in via bamboo tubes – and for the bureaucracy required to manage their trading activities. They had to put up with having their vessels searched for any weapons or Christian literature that crew members might have failed to seal safely away in barrels before docking. And on annual spring trips to pay their respects in Edo, they were treated as tributary low-life. The leader of the mission would enter the shogun's presence on hands and knees, bowing deeply and then withdrawing again in the same manner – 'crawling backwards like a crab', as one observer put it. His men were meanwhile made to perform mini-pantomimes of everyday Dutch life: conversing with one another, taking their clothes off and putting them on again, pretending to kiss one another and to carry babies around in their arms, jumping and dancing and singing songs.

The *bakufu* eventually tired of this vaudeville, requiring the Dutch to put in an appearance at Edo only every two years and later every four years. The number of Dutch ships arriving at Dejima – laden with goods, including Chinese silk thread, to be exchanged for precious metals, porcelain and lacquerware – meanwhile flatlined at just one or two each year for most of the 1700s. Later commentators lamented missed opportunities. The *bakufu* failed to press the Dutch sufficiently on global goings-on, while the Dutch showed precious little interest in Japanese culture, whiling away spare hours on Dejima drinking coffee and playing billiards and badminton.

Honourable exceptions on the Japanese side included the shogun Yoshimune, whose easing of restrictions on importing foreign books in 1720 helped to kick-start *rangaku* in a range of areas, notably science, medicine and art. The Dutch, for their part, did at least employ some inquisitive people as their doctors. Engelbert Kaempfer produced the first Western book on Japanese plants (*Flora Japonica*, 1712). Later in the 1700s, the Swedish naturalist Carl Peter Thunberg conducted studies of local plants and animals, and exchanged medical knowledge with Nagasaki doctors. And in August 1823 the Prussian physician Philipp Franz von Siebold arrived, securing permission to venture into mainland Nagasaki where he taught medicine, performed cataract surgeries, sought out new medicinal herbs and even opened his own medical practice and private boarding school.

Offering tuition in a range of scientific subjects including medicine, botany, chemistry and physics, it was the first European educational institution to be built in Japan since the days of the Portuguese.

Siebold somehow found time for romance too, buying a seventeen-year-old courtesan called Kusumoto Taki out of her contract – into which she had been forced when her father's timber business fell on hard times – and inviting her to move in with him on Dejima. He named a plant after her, *Hydrangea Otaksa* (from 'Otaki': 'Taki' plus the honorific 'O'), and wrote excitedly to his mother claiming to have married a local noblewoman. A few years later, on 6 May 1827, Taki gave birth to a daughter, Ine, and something resembling family life began to take shape. Two wet-nurses were found and supplied with fake professional identities as courtesans so that they could gain access to Dejima. And an Indonesian babysitter called Olson was hired, on one occasion sparking a panicked search of the island after she lost sight of baby Ine while taking a break to swim in Nagasaki Bay.

Siebold continued to take an interest in all things Japanese. He sought out plant samples, built a collection of stuffed animals (mammals, fish, birds and amphibians) and even had a crack at measuring the height of Mount Fuji – he guessed 4,982 metres, over by more than a kilometre. He had his hard-up students in Nagasaki pay him not in cash but in essays, written in Dutch, about Japanese social and religious life. Siebold called them 'dissertations', awarding his students entirely unaccredited 'diplomas' in return. And he built a wide circle of Japanese contacts who supplied him with everything from images of landscapes and architecture to maps of Japan and East Asia.

In 1828, the authorities in Japan began to suspect Siebold's motivations and he was accused of spying for Russia. When letters between Siebold and a Japanese acquaintance called Takahashi Kageyasu were intercepted, Takahashi was found to have sent Siebold a map of Korea while Siebold had been sending Takahashi the fruits of his own research – which looked disturbingly like reconnaissance – on Japanese harbours and cities. Takahashi was arrested, along with more than thirty of Siebold's students, and in late 1829 Siebold himself was banished from Japan. The night before the authorities came for her husband, Taki helped him to make copies of maps that he was sure were about to be confiscated. Later interrogated over her role in his activities, she claimed repeatedly to know nothing about them.

Siebold left his wife and baby daughter what financial support he could: a large quantity of sugar to sell, alongside his clinic and school which he bequeathed to Ine. For a while, Taki and Siebold managed to stay in touch, Taki assuring him that their daughter was 'very clever' and missing her father very much, while Siebold sent gifts and protestations of love, penned in shaky Japanese on floral-patterned paper.

Contact came to an abrupt end in 1831, after Taki finally gave in to familial pressure to remarry, wedding an apprentice ornament artisan and moving into his home. Family was as solid an institution towards the end of the Tokugawa era as it had been at the beginning, making powerful claims on a person's loyalty and governing their prospects in almost every respect. Intimacy and affection mattered, but so too did success and succession. A family with no male heir would adopt one from outside, often by bringing a son-in-law into the fold. This way, samurai families ensured that stipend rice continued to flow, while their merchant counterparts were guaranteed a future for hard-won businesses and reputations.

Taki's role as a mother was to introduce Ine to the behaviour expected of a daughter in a merchant family, rooted in Confucian virtues of filial piety, respect and compassion for others. The finer points were picked up in schools like the one Sakamoto Ryōma briefly attended, and within the home by way of womanly arts including flower-arranging, needlework and the tea ceremony. Taki had been brought up learning to dance and play the koto, and she tried now to interest her daughter in the same pursuits.

But Ine was a bibliophile from early on, preferring the comfort of books to the company of the neighbourhood children, who taunted her over her mixed parentage. Her mother perhaps made the best of this by supplying her with one of the many hundreds of publications dedicated to the cultivation of good daughters, and good daughters' cultivation of themselves. Some were effectively instruction manuals; others were works of fiction presenting ideal and nightmare scenarios for female behaviour. A classic of the first genre was *Imagawa-Style Precepts for Women* (*Onna Imagawa*, 1687), authored in Ihara Sai-kaku's time by a woman called Sawada Kichi and containing the following pieces of advice:

[Do not] scorn or make light of one's husband and flaunt oneself, for this disregards the way of heaven

[Do not] involve yourself with the intrigues of others, nor rejoice in others' suffering

[Do not] dress and adorn yourself beautifully and then eat in a slovenly manner. . .

[Do not] scorn others for their shortcomings while flaunting your own knowledge

Elsewhere, women were urged to be 'cautious' about eating or drink-ing too much, smoking tobacco, singing popular songs, enjoying the theatre and 'wanting things'. Women inclined to lose their temper at such a catalogue of constraints would find 'getting angry' and 'sulk-ing' also on the list.

For mothers or daughters who preferred illustration over abstract instruction, there were books like *Twenty-Four Paragons of Women's Filial Piety in Our Realm* (*Honchō onna nijūshi kō*, 1713). One story told of two sisters who plead repeatedly with their father to desist from his favourite hobby of hunting. At the rate he is dispatching the local wildlife, karma is sure to deal him a terrible hand in the next life. The father at first relents, laying down his gun, only to pick it up again when someone offers him an enormous sum of money to kill a couple of cranes. Waking one night to find their father out in search of his quarry, the girls resolve to teach him a lesson. One of them will dress up in white robes and go to stand by the river, where she will surely be mistaken, in the darkness, for a crane. Her death will force their father to return to the right path.

As the girls argue at length over who should claim this honour, read-ers perhaps began to sense the likely denouement. The man ends up shooting both his daughters dead. Leaving the question of his karma unanswered – presumably now very much worse than before – the anonymous author of the story concludes by praising the girls' filial piety as 'something to be deeply appreciated'.

All but obscured by the story's strangeness was its demonstration of a key quality in Tokugawa-era family values, whose relevance in Japan after 1868 would be hotly contested. The place of men versus women in society was said to be not a matter of inequality but of complementary natures, and the social roles that flowed from them. In the crane story, the girls' father is neither their moral superior nor their controller – quite the opposite. As *Onna Imagawa* put it, men are 'bright' while women are 'shadowy' and 'soft'; for women to follow their men while offering them support and guidance is to live in accordance with the 'logic of heaven, earth and nature'.

Whatever the means of Ine's exposure to expectations like these, they seem to have conjured for her a female version of the dystopian future dreamed up by Ihara Saikaku for the conventionally married man: 'going to bed early every evening until he gradually wastes away'. Growing up on hagiographic tales of her father told by his former students and by Taki – the latter describing him as a 'world-famous man' – Ine took to heading down to Dejima whenever a Dutch ship came in, hoping that he had returned and even asking incomers for their names just in case. In 1845, aged eighteen and impatient with her mother's fretting over her looks (Taki complained that she was a 'tomboy'), Ine resolved to leave home, study medicine and become a doctor. This was a career firmly associated with men, but Ine could invoke filial piety in her favour. Instructed by her mother never to tarnish her father's name, she would go one better: she would follow in his footsteps.

*

Mid-nineteenth-century Japan was home to a mixed medical marketplace, which people tended to navigate on the basis of what was available, what they could afford, what came recommended and what they had already tried – rather than regarding any one medical system as sufficient and infallible. The oldest tradition on offer comprised beliefs and practices with roots in Japan's distant shamanic past. Illness was attributed to evil spirits, or to contact with pollutants like corpses or blood. Healing was a matter of applying herbal and ritual remedies, including the sorts of shamanic and Buddhist incantations that made up the soundtrack to Empress Shōshi's anguished labour in 1008, as recorded by Murasaki Shikibu. Those in search of quieter cures could seek out the therapeutic and purgative properties of *onsen* or hot-spring baths.

A second approach to the body, dating back to the sixth century, involved a Japanese take on Chinese medicine: herbal treatments running alongside techniques like acupuncture, moxibustion and massage, all of it backed up by a Chinese philosophical approach that connected physical with social, emotional and moral health. Much depended on the movement of *qi* or *chi*: energy that courses through the natural world, including around the human body, and whose flow is liable to become blocked or otherwise frustrated by problems with a person's circumstances or conduct.

One of Chinese medicine's strengths was the attention that it paid to prevention as well as cure, concerned as it was with maintaining balance in the body. A major disadvantage, sensed increasingly keenly in Japan during the Tokugawa era, was a heavy reliance on questionable theory. Guidebooks cautioned mothers-to-be to take care with certain food and drink. A meal of sparrow with *sake* was said to turn a foetus lustful and shameless. Attention was paid even to what pregnant women looked at, listened to, thought and felt. Meanwhile, taboos against invasive treatment of the human body, combined with the scholarly status of most Chinese medics (meaning that they were unaccustomed to getting their hands dirty), had served to hamper understanding about how internal organs were arranged and the visceral mechanics of how they did their jobs.

New movements amongst Japanese practitioners of Chinese-style medicine began to bring theory and observation together across the 1600s and 1700s, including in the world of obstetrics. But far more influential on Kusumoto Ine was the *rangaku* tradition, one of whose first heroes was Sugita Genpaku (1733–1817). Watching at the Kotsugahara execution grounds near Edo as the corpse of a fifty-year-old woman – 'Old Mother Green Tea', crime unknown – was opened up and its organs exposed, Sugita became convinced of the superiority of Dutch over Chinese anatomical knowledge. He and a colleague set to work translating *Tafel Anatomia*, a Dutch version of a German anatomy text, into Japanese. After four years of painstaking guesswork, unfamiliar as they were with Dutch, the finished product was published as *Kaitai Shinsho* (*New Book on Anatomy*, 1774). It was the first translation of a Dutch book to be widely circulated, and a spur to *rangaku* in other fields.

Even nativist *kokugaku* thinkers were forced to concede the achievements of Western medicine, with Hirata Atsutane attributing the slow development of its Japanese counterpart to the natural good health of his countrymen. He cautioned them against contact with noxious foreigners – rightly, as it turned out: they brought cholera with them in the 1850s – and warned Japanese doctors against both dissection (which 'smells of the barbarian') and use of the Dutch language ('ludicrous, impure and rather dirty').

Setting out to study in the *rangaku* tradition, Kusumoto chose obstetrics as her specialism. She was aware of the high mortality rates associated with childbirth, and was perhaps also injecting a little pragmatism into her plans for the future. As a woman practising general medicine, she would struggle to attract patients and collegial support. As a midwife, she could bring fresh expertise to what was a long-standing tradition in Japan, commended by Ihara Saikaku with his merchant's hat on, as a way of generating profits without the need for capital investment. In fact, midwifery occupied a rather ambiguous place in Japanese culture: it combined the polluting effects of contact with blood and discharge with grave responsibility at a great moment of cosmic drama and risk, as a soul re-enters the world – 'pulled' into the human realm by the midwife.

Hearing of Kusumoto's intentions, a former student of her father's named Ninomiya Keisaku put her in touch with a second Siebold alumnus: Ishii Sōken, now a recognized expert in obstetrics. Kusumoto left Nagasaki in 1845 to become a medical apprentice at Ishii's clinic in Okayama, in western Honshū. Around the same time, she started using – in private only since she was not samurai – the surname 'Shimoto', based on the Japanese rendering of 'Siebold'.

As was common for these sorts of apprenticeships, known as *gakuboku* (study-serve), Kusumoto lived with Ishii and his wife in their home. She helped out with cooking and cleaning, and was exposed to the knowledge she sought along the way. Training seems to have gone well. Kusumoto's knowledge and skills were soon such that she was allowed to assist Ishii in delivering babies at his clinic, even doing so alone when he was not around.

But an apprenticeship that ought to have lasted close to a decade was suddenly cut short after just five years. Around 1850, Kusumoto's mother came to visit her. When Taki returned to Nagasaki, aboard a ship called the *Tenshin Maru*, Kusumoto and Ishii went to see her off in a smaller boat. At some point after saying goodbye to Taki, Ishii is thought to have made an advance on Kusumoto. Unable to escape the boat, she tried to fend him off with a blade. But he caught her, raped her, and she became pregnant with his child.

Kusumoto condemned Ishii as an 'animal' for what he had done. She could have terminated the pregnancy. Abortion was frowned upon as an infringement of a father's rights over his gestating property, but it was not commonly regarded as the taking of a human life. A child was not thought fully human even at birth, and was sometimes 'pushed' back into the otherworld at this point – particularly if a family was struggling economically and there was a need to 'thin out the seedlings', as the agricultural euphemism had it. But Kusumoto decided to have the baby, moving back to Nagasaki soon after giving birth. The child was a girl, whom Kusumoto named Tadako: 'free of charge'. In Kusumoto's eyes, she was a gift from heaven, no matter what Tadako herself would later claim had been the traumatic means of its bestowal.

Trained in obstetrics and having now given birth herself – she delivered Tadako with no assistance – Kusumoto possessed an understanding of her profession of a kind that few could match. She kept studying nonetheless, leaving Tadako with Taki as she worked first with a doctor in Nagasaki and then, from 1854, with Ninomiya in Uwajima domain, which bordered Sakamoto's home of Tosa on the island of Shikoku. Devastated to hear what his introduction of Kusumoto to Ishii had led to, Ninomiya resolved to do what he could for her career. They worked together for two years in Uwajima, before Ninomiya suffered a stroke and moved to Nagasaki for treatment. Kusumoto joined him, helping him to set up a clinic in her old neighbourhood of Dozamachi. She was there when, in 1859, Japan's controversial reopening to the West gifted her the moment for which, as a child, she had spent so much time waiting and longing. Her father came back.

The family reunion on Dejima was a quiet, tearful affair, with neither Siebold's Japanese nor Kusumoto's and Taki's Dutch proving adequate to the occasion. Siebold produced locks of their hair, which he had taken with him back in 1829. He showed great interest in his grand-daughter, Tadako. But thirty years had passed, and a child from Siebold's second marriage, to Helene von Gagern, was with him here on Dejima. The presence of Alexander, coming up to his thirteenth birthday, made an unpleasant surprise for Kusumoto and Taki when they entered the room.

Worse, for Kusumoto, was her father's interest in politics and commerce over medicine. Having tried and failed to win a place on Commodore Perry's expedition in 1853 (Perry read his writings on Japan, but worried about the spying rumours), Siebold later managed to persuade the Dutch to take him back, selling himself as an experienced builder of cultural bridges. So enthused was he with the task that Kusumoto found him preoccupied and distant, writing to him early in 1860 to ask that he 'treat me properly'. Later that year, he forgot her birthday. 'I prepared a lunch for the two of us,' she told him in a letter. 'But you didn't come. I would still like to offer you something, so please send four plates, and a pot with a lid.' Her father was also failing to keep his hands off the help. When he bought his nineteen-year-old maid, Shio, a suspiciously expensive-looking hair accessory, Kusumoto demanded that he purchase the same thing for his granddaughter. Siebold obliged, but it was not identical, so Kusumoto sent it back to him. When Shio became pregnant, Kusumoto had her fired.

Father and daughter resolved to keep their relationship professional instead. Kusumoto had recently opened her own clinic in Nagasaki, where she treated a wide range of patients – beyond obstetrics alone – and made and prescribed her own medicines. Siebold began helping out on Sundays, donating surgical instruments, advising on difficult cases and helping to acquire medicinal ingredients. Kusumoto made use of Siebold's reputation to bring in new patients and to make contact with some of the experts in Western medicine who were beginning to make their way into Japan.

The arrangement did not last long. Siebold had himself appointed as a shogunal adviser, and moved to Edo. He provided medical aid to members of the British Legation when their residence was attacked by *shishi* in 1861, but his political meddling soon angered both the British and his own Dutch employers. The latter managed, in 1862, to get him banished from Japan for a second and final time.

Kusumoto initially did rather better out of Japan's reopening to the West, finding the 1860s some of the busiest years of her career. She worked shifts at Japan's first Western-style hospital, established in 1861 by the doctor J. L. C. Pompe van Meerdervoort (who praised her 'unlimited zeal' for medicine). And she returned regularly to Uwajima, where she ran a clinic near the castle of the pro-Western *daimyō* Date Munenari, trained two local men in medicine, assisted at the labour of Date's wife Yoshiko, and even – it was rumoured – took a lover: a samurai retainer by the name of Ono Masasaburō. A British doctor in Japan at the time referred to Kusumoto as the 'Chief Physician of the Uwajima family'.

In 1867, the British diplomat Ernest Satow visited Kusumoto's Uwajima clinic, bringing with him the sad news of her father's death in Europe the previous year. Kusumoto rushed from the room, returning to show Satow some of the medical equipment that Siebold had left her. Hardly the perfect father, and a presence in her life only for a few short years, Siebold had nonetheless shaped Kusumoto's existence profoundly.

*

Kusumoto entered Year One at the height of her powers and reputation. She moved to Tokyo in 1870, establishing a clinic in the foreign settlement area of Tsukiji. Just a few kilometres to the north-west lay the country's centre of power. The imperial family was settling into the old shoguns' castle, while former *daimyō* residences to its south were repurposed for the use of the Dajōkan, the imperial armed forces and new government ministries.

From this tiny area of territory came thousands of revolutionary directives across the early 1870s. In 1871, the old domains were swapped for prefectures: around 300 at first and later reduced to fewer than fifty. Japan's *daimyō* completed a steep downward trajectory from domain dynasts to imperial governors to being unemployed, replaced by prefectural governors appointed by the central government in Tokyo. In 1872, a national banking system was established along American lines, as a means of concentrating and disbursing capital – now in 'yen' – for the building up of industry and infrastructure. The same year also saw the issuing of a Fundamental Code of Education, mandating four years of compulsory primary education for girls and boys alike. Temples and private homes would serve as temporary premises, with girls and boys learning side by side from teachers using American textbooks – some in translation, some in the original English.

For Japanese Buddhism, this was part of a dramatic shift in its fortunes in the wake of Year One. It was soon surplus to requirements as a source of intelligence on the local population, superseded in 1872 by a new, centralized family registration system known as *koseki*. With Christianity decriminalized in 1873, under heavy Western pressure, Buddhist temples' hosting of *fumi-e* (picture-treading) ceased too. And after the new government ordered an end to the centuries-old practice of *kami* and Buddhas sharing the same sacred space – both physical and ideological – Buddhist temples and clergy endured a brief but intense wave of violence, as Buddhism was blamed for holding the country back. It would take a new generation of Buddhist reformers, many of them members of Shinran's tradition, to persuade the population once again that the Buddha had something to offer Japan.

While the heavens underwent radical renovation, so too did the Earth. A Land Tax Reform Law in 1873 rid Japan of its old rice tax, based on the expected annual yield of allotted land. Instead, people would now own their own land, handing over 3 per cent of its value each year in cash. A Conscription Law was passed the same year, requiring every man in Japan to serve three years in the army that Yamagata Aritomo was busy creating, followed by four years in the reserves.

Forced to surrender their exclusive warrior prerogative, the samurai were offered – and later required to accept – the conversion of their stipends into interest-bearing government bonds. This was part of a broader shake-up of the old Tokugawa class system that saw courtiers and former *daimyō* incorporated into a single hereditary peerage (*kazoku*). Upper and middling samurai became a 'warrior class' (*shizoku*), while lower samurai found themselves lumped in with the former farming, artisan and merchant classes as 'commoners' (*heimin*). The old restrictions on dress, travel and marriage between classes were lifted, and everyone was permitted the public use of a surname.

One last major change was made to the old status quo, right at the bottom of society. When the corpse of Old Mother Green Tea had been opened up for the enlightenment of the *rangaku* doctor Sugita Genpaku, the person wielding the knife had been a ninety-year-old man of the *eta* class. The word *eta* meant 'abounding in filth' and indicated people pushed beyond the pale of mainstream society by their work with dead flesh – as butchers, leather-workers and furriers; occasionally as harvesters of precious products from deceased human beings, including liver secretions used in medicine. They were usually forced to live at some distance from other communities. In common with *hinin* '(non-people'), who were traditionally involved in low, itinerant occupations like singing and dancing that were scarcely discernible from common vagrancy in the eyes of many Japanese, the *eta* found themselves 'emancipated' in 1871 by government decree. Both outcast groups were given rights on a par with other Japanese, and some began to refer to themselves as *shin-heimin*: 'new commoners' or 'new citizens'. In reality, much of the old stigma was to remain well into the twentieth century.

Alongside education, tax and military service, a fourth connection established during these years between leaders in Tokyo and a population that they hoped to manage with unprecedented efficiency was the mass-circulation newspaper. Most of Japan's first modern newspapers served as mouthpieces for particular individuals or factions within the leadership. *Tokyo Nichi Nichi Shimbun*, established in 1872, was strongly associated with Chōshū men, including Itō Hirobumi.

While most of Japan's new leaders worked away in Tokyo rearranging the country's social and political fundamentals, some of their number – including Kido Takayoshi, Ōkubo Toshimichi and Itō – spent the years 1871–3 abroad on a grand diplomatic and fact-finding mission led by Iwakura Tomomi. Beginning with a Pacific crossing, as Hasekura Tsunenaga had done more than 250 years before, they passed through San Francisco, Chicago, Washington and Boston, London, Liverpool and Glasgow, Paris, Berlin, Stockholm, Vienna, Rome and St Petersburg. Journeying homeward through the new Suez Canal, they stopped at Cairo, Colombo, Singapore, Hong Kong and Shanghai.

This epic journey convinced Ōkubo, head of an influential new Home Ministry after 1873, that *fukoku kyōhei* – 'enrich the country, strengthen the military' – would require, in practice, a period of government-led industrialization, focused on import substitution. Less clear at this point was how the Japanese ought to give substance to a second aspirational slogan of the era: *bunmei kaika* or 'civilization and enlightenment'. For its creator, the one-time *rangakusha* Fukuzawa Yukichi, 'civilization' referred to a spirit, cultivable by anyone, of seeking out practical knowledge. While the fruits of this spirit had become conspicuous of late in the West, from the natural sciences through to factories and hospitals, it seemed to have stagnated in Japan. Where some blamed Buddhism's greedy priests and false cosmology, Fukuzawa, whose writings were amongst the most influential of the age, pointed the finger at deeply *im*practical Confucian scholars: 'rice-consuming dictionaries' who had left the country with nothing to be proud of except its scenery.

How, though, to succeed at civilizational catch-up while retaining all the beautiful qualities that nationalist thinkers had been claiming for Japan in recent decades? Help was at hand, in theory at least, from a third slogan: *wakon yōsai*, or 'Japanese spirit, Western techniques'. Unfortunately, for all its rhetorical attractions 'Japanese spirit' was too nebulous to be of much problem-solving use. Instead, the 1870s ended up playing host to what later generations regarded as excessive, even outlandish suggestions for how to fast-track Japan's rise to parity with the West.

Some advocated replacing the Japanese language with English, or rendering it using the Roman alphabet rather than ideographs. Others suggested doing away with traditional Japanese poetry: its subtle sentiments had lubricated diplomatic gatherings and intimate encounters down the centuries, but now it appeared quaint and effeminate. Mori Arinori, serving as Japan's ambassador to the United States, advised young Japanese men studying in New York to bring an American wife home with them, as a means of importing some 'civilized blood'.

One notion that actually caught on was the introduction of beef into the Japanese diet, as a putative source of Western physical strength. Served to injured soldiers during the Boshin War, it first became a regular fixture on peacetime military menus and then later found its way into upmarket Western-style eateries alongside hundreds of small, steam-befogged 'stew restaurants' where magical things were done with miso and soy sauce.

It was amidst this early love affair with Europe and the United States that Western medicine was adopted as Japan's official medical system. In 1874 guidelines for a national licensing system were laid out, based on a German model. Chinese-style medicine, known since the advent of *rangaku* as *kanpō* (the 'Han method') so as to distinguish it from its Western counterparts, was effectively sidelined. A Medical Bureau (later called the Hygiene Bureau) was established to oversee all this. Its move, in 1875, from the Ministry of Education to the Home Ministry was significant: part of its remit was to keep track of the population's general health and strength, via surveillance carried out in schools and barracks, along with data drawn from Japan's new family registration system. The implications for midwives and medics would be immense.

In 1873, a year before the new rules were announced, Kusumoto found herself head-hunted for one of the most important tasks imaginable for someone in her profession: delivering the first child of the Meiji Emperor.

Negotiations with the imperial family were helped along by Fukuzawa, whose acquaintance Kusumoto had recently made. Kusumoto was first summoned in July for an initial meeting, and a check of the equipment to be used at the labour. Then, on 18 September, came the big day. Unfortunately, all did not go to plan. The baby was stillborn, and the Emperor's consort, Hamuro Mitsuko, died a few days later. In November, the Emperor's second child, a girl, was also stillborn. Her mother, Hashimoto Natsuko, died the following day.

Kusumoto was awarded 100 yen nevertheless for her work in September: despite the tragic outcome, her efforts were lauded as 'remarkable', and she was called back twice to render medical aid to members of the imperial family. And yet what ought to have been a glittering, path-breaking career across the 1870s and into the 1880s was frustrated by a decisive new swing of Japan's experimental pendulum.

In 1879, the Emperor's tutor, a Confucian scholar called Motoda Eifu, authored an Imperial Rescript entitled 'The Great Principles of Education'. In it, he warned about the impact in Japan of Western cultures that valued 'fact-gathering and technique' over and above virtues like benevolence, justice and filial piety. Children, not to say society at large, should be encouraged to look for inspiration to Confucius and to Japanese heroes and heroines of the past whose lives embodied his principles. Others in Japan reacted against the heady pro-Western enthusiasm of the 1870s by arguing that every country advances by way of its own unique history and associated virtues. Japan must therefore seek out and promote its own 'national essence' (*kokusui*).

Across the 1880s, politics largely paralleled this changing mood. An overhaul of the education system led by Mori Arinori, now serving as Education Minister, led to boys receiving longer years of more professionally focused education compared with girls. Western ethics textbooks were replaced with Japanese ones in which Tokugawa Ieyasu was held up as an exemplar – for his personal conduct and his great, nation-unifying achievements – alongside characters of humbler origins, including a seller of soy sauce. In 1890, an Imperial Rescript on Education, again bearing Motoda's imprint, reasserted Confucian values, locating their ultimate source in the Emperor and his 'imperial ancestors'. A copy of the rescript was sent to every school, alongside a photograph of the Emperor and Empress. Text and image alike were treated as sacred objects.

The 1890 rescript made a natural pair with the *Dai-Nippon Teikoku Kenpō*, the 'Constitution of the Empire of Japan', issued the year before, in 1889. Setting out popular rights and new political structures, including a bicameral Diet consisting of an upper 'House of Peers' and a lower 'House of Representatives', it was a continuation of the strategy adopted by Japan's ruling clique back in Year One: strong rule in the Emperor's name. They had reorganized themselves as a 'Cabinet' in 1885, with Itō Hirobumi becoming Japan's first Prime Minister. Now, the Constitution made clear that this Cabinet served at the pleasure of the Emperor, remaining independent of the Diet and of new and liberally inclined political parties, including the Freedom Party (Jiyūtō) and the Constitutional Progressive Party

(Rikken Kaishintō). Elected by men aged twenty-five and over who paid a certain level of tax (in effect, around 5 per cent of the adult male population), the House of Representatives would play a role in drafting and debating legislation, and passing the annual budget. But it would exercise little executive power.

The pre-eminence of the Cabinet was guaranteed by the Emperor's transcendence over mere mortals and institutions alike. He was described in the Constitution as 'sacred', 'inviolable' and of a 'line unbroken for ages eternal'. In him rested control of the armed forces, appointments to the judiciary and House of Peers, and the rights of the people. Encompassing property, assembly, religion and free speech, these were gifts to be withdrawn if their misuse endangered the peace.

The final piece of the puzzle was a new Civil Code in 1898, whose underpinning philosophy was close to that of Tokugawa-era classics on female behaviour and family values. Japan's basic legal unit was to be the *ie* (household) rather than the individual, and its headship would pass from father to eldest son. Women were not permitted to own property, bring legal proceedings, testify in court or divorce their husbands except in cases of desertion or extreme cruelty. Women were already banned, since 1890, from any role in politics.

Most Western women faced similar restrictions in this era. The difference in Japan was made clear in the *Meiji Greater Learning for Women* (*Meiji Onna Daigaku*), published by the Ministry of Education in 1887. 'The home', it declared, 'is a public place.' In other words, women's stewardship of home and family life, in a role that Mori and others talked about in terms of *ryōsai kenbo* ('good wife, wise mother'), was a form of national service.

As girls' education was reorganized to kit them out for this role, with particular attention paid to hygiene lessons and physical fitness, some began to ask whether the traditional women's kimono might need to be abandoned. Its long sleeves restricted movement of the hands, its heavy fabric interfered with posture, gait and the development of breasts, and its tight sash (*obi*) threatened to rearrange a woman's internal organs. Any of these things might hamper the chances of producing future generations of Japanese who would be physically more on a par with Westerners.

Commentators in this era worried that Japanese engineers on secondment at European shipyards seemed to struggle to lift the hammers used there, while Japanese students in European schools seemed to yawn more than their classmates. If such things were to be remedied, girls' upbringings, and the roles of midwives in tending to their pregnancies, would have to be managed more carefully than ever before. Midwifery began to develop into a patriotic and professionalized business. Training was provided by the state, while day-to-day conduct was overseen by organizations like the Osaka Midwives' Association. Its rulebook declared abortion to be the equivalent of murdering the Emperor's own child.

Kusumoto found herself in an unusual situation. Western medicine was in unprecedented demand, but she was less free than before in practising it. Rather than turning medicine into women's work, the effect of Year One had been to lay out women's role in society more clearly and narrowly than ever. Faced with the short-term collapse of healthcare if *kanpō* doctors and unlicensed practitioners of Western medicine were barred from working, the authorities in many prefectures had at first taken a relaxed approach to the 1874 national licensing guidelines. Members of both groups were permitted to see out their careers on temporary licences. But as interpretations of the guidelines steadily tightened and a younger generation of formally trained medics began to come through, Kusumoto ended up returning to Nagasaki and applying there in 1884 for a licence as a midwife, rather than a doctor. No one is quite sure why. A midwifery application involved the submission of a curriculum vitae together with a supporting letter from a doctor, whereas a full medical licence required the sitting of exams grounded in scientific theory. Kusumoto may have doubted her ability to pass them, or perhaps she simply didn't see their value when set against the sort of practical experience of which most Japanese doctors could only dream – and to which her curriculum vitae offered powerful but apparently useless testimony. Whatever the reason, Kusumoto ended her career confined to a role in which, according to the national guidelines, she was forbidden from mixing or dispensing medicines, performing surgery of any kind, or even using the sort of obstetric instruments given to her by her father.

*

February 1896 marked the 100th anniversary of Philipp von Siebold's birth. The occasion was marked with a small celebration in Tokyo, at which Kusumoto and her daughter were welcomed as guests of honour. Precisely what Kusumoto thought of her origins, and where they had left her by this point, remains a mystery. She had changed her surname back from Shimoto to Kusumoto sometime after her father had left Japan. Alexander, along with a second half-brother, Heinrich, made their careers in the country but Kusumoto seemed uninterested in a close relationship with either of them. And when she filled out her family register, she listed her father as 'Kusumoto Shinbei' and her mother as 'unknown'. Taki had died in 1869, with Kusumoto feeding her crushed strawberries on her deathbed, a delicacy Taki had first tasted from the young Siebold's hand many years before, when he cultivated them in a garden on Dejima.

And yet in the best Tokugawa tradition, Kusumoto worked to maintain the Siebold bloodline, by adopting a grandson, born in 1879, as her heir. Naming him Shūzo, Kusumoto supervised his medical education and in 1900 bequeathed him her father's old clinic in Nagasaki. Shūzo went on to make it into medical school in 1904, obtaining the qualifications that had eluded his grandmother and then serving as an army doctor. Kusumoto did not live to see it, passing away on 26 August 1903.

There is little evidence of bitterness on Kusumoto's part about the way that the second half of her life panned out. If she did look back on the 1880s as a moment when high hopes were dashed, then she was not alone. Large numbers of Japanese regarded Year One as a moment of rare promise, only to see the body-building mission of the country's new leaders take them in unwelcome directions. Many refused to take it lying down: the conservative turn of the 1880s would not be the last word on what 'modern Japan' ought to look like.

The accolade, meanwhile, of Japan's first modern female doctor went to Ogino Ginko (1851–1913) in 1885. For many years to come, women doctors would remain a rarity. And yet, as Ogino noted in a magazine interview, plenty of women down the centuries in Japan had operated, unacknowledged, as physicians, often introduced to the profession by their fathers. A case in point she said, lest we forget, was one Kusumoto Ine.

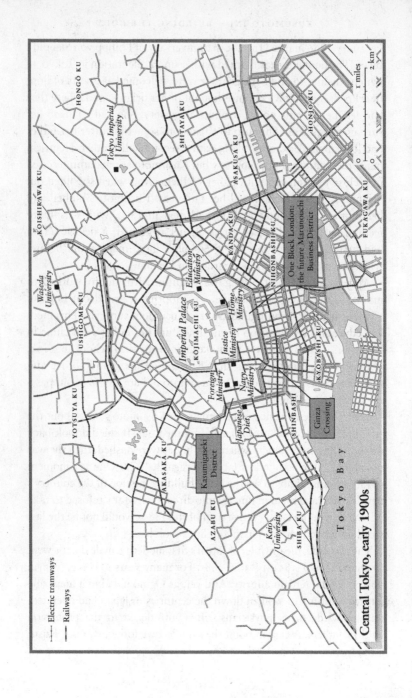

Electric tramways

Railways

Central Tokyo, early 1900s

Tokyo Bay

HONGŌ KU

SHITAYA KU

ASAKUSA KU

HONJO KU

Tokyo Imperial
University

KOISHIKAWA KU

KANDA KU

NIHONBASHI KU

FUKAGAWA KU

Waseda
University

USHIGOME KU

Education
Ministry

Home
Ministry

One Block London:
the future Marunouchi
Business District

Imperial Palace
KOJIMACHI KU

Justice
Ministry

KYOBASHI KU

YOTSUYA KU

Foreign
Ministry

Navy
Ministry

Japanese
Diet

SHINBASHI

Ginza
Crossing

AKASAKA KU

Kasumigaseki
District

AZABU KU

Keio
University

SHIBA KU

1 miles

2 km

PART FOUR

New Lives: 1868–1941

13
Shibusawa Eiichi

(渋沢栄一)

1840–1931

Entrepreneur

Shibusawa Eiichi, photographed
in New York in 1915.

Tonight, in keeping with my promise, I will start to tell you the story
of my life . . . You may well be tempted to yawn and stretch or even to
doze off. But I beg of you please to bear with me, for I speak from a
profound, shall I say, almost doting concern for you, in hopes that my
story may help you in some way – to push yourself to greater effort, to
strengthen your resolve to persevere, or again, to summon up courage,
or perhaps to stay the course of prudence and moderation.

With these words, Shibusawa Eiichi, the 'father of Japanese capitalism', embarked upon his exemplary tale, surrounded by family in his
Tokyo home. His great aim in life was to elevate the business of doing
business, liberating it from the old samurai contempt for merchants
while avoiding the reputation for greed and selfishness that commerce had acquired in some quarters of the West. Shibusawa hoped
to convince his countrymen, via word and deed, that their leaders'
ambitious nation-building plans could be financed by harnessing the
wealth-generating power of capitalism in the collective good. This
would be capitalism for the *kokutai*, the 'national body'.

Shibusawa's faith in the power of personal example revealed the
Tokugawa roots of his project. During the 1700s and into the 1800s,
a new sense of seriousness and self-confidence had entered the upper
reaches of Japan's merchant class. Merchant house histories and
codes emerged as a means of sharing specialized knowledge of economics and commerce with the next generation. Ethics played a
central role: sound business, just like sound behaviour, was said to be
a matter of prudence, modesty, politeness, early rising, hard work
and the avoidance of frivolity and disdain – for other people, and for
the menial tasks that a merchant might sometimes be required to
perform.

At stake for a Tokugawa-era merchant were the achievements of
his ancestors and the prospects of his children: the health, in other

words, of his house. As the leading businessman of the Meiji period, Shibusawa claimed the whole of Japan as his 'house'. In an age marked by the adoption and adaptation of Western models, he hoped to bring Adam Smith and Confucius into conversation; even to raise up a generation of businessmen who would attend to the state of their hearts as well as their finances – who would work, as Shibusawa put it, with the '*Analects* in one hand, and the abacus in the other'.

*

Born in 1840 in the village of Chiaraijima in Musashi Province, Shibusawa Eiichi was introduced to the Confucian classics by his father Yoshimasa and later by his cousin Odaka Atsutada. He read histories of China and Japan too, alongside novels and samurai romances. On one occasion he became so absorbed in a book while walking along that he fell into a ditch. He suffered such a scolding from his mother for dirtying his clothes that he could still recall the moment in detail decades later.

Yoshimasa did not want an intellectual for a son. He wanted help with the farm and with the family's other businesses: growing barley and indigo, raising silkworms and producing indigo dye for the textile trade. Shibusawa obliged, starting as a teenager to mimic his father's patter when buying extra indigo for the family's dye-production business. Tut-tutting theatrically over poor-quality samples, and the mistakes that had obviously been made in their cultivation, he found that he could bring home a fine haul at a good price. He enjoyed the life, save for what he regarded as the country's rotten politics: idle and complacent samurai levying arbitrary taxes. Inspired by the life of Toyotomi Hideyoshi, Shibusawa took the rise of the *shishi* as a cue to embark upon his own heroic adventure.

In 1861, at the age of twenty-two, Shibusawa began to spend short periods of time studying in Edo, attending a fencing school on the side. Two years later, he hatched a grand plan with his cousin Odaka. They would buy some swords, capture a castle, raid its weapons store, head to the treaty port of Yokohama, set it on fire, kill some foreigners, enrage the West, plunge the *bakufu* into an unwinnable foreign war and thus free the country up for more capable and deserving leadership.

Shibusawa was utterly in earnest. He gathered together around seventy men and used money liberated from his father's indigo income to buy swords in Edo. He and Odaka also got hold of armour, paper lanterns and spears – they were, Shibusawa later realized, kitting themselves out like the 'medieval bandits' about whom he had so enjoyed reading as a boy. Surrounded by their arsenal, they meditated on a saying from Confucius: 'If one learns the Way at dawn, one can face death in the evening.'

Shibusawa revealed little of his plan to his father. He asked only to be formally disowned by him, thereby freeing Yoshimasa from any legal responsibility for what his son might get up to. Yoshimasa reluctantly agreed, persuaded by his son's political opinions or perhaps worn down by a long night of hearing about them. Fortunately, Shibusawa did share his plan with another cousin of his, Chōshichirō, who had spent time amongst the *shishi* in Kyoto. Chōshichirō was frank in his feedback. What Shibusawa imagined would be a triumph of *shishi* derring-do, a warrior legend for his times, Chōshichirō assured him would be seen by everyone else as just another peasant protest. Shibusawa and his friends would be hacked to bits by the *bakufu*, and that would be the end of it. It was pointless.

Shibusawa's high sense of self-worth helped Chōshichirō's message to strike home. To die nobly would be a fine thing. To perish as a *peasant* would be quite another. Shibusawa duly called off the attack and left his village to pursue his calling via other means, leaving his wife Chiyo and a young baby behind. Soon finding himself short of funds, especially after a detour through the Yoshiwara pleasure district, Shibusawa was persuaded to enter the service of a *daimyō* called Hitotsubashi Yoshinobu, head of one of the Tokugawa collateral houses and soon to become Japan's last shogun.

Shibusawa thoroughly enjoyed his new status as a samurai retainer. He sometimes travelled by palanquin with a small retinue, including an escorting official who would yell at everyone in the street, 'Get down! Get down on your knees!' And he learned much that would prove useful later in life, from the deployment of charm and pressure in recruiting people for the *daimyō*'s army to overhauling his lord's finances by means of better negotiation on rice prices and better marketing for locally produced cotton cloth. In 1865, Shibusawa was promoted to assistant commissioner of finance.

The next year, everything changed. Yoshinobu took up the poisoned chalice of shogun, and as part of his last-ditch friendship with the French he sent his younger brother Akitake to take part in the 1867 Exposition Universelle in France. The plan was for Akitake to stay on and study, bringing back knowledge and expertise that might yet help the *bakufu* to survive. The men due to depart with Akitake were known to take a dim view of foreigners, and Yoshinobu feared a diplomatic incident. He asked Shibusawa to join the party on their journey, as a smart and moderating influence.

Having moved from rural life into samurai service, Shibusawa's horizons were now about to be expanded once again. Boarding the *Alphée* at Yokohama in February 1867, he encountered French coffee and bread, the latter eaten with a smear of 'congealed cow's milk'. Soon he was looking out over Shanghai's telegraph lines and gaslights, in whose glow Europeans could be seen 'treating the natives like horses or oxen, striking them at will with sticks'. Devoted as he was to Confucius, Shibusawa found the 'ignorance' of contemporary Chinese all the more 'hateful': 'still clinging to their old system, they fall each day into greater and greater poverty'. He discovered similar scenes in Saigon, Singapore and Ceylon, of Europeans lording it over the locals.

Arriving in Paris in April 1867, Shibusawa began to encounter European power at its source: in churches and law courts; in ballrooms and botanical gardens. The low point was a tour of the city's sewage system, simultaneously overpowering and underwhelming. The high point, undoubtedly, was the Exposition Universelle, where French achievements were ranged alongside those of their European and North American friends and rivals. Amongst Shibusawa's favourite items was a British steam engine.

The Exposition also revealed to Shibusawa something of how the Western world viewed Japan. Parisians peered through spyglasses into the interior of a tea-house, set in a garden, where three young

Japanese women were seated on a tatami-mat floor. It garnered good reviews in the papers, as did Japanese porcelain, swords and household goods of lacquered wood with delicate gold and silver inlay. And yet elsewhere in the French media, Shibusawa found the Japanese branded as lazy, with 'loathsome habits' – a reference to perceived promiscuity.

A mini tour of Europe followed in the autumn: Basel, Berne, Geneva, Rotterdam and then The Hague, where the group toured armament factories and a shipyard, and watched the King open a session of Parliament. They moved on to Amsterdam and later Leiden, where Philipp von Siebold's son Alexander, serving as interpreter on the trip, showed them a Japanese garden that his father had planted. They carried on through Brussels and Antwerp, down to Turin, Florence, Milan and Pisa, to see the leaning tower. The final stop was England. Travelling on a special train from Dover to London, they visited Parliament and were received by Queen Victoria for tea at Windsor Castle.

When the group returned to France in mid-December, they found the newspapers full of outlandish claims about the shogun returning his powers to the Emperor. Few of them believed it at first, but Shibusawa was soon left 'gnashing my teeth and clenching my fists' as news reached them of each successive *bakufu* defeat in the Boshin War. Cutting short their stay in Europe, they returned to Japan in 1868 – to a bleak political situation leavened just a little, for Shibusawa, by the comfort of tatami mats and Japanese food.

Shibusawa went first to visit his father in Chiaraijima, before travelling to Shizuoka, a modest corner of the ancestral Tokugawa lands on Honshū's eastern coast to which Yoshinobu had been permitted to retire. There Shibusawa began to experiment with some of what he had picked up in Europe. The French banker Paul Fleury-Herard had advised him to invest some of his group's travel and study funds in public bonds and railway stock. Shibusawa later claimed to have known as much, at this point, about the mechanics of capitalism as he did of the workings of the British steam engine at the Exposition. But he was impressed by the basic idea that wealth could be used to create more wealth, and that the merchants and financiers who made it possible were regarded as 'producing' something – rendering them reasonably respectable people.

Shibusawa set to work bringing together merchants from around Shizuoka to establish a joint-stock company: the Shizuoka Commercial Association. It was a blend of bank and commercial concern, pooling its funds and lending them out to fund new or expanding businesses in the area. Shibusawa referred to this as *gappon*: 'combining resources', money and talent alike, in the public good. Anyone could contribute capital, regardless of their station in life. The aim of the venture would be mutual rather than personal enrichment. As he put it, 'a single wealthy individual does not make the country more prosperous'. *Gappon*, he hoped, would be a means both to rethink commerce in Japan and also to rebrand it – as an ethical enterprise in which a person could take part without risk to their reputation.

Shibusawa's talent as a shrewd businessman helped the new idea to take off. Expecting commodity prices to rise, in part because Japan's new leaders were unknown and untrusted, Shibusawa bought up everything from oil cakes to rice to fertilizer. He was soon able to sell the rice and fertilizer at excellent rates, with the profits becoming part of the association's capital. The company began buying and selling a wide range of other goods, from tea and silk cocoons through to wooden sandals, dried sardines and calligraphy paper. Many of these purchases Shibusawa made himself, heading to Tokyo to negotiate the best prices. Migrants to Shizuoka were meanwhile loaned the capital they needed to set up new businesses, in tea and sericulture especially.

Word got around about Shibusawa, and in 1869 he was called to serve Japan's ruling clique as head of the tax bureau. He became involved in planning the country's new banking and tax systems, alongside some of the new industrial enterprises in which the government was investing – in some cases running them for a time itself as a model, allowing people to train in and test out rival Western technologies. High on the list of priorities were mechanized silk-reeling and cotton-spinning, with both domestic and foreign markets in mind. Shipping was important too, for trade and for security.

Shibusawa respected his new bosses for their heroism in 1868. But he found them bad at balancing budgets and too willing simply to give Japan's nascent armed forces whatever they asked for. He perhaps detected too, in the country's rapidly burgeoning bureaucracy, something of the complacency and stifling of enterprise that had so repulsed him about Pax Tokugawa. He certainly traded, in the years to come, on this frustration with bureaucrats – even while serving as a bridge-builder between them and the business community.

Leaving government in 1873, Shibusawa served as 'superintendent' of the new Dai-Ichi Kokuritsu Ginkō (First National Bank). The first bank to be created within Japan's new American-style system, it was capitalized by two major Tokugawa-era merchant houses: Mitsui and Ono, whom Shibusawa helped to bring into partnership. Many more such banks were chartered, the last of them opening its doors in Kyoto in 1879, as One Hundred and Fifty-Third National Bank.

As superintendent of the Dai-Ichi bank, Shibusawa oversaw the work of senior executives, chaired their meetings and began launching venture after venture. One of the first was the Ōji Paper Company, set up to supply the paper on which new banknotes were printed (until a new Bank of Japan took over the role in 1882, any 'national bank' chartered by the government could issue paper notes). From here, throughout his career, Shibusawa became personally involved in no fewer than 500 companies. He was active in the set-up of more than a hundred of them, and served at the executive level in thirty-four. Many were amongst the first in their field, and included shipyards, ports, railways and modern mining; gas, cotton-spinning, bricks, rope and insurance; and Western-style hotels and breweries – the Sapporo Brewing Company helped to establish beer-drinking in Japan. Shibusawa's Osaka cotton-spinning mill, opened in 1884, boasted steam (rather than water) power, electric lighting and a twenty-four-hour operation, returning dividends to investors of up to 30 per cent by the end of that decade.

As Shibusawa's public reputation grew across the 1880s and 1890s, he came to be regarded as a man who possessed, alongside business nous, a second quality that was indispensable to early Japanese industrialization: trustworthiness. With reliance on foreign capital regarded as a political risk not worth taking, the great national project of 'enriching the country, strengthening the military' depended on Japanese people being willing to pool their resources. But a person would only hand over their money to a novel enterprise like a joint-stock company if they were confident of seeing it again some day, plus interest. That required trust, which Shibusawa cultivated both through his actions and by presenting himself not as a 'merchant', in the old and disreputable sense, but rather a *jitsugyōka*, a 'person of practical affairs'. When a magazine survey was conducted in 1899 of respected national figures, Shibusawa ranked high, alongside Fukuzawa Yukichi.

Seeking to nurture in others the qualities that people admired in him, Shibusawa got involved in one of the great trends of the Meiji era: the establishment of societies and journals by emerging professions and interest groups. Shibusawa's contribution was a bankers' association called the Takuzenkai (Choose Virtue Society), which he later merged with other groups to form the Tokyo Bankers' Association in 1880. He followed up five years later with Ryūmonsha, the 'Dragon Gate Society', named after an old Chinese story about a little fish who manages to jump up a giant waterfall. Beginning with members of Shibusawa's own large household, Ryūmonsha developed into an informal business management school, hosting discussions and lectures featuring leading businessmen alongside the occasional high-ranking politician – including, on one occasion, Itō Hirobumi.

*

When Tokyoites turned out to celebrate their new Constitution in February 1889 – with flags and festival floats, *sake* and sumo wrestling – they did so in a city that had been changed forever by the work of companies and industries sponsored by Shibusawa and by the government spending on infrastructure that their profits had made possible. The heart of the city, and the focal point of the celebrations, was a brand new Imperial Palace. It had been completed just a year ago on the site of the old shoguns' castle, lost to fire a few years before. To the south, the government district of Kasumigaseki continued to take shape.

Prime land to the east of the palace was sold, in 1890, to Iwasaki Yanosuke, who planned to build headquarters there for the up-and-coming company that he had recently inherited: Mitsubishi.

Here was a second model for business and industrialization in Japan. While Shibusawa championed what he hoped would be open and democratic joint-stock companies, governed by an elected board of directors, Mitsubishi was one of the four most powerful *zaibatsu*, as they became known: family-run, heavily hierarchical conglomerates comprising firms spanning a range of industries and services. By coordinating their goals, capital and expertise, and developing close links with Japan's political elite, they were able to take leading roles in industries like shipbuilding, chemicals, machinery and mining. The other three major *zaibatsu* were Yasuda – like Mitsubishi a relatively new concern – alongside two Tokugawa-era merchant houses already doing very well in the new Japan: Sumitomo of Osaka and Mitsui of Edo/Tokyo.

The two differing ways of doing business ended up sharing a neighbourhood in Tokyo. Mitsubishi's new HQ grew into the Marunouchi business district, known as 'Icchō Rondon' – 'One Block London' – for its Victorian architecture. Just to its east in Nihonbashi was Mitsui, with Shibusawa's First National Bank using office space there for a while. Shibusawa had his personal base in Nihonbashi too. In 1888, he built himself a large Venetian Gothic mansion overlooking a canal. It was a home for his new family – after his wife Chiyo passed away in 1882, he had married again, a woman named Kaneko – and a place where colleagues from the business districts nearby could come for meetings.

South-east of the palace, one could find the great architectural hangover of Japan's love affair with the West in the 1870s. Razed by fire in 1872, leaving 50,000 people homeless, the Ginza neighbourhood had been resurrected in brick and stone, with wide and airy tree-lined streets whose fashionable focal point was soon the 'Ginza crossing', where Harumi and Chuo streets intersected. People could be found there pounding the country's first pavements in avant-garde combinations of Japanese and Western dress, from kimono worn over trousers to hefty mutton-chop sideburns and chunky diamond rings. What became known as 'Gin-bura' – 'aimless strolling in Ginza' – could be enjoyed day or night, courtesy of the capital's first gas-powered street lights.

Ginza was home, too, to the Tokyo offices of more than fifty newspapers and magazines: Japan's answer to Fleet Street in London. Conveniently located nearby, in the Shinbashi district, was the Tokyo terminus for Japan's first railway line. Completed in 1872, using British narrow gauge tracks and locomotives, it ran – with traffic on the left – between Yokohama and the impressive Shinbashi station. Featuring pavilions of stone, glass and painted metal, it had been opened by the Emperor himself to the strains of *gagaku* (ancient court music) alongside a Western-style military band. By 1889, the line had been extended to link Tokyo and Yokohama with Kyoto, Osaka and Kobe.

Transport within Tokyo was developing, too. Here, as in other large cities like Osaka, there had been a steady shift from waterways to roadways, as surfaces improved and travel increased by rickshaw and horse-drawn tram. Communications had been revolutionized, thanks to nationwide postal and telegraph networks established on the basis of British models. By 1890, Japan was home to 5,000 post offices, soon handling hundreds of millions of items per year. Tokyo and Yokohama boasted the telephone. The security of the capital, meanwhile, lay in the hands of a police force based on a Parisian model.

Stories abounded, in these years, of a rapidly changing environment being met with opposition or alarm. Some unexpected early maintenance work had to be carried out on the telegraph system after members of the struggling samurai class took out their frustrations on telegraph posts, chopping down hundreds of them in 1873. Rumours spread in parts of western Japan around the same time that the system worked by means of virgins' blood flowing through the wires. Anxious girls began shaving their eyebrows and blackening their teeth, faking the appearance of married women. Meanwhile, a newspaper report told of a young geisha who fainted when a customer lit a match, convinced that a ghost had manifested in the room.

Shibusawa's influence was everywhere in this new world. He helped to form the Tokyo Electric Light Company, Japan's first, which began supplying electric power to Tokyo in 1887. Electricity was a triple win: it offered a powerful marker of modernity, it curbed Japan's reliance on foreign lamp oil and it cut the risk of homes and buildings going up in flames. Shibusawa also chaired Tokyo Gas, providing the city with gas-lighting in its public spaces. And he helped Iwakura Tomomi in bringing together a group of nobles to invest in a new railway line, running from Tokyo to Aomori, in northern Honshū. The government was persuaded to guarantee a return on the investment of 8 per cent, along with helping to find Japanese engineers to work on the project. Shibusawa established Nippon Railway in 1881 to run the venture and the line was opened ten years later.

One of the few things that Shibusawa saw in Europe which hadn't yet made it to Japan was a sewage system: that would have to wait until well into the 1900s. Until then, one of the capital's least desirable new addresses was the far western district of Shinjuku. Its evening rush-hour of sewage carts heading out of the city centre earned it the nickname 'great anus of Tokyo'.

By the time Japan held its first elections to the new Diet in 1890, achieving a 97 per cent turnout, politics and industry alike had begun to take clear shape. A speech to the Diet that year by Yamagata Aritomo, serving now as Prime Minister, gave a hint as to where the country would need to turn its attention next.

Japan's northern border was reasonably secure. In 1869, the island of Ezo had been renamed Hokkaidō and been brought firmly under Tokyo's control. Its indigenous people, the Ainu, had been set on a tragic, decades-long downward trajectory, starting with an influx of Japanese settlers, the effective theft of their land and attempts to assimilate them into mainstream Japanese culture (notably via the schooling of their young in appropriate manners and morals). The result was poverty, indebtedness and alcoholism. Further north still, an 1875 agreement with Russia left the Kuril Islands in Japanese hands while Sakhalin went to Russia. After 1879, Japan's far southern border was extended to encompass the Ryūkyū Islands, annexed that year and turned into 'Okinawa prefecture'. As with the Ainu, the Ryūkyūans had a history and a culture all their own, running alongside centuries-old political and trading contacts with Japan. And like the Ainu, many Ryūkyūans were to find their inclusion in Japan's new national project, as peripheral 'Japanese', turning out very much to their disadvantage.

Matters to the west of the Japanese archipelago represented the biggest concern for Japan's leaders. Russia was finishing work on a trans-Siberian railway line to Vladivostok, which might all too easily be extended south towards a politically unstable Korea. A handful of Western countries continued, meanwhile, to feast on a once-great China, whose weakened leaders still insisted on their suzerainty over Korea. For Yamagata, addressing the Diet in 1890, all this uncertainty in East Asia meant that Japan's security would henceforth require the maintenance of a sphere of influence beyond its borders – a 'line of advantage', as he put it. Korea was key. Taking his cue from one of his Prussian military advisers, Yamagata described the peninsula as a 'dagger aimed at the heart of Japan': should the wrong people be permitted to come into possession of the peninsula they could use it as a base from which to intimidate or even attack Japan – as Kublai Khan's Mongol forces had demonstrated back in the 1200s.

Tensions over the peninsula, between China and Japan in particular, continued to rise across the early 1890s until in 1894 the Sino-Japanese War broke out. The outcome was a spectacular illustration of Japan's epoch-making pivot away from China and towards the modern West. Japan's new army and navy, based on Prussian and British models respectively, were victorious. And the subsequent peace treaty, signed at Shimonoseki in April 1895, helped to establish Japan as East Asia's paramount power. The independence of Korea from China was secured. A lease was obtained on the Liaotung Peninsula on the southern tip of Manchuria, close enough to the northern part of Korea for the security of the two peninsulas to be regarded as intertwined. The Chinese were made to pay a hefty indemnity in silver. And Japan's southern border was extended once again, this time to include the island of Taiwan.

All this was enormously popular with the general public. Thirty years spent pooling the nation's resources – through taxation, education, conscription and now an early form of industrialization – were at last yielding tangible results: security, influence and even a degree of Western respect, evident in the steady revision during the 1890s of the infamous 'unequal treaties' signed in the late 1850s and early 1860s. At the same time, Japanese exports had now overtaken imports, a transformation led by cotton yarn and raw silk, along with raw cotton and finished textiles.

But the national pride that a growing newspaper industry helped to whip up in the wake of the China war was frustrated almost immediately, as Russia, backed by France and Germany, demanded that the Liaotung Peninsula be restored to the Chinese – in the interests, it was rather grandly claimed, of the 'peace of Asia'. Japan's leaders had little option but to acquiesce to what became known as the Triple Intervention, only to see the Russians begin to strengthen their own position in Manchuria, obtaining in 1898 a long-term lease on the very Liaotung Peninsula that the Japanese had been forced to give up. Construction of a railway network was soon underway, with a hub at Harbin connecting Vladivostok in the east, Russia's new warm-water naval base at Port Arthur on the southern tip of the Liaotung Peninsula, and Moscow far to the west.

Shibusawa counted himself amongst his country's 'Pan-Asianists': he was keen to see China, Korea and Japan work together to keep their region as free as possible of Western colonial influence. For critics, such views amounted to little more than a rhetorical fig-leaf for the assertion of Japanese power, backed by xenophobic notions old and new: the ancient barbarians-on-the-periphery idea familiar to Emperor Kanmu, the nativism of Tokugawa-era *kokugaku* thinkers and most recently Western pseudo-scientific racism. But plenty of people in Japan really did hope to make of *bunmei kaika* – 'civilization and enlightenment' – not just a domestic slogan but a thriving export.

For the influential educator and government adviser Nitobe Inazō, this went beyond politics and strategic advantage to become a question of basic humanity and humanitarianism. He worked for a while with a German-trained doctor by the name of Gotō Shinpei, assisting him in turning Taiwan into what Gotō called a 'laboratory' for testing the potential abroad of the state- and infrastructure-building techniques and technologies that Shibusawa was helping to develop at home. Advocates of early Japanese colonialism pointed to Taiwan's rapidly rising GDP as a sign of success, along with the schools, hospitals and businesses that soon opened there.

Shibusawa worried about the heavy military spending required to give shape to civilizing ambitions such as these. But he was willing to play his part in the economic development – detractors would say 'exploitation' – of Taiwan and the Korean peninsula. His Dai-Ichi bank operated in Seoul and Pusan, and for a time his face appeared on banknotes issued there. In 1901, he became president of the Seoul–Pusan Railway Company, working to raise enough capital to link those two cities by rail. The aim, he said, was to increase Korean prosperity, and in so doing turn it into a richer market for Japanese products. All this could help to secure Korea against Western aggression, aiding Japan's own security into the bargain. China too could, with Japanese help, be saved from itself. Here was an extension of the 'public good' that underpinned Shibusawa's ethic of capitalism, from the Japanese public to an imagined Pan-Asian one.

The Russians continued to menace such hopes. As their presence in north-east Asia grew, an Anglo-Japanese Alliance was signed in 1902, binding Britain and Japan together in defending their Chinese and Korean interests against Russia. Negotiating with Russia from a position of increased strength, Itō Hirobumi thought that the most straightforward solution would be for his Russian counterparts to recognize Japan's interests in Korea while the Japanese did the same for Russia in Manchuria. But talks went nowhere, and in February 1904 the Japanese navy furnished patriots back home with their biggest boost yet: a surprise attack on Russian ships at Port Arthur.

During the war that followed, Shibusawa's support was considered sufficiently important that when at first he spoke out against the conflict he received a visit from a Japanese army general, insisting that if nothing were done the Russians might end up occupying the Korean peninsula. Shibusawa was persuaded, and began to rally Japanese business leaders to raise money for what became a colossally expensive venture in lives and funds alike.

Two military heroes emerged during the conflict. On land, General Nogi Maresuke captured Port Arthur for the second time – the first occasion was during the Sino-Japanese War. And at sea, Admiral Tōgō Heihachirō welcomed the Russian Baltic Fleet to Asia with destruction almost down to the last vessel. The British gave their new ally the most precious of congratulatory gifts: a lock of hair from the head of Admiral Lord Nelson himself, a legend amongst Japanese seamen for what they regarded as his samurai spirit.

But with more than 100,000 soldiers dead by May 1905 on the Japanese side alone, both the Japanese and the Russians were soon in the mood to make peace. US President Theodore Roosevelt brokered the Treaty of Portsmouth in September that year, bringing to an end a war that most international observers regarded as a Japanese victory – the first for an Asian over a modern Western imperial power.

Japan soon saw benefits to match the plaudits. The lease of the Liaotung Peninsula once again came their way, now with Russia's railway infrastructure and Manchurian mining rights into the bargain. From 1906, security in the area, known as the Kwantung Leased Territory, was provided by a new Kwantung garrison (later 'Army'). Civilian administration and business affairs along the railway corridor became the responsibility of the South Manchuria Railway Company (SMR). Gotō Shinpei's reputation in Taiwan won him the post of first company president in 1906, with government and private backers of the SMR hoping that he would work similar magic with their new investment. The southern portion of Sakhalin was meanwhile added to the Japanese empire and renamed Karafuto. Finally, Japan's priority interest in Korea was officially recognized, with the Russians agreeing not to interfere with whatever the Japanese might decide to do there.

What the Japanese decided to do was to turn Korea into a Japanese protectorate later in 1905, and then fully annex the country in 1910 at the cost of fighting that ended many thousands of Korean lives. Japanese money, migrants and goods poured into the peninsula, the beginning of attempts to turn Korea into a 'civilized' market and source of raw materials. Shibusawa was once again in the thick of the action. The Seoul branch of his Dai-Ichi bank became the Bank of Korea (renamed 'Bank of Chosen' in 1911). He brought together three major Osaka cotton producers, including his own mill, to establish a cartel for exporting cotton to Korea. And he helped to set up a new 'Oriental Development Company' in 1908, with the extraordinary ambition of settling 2 million Japanese farmers in Korea over ten years. The figure by 1926 was a comparatively disappointing 20,000 farmers, with more land than expected turning out to be already under cultivation by Koreans. Undeterred, the company grew to become a significant landlord itself, controlling 80,000 Korean

tenants across more than 150,000 hectares by the time of Shibusawa's death.

Shibusawa began calling for greater cooperation between government and business in setting policy goals, given that businesses were
being asked to make significant contributions to Japanese foreign
policy: from the waging of the Russo-Japanese War, which cost Japan
around 1.7 billion yen (around a billion of which had to be borrowed
abroad), to the setting up of industry and infrastructure in places like
Korea and the territory controlled by the SMR. He was also worried
that Japan's increasingly aggressive pursuit of its interests in East
Asia was harming its international reputation, not to mention the
costs of administering an ever-larger empire.

Shibusawa even began to wonder whether Japan was reaching a
tipping point, beyond which the further deployment of its military
would actually endanger its interests. He argued that the old 'way of
the warrior' (*bushidō*) ought now to become the 'way of business'
(*jitsugyōdō*), with businessmen rather than the armed forces being
the true inheritors of the old samurai spirit. Where some still used the
slogan *wakon yōsai*, 'Japanese spirit, Western techniques', Shibusawa
advocated *shikon shōsai*: 'samurai spirit, merchant talent'.

*

In 1912, just a few years into Japan's colonial experiments in Manchuria and Korea, the country found itself at the end of an era. The
Emperor had gone from an obscure teenager co-opted by coup leaders in 1868 to the single greatest symbol of Japan's modern rise to
power. He passed away on 30 July 1912, followed into death by the
war hero General Nogi and his wife in a widely publicized act of
junshi: a centuries-old custom whereby a samurai would take his
own life when his master died. Public mourning was tinged with anxiety at the loss of a stabilizing figure. Japan had prospered of late, but
where would the country go next?

Shibusawa's role in building that prosperity shifted around this time
from commerce to philanthropy. His aim now, he said, was to ensure
harmony between labour and capital, and to work for the relief of
poverty. He had already long been involved with one of Japan's first

welfare institutions: the Tokyo Yōikuin, combining an orphanage, a juvenile reformatory, a hospital, and a nursing home for the elderly. It became just one of hundreds of charitable concerns in which he was involved, in one capacity or another.

Shibusawa's approach to welfare was firmly in tune with his overall ethic of *kokutai* capitalism. The Tokyo Yōikuin cared for those who could not currently take care of themselves; in as many cases as possible, Shibusawa hoped that people would return to lives of self-sufficiency. The same applied to the Tōhoku region of northern Honshū. Referred to in the press as 'Japan's Tibet', it suffered more than most other parts of the country from poverty and famine. Shibusawa argued that investment in industry and infrastructure was a better way to help the region – and, in turn, the country – than simply doling out relief money and leaving it at that. Such initiatives should be led, he insisted, by business and philanthropic organizations rather than the state. Here, as elsewhere in Japan's affairs, private enterprise, acting ethically and as free as possible of bureaucratic interference, was the way forward.

When it came to labour relations – a growing concern in the 1890s and early 1900s – Shibusawa hoped to see managers and workers establish relationships governed by Confucian virtues of benevolence and responsibility. Such virtues were easily practised in small businesses, where interactions were regular and personal; the challenge, he thought, would be to see them take root in large factories and mills. To this end, Shibusawa became vice-president of the Kyōchōkai (Co-operation Society), a new organization formed in 1919, bringing together businessmen and government bureaucrats to provide education for workers, mediate in labour disputes and advise on labour reform. Where bad capitalism, for Shibusawa, focused on individual profit, so bad labour relations focused on workers' 'rights'. The keynote ought to be collaboration.

Critics argued that organizations like the Kyōchōkai were to labour relations what Pan-Asianism was to international relations: the language of mutuality dishonestly deployed in the service of rapacious self-interest. Others pointed to Shibusawa's enormous personal fortune, or to his rumoured fathering of around thirty illegitimate children, asking how such things fitted in with his much-trumpeted professional and personal morality. Shibusawa tried to give the latter a positive spin, saying that 'Besides relations with women, I have no reason for shame before Heaven'. His second wife Kaneko was later more straightforward: 'Lucky he was a Confucian; it would have been rough if he had been a Christian.'

Shibusawa continued to press his vision of capitalism and welfare right up until his death in 1931 at the age of ninety-one, a diet that he confessed was rich in sugar and fat having apparently done him little harm. The country boy who once haggled over indigo had grown up to be feted in the *Washington Herald* as 'the [J. P.] Morgan of Japan'.

14
Tsuda Umeko

(津田梅子)

1864–1929

Culture Shock

Tsuda Umeko as a student, at Bryn Mawr College, Pennsylvania, 1889–92.

Thursday, November 23, 1882

Oh, Mrs. Lanman . . . you would be astonished to see how easily
we Japanese take to Japanese ways. I now bow low to everybody
and have to sit on the floor and talk, though we have a foreign
parlor with chairs . . . Japanese food tastes very nice and I have
taken to it as naturally as fish to water, but at every meal there is
bread and something foreign for me as they don't want me to get
sick. They wanted to sugar and milk my tea and have butter for
bread, but I would not let them.

Tsuda Ume's letter continued for a while in this vein. It was annoying
to have to take her shoes off when entering a house. She looked
'funny' in Japanese clothes. It was hard to sit down in the Japanese
style without looking uncouth. Japanese etiquette in general was so
strict – at mealtimes, it was considered disrespectful to leave even a
single kernel of rice uneaten in one's bowl – that Tsuda expected to
make a 'bad blunder' at any moment. 'How different', she concluded,
'from "American ways".'

Eleven years before, when she was just six years old, Tsuda had
been the youngest member of the Iwakura Mission. Where Itō
Hirobumi and the others had set out around the world to make contacts and copious notes covering all areas of modern governance and
society, Tsuda and four other girls were charged with establishing
much deeper relationships with the West. The men would learn. The
girls would *become*. American women were seen as the ideal model:
happy, educated and expert modern homemakers.

Brought up as an American girl in Washington DC, a seventeen-
year-old Tsuda returned in 1882 to a country that she barely recognized.
Her culture shock was profound and unusual, but she was far from
alone in regarding Meiji-era Japan as an alien place. Nor was she the

only one in the late 1800s and early 1900s to seek alternatives to the world that Japan's new political and military leaders were building with assistance from the likes of Shibusawa Eiichi. What marked Tsuda out was her ex-pat take on her country's problems, and her sponsorship of surprisingly enduring solutions based on her own unique blend of Japanese, Western and Christian values.

*

Tsuda Ume was born on 31 December 1864. She was named by her mother Hatsuko after a bonsai plum tree (*ume*) by her bedside. It had been keeping her company while her husband Sen was away. On learning that his eagerly awaited child was a girl, he had left the house in a huff and had still not returned seven days later, when it came time to name her.

Back in July 1853, Sen had been one of the samurai guards looking on as Commodore Perry came ashore to get US–Japanese relations off to their famously tense beginning. He did his best to turn the years of crisis that followed to his own advantage, studying Dutch and English, working as an interpreter for the *bakufu* and then marrying Hatsuko in 1860 and having himself adopted into her family: they were retainers to a branch family of the Tokugawa.

Sen visited the United States on behalf of the *bakufu* in 1867 and then in 1869 became a manager at Japan's very first Western-style hotel in Tsukiji, the foreign settlement area of Tokyo. The Edo Hotel, as it was known by its mainly foreign clientele, was an early experiment in the adoption of Western architectural styles, turning it into something of a tourist attraction amongst local Japanese. The actual guests were less impressed. One of them described it as 'an apology for a hotel', badly built and equally badly managed. By the time Kusumoto Ine moved to the area in 1870 to establish her clinic, most of the rooms were empty. Sen left the next year.

Anxious about his future prospects in rapidly changing times, Sen found himself tempted by an unusual government advertisement that came to his attention in 1871. A handful of young girls were to be given ten years of education in the United States, all expenses paid and some pocket money thrown in. With an eye, perhaps, to turning his daughter into a valuable marriage prospect down the line, Sen put Ume's name forward. He did not regard her as central to the family's fortunes, pinning his real hopes instead on his two youngest boys – naming them Kingo ('my gold') and Gingo ('my silver').

Only five applications were received in answer to the government ad. This was, after all, a brand new national leadership pitching a truly unconventional idea. Wondering whether she would ever see her daughter again, the mother of one of the other applicants renamed her 'Sutematsu' shortly before departure – 'thrown-away pine'. Tsuda herself later recalled being daunted by what she imagined was to come, but also curious about where her adventure would take her. At just six years of age, she found herself presented to the Empress in November 1871, along with the other four applicants – all of whom had been accepted. The Empress addressed the girls from seclusion behind a 'heavy hanging screen'. They were given some sacred 'court cake', believed to cure all illness, along with a length of red silk and a document urging them to 'study for the good of our countrywomen'.

The next month, Tsuda packed her bags: paper, ink and brushes for writing home; some illustrated histories of Japan; a red Western-style shawl from her father; a dictionary and an English primer. Then she and the other girls boarded a skiff at Yokohama, heading for the *America*, the vessel that would carry them across the Pacific. A crowd gathered to see them off, and Tsuda's aunt was sure that she heard one person whispering about 'heartless parents' sending their children to a 'barbarous land'.

Having celebrated her seventh birthday in the middle of the Pacific Ocean, in a cramped cabin with four sea-sick girls, Tsuda and the rest of the Iwakura Mission arrived to welcoming crowds in San Francisco, early in 1872. The girls found themselves feted all the way across America – stares, kisses, toys waved in their faces – until finally the 'princesses', as the media described them, parted ways with the rest of the mission in February 1872 in a snowy Washington DC. There, Japan's ambassador to the United States, Mori Arinori, arranged for Tsuda to stay with his secretary, Charles Lanman, and his wife Adeline.

Childless in their fifties, the Lanmans welcomed Tsuda with open arms. Charles cherished her as his 'sunbeam from the land of the Rising Sun', while a letter written by Tsuda to Adeline just a few weeks after her arrival spoke for itself:

> I am very happy. I gave you this to make a presant a for you. I hope
> you would like it. I think your very nice lady. I think you like me. I love
> you better then you love me. good bye you friend Mume.

Tsuda spent the next ten years living with the Lanmans in a Georgetown home which, thanks to Mr Lanman's career as a writer, had seen literary celebrities including Washington Irving and Charles Dickens pass through. Tsuda attended a small private school, and a little over a year after her arrival in the United States she declared her wish to be baptized. Religious conversion was against the rules for Japanese students studying abroad. But the country's centuries-old ban on Christianity had recently been lifted, and after approval from Mori, Tsuda got her wish. When she received the news, a few weeks later, that her little brother Kingo had died, Tsuda wrote to her mother to assure her that he was now with God in heaven. Her mother and father became Christians a little while later.

Within a few years, a girl who had arrived in the United States knowing just three words of English – 'yes', 'no' and 'thank you' – was raiding the Lanmans' library for works by Dickens, Shakespeare and Wordsworth, along with biographies ranging from Caesar to Charles Darwin. Tsuda was a promising mathematician and linguist too. She also wrote, painted and enjoyed the theatre. She played chess, croquet and tennis. For company, she had a pet cat, upon whom – either missing her native language or preferring the straightforward approach in life – she bestowed the name 'Neko' ('Cat').

Not everyone in America showed Tsuda as much warmth as the Lanmans. Boys sometimes shouted at her in the streets – 'Chinamen eat rats!' And while adults were more polite, these were years in which even those intending to compliment the Japanese did so by noting their hunger for (Western) civilization or by dubbing them 'the British of Asia'. Tsuda carried all this back with her to Japan in 1882, along with gifts from the Lanmans to help her live a suitably civilized life there: several hundred books, some works of art and a piano.

Arriving back in Tokyo, Tsuda found herself as much a curiosity in Japan as she had been ten years before in America. People wanted to see her American dresses and hats, and they laughed when she tried to combine kimono with layer upon layer of American underwear – corset and camisole, stockings, garters, petticoats and knickers. In her letters to Adeline Lanman, the Japanese were to Tsuda sometimes a matter of 'we' but often of 'they' – as in 'they are a slow, languid . . . race'.

Tsuda hoped to fulfil the Empress's wishes, sharing with her countrywomen the blessings of her foreign education. But while the male Japanese students with whom she shared a ship home sailed on straight into government jobs, her country appeared to have no use for her. She ended up stuck at home, helping her father to write letters, looking after her younger siblings and struggling to reacquire the Japanese language.

All that changed in December 1883, when an offer of work came through from Itō Hirobumi. He was due to take over as Foreign Minister and was in need of someone to help his wife play hostess to foreign guests. Mrs Itō was a former geisha, so a skilled entertainer in the traditional sense, but she lacked a command of foreign languages and customs. Itō's daughter, too, could benefit from having a Western-educated lady as a companion. Tsuda was invited to move into the Itō home, and was given a job on the side at the Tōyō Jojuku, a small school for upper-class women. Both roles allowed Tsuda to trade her knowledge of the English language and American ways for a training in elite Japanese conversation and manners.

It was the kind of life of which Tsuda had long dreamed. She joined a household consisting of mother, father and three children, all shuttling back and forth between an old Japanese house and a new Western-style one on a hill nearby, where they ate Western meals – soup, fish, meat, desserts – and Itō had his office. Tsuda was given her own rooms and servants, and could wear her American clothes without embarrassment. She even advised Itō's wife and daughter on foreign fashion, taking them shopping in Yokohama.

Itō himself, with whom Tsuda spoke in English, seemed progressive and energetic – even 'impulsive': ready to go all out for something he believed in. But he always travelled with a retinue of footmen, coachmen and policemen. By 1886, he was 'rarely leav[ing] his office or his home for fear of assassination'. Here was evidence of another side to the purposeful political and economic strides that Japan had been taking during the 1870s and 1880s – one of disagreement and resistance, even rebellion.

Amongst the first to show their displeasure had been the samurai, many of whom had supported the pro-imperial cause in 1868 only to lose their domain lords, their stipends and their privileged place in the class system and on the battlefield. Violent anger peaked with the Satsuma Rebellion in 1877. Tens of thousands of disgruntled samurai joined one of the heroes of 1868, Saigō Takamori, on a march towards Tokyo. Having quit Japan's governing clique in disgust a few years before, Saigō intended to speak with the Emperor himself about the wrong turn that the country was taking. What started as a protest march turned into a second civil war, pitting Yamagata Aritomo's conscript army against Saigō's samurai. After months of fighting that killed 6,000 conscripts, left three times as many dead or wounded on Saigō's side and consumed a significant proportion of the national budget – some of it handed to Mitsubishi, whose ships ferried government troops around – the uprising finally ended with Saigō's defeat and death.

Elsewhere in Japan, some were seeing their tax bills rise while payment terms became less flexible: in place of the old tax collectors – local men usually willing to negotiate – came relatively intransigent centrally appointed officials. Other people were disturbed by rumours, sparked by talk of conscription as a 'blood tax' (a term used in the West), that government agents were criss-crossing the land armed with glass vials into which they siphoned conscripts' blood for sale abroad – perhaps as wine. Discontent spilled over into violent demonstration across the 1870s and early 1880s, drawing in tens of thousands of protesters. Government offices were amongst the most popular targets, alongside the homes of money-lenders. The official response to unrest, now as in later decades, was to combine the deployment of a well-funded police force with a concession or two – including, in 1877, a 20 per cent cut in the tax rate.

By the time that Tsuda took up her post with the Itōs, opposition to the emerging status quo in Japan was coalescing around the country's future political arrangements. Activists in a 'Freedom and People's Rights movement' held meetings around the country – sometimes on barges in the middle of rivers or lakes, to avoid police interference – urging the adoption of a liberal settlement in Japan, complete with inalienable rights. Japan's two major political parties, the Freedom Party and the Constitutional Progressive Party, stood at one end of this activist spectrum, with sporadic outbreaks of political violence at the other.

Amidst this widespread anxiety and discontent, Tsuda homed in on two particular groups of Japanese whose fortunes she saw as being under threat: women and Christians. Writing to Adeline Lanman, she noted that women seemed to have precious few rights in Japan, while the enthusiasm for women's education that had sent her to America back in 1871 seemed to have disappeared. Girls were instead forced, at a young age, into arranged marriages, living effectively as their husbands' maids.

Most disturbing of all, for Tsuda, was the power of culture in persuading women to be happy with their sorry situation. The rot reached all the way to the top – perhaps even starting there – with a political elite mired in immorality; many were heavy drinkers, often married to former geisha while keeping concubines on the side. What was needed, thought Tsuda, was for Japan's well-born women to receive the sort of education that she herself had enjoyed in the United States. Such women would aspire higher, assert themselves properly, and be sufficiently intellectual company for their husbands that fishing for wives and mistresses in tea-houses and pleasure districts would become a thing of the past. A former geisha twanging away on a shamisen would never be able to compete with a well-educated wife playing Beethoven on the piano.

Tsuda's unusual upbringing meant that she tended to conflate progressive, American and Christian values in seeking culture change for Japan. She talked at length with Itō about religion, becoming excited about the prospect of his conversion to Christianity, but fearing that she possessed little talent as an evangelist. 'I can hardly give reasons for my own belief,' she wrote in a letter to Adeline Lanman. 'I only know I do believe . . . How much I wish some better and wiser person were in my place, and had this chance!'

Japan's Protestant Christian population was on the rise at this point, hitting 30,000 in 1893. The Orthodox and Catholic Churches were making modest inroads too, the latter having in 1862 made saints of the twenty-six Christians crucified by Hideyoshi. Most promising of all for Tsuda, a great many converts were people of influence: former samurai, attracted by compelling parallels between the gospels and the austere, selfless spirit of *bushidō* (the 'way of the warrior'). The apostle Paul, claimed the Christian leader Uchimura Kanzō, had been a 'true samurai': loyal, independent of mind and possessed of a healthy hatred for money.

One of the problems Tsuda quickly picked up on was the poor quality of some of the foreign missionaries. They were 'fussy about sect' and came across as superior, even arrogant – unwilling, Tsuda noted of the American contingent, to appreciate 'anything good in Japan or anywhere outside of America'. This failure to distinguish between the gospel and Western culture led missionaries to be described – based on their noted fondness for dairy products – as *bata kusai*, 'stinking of butter'. Many refused to enter Japanese homes, or if they did, would not take off their shoes. Others lived in luxury and enjoyed three-course meals, plus dessert, while serving up terrible food in their mission schools. 'Are their consciences, so tender in talking religion and distributing tracts, hard on this?' asked Tsuda in a letter to Mrs Lanman. 'Are they blind?'

Against the backdrop of a rising sense of cultural nationalism in Japan, the continued association of Christianity with the West had the makings of a serious political problem for Japanese Christians. Buddhism might have lost some of the privileges it had enjoyed under the Tokugawa shoguns, but it was still regarded by most people as thoroughly Japanese. Its ideas, architecture and rituals loomed large in their lives, while reformers worked hard to find a credible place for Buddhist philosophy amidst the claims and nation-building utility of Western science. Shintō was enjoying a revival thanks to the rooted-ness of the new regime in a divinely descended emperor. Christianity, by contrast, faced rising scepticism over the ultimate compatibility of love for the 'two Js': Jesus and Japan. Tsuda experienced these tensions at first hand in 1884 when newspapers splashed on claims that Itō was hoping the Emperor himself would become a Christian. Tsuda's presence in the Itō household suddenly seemed impolitic, and she left later that year.

Assisting the Women's Charity Society in organizing a three-day bazaar in 1884, Tsuda was impressed at the hard bargaining of Japan's womanly elite. They were ruthless in driving up prices on dresses, clocks, caps, fans, toys and cushions, and refused to give small change. And yet these women seemed to Tsuda to be helplessly hooked on the high life of entertainment and socializing. Hoping for better things from the younger generation, she took up a teaching post at the Peeresses' School in 1885. This was a new institution, intended as a female counterpart to the Peers' School, which had been established in 1877 to educate the children of the nobility. As Tsuda put it in a letter to Mrs Lanman, they were 'the highest girls, the best girls of the land . . . Think of the influence [they] will have in the after fate of this nation'.

A sense of excitement and possibility kept Tsuda going for a while. She watched students arrive in coaches and rickshaws at the school's smart complex of Western-style buildings in central Tokyo, vehicles and drivers alike sporting family crests. Some brought their own stewards or maids. But the school ended up offering little more than a gilded version of 'good wives, wise mothers'. History, science and languages vied for timetable space with needlework, cooking, etiquette and state-sponsored ethics. Murasaki Shikibu and Joan of Arc were domesticated as models of good behaviour, alongside a daughter who sold her front teeth to a dentist in order to help her poverty-stricken parents.

Tsuda already had her doubts about Murasaki Shikibu, having, it seems, read the first English translation of *The Tale of Genji* the year before. It was 'a famous Japanese work . . . written by a woman', she reported to Mrs Lanman, 'a luxurious, dreamy, poetical thing, but full of Oriental immorality'. It was possibly a little too aristocratic for her tastes too. Finding herself culturally adrift at the Peeresses' School – she was too middle-class, too American, intent upon an ideal of intellectual and independent womanhood for which she found few takers – Tsuda took a leave of absence in 1889 and returned to the United States. There she studied biology at Bryn Mawr College – another new institution, but one far closer to her heart. Its dean was the educator and suffragist M. Carey Thomas, who famously was determined to provide an education for women that would match Harvard's in its rigour.

Time away from Japan brought Tsuda's concerns about her countrywomen into clearer relief. The result was a book, co-authored with her friend Alice Mabel Bacon, an American educator. *Japanese Girls and Women* (1891) laid out the problem, alongside a range of suggested solutions: a broader, more challenging education, the right to own property, less reliance on men, and more equal marriages. Women of the former samurai class were offered up as the ideal raw material for such opportunities, possessing the energy and sense of virtue required to make the most of them. Geisha, meanwhile, were holding women – and men – back; they were the very antithesis of Christian morality and the progressive spirit.

Reactions to the book back in Japan were mixed, but Americans embraced it as a vindication of the sort of civilizing influence they believed they were exercising in Asia. Tsuda found herself in demand as a public speaker across the United States, using the role as a means of raising funds – under the auspices of a new Japanese Scholarship Committee – to allow a few fortunate Japanese girls to complete their educations in the US. Tsuda seems to have modelled herself here on Pandita Ramabai, an Indian advocate for women's education. Tsuda had attended a lecture of hers in Japan, and was impressed by her intelligence, earnestness, confidence and ability to find funding for her cause in America.

Returning to Japan refreshed in 1892, Tsuda began, alongside her teaching work, to publish her thinking on the future of women in her country. In some ways, it mirrored that of Shibusawa on workers. Both focused on education, and on the respect – from others and for oneself – to which it naturally gave rise. And both played on Japanese fears of being thought backward by their international peers, warning, respectively, that business conduct and men's treatment of women would be viewed abroad as a reflection on the country as a whole.

A second foreign tour in 1898 took Tsuda once again to America and also to Europe. She met Helen Keller and Florence Nightingale, and visited a number of pioneering institutions for women's education, including Girton and Newnham at Cambridge University, St Hilda's at Oxford University, and Cheltenham Ladies College. She now felt ready to get her own educational venture off the ground, resigning from the Peeresses' School in 1900 and opening the Joshi Eigaku Juku (Women's English School) the same year.

They were modest beginnings: four teachers and fifteen students crammed into leaky rented premises, with a blackboard, a typewriter, some books and Tsuda's well-travelled piano. An eclectic opening ceremony was held, comprising a reading of the 1890 Imperial Rescript on Education, a hymn (in Japanese), some psalms (in English) and finally a prayer (Japanese).

The school accepted day-students and boarders, and its purpose was to prepare women to take the government exams for a teaching licence in English, by offering them a three-year course in English language, literature, translation and composition. Girls would gain a rare and valuable route to financial independence (teaching was one of the few professions open to women at this point), alongside the broader autonomy and self-respect that Tsuda was confident – on the basis of her own childhood – would be the fruits of an immersion in the classics of English literature.

Current affairs were also discussed in class (in English), at a time when women's participation in politics continued to be outlawed. Students were encouraged to reflect on the status of women around the world, with coverage of the suffragette movement in the US and Europe helping to foster a degree of cosmopolitanism and international solidarity found in few other girls' schools at the time. A year before Joshi Eigaku Juku opened, the Ministry of Education had ordered the building of at least one girls' Higher School in each of Japan's prefectures. Few availed themselves of these extra years of education in the early 1900s, with only around 3 per cent of the number of girls in primary education taking up places. All who did found themselves, in common with their Western counterparts, using textbooks that focused heavily on their natural suitability for housework.

Where most schooling in Japan around this time involved learning by rote, boys attending elite Higher Schools were encouraged to develop the independence of spirit required of national leaders in politics, business and the sciences. Tsuda sought something similar for her school, surprising – sometimes upsetting – her students by getting them to voice their own opinions, even to argue with their teachers. Most girls, in Tsuda's view, grew up 'timid, lack[ing] confidence and independence'. They could also be 'over-sensitive', preferring to have others formulate, and so take responsibility for, their opinions.

Tsuda was, by all accounts, a force to be reckoned with in the classroom, demanding a response from students that would equal her own passion. She pressed her girls on their English and powers of reasoning alike, using composition assignments to test and sharpen their logic. Those who managed to keep up with the pace were rewarded, at the end of the class, with a smile and an English joke. Boarders even got to see their teacher dance of an evening, picking up some of her favourite American country-dancing moves. Tsuda was proud of them all, pinning little red flags into a map to show where graduates of Joshi Eigaku Juku had gone on to live and work.

There were risks attached to what Tsuda was doing. Advanced education for women was popularly associated, both in the West and in Japan, with an array of undesirable outcomes ranging from physical depletion, including under-developed ovaries, to 'mannishness and promiscuity'. Tsuda was well aware that her great venture would be judged less on girls' intellectual and spiritual development than on relatively 'insignificant matters' such as speech, manners, etiquette and dress. For this reason, she cautioned her students always to 'exhibit grace and modesty, civility and care', preserving the good name of the school and learning how to live independently in a society that for the moment continued to fear that quality in its women.

Students and parents liked what they saw of Joshi Eigaku Juku. Within three years, it had more than 100 students on its books. Its resources were growing, too, thanks to reading material donated by Bryn Mawr and St Hilda's College, Oxford, and a combination of books and funds sent by the Japanese Scholarship Committee (now the 'Committee for Miss Tsuda's School for Girls'). Just like her ladies at the charity bazaar many years before, Tsuda was not ashamed to ask people to empty their pockets for a good cause, or to cajole Western missionaries and teachers from major men's institutions – including Tokyo Imperial University and the Peers' School – to give guest lectures. One of her star turns was Nitobe Inazō: Pan-Asianist, advocate of a 'humanitarian' colonialism, Christian convert, author in 1900 of *Bushidō: The Soul of Japan* (in which he likened samurai culture to Europe's chivalric tradition) and later headmaster of the elite First Higher School – effectively a prep school for Tokyo Imperial University.

By the end of 1905, Tsuda's school was operating in new premises, thanks to a particularly generous American benefactor, and had received from the government the highest ranking available to a women's private school: *senmon gakkō* (vocational school). Its graduates were no longer required to sit the teachers' exams. This was due in part to a shortage of teachers, the profession's reputation having dipped in recent years. But it was an accolade nonetheless: Tsuda's school was deemed good enough that graduation from it was sufficient proof of students' readiness for the teaching profession.

Tsuda's success mattered all the more as the economic and social strains of the Russo-Japanese War of 1904–5 threatened to set both her favourite causes back. With soldiers dying at an alarming rate, the responsibility of women to produce more was emphasized afresh, at the cost of other considerations in a girl's education. Christians, meanwhile, saw their patriotism questioned with new intensity. Already, in the early 1890s, Japan's first full Professor of Philosophy at Tokyo University, Inoue Tetsujirō, had attacked Christianity as antithetical to Japanese security, within and beyond its borders: it bred a dangerous sympathy for the Christian West (including Russia), the Sermon on the Mount was full of defeatist nonsense and Jesus seemed to have had precious little respect for his parents. When war broke out in 1904, critiques of this kind were joined by Buddhist reformers hoping to see both Russia and Christianity defeated in battle. While Japanese Christians fought and died in the conflict, at home their families came under greater pressure than anyone else to be vocal in their support and generous in their donations to the cause.

For Tsuda, these and subsequent years became difficult ones in personal terms too. Having discovered her vocation, she found she could not stop. She worked long hours as a teacher, also serving as the school's chief administrator and fundraiser, compiled new textbooks and helped to edit not one but two magazines aimed at students of English. It all began to take a toll on her health.

She took a brief break in the United States in 1907, during the course of which she visited the White House and was questioned by Theodore Roosevelt about the fabled 'Japanese spirit', on display in the war that he had helped to bring to a conclusion two years before. The First Lady had read *Japanese Girls and Women*, and she asked Tsuda what values she hoped to see the Japanese people hold on to as modernization proceeded. 'The spirit of sacrifice and loyalty' was the answer: for all her love of American and English literature, Tsuda was less wedded to the West than her critics tended to allow.

Soon after Tsuda's return to Japan in 1908, her father died, followed in 1909 by her mother and by her friend and former employer, Itō Hirobumi. The latter became an early casualty of Japan's newly assertive foreign policy on the mainland: shot dead by a Korean nationalist shortly after retiring as Resident General of Korea. Tsuda's sister Koto died in 1911, followed by Adeline Lanman – who had long since lost her husband – in 1914.

Tsuda continued to receive plaudits throughout the 1910s, including the Sixth Order of Merit for services to women's education. But ill health, including diabetes, forced her to begin winding down her activities, around the same time as her conservative counterpart in the world of business, Shibusawa Eiichi.

*

Adding to Tsuda's woes during the final decade of her career was a piece of writing, part poem and part manifesto, published in 1911:

> In the beginning, woman was the sun, and a true being.
> Now woman is the moon.
> She lives through others, and shines through the light of others.
> Her countenance is pale, like a patient.

Let us reveal our hidden sun, our unrecognized genius!
We must restore the sun.

Composed by a former student of Tsuda's, Hiratsuka Raichō, this was the opening salvo in a war that Tsuda had always counselled her girls against fighting. Back in 1902, she had established her own household, legally freeing herself of her father's influence and altering her name from 'Ume' to 'Umeko'. (*Ko*, meaning 'girl' or 'princess', had been used for centuries by women of noble rank in Japan. Free, in the Meiji era, to change their own names, many commoner women chose it for themselves.) But Tsuda still cherished Japan's old cooperative ethic, within families and across society, and hoped to see women reform it from within. Hiratsuka preferred to attack it. She mounted an assault on unequal marriage (which rendered women 'slaves during the daytime and prostitutes at night'), on the demeaning terms of the Civil Code, and on the kind of life-limiting domesticity peddled not just in schools but by magazines like *Woman's Friend* (*Fujin no Tomo*). Such publications were stuffed full of tips on housekeeping and cookery alongside adverts for products designed to confirm the kitchen as a woman's natural sphere, from handy stand-up workspaces to gas-burning rice cookers. Japan's first department store, Mitsukoshi, opened in 1904 in Nihonbashi, bringing magazine adverts to life and promoting a tie-up of commerce and conservative social values that helped to define women's lives for many years to come.

Hiratsuka wanted women to read journals like hers instead. *Bluestocking* (*Seitō*) featured 'In the beginning' in its very first issue, reminding people that whatever the Civil Code might say, Japan's origins lay not with a man but with a Sun Goddess. Tsuda was willing to acknowledge that the associated literary group, Seitōsha (Bluestocking Society), was home to some 'clever' writers. But she denounced the likes of Hiratsuka nonetheless as 'immoral', 'lawless' – even as 'agents of the devil' – for promoting ideas that were 'foreign' to Japan.

Despite their differences, Tsuda and Hiratsuka were similar in that they both targeted women of relatively high social status, and found liberation in the life of the mind. Elsewhere in Japan during these same years, sorrier circumstances were pushing women towards more radical solutions. One of the dark sides of the great industrial strides made thanks to men like Shibusawa was the treatment of textile workers. Many were young girls, recruited to live and work in factory-dormitory complexes in return for an up-front payment to their parents. Songs of the time told of harsh conditions: twelve-hour shifts worked at pace, meals of rice mixed with sand, pay deductions for the smallest infraction, violence and sexual abuse. Some girls ran away. Others pressed on, their music and writings revealing them as unlikely recruits to Shibusawa's mutual-aid model of labour relations: 'Let's wrench the balls of the hateful men!'; 'Bosses are vipers, our bitterest enemies'.

Socialism and anarchism flourished amongst some of these women, giving rise in 1910 to a failed attempt on the Emperor's life. A woman called Kanno Sugako had been due to throw the first bomb. She used her treason trial, held in secret, to denounce the malignant role that the imperial institution was playing in a country that she now struggled to call home:

Although I feel sorry for him personally, [the Meiji Emperor] is the chief person responsible for the exploitation of the people economically. Politically he is at the root of all the crimes being committed, and intellectually he is the fundamental cause of superstitious beliefs. A person in such a position, I concluded, must be killed.

Other activists pushed for the sort of legislation on industrial labour standards that businessmen resisted but which the government was forced in 1911 to concede. A minimum working age of twelve was established, alongside – for women and children – a maximum shift length of twelve hours with at least two rest days per month.

Against the backdrop of feminist and industrial activism, Tsuda's focus on elite education appeared to her critics to be uncomfortably out of date. It had perhaps always been a little too self-referential, too narrowly rooted in her own experience of moving between two cultures – her textbooks featured lonely yet optimistic young women who triumph in the end. And yet Tsuda had achieved something remarkable. Arriving home in 1882 after a decade in America, she had coped with her culture shock by administering one of her own:

pioneering a form of education that blended Japanese with Western values, shaping women who did not have to ask for respect because they commanded it. That Tsuda herself embodied this ideal was clear from the testimony of her students, from the funds and accolades she attracted, and from the fact that a year after her death, in Kamakura in 1929, the administrators of her school took what was a highly unusual step at the time: they renamed it after her – 'Tsuda Eigaku Juku' – and buried her ashes on campus.

15
Ikeda Kikunae
(池田菊苗)

1864–1936

Taste-Maker

Ikeda Kikunae and his great discovery: *umami*,
as a chemical formula and a bottled product.

UNITED STATES PATENT OFFICE
Patented Aug. 13, 1912

Be it known that we, KIKUNAE IKEDA and SABUROSUKE
SUZUKI, subjects of the Emperor of Japan . . . have invented certain
new and useful Improvements in Nutritive and Flavoring Substances
and Processes of Making Same . . . The fact that the monovalent
anion $C_5H_3NO_4$ of glutamic acid presents intense meat-like taste,
has been discovered by us in the course of chemical investigation of
the constituents of the sea-weed Laminaria japonica.

Presented as tribute by Emishi 'barbarians' to Emperor Kanmu's
court in the late 700s. Harvested by the two long-suffering sisters at
the centre of Zeami's play *Wind Through the Pines*. Now, at the
dawn of the post-Meiji era, the edible seaweed known in Japanese as
konbu was about to find itself the source of a seasoning sensation at
home and abroad: monosodium glutamate, or MSG.

It began with Ikeda Kikunae, a chemist whose concern for his
nation's nutrition sent him on a search for a way of making even the
meanest of meals more nourishing and more flavoursome. And it
continued with Suzuki Saburosuke, who used his marketing nous to
help establish Ikeda's discovery as one of the flavours of the new age
in Japan. This new era was named Taishō, or 'Great Righteousness',
and lasted from the accession of the Meiji Emperor's son and successor Yoshihito in 1912 to his death in 1926. Yoshihito personally
was too weak to make his era his own. The fifth child of the Meiji
Emperor, he was the first to survive into adulthood and was beset by
physical and mental ill health. Taishō Japan came to be defined
instead by a fresh series of experiments in building a modern country: the managing of a mass industrial society, the widening of
participation in politics, the emergence of a consumer culture – in

which food was a key ingredient – and the maturing of Japan's international relationships.

Those, like Nitobe Inazō, who hoped that the Japanese would now become 'citizens of the world' saw scientists as helping to lead the way. They were idealized as members of a global scientific community, working to expand the frontiers of human knowledge in key areas including physics, chemistry and medicine. Entrepreneurs like Suzuki had their own part to play by bringing Japanese products to the world and helping to create a more cosmopolitan culture back at home.

Ikeda's life, and that of his great invention, offers a taste of the Taishō period and the later 1920s. Notes of confidence, optimism and good living – for middle-class urbanites especially, from doctors and lawyers to bureaucrats and businessmen – can be found mixed in with elements of frustration, suspicion and disillusionment with where Japan seemed to be heading as a country and the way the rest of the world was treating it.

*

Japan's global standing received a major boost early in the Taishō era when it entered the First World War on the side of its ally Great Britain. The Imperial Japanese Navy saw action in the Mediterranean, protecting Allied shipping, while Japanese Red Cross nurses tended soldiers serving on the Western front. The real significance of the war for Japan, however, lay closer to home. Japanese forces targeted German colonies in the South Pacific and on the Shandong peninsula in China. Soldiers were followed into action by diplomats, winning possession of both Shandong and some of the German Pacific Islands (part of the former Spanish East Indies) at Versailles in 1919, and establishing Japan as a founding member of the League of Nations. Nitobe Inazō became one of the League's first Under-Secretaries General.

Industry, too, profited handsomely during the conflict, supplying Japan's allies and capitalizing on the disruption caused to international rivals. As giants of heavy industry like Mitsubishi and

Kawasaki expanded their operations, the country's population of factory workers soared from around 950,000 in 1914 to 1.5 million in 1919. Gross National Product jumped by more than 40 per cent across the same period.

Consumers did less well. The cost of living rose steadily, and then in 1918 the price of rice suddenly shot up by as much as 60 per cent. Violent protests erupted across the country that summer, drawing in a million people and requiring the deployment of the army alongside the police to restore order. The largest demonstrations in Japanese history, they helped to shift politics in brand new directions.

The Japanese had become accustomed by this point to the separation of the Diet, serving primarily as a debating chamber, from an independent, imperially appointed Cabinet through which the leaders of 1868 and their protégés wielded real executive power. The premiership was passed around between members of this narrow clique: Itō Hirobumi served four terms as prime minister; Yamagata Aritomo two terms. But amidst a political crisis caused by the unrest of 1918, Yamagata recommended someone new for the post of prime minister: Hara Kei, the Catholic leader of the conservative Seiyūkai, one of two main political parties in the Diet at this point, alongside the more progressive Kenseikai. For the first time, the premiership passed to a commoner, on the basis of his leadership of a political party.

For those in Japan who hoped that this would mark a turn towards greater democracy, the years that followed offered much to celebrate. In 1922, the ban on women's participation in politics was finally lifted. From 1924 onwards, it became customary to appoint the leader of the Diet's largest party or coalition as prime minister. Then, in 1925, Japan instituted universal male suffrage, quadrupling the size of the electorate. A trend towards parliamentarianism was confirmed as civil servants, businessmen and military men increasingly looked to electoral politics – joining or sponsoring political parties – as a way of getting things done.

Continuing the Meiji theme of controlling the population and channelling the country's resources, the Taishō-era state adapted itself to confront two new, interrelated dangers: an industrial working class making demands en masse, and the filtering into Japan of foreign ideologies – socialism and communism the most pernicious amongst them. Police powers were strengthened: under the terms of a Peace Preservation Law in 1925, crimes against the *kokutai* became punishable with a lengthy prison sentence – upped, in 1928, to the death penalty. And a Special Higher Police (Tokkō), formed in response to the attempt on the Emperor's life in 1910, kept careful track of the left-wing parties that had formed in response to the granting of universal male suffrage, making sure that their policy platforms did not seriously threaten the status quo.

Where possible, the authorities preferred guidance to punishment. The Kasumigaseki government district in central Tokyo was home now to a new generation of professional bureaucrats, inheritors of the Meiji ideal of enlightened, public-spirited and technocratic leadership. Styling themselves 'shepherds of the people', they worked away in the Home, Education and other ministries to stave off revolution by researching social problems and making concessions where they could. This included promoting a model of industrial relations very similar to the one favoured by Shibusawa. Hundreds of strikes took place during the 1920s. But with government encouragement, and spurred on by a shortage of skilled labour in many industries, employers began to offer the kinds of concessions – complaint boxes, games rooms, healthcare, promises of permanent employment – that gave real substance to calls for mutuality and respect between workers and managers.

Where the population at large was concerned, bureaucrats favoured a way of working that their Tokugawa-era predecessors would have understood well: *kyōka*, or 'moral suasion'. They made skilled use of a national network of state employees, including police officers and school teachers (overall, more than a million people were on government payrolls in the 1920s), working also with local interest groups around the country. Helped by a media that delighted in linking liberal or left-wing ideologies with moral and sexual deviancy – Hiratsuka Raichō and her friends had a particularly torrid time of it in the press – the Taishō authorities proved largely successful in promoting gradual over radical change.

Much was expected in this new age, as it had been in the Meiji era, of science and technology. The Japanese word chosen after 1868 for 'science' was *kagaku*: literally 'department-study'. It emphasized the division of established knowledge into practically relevant specialisms, confirming science's place in the broader culture of nation-building pragmatism established by the likes of Fukuzawa Yukichi and Shibusawa Eiichi. Many of Japan's first scientists were samurai, carrying their tradition of public service from the battlefield into the laboratory, the lecture hall and the pages of popular magazines – fulfilling a government-imposed responsibility to enter and elevate public discourse.

Complementing his work as imperial family physician and Professor of Medicine at Tokyo University with a sideline in social commentary, Erwin Bälz complained that this approach to science risked treating it as a 'machine' for getting things done, rather than a mode of enquiry into the world. But discovery was a luxury that Meiji-era leaders felt they could ill afford. Their priority was the acquisition of expertise and the founding of institutions where that expertise could be passed around. Crucially important to the task were Japan's *ryūgakusei*, the promising young students sent abroad in their thousands to work with acknowledged experts in their fields, and then returning to staff a network of imperial universities. Prime amongst them was Tokyo University, established in 1877 and becoming Tokyo Imperial University in 1886. Similar state-funded institutions followed in Kyoto, Tōhoku and Kyūshū, competing with private counterparts in the capital, including Keio (founded by Fukuzawa) and Waseda (established by Ōkuma Shigenobu).

Ikeda Kikunae exemplified these foundational trends in Japanese science. He was born in Kyoto on 8 October 1864 into a branch of the southern Satsuma clan. As with many samurai families, the transition to Meiji did not go smoothly for Ikeda. When he left home to read chemistry at Tokyo University in 1885, he was forced to sell his futon in order to help fund his studies. While there he switched back and forth between science and Shakespeare, giving lectures on the Bard at a private college as a means of generating extra income.

After graduation, Ikeda spend a few years training secondary school teachers in chemistry, before landing a job as Assistant Professor of Chemistry back at his alma mater. In 1899 he departed for Germany as one of the *ryūgakusei*, studying physical chemistry (the behaviour of matter at the atomic and molecular levels) for a year and a half at Leipzig University under the future Nobel laureate Wilhelm Ostwald. Looking around the city, Ikeda noticed that the Germans seemed to have more powerful physiques than most Japanese. That got him thinking about diet: too many people in Japan were still eating poorly, and this surely boded ill for the future.

Returning to Tokyo University in 1901 to take up a professorship and help to introduce the study of physical chemistry to Japan, Ikeda set about tackling this question of food, nutrition and national strength. At first, he didn't have very much luck. Then, seated at the dinner table one day, he experienced his very own eureka moment. Here, steaming in a bowl before him, staring him in the face, was the answer: a boiled tofu dish flavoured, as such dishes had been for centuries, with *konbu*. The taste wasn't sweet, sour or bitter. It wasn't exactly salty either. It was something else, something meaty and savoury. It reminded him of the tomatoes, cheese and asparagus he had sampled in Germany, and it struck him now as lying entirely outside the four-part taste typology in use since the days of Aristotle. Ikeda appeared to have stumbled upon taste number five.

Such things were subjective to a degree, Ikeda conceded. But he knew plenty of people who were capable of discerning this particular brothy flavour. None of them seem to have been gifted gourmands, referring to it simply as *umai* – 'tasty'. Ikeda took his cue from them nonetheless, coining the term *umami*, 'tasty taste', to refer to the culinary spell cast by an ingredient whose nature he didn't yet know, but which held out the promise of rendering even the humblest of meals a delight.

Ikeda began his investigations in earnest in 1907, simmering 38 kilograms of dried *konbu* in water. He treated the resulting liquid to a range of complex chemical processes, culminating in a very simple one: he put it in his mouth. And there it was: a little on the sour side, to be sure, but unmistakable nonetheless. Ikeda had isolated the source of *umami*, more or less literally boiling it down to its essentials.

Further tests revealed that this mystery substance, the essence of what scientists working decades later would establish officially as the world's fifth flavour, was none other than glutamate. Glutamic acid was already well understood, thanks to work by the German chemists Karl Ritthausen and Emil Fischer. But where Fischer had tasted the acid, finding nothing to recommend it, Ikeda tasted it in glutamate form. Based on the notion that evolution selects animals' food preferences for their nutritional value, and that taste is somehow related to digestion, Ikeda concluded that *umami* must be good for you. To consume it as a seasoning would therefore be a win-win: better tasting *and* healthier food.

The tastiest and most practical form for such a seasoning to take, Ikeda decided, would be a salt of sorts: (mono)sodium glutamate. In 1908, he developed and secured a Japanese patent for the chemical process required to create it, later following up with British, French and American patents. Having secured Home Ministry approval, he sought out Suzuki Saburosuke to suggest that Suzuki Pharmaceutical Company take care of production and marketing. Suzuki agreed, and decided on the brand name Ajinomoto: 'quintessence of flavour'.

A promising precedent existed for Ikeda's and Suzuki's new venture. Like Ikeda, the German scientist Justus von Liebig had been interested in cheap nutrition, finding it in a method for producing beef extract. 'Liebig's Extract of Meat Company' was established in 1865, producing first a viscous liquid – making it possible to enjoy something called 'Liebig on toast' – and then a few decades later coming up with the Oxo cube. Liebig made similar discoveries in relation to yeast extraction, helping to bring Marmite into the world around the turn of the twentieth century. But Ajinomoto represented the first time, anywhere in the world, that an amino acid had been produced on an industrial scale. It was also the first successful cooperative venture in Japan between a university and industry.

In 1909, Suzuki changed his own company name to Ajinomoto and set about finding a place for this new product in a Japanese food culture that was continuing to evolve with the times. Year One – 1868 – had done nothing to dislodge the nation's staples: rice, vegetables and fish – the last offering tasty and relatively guilt-free flesh, in the eyes of some Japanese Buddhists. But meat was soon added to the mix: in military barracks, in restaurants and later in ordinary homes where fastidious families covered the household shrine or altar with paper while cooking, out of respect for godly nostrils. One of the most popular new dishes was *sukiyaki*: thinly sliced beef cooked with onions and tofu in a blend of soy sauce and sugar, then served with a beaten raw egg. For soldiers on the battlefield and civilians on the go, there was *yamatoni*: tinned beef prepared with ginger and soy sauce.

Chefs returning from studies abroad added to this expanding menu, creating dishes with international inflections that soon became 'Japanese' standards: curry rice, potato croquettes, omelettes, beef steak and fried prawns. The ever-present modernizing theme of adoption and adaptation was extended to Worcestershire sauce, produced in Japan using soy sauce as the base.

Chefs became an early target market for Ajinomoto, but Suzuki found them surprisingly hostile. Great taste was a matter of craft and graft, they told him, not of tipping some powder into a pan. Fortunately, Meiji-era family values, carrying over into Taishō, helped to save the day. Despite Tsuda Umeko's best efforts, the vast majority of young women were still brought up – at home, in schools and as readers of newspapers and magazines – to regard nutrition as a national security issue, and as one of their many responsibilities in life.

Ajinomoto ticked, or claimed to tick, this nutrition box, alongside several others. The product bore the imprimatur of cutting-edge science, cooked up at no less an institution than Tokyo Imperial University – 'Invented by Doctor of Science Ikeda Kikunae', as early adverts put it. And because Ajinomoto could accomplish in a second what would otherwise require long periods spent boiling *konbu*, it fulfilled the requirements of practicality and convenience too – earning itself a place in the pages of home economics textbooks.

One of the greatest challenges for Ajinomoto's marketers was the speed at which urban life was changing. By 1923, Tokyo's population had doubled in a single generation, from 2 million to 4 million inhabitants. Central parts of the city were now dense and noisy with shops, trams, cars, telegraph and electric cabling and all the trappings of consumer culture, including sandwich-board men (one of whom was Suzuki himself, in the early days of promoting Ajinomoto), fashion models and advertising balloons. Tokyo's outer edges, meanwhile, seemed constantly to be on the move, as an expanding network of intra-city railway lines brought department stores and new neighbourhoods in their wake. The iconic Yamanote Line, a full city loop, was completed in 1925.

Japan's cities were also home to countless theatres, cinemas, jazz clubs and dance halls. They helped to bring Western pop culture to the masses, giving rise, in turn, to a notable new presence out on the streets: *modan gāru* ('modern girl') and *modan boi* ('modern boy'). The former were regarded as particularly outrageous. They cut their hair short, smoked in public, dressed like stars of stage and screen and generally epitomized what more conservative Japanese − their indignation stoked by a scandal-hungry media − viewed as the degeneration of Meiji-era nation-centredness into a Taishō-era preoccupation with the self. Indulgent poetizing and philosophizing were key symptoms of this particular malaise, alongside the careless pursuit of pleasure.

While some wrote letters to the newspapers, harrumphing about how Japan was losing its way, others looked to the arts for an outlet. The fiction of Edogawa Ranpo, who took his name from Edgar Allan Poe, was full of nefarious characters and deeds shaped by seedy and anonymous cities − theft, murder, even the corruption of science by a man who killed his unfaithful wife and then found a way to preserve her body as a mannequin in his shop window. Film was similarly adept at stoking anxiety and then providing catharsis. Alongside American and French fare, cinema-goers enjoyed *kaiki eiga*, 'strange films', which brought old ghost stories up to date through special effects, and scripts that played on the latest popular fears.

Culture was no less of a concern for Japan's 'shepherds of the people' than activism and industrial relations. Just because a person wasn't espousing Marx or out on a march, that didn't mean that they weren't harbouring corrosive opinions or at risk of picking them up. Films and music were carefully censored for political and sexual suggestiveness. And when Asia's first radio transmissions went out in 1925 across Tokyo, Osaka and Nagoya, they were accompanied by strict regulations for Japan's new national broadcaster,

NHK (Nippon Hōsō Kyōkai): no politics, no excitable voices or turns of phrase, and circuit breakers to bring a broadcast to an immediate halt in case of an infraction.

There was a difference, of course, between making rules and shaping tastes. Where the latter was concerned, real power lay with Japan's commercial and creative industries. Official attempts to ban the shamisen and the koto as vulgar and outmoded lost out to the country's film directors and music producers, who understood the evocative power of these instruments. Heard for centuries in shrines, tea-houses and private homes, musicians were now being corralled into recording booths where technicians tried to explain '78 rpm', and why it meant that they had to stop playing after three and a half minutes.

This was a formative decade for music in Japan, as record companies moved from releasing recordings of well-known songs to taking the creative initiative themselves, putting together their own stables of writers, singers, backing bands and promoters. Alongside recordings in a traditional Japanese vein, these companies dabbled in a range of styles befitting Japan's cosmopolitan 1920s: French chanson, Cuban rumba, Hawaiian hula and, most of all, American jazz. Gramophone records aside, residents of cities like Tokyo and Osaka could enjoy much of this music live, in cinemas, department stores, concert venues and dance halls. The last were frequently targeted by newspaper critics and the police, on the grounds that men and women jumping around and getting sweaty in one another's arms was not conducive to sound public morality.

Ajinomoto became a prime example of the power of commerce and culture to influence people's preferences in this era. Its marketers attuned themselves to what they recognized was a new emphasis, amongst housewives in the 1910s and 1920s, on cosmopolitanism and 'cultured living'. They pitched their product – which at 50 sen for the larger-sized bottle in 1912 was not especially cheap – as a luxury, high-culture item, selling it in a slim glass container roughly the size and shape of a perfume bottle. For their logo they chose a smartly dressed woman with a white apron and Western-style pompadour hair.

At the same time, they hired well-known media commentators on

nutrition and household management to write newspaper and magazine columns extolling Ikeda's creation. In 1922, they went as far as
obtaining details for all girls graduating from higher schools – a small
number still, but reliably middle-class. Each girl received her own
free bottle of Ajinomoto, along with a cookbook. The scheme proved
so successful that it was repeated every year, all the way until 1937.

*

Ikeda Kikunae did more, after 1909, than sit back and watch the
money roll in. He continued his research, working with others to
tease out a range of glutamate-containing foods, including asparagus, soybeans, Parmesan cheese, prawns, sardines, ripe tomatoes
and breast milk. And he helped to move Japan's scientific establishment into a new phase, away from state funding and the import of
foreign findings and towards privately sponsored innovation in partnership with industries like shipbuilding and electronics. In 1917 he
became, alongside the seemingly ever-present Shibusawa, one of the
founding members of the Institute of Physical and Chemical Research,
known by an abbreviation of its Japanese name: RIKEN. 'If you only
ever learn by absorbing from others,' Ikeda declared, 'you will stop
actively thinking about things.'

With patent filings and conference appearances in Europe and the
United States, Ikeda also became part of Japanese efforts to promote
international scientific and industrial collaboration. One of the pioneers here was Noguchi Hideyo, who had moved to the US at the
turn of the century. There he had picked up English and advanced
bacteriology alongside one another, once marking an experiment
with the warning words 'No-touchi, No-guchi'. He became known
amongst his American colleagues for an unruly head of hair, great
technical skill with a microscope and a punishing work ethic, pulling
all-nighters with the help of cigars, tea and whiskey. Studying at New
York's Rockefeller Institute for Medical Research with his mentor
Simon Flexner, Noguchi often had his name in the newspapers for
discoveries relating to the causes of rabies and syphilis, and also for
his and Flexner's controversial use of sick adults and healthy children
in their experiments. Noguchi ended an intrepid international career

in West Africa, studying yellow fever and succumbing to the disease himself in 1928.

Ikeda's own big break in the United States came around the time of Noguchi's death. For a while, Ajinomoto's prospects there had looked bleak, with American housewives more resistant to its charms than their Japanese counterparts. But canned food companies, including Heinz and Campbell's Soup, now discovered Ajinomoto, as just the sort of economical flavour-enhancer that they had been seeking. They began to place enormous orders, in some cases for 100 tons or more.

Ajinomoto was doing well closer to home, too. Restaurants in the Japanese colony of Taiwan were using it, and its marketers were now reaching out to a wider public: putting up signs on lamp-posts and sending sachets of the product to primary schools, along with quizzes to give the initiative an educational gloss. Street vendors supplied free advertising, displaying their cans of Ajinomoto to customers, perhaps as reassurance that they were using quality, branded ingredients in their food.

China was more of a challenge. Ikeda's invention faced two serious problems there: cheaper imitations and a mounting dislike of the Japanese. Shanghai's upmarket internationalism helped sales, to a degree. But billboard advertisements and retail outlets were met with protests, while the marketing blurb for a Chinese product called 'Buddha's Hand' left little room for misunderstanding:

> The national taste essence! An entirely domestic product! Not the same as the import! Better than Ajinomoto!

Sino-Japanese relations had been lukewarm at best since the war of 1894–5, fuelled on the Japanese side by nearly 2 million yen's worth of canned *yamatoni* beef. Ten years later, the Liaotung Peninsula and the South Manchurian railway network had been ceded to Japan in the wake of the Russo-Japanese War. Matters were made worse in 1915, when Japan took advantage of the upheaval of the First World War to issue China – reborn as a republic in 1911 and mired in political chaos – with its infamous 'Twenty-One Demands'. These included acquiescence to Japan's temporary management of former German possessions in Shandong, a lengthy extension on the lease of the

South Manchurian railway and its associated land corridors, agreement to an expansion of Japanese interests in Manchuria, and the hiring of Japanese 'advisers' to help manage China's finances and police force. Retired leaders of the 1868 generation, referred to now as *genrō*, 'elder statesmen', regarded this last demand as especially reckless and intervened to have it taken off the table. When the Chinese government found itself with few options but to accept the revised proposal, student activists declared a 'National Humiliation Day'.

Ajinomoto did badly too in Korea, where on 1 March 1919 students staged an anti-colonial protest during which a declaration of independence from Japan was read out, referencing Wilsonian self-determination. Protests spread from there and continued on for months, involving more than a million Koreans and resulting in a level of violence on the part of the Japanese authorities that helped to poison Japanese–Korean relations for the long term. Seven thousand Koreans were killed, and tens of thousands wounded. The influential political theorist Yoshino Sakuzō called it a 'great stain on the history of the Taishō period'.

A fresh blemish appeared four years later. On 1 September 1923, a great earthquake and associated fires killed around 100,000 people in the Tokyo region and destroyed more than half the city's homes. It said much about the feelings towards Korea of some Japanese – a consequence of violence on the peninsula and the perception that Korean migrants to Japan were undermining Japanese workers – that rumours quickly spread of Korean residents in Tokyo using the upheaval to launch an uprising. Police and army officers, some with experience of service four years previously on the Korean peninsula, stood aside as around 6,000 Koreans were murdered. Many others survived only because fellow Tokyoites took them into their homes, out of harm's way.

Here was the vexed undercurrent to Japanese attempts at internationalism in the Taishō era: deep uncertainty, carried over from the Meiji era, about Japan's relationships with the West and about its place in Asia. American and European culture, commerce and cuisine were helping to give cities like Tokyo an increasingly cosmopolitan feel. But they had their critics, who linked them with declining moral standards, an increase in selfishness, a failure to assert Japan's rights on the international stage and a disregard for traditional Japanese culture and norms of behaviour.

When it came to Asia, opinion had long been split between avoiding the contagion of a declining region and seeking – in the spirit of Pan-Asianism – to treat its ills by exporting the Japanese model of modernization. A powerful racial dynamic was at play on both sides of the debate, contributing to violence against Koreans and attempts to 'reform' the culture and habits of peoples at both ends of the Japanese archipelago: the Ainu and Ryūkyūans of what were now Hokkaidō and Okinawa prefectures, respectively.

While arguments continued in Japan over its international relations, Western concerns about Japan began to mount. The Twenty-One Demands had worried the United States and Britain, raising as they did the prospect of Japan seeking a protectorate in China, thus damaging Western trading and political influence in mainland Asia. Outright criticism of Japanese imperialism risked the obvious charge of hypocrisy, with so much of Asia under Western colonial control – India, Burma, Singapore, Indochina, Hong Kong and the Philippines. Instead, the 1920s saw attempts to moderate Japanese influence. The Washington Naval Conference of 1921 agreed that Britain, the United States and Japan would maintain a tonnage ratio of 5:5:3, respectively, across major parts of their fleets.

Claims by Japanese critics of this deal that a westernized global order would never truly make room for an Asian upstart were given potency by the persistence into the era of Wilsonian idealism not just of Western empire but of the racism that so often attended it. Japanese diplomats at Versailles in 1919 had been refused their request for a statement on racial equality. Meanwhile, Japanese travellers to the United States had become used to casual racism of all kinds. Noguchi Hideyo was lovingly nicknamed 'the yellow peril' by one of his colleagues, while anti-vivisection campaigners thought him a harmless copy-cat 'Oriental', insufficiently original in his thinking to share the guilt of his American colleagues in their research methods. The earthquake of 1923 was met with $12 million in fundraising by the American Red Cross. But the next year brought the Immigration Act, under whose auspices no one who was ineligible for American citizenship – a category into which all Japanese had recently been placed by the Supreme Court – was allowed to enter the country as an immigrant.

Against this backdrop, liberal internationalists like Shidehara Kijūrō, who served as Foreign Minister across much of the 1920s, were denounced by some in Japan as the useful idiots of a cynical and self-interested West. There seemed to be little that Western countries could propose, in international negotiations, to which such men would not readily agree. Opinions hardened as Japan's economy suffered a series of shocks during this decade, culminating in the Wall Street Crash of 1929. The likes of Britain could fall back on their empires during tough times – why, argued Japan's hawks, should our country not set itself up to do the same?

*

Retiring from Tokyo Imperial University in 1923, Ikeda left Japan in 1925 for a late-life stint as a *ryūgakusei* back in Leipzig. He stayed, this time, for six years. While he was away, the Taishō Emperor died and was succeeded by his son Hirohito. The new era, beginning in 1926, was proclaimed as Shōwa, or 'Enlightened Peace'. And for people of means in Japan it lived up to its billing, at least initially. The liberal cosmopolitanism of the Taishō years carried over, and Ajinomoto reached its commercial peak. By the end of the 1920s, the company was manufacturing around a thousand tons of its product every year. Even some chefs were at last brought on board, now that people enjoying Ajinomoto at home found restaurant fare a little tame without it.

Ikeda's invention reached another milestone in 1931 when its application became a matter not just for the housewives preparing the dish but for family members consuming it: a shaker-bottle was produced for use at the dining table. Returning to Japan that year to live out the rest of his life at home, Ikeda found the rewards from his discovery continuing to flow in. But it would soon prove a great commercial blessing that Ajinomoto in the United States was hidden away in soup, behind reliable American branding, rather than out on dinner-table display. Mild hostility there towards the Japanese was turning into something stronger. Here, now, was a regional rival, not to be trusted; and powerful enough to warrant the first iterations, in the 1920s, of 'War Plan Orange': a strategy for war with Japan that centred on American naval bases in Hawaii, Guam and the Philippines.

Shibusawa once warned that a younger generation in Japan were at risk of forgetting all that their country owed to America, in building itself up after 1868. The forgetting of a debt, he said, was at variance with the *bushidō* ethic. He helped to establish a Japanese wire service in 1914, cooperating with Reuters in the hope that if Japanese and Americans received timely and accurate information about one another then relationships might improve. As the last leaders of 1868 passed away during the course of the 1920s, that younger generation found itself with unfettered access to the impressive levers of control that their forebears had established after Year One. They inherited, alongside, a series of unanswered questions about modern Japan's proper place in the world.

Some, especially in the military, now expected those questions to be answered in the manner they had first been asked back in 1853: in a confrontation with American ambition and power in the Pacific. One of those men was Lieutenant Colonel Ishiwara Kanji of the Kwantung Army. Like Ikeda, he had studied for a time in Germany, though in military affairs rather than chemistry. And, like Ikeda, he later established a presence of sorts on the tracks of the strategically important South Manchurian railway. Ikeda's was a modest matter: some of the trains trundling along those tracks bore adverts for his wonder-substance, Ajinomoto, on their sides. Ishiwara's was more dramatic: explosives, detonated on 18 September 1931, near a section of railway just outside Mukden, helping to launch Japan into long, disastrous years of war.

16
Yosano Akiko

(与謝野晶子)

1878–1942

Poet of Peace and War

Yosano Akiko, pictured at home in Tokyo in 1936.

Events moved rapidly after Ishiwara Kanji's explosives went off outside Mukden. Ministers back in Tokyo, correctly suspecting elements in the Kwantung Army of planting the devices, warned against widening the conflict beyond the skirmishes with Chinese troops that Ishiwara had succeeded in provoking. From the commander of the Kwantung Army, however, came permission to do just that. The cities of Mukden and Changchun fell to Japanese forces within days, followed throughout the autumn of 1931 and into 1932 by key targets across Manchuria.

As the government reluctantly granted retrospective approval for each new military action – the only way to maintain the illusion of control – crowds began cramming into public halls and parks around Japan to cheer newsreels of their soldiers 'fighting back' after what they were told had been Chinese attacks. Newspapers vied with one another and with NHK radio to break the latest news and stir the patriotic pot, while restaurants offered celebratory Manchurian menus and record companies rushed out songs with names like 'Manchurian Maiden, My Manchurian Lover'. Films appeared in a similar vein, including *Love in the Frozen Plain* (*Tōgen ni fuku ai*) – shot on location in newly occupied territory.

A modern mass culture built on leisure, consumption and westernized schmaltz was shifting into a nationalistic high gear, its producers supplying what they thought people now wanted. Few in Japan hungered for war, or could yet know where the 1930s would take them. But such were the dwindling reputations by this point of civilian politics, diplomacy and big business that the armed forces could claim with increasing public credibility to be one of the few remaining institutions truly to embody cherished 'Japanese' values of selflessness, cooperation and exertion in the national interest. Influential, too, in generating broad public support for Japanese forces was the backing of celebrity intellectuals. A surprise addition to their ranks, from the early 1930s, was the widely respected poet Yosano Akiko.

The quintessential Taishō liberal, Yosano made her name creating poetry for a generation of young women who aspired to more than the sorts of marriages memorably described by Hiratsuka Raichō as slavery during the daytime and prostitution at night. Yosano saw herself as a cosmopolitan citizen of the world; a 'human being,' she often said, neither rejecting nor tightly bound to any one identity, whether housewife or imperial subject. But then her outlook and her poetry appeared to change radically, the latter becoming clichéd and cloyingly nationalistic. Readers were dismayed, biographers stumped.

Yosano did not suddenly turn from poet of peace to poet of war, any more than ordinary Japanese who felt enthusiastic about the possibilities of resource-rich Manchuria were transformed overnight into ravenous imperialists. For decades, a culture of misgiving had been building up in Japan about the impact of its modern interactions with the West on family relationships, the quality of politics and the tone of public life. By the early 1930s, hawks in government and the military found much here that they could play to their benefit.

It would suit later generations to imagine the story of 1930s' Japan as one of militarism gone mad, grinding a helpless civilian population under its tank tracks. Yosano Akiko's life hints at a more uncomfortable truth: that under the pressures of recent history, and seeing few other options, large numbers of Japanese chose to place their trust – partially and with mixed feelings – in the country's armed forces and in the salvific mission that military leaders claimed for themselves both on the Asian mainland and at home in Japan.

*

Yosano Akiko was born Ōtori Shō on 7 December 1878 in the city of Sakai, not far from Osaka. One of her earliest memories was of spilling a bowl of rice at the age of three. Her merchant father Sōshichi had helped her to clear it up – though not out of any particular affection for her: like Tsuda Umeko's father, he had wanted a son and had left home for a week upon discovering that his new baby was a girl.

Rather, he was terrified of his wife Tsune. So too was Akiko, whose 'dread' of her mother's coldness and neuroticism contributed to a sense – despite having two brothers and a sister – of deep loneliness as a child, sometimes darkening into an obsessive fear of death.

The saving grace of Akiko's childhood was literature. Her father was a bibliophile, a modernizer, a scientific materialist and a history-lover, who used to refer to great figures from the Japanese past as though they were acquaintances of his: 'Hideyoshi-san', 'Ieyasu-san'. He was also a part-time poet. Disappointed though he was by Akiko's sex, he encouraged her reading, pleased to see her finish her chores in the family sweet shop and go immediately to curl up with a book.

Sōshichi's encouragement stopped short of sending Akiko to university, still a rare privilege for women at this time. Instead, like Murasaki Shikibu centuries before, Akiko watched as her elder brother Shūtarō received a level of education – at Tokyo Imperial University – which she knew she was worthy of herself. Her younger brother Chūsaburō followed suit a little while later, studying at Waseda.

Left to feast alone on whatever she could find, at home and in the local library, Akiko read the *Chronicles of Japan* and the *Record of Ancient Matters*, imperial poetry anthologies and historical epics, Heian-era diaries and the work of Tokugawa luminaries like the playwright Chikamatsu Monzaemon and the haiku poet Matsuo Bashō. Closest to Akiko's heart was *The Tale of Genji* and its author. 'Murasaki has been my teacher', she once wrote, 'since I was nine or ten . . . I felt as though I heard this great female writer tell me *The Tale of Genji* with her own lips.'

Akiko published her first poem at the age of sixteen. She later recalled being motivated in part by shock at the terrible poetry that other women were producing – so bad, she feared, that it risked damaging their prospects of equality with men. Writing brought Akiko into contact, in 1900, with her future husband Yosano Tekkan. Hailing from a line of Jōdo Shinshū Buddhist priests, he had rejected religion in favour of helping to take traditional Japanese *waka* poetry – the five-line form used in the old imperial anthologies, often referred to in Akiko's time as *tanka* – in a modern direction: via his own poetry, and through a New Poetry Society that he helped to establish, its members counting Byron and Goethe amongst their heroes and guiding lights.

Akiko found Tekkan smart and attractive – but also married, to a woman called Hayashi Takino, with a baby on the way. The two nevertheless launched themselves upon the sort of flirtatious exchange of poetry that Murasaki would have understood well, if perhaps not condoned, wary as she was of predatory men posing as sensitive souls. In November 1900, the pair travelled to Kyoto to view the autumn maple leaves, in the company of a mutual friend and fellow member of the New Poetry Society, Yamakawa Tomiko.

It was an emotional few days. Tekkan wasn't certain that he wanted to end the relationship with his wife. Akiko was fairly sure what she wanted. Tomiko, unfortunately, was after the same thing. The three stayed together at an inn, with only a wood-and-paper partition separating the two women in one room from Tekkan in the other. Such sleeping arrangements cried out for poetry, and Akiko obliged, referring to Tekkan by the name of one of his favourite flowers:

> From one room over
> now and then your breathing found
> its way and that night in a dream
> my arms embraced the flowering
> white plum.

Tomiko offered her own contributions, one in particular making painfully clear her place, by the end of the trip, in this literary love triangle:

> Casually I left
> to my friend all the crimson
> flowers, turned my
> back and weeping plucked
> the grasses of forgetting.

Kyoto made a couple of Akiko and Tekkan, but Tekkan kept putting off the moment of truth with his wife. Takino was the mother of his child, and a key supporter of the New Poetry Society's magazine, helping to run and fund it. She probably didn't enjoy the March 1901 issue very much, crammed as it was with romantic verse passing between her husband and his new lover. Akiko, for her part, was neither immune to jealousy nor willing to be kept waiting by Tekkan. From her home base in Sakai, she peppered him with poetry:

> Aren't you nice, Genji and Narihira,
> promising to share the same lotus with them all in the world to come!
> But let me ask you –
> how many people can one lotus hold?

At last, in the summer of 1901, Tekkan's wife left him and Akiko moved into his home in the village of Shibuya, linked by rail with nearby Tokyo and shortly to be swallowed up by it. Neighbours were kind enough to tell Akiko how amazing Takino had been, and how she couldn't hope to compare. But Akiko was undeterred. She married Tekkan in October, making her name as a poet the same year with *Midaregami* (*Tangled Hair*). It was a compilation of 399 poems, whose *tanka* form was deeply traditional but whose content – full of the sensuousness and passion of young womanhood – was anything but:

> In my bath –
> Submerged like some graceful lily
> At the bottom of a spring,
> How beautiful
> This body of twenty summers.

> To punish
> Men for their endless sins,
> God gave me
> This fair skin,
> This long black hair.

> She calls out
> To awaken the tender young priest:
> A window in spring.
> Touched by a long trailing sleeve
> The sutras topple.

Reviewers were divided over Akiko's debut. Her mention of breasts in one poem was denounced as the kind of thing you might hear 'from the mouth of a whore'. Another critic found the whole collection tiresome and self-indulgent: the 'precocious prattle of a young girl'. Worse was said, and Akiko's house was stoned. Younger Japanese, on the other hand, found *Midaregami* marvellously refreshing, catapulting its author to a level of fame that quickly outstripped her husband's.

Akiko found new fans and made new enemies a few years later during the Russo-Japanese War, when she published in the New Poetry Society's magazine a poem entitled 'Thou Shalt Not Die' ('*Kimi shinitamō koto nakare*'). It took the form of a letter to her little brother Chūsaburō, whom Akiko feared might sign up for a suicide mission with the military at Port Arthur:

> Oh, my brother, I weep for you.
> Do not give your life.
> Last-born among us,
> You are the most beloved of our parents.
> Did they make you grasp the sword
> And teach you to kill?
> Did they raise you to the age of twenty-four,
> Telling you to kill and die?
>
> Heir to our family name,
> You will be master of this store, old and honored, in Sakai.
> Brother, do not give your life.
> For you, what does it matter
> Whether Port Arthur fortress falls or not?
> The code of merchant houses
> Says nothing about this.
>
> Brother, do not give your life.
> His Majesty the Emperor
> Goes not himself into the battle.
> Could he, with such deeply noble heart,
> Think it an honor for men
> To spill one another's blood
> And die like beasts?

Supporters of the war were incensed by what appeared to be a toxic combination of defeatism, pacifism and disrespect for the monarchy.

Anti-war socialists, too, expressed distaste at the incorrigibly bourgeois mentality revealed in the poet's narrow concern for her own
family. 'Thou Shalt Not Die' became an anti-war anthem, nonetheless, and busy years followed for Akiko: collaborations with other
leading feminists, including Hiratsuka Raichō; travel to Europe with
Tekkan; fresh poetry and prose; a translation into modern Japanese of
The Tale of Genji; and the upbringing of eleven children.

This broad array of achievements made it easier for Akiko to argue
against any attempt, by society or the state, to define her proper
role in life. Despite struggling financially, she objected strongly to
the idea, advocated by Hiratsuka and others, that the government
should step in to offer economic support to mothers, as curators of
a precious national resource. The state, Akiko argued, had done
quite enough already in attempting to shape womanhood in Japan.
It should step back.

Childhood too, Akiko thought, needed to be liberated from the state's
narrowly utilitarian outlook. To that end, she co-founded a new school
in 1921: the Bunkagakuin in Tokyo. Its mission was to promote 'a cultured human life' by helping girls and boys to be 'their own masters'
rather than 'slaves to money and employment'. Music, dance, crafts
and painting were worked into a curriculum to which Akiko herself
contributed by teaching creative writing and Japanese literature.
She produced a new literature textbook, having found the existing
ones too intent upon 'making students useful to the state'. The Tale
of Genji was, of course, front and centre. One student of Akiko's later
recalled the mysterious power of their teacher's soft, Osaka-accented
recitations, transforming a difficult and culturally distant text into
something so natural and intimate that it was as though Yosano-sensei
were 'breathing the air of the Genji' into the classroom.

*

The broadening of Yosano Akiko's concern for her compatriots to
encompass their international predicament was inspired by a forty-
day tour through Japanese-controlled areas of Manchuria that she
and her husband undertook in the summer of 1928 at the invitation
and expense of Japan's largest corporation, the South Manchuria

Railway Company (SMR). Since Gotō Shinpei's appointment as the first company president in 1906, the railway and its associated land corridors had become the site of economic experiments of all kinds: mining and freight services, harbours and hotels, iron and steel works, together with new forms of agriculture. A grand social experiment ran alongside. New communities were created of Japanese settlers, protected by the Kwantung Army and provided with their own shops, schools and hospitals. The SMR saw itself as turning Manchuria into a frontier for Japan's civilizing influence in Asia, and it sought celebrities like Yosano to help spread that message back home.

And yet, so old and intimate were Japan's links to the mainland that a visit there inevitably prompted broader and more mixed reflections. Some of the first to journey to China in the years immediately after the 1868 Meiji Restoration found much to enjoy. Here, in its full and glorious reality, was the landscape of mountains and plains, forests and waterfalls, which Chinese art and literature had helped to embed in the Japanese imagination. Travellers savoured, at the same time, signs of a dramatic swing of history's pendulum since the 1850s. China was clearly now, in the words of one, the 'sick old man' to Japan's 'lively youth'.

By the time that well-known writers began to visit Manchuria, with encouragement from the SMR, curiosity was tinged with ambivalence. The novelist Natsume Sōseki toured parts of Manchuria and Korea in 1909 as a correspondent for the *Asahi* newspaper. He wrote warmly, in private correspondence, of the 'vigour' of the ex-pat Japanese. But he worried about the shallow roots of seemingly purposeful activity. There had been a hurriedness and a superficiality, he thought, to Japan's quest for the Western-style 'civilization and enlightenment' that it was seeking now to export to the continent. The result was a spiritual homelessness amongst Japanese, suffered in his 1914 novel *The Heart of Things* (*Kokoro*) by a small group of university friends whose relationships are tragically undermined by confusions over old and new values. In a lecture given at a school around the same time, Sōseki set out a prescient warning about where social and psychological dislocation might lead people – into a narcissistic individualism or a slavish communitarianism. 'What a horror', he declared, 'if we have to eat for the nation, wash our faces for the nation, go to the toilet for the nation!'

Later generations of writers found that a short trip to a place like Shanghai, Asia's second-largest city after Tokyo, brought into sharp relief the potential peril to Japan presented by the darker sides of Western modernity. The 'Paris of the East' boasted a cosmopolitan high life of nightclubs, casinos, dance halls, cabarets and upscale restaurants. But it was famous as well for violence, debauchery and a certain sort of hopelessness, with an estimated one in every thirty residents making their living from sex work.

Visiting in 1921, the short-story writer Akutagawa Ryūnosuke was disturbed to find much of what he had grown up knowing and loving about China through its literature tarnished now by a combination of colonialism, consumerism and mass culture. On the evidence of Shanghai at least, when China and the modern West came together, these two great cultures seemed not so much to complement as to cancel one another out. Authenticity, refinement and charm ended up in desperately short supply. For Akutagawa, a glance at the famed Pavilion of the Lake said it all: a 'decrepit tea-house', set in water turned 'sickly green' by algae. He looked on as a Chinese man languidly relieved himself into it – 'a bitter symbol', he concluded, of what had become of a 'grand old country'.

Akutagawa's contemporary Tanizaki Junichirō travelled to China in 1918 and again in 1926. He seemed to have more fun than Akutagawa, enjoying 'magical' food and developing a monstrous hangover after partying in Shanghai with China's literati, many of whom knew and admired his work. But while Beijing retained something of its traditional identity, Shanghai bothered him in a similar way to Akutagawa. Its mix of cultures had the effect of rendering life not richer but somehow more prosaic. Here was a window, perhaps, into Japan's near future.

In 1927, Akutagawa's short story 'Spinning Gears' ('*Haguruma*') revealed his deep despair at the soullessness and fakery of urban culture in Japan. He took his own life later that year, at the age of just thirty-five. Tanizaki found refuge in Japan's old capital Kyoto, from where he set about exploring his country's cultural heritage. He later argued in an essay entitled 'In Praise of Shadows' ('*In'ei Raisan*') that Japanese people live in the world – ideally at least – as though in a room illuminated by candlelight, experiencing life as a subtle and affecting play of movement. Modern Western existences, by contrast, are marred by a bland this-or-that literalism – the room is lit by an electric light, which is either on or off. In common with Akutagawa, Tanizaki found much in Western culture to respect and enjoy, but feared that its more corrosive elements were proving to be the ones most influential in shaping Japanese life.

For Yosano Akiko too, a trip to the mainland prompted uncomfortable thoughts. She was deeply moved, early on in her travels, by the vast natural beauty of the mountainous Qianshan region and by what she referred to in her later account – *Travelogue of Manchuria and Mongolia (Man-Mō Yūki)* – as the 'utter solemnity' of Buddhist worship there. The chanting amidst candles, incense, bells and gongs contrasted sharply with the drily 'formulaic' sutra recitations that she associated with contemporary Japanese priests. Having succumbed, at home, to modernity's disenchantment of the world, the Japanese now risked becoming its carriers on the continent. The Japanese-controlled city of Liaoyang still boasted its fabled elms, willows and White Pagoda, in whose ancient upper storey she watched swallows making a nest. But 'the sight close by of new Japanese and Western buildings struck a sharply discordant note'.

Civilizing and spoiling might be tough to tease apart, but the former was, for Yosano, no empty piety. She was impressed by the schools she visited, built and run for locals and ex-pats alike. She toured a new prison too, encountering heated cells, clean straw matting, neatly folded bedding and inmates sitting placidly, lotus-legged, in smart blue uniforms. And yet, in one of those incongruous new Liaoyang buildings, Yosano also found Japanese troops moving around excitedly, 'as though a war was commencing . . . imperialism and the smell of liquor rippled through'. Not everyone appreciated the SMR's presence. Sino-Japanese tensions were so high by 1928 that Beijing had to be removed from Yosano's itinerary for the sake of her security. In Manchuria, she travelled – by rail, horse-drawn carriage and palanquin – mostly in the company of ex-pat Japanese, finding the Japanese military guards on trains especially comforting.

The city of Mukden seemed especially unsettled. Yosano witnessed a 'menacing spectacle' at the railway station: 'officers with squared shoulders coming and going with Japanese swords . . . the glint of agitated eyes'. She returned later in her trip, writing away in her room at the Yamato Hotel on the morning of 4 June when she heard a 'faint, strange noise' in the distance. The Kwantung Army had done its best to help the SMR weather the mainland's tempestuous polit- ics, after the overthrow of China's imperial dynasty in 1911 and the rapid degeneration of its republican experiment into a tangle of com- peting regional warlords. It had built and maintained a pragmatic security alliance with the dominant warlord in Manchuria, Zhang Zuolin. But elements in the army had decided that that relationship was more trouble than it was worth. Yosano had just heard Zhang die, his railway carriage blown up as it passed through.

Mukden was suddenly 'gripped with fear, the threat of danger, and chaos'. Yosano's 'heart ran cold' as she watched Japanese forces set- ting up artillery positions and camouflaging train carriages as trees. The director of the local railway office told her that Chinese residents could now be overheard saying 'alarming, frightening things about us Japanese'. His own office had been daubed with threatening graffiti, which was then hurriedly cleaned away.

Yosano seems to have been unsure quite what to make of these developments. Congratulating, 'in the name of humanity', the aspir- ational nationalism of young Chinese, she hoped that Chinese leaders would manage those sentiments with 'discretion' rather than chan- nelling them into an unwarranted hatred of the Japanese. Worrying that one day soon 'Japan will end up isolated from the world', she seemed to imply that such a fate would not be entirely of her country- men's own making.

*

Just a few months after Yosano Akiko left Manchuria, Lieutenant Colonel Ishiwara Kanji arrived, having arranged for himself a trans- fer to the Kwantung Army. Where the misgivings of writers like Akutagawa, Tanizaki and Yosano focused mostly on what was hap- pening to their country's culture and its people's sensibilities, Ishiwara was more concerned with Japan's strategic weakness. By late 1928, warlordism in China was ebbing away as Chiang Kai-shek's Nation- alist troops completed a unifying push northwards. Chiang now posed a threat to Japan's interests in Manchuria just as the Soviets were building up their own forces in the area.

Two years later, the London Naval Treaty was agreed, updating the Washington Naval Treaty of nearly a decade before. Its terms were so damaging to Japan, relative to Great Britain and the United States, that fights broke out in the Diet when it was debated. The United States, meanwhile, was fortifying its position in the Pacific. Inspired by Nichiren, a leading light of Buddhist reform back in the Kamakura era, Ishiwara read these events as harbingers of a 'titanic world conflict'. Japan and the United States would at last do battle, ushering in an age of everlasting peace.

A sense of impending crisis abroad was sharpened by economic hardship at home as the Wall Street Crash and subsequent worldwide Depression caused Japanese exports to fall by a half between 1929 and 1931. A million city-dwellers lost their jobs, while farmers saw rice prices tumble. Thousands of starving families were forced into desperate measures, from stripping the bark off trees in search of edible insects to selling their daughters into prostitution. Rural distress was all the more serious because the Imperial Japanese Army recruited overwhelmingly from the countryside. Since the death in 1922 of its founding father Yamagata Aritomo, a younger generation of leaders had been vying for control of this important institution. An Imperial Way faction (Kōdōha) had emerged, energized by an almost millenarian emphasis on what the 'Japanese spirit' could accomplish, combined with a conviction that pusillanimous politicians were impoverishing rural Japanese while endangering the country's security abroad.

It was against this backdrop of broad-based and rising discontent that on 18 September 1931 Ishiwara and his co-conspirators put their plan for a full takeover of Manchuria into action. Shortly after the bombs went off outside Mukden, Japanese forces launched an assault on a nearby Chinese base. The conflict widened from there, until on 1 March 1932 a new state was declared: Manchukuo. For centuries, the Japanese had regarded Chinese emperors with awe. Now, the very last in that long and illustrious line found himself the puppet of Japanese power: Puyi, the final Emperor of the Qing dynasty, served as the nominal ruler of Manchukuo, doing the bidding of the Kwantung Army. Conquest of the region was completed in 1933, fulfilling

Ishiwara's aim of securing its fertile lands and raw materials for Japan's upcoming war – while denying them to the Chinese and the Soviets.

People at home in Japan began to talk about Manchuria as a 'lifeline'. While Western countries fell back on their colonies for support in weathering the Depression, Japanese newspapers and magazines extolled Manchuria as a 'bottomless treasure house'. It was a 'new paradise', whose 'inexhaustible resources' of sheep, cattle, sorghum and wheat would be husbanded by communities of continental Japanese, making peaceful and legitimate lives there while advancing the prospects of their Chinese brethren. The Japanese population of Manchuria stood at a quarter of a million in 1931. The dream was for millions more to join them.

The usefulness of pastoral Pan-Asian fantasies to the likes of Ishiwara lay in their potential as a pretext for armed intervention on the mainland. That logic was tested in January 1932 in Shanghai, whose Hongkou district was known as 'Little Tokyo' for its thousands of Japanese residents. Army plotters sent five members of a militant Japanese Buddhist sect marching into a Chinese factory district in the city, chanting sutras, banging drums and taking the inevitable beating. Two of the five died, and the hoped-for conflict quickly broke out between Japanese forces and Chinese troops of the 19th Route Army. Thousands of Chinese soldiers and civilians ended up losing their lives, some in air raids carried out by Japanese planes on civilian neighbourhoods. Around 10,000 Chinese went missing, many of them later thought to have been dumped from Japanese vessels into the Yangtze River. More than a million Chinese were left homeless.

As news came in of the 'Shanghai Incident', Yosano published a poetic reflection that must have surprised fans of her earlier work:

> To the west of the river
> We see something in the trenches.
> Approaching, we find enemy corpses –
> Enemy corpses, lying one upon another.
>
> The saddest among them
> Are the 200 student soldiers.
> Youthful at 17 or 18,
> None have faces over 20.

How could their gentle mothers
Bear to see this?
Some even have pretty fiancées,
Chosen for them in the old Chinese custom . . .

Who is it that deceives them,
With their youthful naive hearts,
Teaching them to hate
Their good neighbor, Japan?

Who is it that entices them
To turn in their pens for swords,
And scatters their young lives to the winds
Before the plum flowers bloom in spring?

It is the foolish Ts'ai T'ing-k'ai,
Commander of the 19th Route Army.
He does not know that before the day is out
His regiments must fall.

To the west of the river
We see something in the trenches.
200 rosy-cheeked youths
Lie mired in blood and dirt.

'Rosy-Cheeked Death' ('*Kōgao no Shi*') was not entirely at odds
with the spirit of 1904's anti-war 'Thou Shalt Not Die'. Both poems
were more concerned with innocent victims and high human ideals –
friendship, nobility, neighbourliness – than with political nitty-gritty.
But much here was new, indebted to Yosano's travels on the mainland
and to her mixed feelings about Japan's presence there. Now, as then,
she concluded that the real corrupting force was dishonest Chinese
leadership: 'foolish' men, tarnishing a place of purity and tradition
with its 'gentle mothers', 'pretty fiancées' and 'old custom'. Her views
reflected a broader trend in the Japanese media at this point. Everywhere from children's magazines to highbrow periodicals one could
find the claim that Japan was extending a hand of friendship and support, only to have its generosity thrown back in its face.

A second new poem, in June 1932, showed Yosano's sense of anger and hurt morphing into righteous aggression. 'Citizens of Japan, A Morning Song' ('*Nihon Kokumin Asa no Uta*') included a celebration of the sacrifices made in Shanghai by three Japanese soldiers, who became famous back home thanks to a controversial incident that the army quickly claimed was a successful suicide attack:

Ah, the augustness of His Majesty's Reign
That inspires people's hearts!
It is a time that ignites our sense of duty.

It is a time to cease empty arguments,
And smash sissified dreams of compromise.
Knowing their course to be just,
Our forces attack through sufferings a hundredfold.

Though his is the body of one soldier,
Carrying the canister of destruction,
He dances through the barbed wire,
And transforms that body into powder.

Though his is the body of one major,
He expects no mercy from the enemy,
And scatters that body, purer than a flower,
Giving life to a samurai's honour.

And these men are not alone.
Patriotic heroes with hearts like theirs
Rise to the challenge wherever the Emperor's forces go,
To the north and to the south.

The 'three human bombs' of Shanghai became a popular sensation in the first half of 1932. Alongside a starring role in 'Citizens', they featured in plays, films and *gunka* (martial songs), the best known of which was composed by Yosano's husband Tekkan. 'Human bombs *sake*' was sold, along with 'human bombs candy'. An Osaka department store went as far as serving up a 'three human bombs special': butterbur for the three men, with radishes cut to resemble their canisters of explosives.

By the time attention shifted to the Los Angeles Summer Olympics in July, the days of enjoying militarism and ultranationalism as a spectator sport from the comfort of strife-free home islands were well and truly over. Violent radicals, some styling themselves on the *shishi* ('men of high purpose') of the late 1850s and early 1860s, resolved to rid the country of the greedy and ineffectual business and political classes whom they blamed for bringing it down. They called for a 'Shōwa Restoration' to make good the unfulfilled promise of the Meiji Restoration, giving the Emperor direct control and allowing the country to claim its rightful place in Asia.

The first shots in this domestic battle for Japan were fired in February 1932 – into the body of a former finance minister by an assassin belonging to a civilian ultranationalist organization called the Blood Brotherhood (Ketsumeidan). In March, other members of the same group murdered Dan Takuma, the managing director of the Mitsui *zaibatsu*, right outside his central Tokyo HQ. Big business was accused, by Japan's ultranationalists, of pulling the strings of corrupt and ineffectual political parties. Seiyūkai was backed financially by Mitsui. Minseitō (formerly Kenseikai, the progressive party) was supported by Mitsubishi. Worse, when Japan left the gold standard in 1931, as part of a package of reforms designed to tackle the country's economic misery, Mitsui and others had made huge sums of money speculating against the yen. Dan had, in effect, bet against Japan. And now he had paid the price.

The revolutionary violence stepped up a gear on 15 May 1932, with an attempted *coup d'état*. Prime Minister Inukai Tsuyoshi was assassinated at his official residence by a group of young naval officers. Co-conspirators took to the streets elsewhere in Tokyo, throwing hand grenades at the Bank of Japan, the Seiyūkai headquarters and the country's main police stations. Lest anyone miss the symbolism in this choice of targets, the attackers issued a statement identifying those responsible for undermining the 'godliness of the Imperial Country of Japan':

> Political parties are blind in their pursuit of power and egoistic gain. Large enterprises are firmly in collusion with politicians, as they suck the sweat and blood of the common people. Bureaucrats and police are busy defending the politico-industrial complex. Diplomacy is weak-kneed. Education is rotten to the core.

The coup failed, but the violence of 1932 succeeded in bringing Japan's era of party political Cabinets to an end, amidst claims that only governments of national unity could hope to tackle mounting domestic and foreign crises. The latter intensified considerably in February 1933 when, at a meeting of the League of Nations, Japan was censured for its actions in Manchuria. The Japanese delegation walked out, and in March an imperial edict took Japan out of the organization altogether. Japan's chief delegate to the League, Matsuoka Yōsuke, was every bit as in tune with the mood in his country as Yosano Akiko. He defended the innocence of Japan's cause, drawing a comparison with the crucifixion of Jesus Christ. (Matsuoka himself was a Christian, converting, as Tsuda Umeko had done, during a lengthy stay in the United States.) Jesus, Matsuoka declared, had eventually been understood. So, too – one day – Japan. In the meantime, as a newspaper cartoon showed a samurai using a sword of righteousness to sever himself free of the iron ball of the League, an isolated and resource-poor country looked more than ever to mainland Asia for its lifeline.

*

A few years of relative peace followed as Japan's economy recovered from the Depression. But a second coup attempt, on 26 February 1936, served as a reminder of powerful opposition to the domestic status quo in parts of the army and amongst their civilian supporters. More than a thousand rebel soldiers surrounded the Diet building that day, and were persuaded to return to barracks only when loyalist army units arrived, naval vessels in Tokyo Bay pointed their guns at them and the Emperor himself intervened to make known his displeasure.

Tensions on the mainland had meanwhile remained high, to the point where all it took was a brief exchange of fire in July 1937 between Japanese and Chinese Nationalist troops at the Marco Polo Bridge near Beijing to plunge the two countries into all-out conflict. Chiang Kai-shek was under pressure from his supporters and from his emerging Communist rivals to deal with the Japanese presence on the mainland once and for all. Japan's new Prime Minister, Konoe Fumimarō, was seeking a solution to raids being made into

Japanese-held Manchuria by Chinese peasants, Chiang Kai-shek's forces and Communist guerrillas. Neither man wanted war. Neither was able to avoid it.

Japanese units quickly overran Beijing, while a more protracted and costly battle for Shanghai was won in November. Veterans of the latter campaign began trekking west towards the Nationalist capital, Nanjing. Chiang and most of his government flew to safety, leaving Chinese troops to mount a brief defence before Japanese forces burst through in early December. Brutal army training, a demand for absolute obedience to superiors, field handbook instructions not to surrender or allow oneself to be captured, and finally a powerful belief not just in Chinese cultural backwardness of late but in their sub-humanity, all combined with weariness and fear in the ranks to produce one of modern history's most notorious episodes. Japanese troops went on a rampage, murdering tens of thousands of civilians. Some later estimates put the number of deaths at 200,000, even 300,000.

By the end of 1938, 850,000 Japanese troops had been committed to a conflict that seemed to have no end in sight, as Chiang Kai-shek led his forces ever further into south-west China. A flurry of laws were passed to give the Japanese government the economic control it needed to keep up the effort, extending by the end of 1939 to cover production in key industries, power generation, price and wage levels, and the allocation of capital and labour to parts of the economy where they were needed most.

Great efforts were made, too, for the 'spiritual mobilization' of the population. Japan's leaders drew heavily here on the culture of misgiving that had built up over past decades, transforming it into a national manifesto. A government booklet entitled *Kokutai no Hongi* ('Fundamentals of Our National Polity'), sent out to schools in 1937, blamed an escalating global crisis – from an Asian continent at war to a European one poised on the brink – on a selfish individualism whose roots lay in European Enlightenment thought. The Japanese, as a community, must hold fast to the Emperor and to an imperial line going back to the gods, allowing their small single selves to be absorbed into this greater life.

Yosano continued to teach at the Bunkagakuin throughout the 1930s. She managed to reconcile her school's liberal principles with her support of war on the mainland by clinging to a Pan-Asian vision that distinguished the good people of China from their deeply unfortunate leadership. Others did the same, for a while believing the best of Matsuoka Yōsuke when in the summer of 1940 he announced, in his capacity as Foreign Minister, Japan's intention to build a 'Greater East Asia Co-Prosperity Sphere' (GEACPS). Rooted in shared culture and common economic interests, this bloc of brother nations spanning Japan, China, Manchukuo and parts of South East Asia would together force Western colonial power out of their region. While Yosano hoped that the establishment of Manchukuo would help to facilitate 'reconciliation' between the Japanese and the Chinese, one of Japan's great philosophers, Nishida Kitarō, wished GEACPS well – while warning the army against turning it into a 'coercion sphere'.

Such fears were soon realized, as the conflict in China dragged on, tensions deepened with America and new opportunities arose from the war in Europe. A Tripartite Pact was signed with Mussolini's Italy and Hitler's Germany in the autumn of 1940, and the following summer Japanese forces completed an occupation of French Indochina, intended to deprive Chiang's forces of a key supply route. President Franklin D. Roosevelt ordered Japanese assets in the US frozen and placed a ban on oil exports. In August 1941, he signed the Atlantic Charter with Winston Churchill, a move that was interpreted in Tokyo as a hostile act.

Talks between the United States and Japan foundered on the latter's now unbreakable link with the mainland. Roosevelt wanted the Japanese out of China. But Prime Minister Konoe could not tell the families of soldiers fighting and dying there that what his government had previously billed as an existential cause was now to be laid aside. Unable to find a way through, he resigned as prime minister in the autumn of 1941. His replacement, Tōjō Hideki, a former head of the Kwantung Army, fared no better as a negotiator. At the beginning of December, the decision was made that ended up giving the likes of Ishiwara Kanji the war they had been waiting for.

Early on Sunday morning, 7 December 1941, residents of the Hawaiian island of Oahu awoke to the sound of explosions at Wheeler Army Airfield and around Pearl Harbor: 350 Japanese fighters and bombers were in the process of destroying nearly 200 American planes, sinking two battleships and wreaking all sorts of damage besides. More than 2,400 American personnel were killed. Japanese losses were light by comparison: 129 men, twenty-nine aircraft and five midget submarines.

An Imperial Rescript was promulgated at 11 a.m. on 8 December, Japan-time, declaring war on the United States and the British Empire. Once again, worries and grievances stretching back to Japan's reopening to the West in the 1850s were woven into a justification for war. And, once again, China was the main focus. Its leaders had failed to understand Japan's responsibility for ensuring peace and stability in East Asia. They had brought disaster on their region as a result.

An era of conflict that had begun in hope and kitsch celebration in the autumn of 1931 was set now to plumb depths of privation and suffering that few back then could have imagined. Even Ishiwara thought Japan's attack on America to be premature. Yosano was by this time confined to bed and slowly dying, following a brain haemorrhage in 1940. She did her best, nevertheless, to respond in verse to the attack on Pearl Harbor and Japan's declaration of war. Her political outlook remained the same and her poetry was still a thicket of militarist cliché, but a glimpse of the sort of trouble that her country was now in seemed to revive in Yosano a hint of her earlier lyricism and restraint. 'It is a time for falling tears', she wrote, 'as we enter the bitter cold / of the twelfth lunar month.'

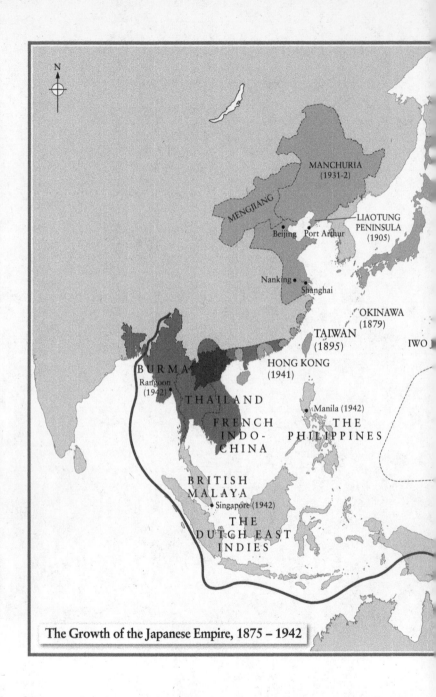

The Growth of the Japanese Empire, 1875 – 1942

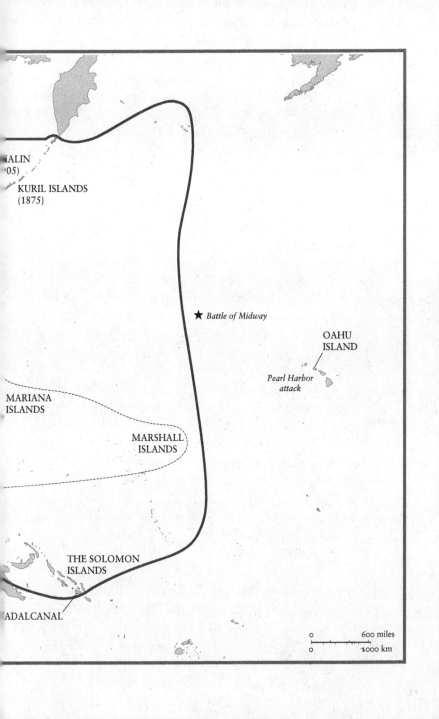

ALIN
05)

KURIL ISLANDS
(1875)

★ Battle of Midway

OAHU
ISLAND

Pearl Harbor
attack

MARIANA
ISLANDS

MARSHALL
ISLANDS

THE SOLOMON
ISLANDS

ADALCANAL

0   600 miles

0   1000 km

PART FIVE

'Forward with Culture': 1942 to the Present

17
Misora Hibari
（美空ひばり）

1937–1989

Starlet / Harlot

Misora Hibari, performing her hit song 'Kanashiki Kuchibue' ('Mournful Whistle') in 1949.

The Pearl Harbor raid, in December 1941, seemed at first to have been a success: a great deal of damage was done to American capabilities in return for minimal Japanese losses. Japan's armed forces quickly followed up by capturing a string of major Western colonial territories in East and South East Asia, and the south-western Pacific: Hong Kong (December 1941), Manila (January 1942), Malaya and Singapore (January–February 1942), Rangoon (March 1942), Java in the Dutch East Indies (March 1942) and Guadalcanal in the Solomon Islands (May 1942). Tens of thousands of Allied soldiers were taken prisoner, while anti-colonial Asian nationalists including Burma's Aung San greeted the Japanese as liberators at first – only to discover that Asia's political aspirations ranked a distant second, in Japanese priorities, to its natural resources. Oil from the Dutch East Indies. Copper, chromium and iron ore from the Philippines. Rubber and tin from French Indochina and British Malaya.

As far back as the 1890s, Japan's empire builders had been willing to shed foreign blood for the sake of the nation's strategic interests. But early additions to the empire – Taiwan from 1895, the South Manchurian railway corridor from 1905, Korea from 1910 – had also been the focus of civilian-led 'civilizing' experiments, notably in schooling, healthcare and infrastructure. War in Asia from 1937 and the Pacific from 1941 changed all that. What had long been obvious to Korean nationalists was now exposed for all to see: underpinning Japanese talk of civilization and shared prosperity was a willingness, if it came to it, to extinguish any and all opposition – from people, institutions and cultural forms including local languages and literatures.

Decades of work by pro-imperial intellectuals like Nitobe Inazō were undone in a few short years by Japanese soldiers who were encouraged – by their upbringing, training, commanders and sometimes desperate circumstances – to blur or ignore the distinction between enemy combatants and ordinary civilians. They shouted, shoved and slapped. They commandeered or destroyed property. They made of 'Co-Prosperity' a grim reality of starvation, rape, forced labour and summary execution, in which captured Westerners were caught up alongside the peoples of Asia. All in all, they earned for 'the Japanese' an international reputation for a depravity of violence that went beyond the exigencies even of total war. The Thai-Burma 'Death' Railway, built at a cost of tens of thousands of lives, would be held to have revealed something about the psychology of the people whose soldiery managed its construction. Likewise the dragooning of around 200,000 women – Korean, Chinese, Filipino, Malay and Dutch – into working in military brothels. So much for freeing Asia from colonial tyranny. 'If the British sucked our blood,' concluded a deeply disillusioned Aung San, 'the Japanese ground our bones.'

The misery went on long after the tide of war had turned against Japan. All three of the US Pacific Fleet's aircraft carriers survived the Pearl Harbor attack, having been out at sea that day. Much of Pearl Harbor's vital infrastructure had remained intact, too, including oil tanks, ammunition stores and repair facilities. Meanwhile, the American public proved much more willing to fight, and American industry more swiftly adapted to the prospect, than Japanese military strategists had hoped. As early as 1942, the United States started out-producing Japan in war-related materials, winning major engagements – famously at Midway in the central Pacific, where four Japanese aircraft carriers were sunk – and planning in due course for an occupation. Prime Minister Tōjō Hideki did what he could to keep the truth of the war's progress from the Japanese public. But that job became more difficult the closer that forces led by General Douglas MacArthur and Admiral Chester Nimitz came to Japan's home islands, via hard-fought victories including Guadalcanal (1942–3), Saipan in the Marianas (July 1944) and Leyte in the Philippines (October–December 1944).

By the time that Tōjō was forced to resign – after the fall of Saipan – everyday life in Japan had been utterly transformed. Entertainment venues were shut and neon signs switched off to save power. Food was rationed and clothing confined to the coarse basics of a 'national civilian uniform' for men and peasant-style pantaloons for women. Golf courses were dug up for use as farmland. Pots, pans, railings, statues and temple bells were melted down to reappear as armour and bullets. More than a million 'neighbourhood associations' – groups of between ten and fifteen households – were required to cooperate in fighting crime, fires, espionage and extravagant living. They distributed rations amongst themselves and circulated government information using a communal noticeboard, which each household stamped in red ink to confirm that they had absorbed the latest instructions.

Born in Yokohama in 1937, Katō Kazue – the future Misora Hibari – found solace amidst all this in music. Her father Masukichi was a fishmonger, accustomed to spending his spare time in his local music shop, sampling the latest records. Kazue began joining him there in 1942, at the age of five. Inspired by what she heard, she staged mini song and dance performances at home, gathering family and friends together on one side of some *fusama* (sliding partition doors) and then opening them with great drama, smiling and breaking into song as she swanned through. She was a natural performer, with a prodigious memory for lyrics. But what really impressed these first audiences was an emotional maturity far beyond her years. It was on vivid display in 1943 when Kazue endured an experience familiar to countless other children around the world in this era: saying goodbye to her father as he was called up for military service. She sang so powerfully at Masukichi's neighbourhood send-off that other families began asking her to do the same for them. The pain of her father's departure, she later recalled, was eased considerably by the pleasures of 'singing for so many – and being applauded'.

While Kazue was exploring her potential as a performer, girls a few years older were being drafted to work in Japan's factories, as the authorities tried desperately to keep the war effort going. Women, retirees and prisoners were enlisted too, alongside Korean and Chinese workers – some volunteering, the majority compelled. In 1944, university students found themselves hauled out of classes, crammed into aeroplane cockpits alongside stacks of explosives and waved off on one-way journeys towards the American navy vessels creeping ever closer to Japan's home islands. They had joined – often with very little say in the matter – the Kamikaze ('Divine Wind') Special Attack Corps, named after the storms that saw off Japan's Mongol invaders back in the late 1200s and first deployed during the Battle of Leyte Gulf in the autumn of 1944.

On Kazue's eighth birthday, 29 May 1945, it became spectacularly clear to the people of Yokohama just how little was being achieved by the Special Attack Corps in return for around 5,000 young aviators' lives. Air raid sirens started up and people fled for the relative safety of caves converted into bomb shelters, as the first of 500 American B-29 Superfortress bombers appeared in the sky and began releasing some 3,000 tons of oil, petrol, phosphorus and napalm on to densely packed wooden buildings below. The people of Yokohama returned to their city to find nearly half of it gone.

Most of Japan's major cities were targeted in a similar way that spring and summer, including Tokyo in March, where the most destructive air raid in history killed 100,000 people in one night and destroyed a quarter of the country's sprawling capital. An anti-war faction led by former Prime Minister Konoe Fumimarō and an ex-diplomat named Yoshida Shigeru managed, in June, to persuade the Emperor to consider negotiating an end to the war – before total devastation or Communist revolution effectively brought an end to Japan.

It was too late. Preparations were well underway in the deserts of New Mexico by this point for the testing of a device nicknamed 'The Gadget'. US President Harry Truman was notified of the test's success just as the Allies were gathering for a conference in Potsdam on 16 July. Bitterly angry with Japan's leaders for starting a war and conducting it as they had, mistrustful of any promises they might make and determined to keep the Soviet Union from making a late and opportunistic entry into the fighting, Truman now had the means required for ending the war quickly and on his own terms. The Potsdam Declaration of 26 July duly demanded that the Japanese surrender unconditionally or face 'prompt and utter destruction'.

With no mention made in the Declaration of the fate of the Emperor, Japan's leaders decided to avoid either accepting or rejecting it. Their attempt to thread the diplomatic needle was interpreted as a flat 'no' by the Americans. The response arrived on 6 August. In place of the usual swarm of B-29s came a single plane, the *Enola Gay*, releasing a single bomb into the morning air over Hiroshima. It exploded half a kilometre above ground, transforming the city below into a flaming chaos of suffering and disfigurement that witnesses later compared with medieval Buddhist imagery of hell. One hundred and forty thousand people died in the blast and from radioactive fallout. Another 70,000 were killed in Nagasaki, after Japan's centuries-old gateway to the world was struck by a second atomic bomb on 9 August.

Even now, and despite the Soviet Union declaring war on Japan on 8 August and pouring forces into its 'lifeline' of Manchuria – ending any prospect of Stalin serving as a diplomatic intermediary with the Americans and the British – Japanese army and navy chiefs of staff, along with the army minister, argued for the conflict to continue. The Emperor himself finally intervened, announcing in a radio address to his subjects on 15 August that he had ordered his government to accept the provisions of the Potsdam Declaration. Hearing their Emperor's voice for the very first time, the people of Japan were reminded that they had been fighting for the stability of East Asia. Now they faced a 'new and most cruel bomb', which threatened their country's continued existence and perhaps that of human civilization itself. Using an archaic form of Japanese, and drawing on the language of a Buddhist sutra, the Emperor asked his subjects to 'endure the unendurable, suffer the insufferable'. On 2 September 1945, his representatives boarded the USS *Missouri* in Tokyo Bay (part of a vast armada of Allied warships with their guns trained on the city) to sign the instrument of surrender.

When the Emperor addressed his people again a little while later, this time in an Imperial Rescript, he exchanged religious texts for a more modern point of reference: the Charter Oath of 1868, whose text had been inspired by Sakamoto Ryōma's manifesto. In some ways, it was a strange selection. The year 1868 had been a moment of elite revolution. This was a time of national devastation. Two million Japanese soldiers and nearly 700,000 Japanese civilians were dead. Nine million people were homeless. Malnourishment, disease and mass unemployment ran alongside bewilderment and disgust – at

Japan's former leaders, and at the country's soldiery, as news filtered through of their conduct abroad.

And yet in one crucial respect, 1945 was very much like 1868. It was Year One. A deeply discredited old order was giving way to something new, with the scale and scope of change as yet unknowable but sure to be contested as time went on. A few things were clear from the content and context of the Potsdam Declaration. Japan's transformation this time would be led by America, as the most influential player by far in an Allied Occupation. Japan's old political elite would play a much-reduced role in the nation's life – the days were gone of a small clique effectively hoarding national sovereignty for themselves. And Japan's armed forces, set to be disbanded, would have no role at all. Instead, in the words of Japan's Education Minister in September 1945, 'We go forward with culture.'

From Queen Himiko's shamanic hold on her people's imaginations and the Buddhist art and ideas of Prince Shōtoku's era, through the sophistication of Murasaki Shikibu's Heian court and Ihara Saikaku's social satire, 'culture' – broadly defined – had always been closely bound up with power in Japan. Now, it was set to be more influential than ever in how the Japanese understood themselves, organized their affairs and repaired their image and their relationships around the world. A shattered population, profoundly uncertain about the future, looked to literature, radio, film and music not just for light relief but for signs of the country's direction of travel.

One of the first to understand this major feature of post-war life, to her joy and to her cost, was a little girl who soon after the surrender began to graduate from home-made shows and neighbourhood send-offs to theatre gigs, recording contracts and film work. For the legions of fans who helped turn her into a child star, Katō Kazue represented hope for the future. She was young, bright and strong, brimming with talent and optimism. Others were unnerved by her precociousness, her uncanny imitations of adult song and dance routines. She was a painful reminder of the way the war had destroyed the old distinctions between children and adults, along with the nation-defining covenant that used to exist between them: filial duty passing one way, benevolent care the other. This girl might even be a portent. Perhaps losing a war was not the worst thing that could happen to a nation. Maybe the real destruction came later, as military defeat gave way to irreversible cultural and moral decay.

*

In the ninth and tenth centuries, it had been the aristocratic Fujiwara family. From the twelfth century through to the nineteenth, turns were taken by the Kamakura and Ashikaga shoguns, bloodstained warlords, the Tokugawa dynasty and finally a clique of lower-ranking samurai intent on opening Japan up to the modern world. Time and again, across history, Japanese emperors found themselves effectively the captives of some new political force in the country, seeking to exercise nationwide authority in their name. In September 1945, the phenomenon was captured on camera: the Shōwa Emperor standing to attention, about nose-height to General Douglas MacArthur, Supreme Commander for the Allied Powers (SCAP).

For all MacArthur's fabled authority as the 'Blue-Eyed Shogun', ruling from a high-rise Tokyo office building that loomed meaningfully over the Imperial Palace next door, his job was to implement a plan for Japan that had been developed back in Washington DC. Substantially achieved by the end of 1948, it broke down into three parts. First, 'Japan' was cut back down to size. Its borders were returned to those of 1868. Its armed forces were completely disbanded. And twenty-eight senior leaders were tried for war crimes by an International Military Tribunal for the Far East convened in Tokyo in 1946. Tōjō Hideki was amongst seven men to be sentenced to death, while a further eighteen received prison terms. Ishiwara Kanji, who had helped mastermind the bomb plot that tipped Manchuria into war in 1931, managed to avoid even being indicted – a turn of events that the man himself was said to have found puzzling.

Second, measures were introduced to tackle the *zaibatsu* conglomerates, defined by MacArthur and his staff at GHQ (General Headquarters) as any large business organization with enough influence to frustrate free competition in their sector. The 'Big Four' *zaibatsu* alone – Mitsui, Mitsubishi, Sumitomo and Yasuda – had ended up controlling a third of Japan's total capital in heavy industry and a good half in finance and insurance. This sheer concentration of economic power, combined with closed familial forms of governance (much criticized by Shibusawa Eiichi) and political connections at the highest levels had had the effect, it was argued, of undermining civil society. The assets of the largest *zaibatsu* were duly redistributed, while leading businessmen joined around 200,000 influential war-time figures – journalists, teachers, publishers, policemen and military officers – in being barred from public life. Conspicuous by their absence from the 'purge' lists were central government bureaucrats, whom MacArthur valued as administrative allies.

All of this was intended to render Japan's soil more fertile for the third and grandest part of Pax Americana: democracy. Its centrepiece was a new Constitution, drafted in just six days in early 1946 by American staffers at GHQ. The Emperor was henceforth to be a 'symbol of the state' and no more. His invocation of the Charter Oath was part of a New Year's Day rescript in 1946, in which he renounced his divinity. Known in English as the 'Declaration of Humanity', its original Japanese text was careful to leave open the question of whether the imperial family might nevertheless be *descendants* of Amaterasu, the Sun Goddess. Sovereignty was hence-forth to reside with the Japanese as a people, who would elect representatives to a bicameral Diet. The Prime Minister would be drawn from the largest party in the Lower House. And executive authority would be wielded collectively by his Cabinet.

'His' Cabinet – or 'hers'? Women were given the vote, and permitted to stand for election. Thirty-nine women won seats in the Lower House when the Japanese went to the polls in April 1946. They joined their male colleagues in debating and then approving, with only minor alterations, a Constitution that guaranteed the Japanese a broader range of inalienable rights than even their American mentors enjoyed: free universal education, the protection of public health and collective bargaining for workers (fully half of whom soon formed unions, mostly within individual companies rather than across industries). A strict separation was ensured between religion and state, given the role, as the Americans saw it, of Shintō doctrines and functionaries in supporting the war. Finally, to add to the startling phenomenon of one country writing another's Constitution, Article

Nine of that document laid out Japan's renunciation, for all time, of the right to wage war.

Major legislation followed, including a land redistribution scheme in October 1946 that eventually turned 5 million tenants into owner-farmers, and a Fundamental Law on Education (1947) that exchanged the state-oriented schooling criticized by Yosano Akiko for an American-style education premised on 'individual dignity and endeavour'. Japan's teachers, purged of their ultraconservative colleagues and mourning the children whose enthusiasm for military service they had helped to kindle, emerged as one of the country's most staunchly left-wing and pacifistic political constituencies. Some even tasked their students with learning Yosano's anti-war poem 'Thou Shalt Not Die' by heart. Finally, in 1948, the Meiji-era Civil Code was replaced, putting women on an equal footing with men in matters such as inheritance and divorce.

Amongst the early beneficiaries of this new, American-style democratic spirit was one Katō Kazue. Keen to advertise their commitment to opportunity for all, the Japanese arts world began promoting amateurs alongside professionals in a range of areas, from art exhibitions to poetry and song contests. Japan's national broadcaster, NHK Radio, created a competitive singing challenge called *Proud of My Voice* (*Nodo Jiman*). When the programme visited Yokohama in 1946, they invited Kazue to compete.

Kazue's home town was by this time beginning to regain a reputation for musical innovation that it had enjoyed for almost a century. A Japanese musical tradition spanning ancient Chinese- and Korean-influenced court music (*gagaku*), Buddhist chants, Nō ensembles, festival songs and a plethora of regional folk styles had mixed and mingled in Yokohama, from the 1850s onwards, with Western classical, choral and folk music. Pianos, violins, organs and brass had been briefly 'foreign' and then thoroughly 'Japanese', finding space alongside an older array of instruments including the shakuhachi (Japanese flute), koto, shamisen, mouth organ and drums. Immigrant tunes had received new identities: 'Auld Lang Syne' became the beloved 'Glow of the Firefly' ('*Hotaru no Hikari*'), featuring in songbooks used by a first generation of Japanese schoolchildren learning to sing in unison. Military bands and shop-front 'ding-dong bands' had trumpeted the power of Japan's new political and commercial establishments, while Freedom and People's Rights activists and ill-treated factory girls protested against them in songs of their own.

Kazue's father, Masukichi, had grown up in the 1920s and early 1930s with a magnificently capacious new musical genre called *ryūkōka*, 'popular song'. Much of the inspiration came from North and South America, Asia and Western Europe, courtesy of ocean-liner bands performing in port cities like Yokohama and leaving recorded and sheet music behind. In this way, American jazz, *chansons*, tango, rumba, Hawaiian music and many other styles besides became formative influences in early Japanese pop, with Japanese composers and performers adding new elements from mainland Asia as a result of time spent living and working in Japan's expanding empire. The celebrated composer Hattori Ryōichi lived for a while in Shanghai, whose seedy nightlife enhanced its jazz scene's reputation for gritty authenticity. Composer and guitarist Koga Masao's upbringing in colonial Korea allowed him to work Korean folk influences into his songs.

Kazue had first enjoyed the fruits of all this as a toddler, on record-shop outings with her father. She particularly enjoyed songs with strong stories attached. Wartime censorship steadily thinned the pickings, with more than a thousand songs eventually banned by name as part of attempts to cleanse Japan of Anglo-American taint. But from the summer of 1945, American GIs began bringing in the latest boogie-woogie, big-band jazz, mambo, country and blues. Masukichi took full advantage when he returned home from the war, using musical instruments liberated from Japanese military stores to establish a backing group for Kazue, whose mother Kimie picked 'Misora' – 'beautiful sky' – for her stage name.

The 'Star Misora Band' – violin, guitar, accordion, trumpet and drums – made its debut in September 1946 with a three-day run of matinee and evening performances at Yokohama's Athens Theatre (a rather grand name for what Kazue later recalled was basically a 'shack'). Kazue took centre-stage with a ukulele, while outside the venue her father turned his fishmonger patter to the hawking of his daughter's musical wares. The band offered a mixture of children's and adult songs, while for an encore Kazue led her audience – just twenty people at first – in a rendition of '*Ringo no Uta*' ('Apple Song'). This was one of the big hits of the day, taken from the film *Soyokaze* (*Soft Breeze*), in whose wholesome delights a war-weary population had been taking grateful refuge of late. The film's fresh-faced young star sang the 'Apple Song' as she skipped her merry way through an orchard.

It was to '*Ringo no Uta*' – a sure-fire winner – that Kazue turned when NHK came calling. But all did not go as planned. The judges greeted her first two verses in mysterious, ominous silence, and then the announcer cut her off as she embarked on the third. The problem was not the song. It was a little banal – 'the apple's lovable, lovable's the apple' – but hardly risqué. The problem was the singer. 'It would be a bad influence', declared one of the judges, 'for a child to sing an adult song.' No grade was given, landing Kazue with a default 'Fail' according to the programme's rules.

It was a dispiriting moment, but for a while it seemed a one-off. Kazue's fame continued to grow off the back of her live concerts, and in 1948 she landed herself a place on an all-star bill at the new Yoko-hama International Theatre. Her performance that day showed up the other artists to such an extent that the theatre's manager first worried for their morale and then quit his job to become Kazue's manager. He helped her to find work in Tokyo, where a theatre pro-ducer suggested that she change her name from Kazue, which he found rather dull, to Hibari, meaning 'skylark'. The transformation was complete: Katō Kazue was now Misora Hibari: 'lark in a beauti-ful sky'.

For her growing army of fans, Hibari provided liberation of a kind that was not on offer from the Americans. Getting to one of her con-certs might well involve weaving one's way around rubble, bomb craters and makeshift homeless shelters. Those lucky enough to have sufficient to eat could vividly recall bartering for food in black mar-kets around these streets, or forcing their way on to jam-packed trains to go foraging in the countryside. Many were still waiting for new homes, jobs or news of missing loved ones. People would bring all this sadness and trepidation into the theatre and take their seats. The auditorium lights would dim and the stage lights would come up.

A little girl would appear on stage, breaking into a cheeky smile, a bashful jig and a song of luminescent joy or sorrow. And, under cover of darkness and the sound of the band, everyone would dissolve into tears.

Some in Yokohama and Tokyo felt rather differently about Hibari. They doubted her motives, or at least those of her adult backers. And they questioned the tone of some of her performances. One of the most disturbing aspects of life on city streets in 1948 was the presence of children orphaned by the war; left to fend for themselves in railway stations or underground passageways, some were forced to offer sex in return for money or food. So potent a symbol of Japan's defeat were the war orphans that Occupation censors warned filmmakers to treat the topic with especial care, for fear of stoking the sort of furious anti-American anger from which the Occupation had so far remained largely free. What, then, were Hibari's handlers thinking when they sent her out on stage in 1948 with a cigarette in her hand, a bag slung over her shoulder and tears in her eyes, singing a song – 'In the Flow of the Stars' ('*Hoshi no nagare ni*') – about a young woman turning to prostitution amidst the hardships of war?

> In the flow of the stars, I go,
> Where will I sleep tonight, where will I stay?
> My heart is hard,
> My tears have dried,
> Who turned me into a woman like this?

'Monster.' 'Beast.' 'A deformed adult.' 'Drenched in evil.' 'A sin.' 'It chills my blood.' 'I wanted to throw up.' Such were the responses of newspaper columnists and letter-writers to this and similar performances around the same time. Most controversial of all was Hibari's close emulation of one of the country's biggest adult stars, Kasagi Shizuko. Kasagi was Japan's 'Boogie Queen', howling, growling and swinging her hips as she belted out songs like 'Hey Hey Boogie' and 'Tokyo Boogie-Woogie', both by Hattori Ryōichi. During orchestral interludes, she would skip and march around the stage, abetted by a troupe of scantily clad chorus girls.

Kasagi's act appeared to overlap, in content and clientele, with a post-war '*kasutori* culture' that saw Japanese men drowning their failures and lack of future prospects in *sake* dregs (*kasutori*) and in a genre of pulp literature and live shows whose dominant theme was naked and semi-naked women. At the same time, Kasagi's raunchy Americanized style provided some of the clearest evidence yet that, having humiliated Japan's menfolk on the battlefield, the United States was now coming for their women: making prostitutes of some of them, particularly around American military bases in places like Yokohama, and poisoning the rest with music whose lyrics cheapened and sexualized them. To witness an eleven-year-old girl imitating all this – the boogie-woogie songs, the make-up and jewellery, the suggestive dance moves – was to have one's definition of 'defeat' subjected to unwelcome revision: from a moment in the summer of 1945 to an ongoing process, with no end or saviour in sight.

Some of Hibari's critics focused on her exploitation by 'lowly' and irresponsible adults around her. One newspaper published photos of her on a train, looking exhausted, and of her manager having to carry her on his shoulders. Might he be breaking the country's stringent new labour laws, some wondered? Others homed in on the vulgarity of a fishmonger's family grown suddenly wealthy from their daughter's lucrative yet shameful exertions – one remarked on Kimie's fondness for putting 'a ring on every finger'.

Such was the vitriol poured on Hibari herself that she and her supporters learned early on to build setbacks into her personal myth. When her tour bus crashed in mountainous Shikoku, leaving her with broken bones, injuries to her face and chest, and a severed artery in her wrist, stories were told of Hibari struggling from her hospital bed to visit a village shrine, beseeching the *kami* of a cedar tree there to help her become the 'number one singer in Japan'. And when a particularly noxious piece of commentary likened her to a freakish circus act – the 'boogie-woogie girl' born to share the big-top with the 'bear girl', the 'spider man' and the 'long-necked woman' – her mother cut the piece out of the newspaper and stuffed it in Hibari's *omamori* pouch (a small amulet, carried for luck and protection), so that she could keep her critics close.

Hibari was not the first child star to unnerve people. The year that she was born, 1937, Graham Greene wrote a review of the Shirley Temple film *Wee Willie Winkie* in which he suggested that

Temple's real appeal was not the innocence of the infant but something 'more secret and more adult': her 'neat and well-developed rump', the 'side-long, searching coquetry' of her eyes. Twentieth Century Fox launched a successful libel action in response, alleging that Greene had effectively accused them of 'procuring' Temple for 'immoral purposes'. The difference with Hibari was revealed in the words of one critic in particular, who described her songs as the 'music of a ruined nation'. Opinion polls suggested that the majority of Japanese were broadly in agreement with General MacArthur's political reforms. And turnout had been high at the country's first post-war elections. But Hibari's act spoke to some of a country threatened with – already undergoing, in fact – far broader, deeper change. They worried, in short, about the scale of the Americans' ultimate ambitions in Japan.

They were right to do so. Japanese representatives aboard the USS *Missouri* had signed the instrument of surrender as two United States flags fluttered overhead. One had been flying above the White House at the time of the attack on Pearl Harbor. The other had flown from the mast of Commodore Matthew C. Perry's ship when he weighed anchor off the Japanese coast back in 1853. Wartime American strategists asking themselves how a promising process of Japanese modernization could have gone so disastrously off track, had gone back not ten or fifteen years in search of answers, but almost a hundred. They had alighted on a deep-set 'feudal' mentality, frustrating from the get-go the development of the individual responsibility and civic-mindedness so crucial to a functioning democracy. The Japanese had acquired modern banks and industry, sciences and suits. And yet too many people had remained willing, instinctively and to a destructive degree, to do whatever fathers, bosses or military superiors demanded of them. Unquestioning obedience had remained the default position, recently encountered in raw form on battlefields and in POW camps.

A cleansing of the culture was called for, which included the reshaping of Japan's arts and mass media. Alongside cautions about depicting war orphans or offering other similarly implicit criticisms of America and the Allies, kabuki performances and period films were targeted for their feudal values and dramatic tales of violent revenge. Restrictions were placed on the use of powerful pre-war and wartime symbols like Mount Fuji and the red *torii* gates of Shintō shrines. Bowing was discouraged. The 1945 film *The Men Who Tread on the Tiger's Tail (Tora no o wo fumu otokotachi)*, by an up-and-coming film director named Kurosawa Akira, found itself banned first by wartime Japanese censors as 'too democratic' and then by the Americans as 'too feudal'.

Yoshida Shigeru, member of 1945's anti-war faction and leader now of a new Japan Liberal Party, disagreed profoundly with this reading of Japan's recent history. He regarded the Meiji and Taishō eras as purposeful, prosperous and proud, with the 1930s and early 1940s a tragic deviation rather than the inevitable outcome of botched modernization across the longer term. Nicknamed 'the Pocket Churchill' for his combination of Anglophilia, conservatism, stubbornness and love of cigars, he served as Japan's prime minister from 1946 to 1947 and again from 1948 to 1954. As the Occupation dragged on and American military bases came to be associated not so much with a cleansing of Japanese culture as its corruption with prostitution, crime and the disturbingly popular boogie-woogie of Kasagi and Hibari, Yoshida took to saying that 'GHQ' ought to stand for 'Go Home Quickly'.

*

Inside Yokohama's exclusive Cabaret Orion club, the lights have been turned down low. Clients in lounge suits and ballgowns line the edges of the room, turning towards the stage as a tuxedoed band – violins, double bass, saxophone and drums – launches into a slightly melancholy tune, with a gentle jazzy swing. A spotlight blinks into life, picking out the club's decorative centrepiece: an ornate water-fountain, at whose edge stands a diminutive figure in top hat and tails. He greets his audience with a gentlemanly bow, a swing of his cane and a doffing of his hat. At which point 'he' is revealed as 'she': a twelve-year-old girl, long hair tied back to reveal a beaming, benevolent smile. Declining a proffered glass of *sake* with an understated gesture from her white-gloved hand, she begins to sing in a smooth low voice:

> More than the *sake* in the glasses at night,
> That burning crimson, shining bright.
> I put my lips to the flower of love.
> But . . . the rose that I gave you,
> Trembles with sadness,
> Then falls away with my dreams.

With that, the girl casts a white rose into the waters of the fountain and sets off around the room, strolling and striking poses with her cane as the band plays on. There is a touch of Fred Astaire to her: charming and urbane, at one point taking a turn on the dance floor with an elegant woman who might be twice her age or more, reaching up to mime a kiss on her forehead before waving her regretfully away. The song ends on wistful lines about laughter, loneliness and innocence one day restored.

What would a twelve-year-old know about lost innocence? In Mitsuko's case, quite a bit. She is a war orphan, a child of the streets. Most days, she can be found hanging out down by the river with other homeless children, alongside dirty-faced day labourers. Some of her gang are crowded around outside the club's windows this evening, looking in. Unkempt and uncouth, they mean the world to her: a makeshift family, to whom she blows a discreet kiss as she performs.

Mitsuko is not a real orphan. She is a masterpiece of rebranding: a character in a film called *Mournful Whistle* (*Kanashiki Kuchibue*, 1949), given to Misora Hibari to play as a way of persuading people to see her precociousness in a fresh light – not as the product of exploitation or premature sexualization, but as wisdom and maturity, hard won during a time of war. Mitsuko is cheerful and resourceful, with a talent both for singing and for bringing people together. In the audience for her performance of the film's title song is her brother Kenzo, whom Mitsuko had thought lost to the war. Reunited at last, Mitsuko helps him to put a hopeless, dissolute life back together. War orphans, it turns out, are capable of being more than mere passive victims of conflict, or of Occupation-era licentiousness. The destruction wrought upon children by adults sometimes gives them precisely the sort of moral clarity and independence that so many early post-war thinkers – American and Japanese alike – agreed was essential for Japan's regeneration.

In Mitsuko, some of the most powerful of Japan's post-war culture-brokers – Hibari herself; Shōchiku studios, who produced the film; and Nippon Columbia, who signed Hibari to their label and helped to manage her image – presented audiences with the perfect, natural blend of traditional Japanese family values and fresh democratizing energy. And they loved it. The film was a hit, and sales of the song 'Mournful Whistle' topped half a million – a post-war record. The year 1949 became a turning point for Hibari, helping to launch her as a film and musical sensation across Japan, and even beyond. In 1950, she was invited out to Hawaii by the US Army's history-making 442nd Regimental Combat Team, comprised almost entirely of Japanese-American soldiers and fresh from distinguished service in the Second World War's European theatre. Hibari was treated, in Honolulu and elsewhere, as a bona fide star: greeted upon her arrival by adoring, flower-bearing fans, a police motorcade – even a Hawaiian Hibari impersonator, with whom she performed in matching hula skirts. While there, she filmed scenes for a new film, *Tokyo Kid (Tokyo Kiddo)*, released later that year and promoted heavily off the back of an American tour that took her from Hawaii through a string of West Coast venues including Los Angeles and San Francisco.

Kasagi Shizuko made her own tour of America later in 1950. Friendly with Hibari back in Japan – they sometimes played together in the green room when they were on the same bill – she was concerned that in the United States the little girl's popularity might obscure her own. She need not have worried. Part of the genius of 'Mournful Whistle' in reshaping Hibari's image had been the song's use of a pentatonic *yonanuki*-minor key, formed by having the fourth (*yo*) and seventh (*na*) notes removed (*nuki*) from its Western minor counterpart. A staple of pre-war Japanese pop, it served now to shift Hibari's associations away from sleazy Americana and to reassure her audiences that in musical terms at least all had not been lost with the war.

A glance at the sales figures for 'Mournful Whistle' was enough to persuade her handlers that this had been the right move. They duly followed up in 1950 with 'Echigo Lion Dance Song' ('*Echigo Shishi no Uta*'), combining a *yonanuki*-minor key with lyrics inspired by folk songs from the Echigo region of Japan. Western instruments were used, but played in a way that resembled the traditional Japanese shamisen, shakuhachi and *taiko* drums.

Two years later, Hibari completed her transition with 'Apple Folk Song' ('*Ringo oiwake*', 1952). Sung in an affected north-eastern Japanese regional accent and recalling the sorrows of wartime, it set the tone for Hibari's adult career, featuring storytelling, heartache, husky spoken passages, and vocal tricks including vibrato and melisma (several notes sung to a single syllable):

> Over the mountain peak,
> Float clouds as white as cotton.
> The peach blossoms bloom,
> The cherry blossoms bloom,
> And then come the early apple blossoms.
> For us, there is no more beautiful time of year.
> But when the heartless rains fall,
> Scattering the white petals,
> I recall my mother,
> Who died around this time of year in Tokyo.

Where much of Japanese pop over the decades to come would track Western progress through rockabilly, rock and punk, Hibari helped to shape a genre of sentimental ballads, crystallizing in the 1960s as '*enka*', in which time appeared to stand still. *Yonanuki*-minor melodies and lyrics arranged into lines of five and seven syllables – inspired by ancient poetry rather than modern pop – together helped to conjure the nostalgic sadness and small-town values of the 'real' Japan.

'Apple Folk Song' sold 700,000 copies on its release – another postwar record. And now Hibari found herself facing a fresh set of critics. The year 1949 had become a turning point, not just for her but for the Japanese people as a whole. As American relations with the Soviet Union soured and a Communist 'People's Republic' was declared in China, Japan's future, in American eyes, was shifting from liberal democratic experiment to robust Pacific ally. Japan was now envisaged as a reliably conservative country, flying the flag for capitalism in East Asia and providing American businesses – acutely aware of the cost in taxpayer dollars of the Occupation – with a profitable trading and investment partner, rather than the aid-hungry socialist basket case that some investors feared. Labour unions were duly reined in and Japan's finances tightened up, with restrictions placed on credit, wage levels and public spending. Measures against large conglomerates were softened and a 'red purge' was undertaken of left-wing elements in government, the unions, the business world and wider society.

The outbreak of the Korean War in 1950 accelerated the transformation. After Japan's defeat, the peninsula had been divided into a US-occupied southern portion and a Soviet-occupied north. What was intended to be a temporary division began to look more permanent after separate states were declared in 1948: the Republic of Korea in the south, and Kim Il-sung's Democratic People's Republic of Korea in the north. Kim's decision to invade South Korea in June 1950 prompted the formation of a United Nations force in its defence, which Douglas MacArthur was appointed to lead. The Occupation authorities now demanded that the Japanese establish their own heavily armed 'National Police Reserve' (NPR), to help take care of internal security while a large contingent of American soldiers left for Korea. Around $800 million a year in American military procurement orders began to flow Japan's way, helping to move its economy towards significant growth, but heightening fears that Japan was heading for long-term status as a military-industrial handmaiden to the United States.

MacArthur was relieved of his Korea and SCAP commands in April 1951, after President Truman discovered that he was hoping to escalate hostilities on the peninsula into an all-out war with Communist China. The American diplomat John Foster Dulles was meanwhile consulting widely on a peace treaty with Japan, designed to give lasting legal form to what America was beginning to ask of the Japanese. South East Asian nations who had borne the brunt of 'Co-Prosperity' during the war sought reparations. Great Britain, adjusting to the loss of India from its empire in 1947, hoped to limit Japanese competitiveness in exports. Pragmatic, and ever the internationalist, Prime Minister Yoshida Shigeru was willing to acquiesce to the inevitable post-Occupation alliance with America as long as Japan's economic freedom of movement was not restricted. Five other players with demands of their own were absent from the discussions. The Soviet Union decided to boycott talks, deeply suspicious as it was of a US–Japan Security Treaty due to be signed alongside a peace deal. The two Koreas were at war. And the source of legitimate Chinese government remained an open question, with the People's Republic of China consolidating its position on the mainland while Chiang Kai-shek's defeated Nationalists hunkered down on the recently vacated Japanese colony Taiwan.

The Treaty of San Francisco was signed in September 1951 by forty-eight of the countries that had ended up at war with Japan in the late 1930s and early 1940s. Yoshida could claim it as a win: it was far less punitive than it might have been, and restored Japan to full sovereignty. The Security Treaty signed at the same time was more controversial. It provided for the maintenance of American military bases in Japan – putting the country at risk of attack from America's enemies – and permitted American forces to put down insurrections in Japan, if asked to do so by Japanese officials.

Japanese liberals feared that the Occupation's 'reverse course' after 1949, together with these two new treaties, portended a return to authoritarianism in Japan, after a few years of respite. They noted with alarm a parallel reverse course in popular culture – the crawling back under the comfort blanket of collectivism and cheap sentimentality. A swathe of new period dramas romanticized traditional Japan, while film studios started to make weepy films about the war – kamikaze pilots included – focusing on tragedy, duty and suffering rather than culpably misguided leadership.

Hibari was amongst those implicated. She starred now and again in samurai films, and recorded songs – including 'Mournful Whistle' and 'Echigo Lion Dance Song'– that had been written by a man named Manjōme Tadashi, a successful wartime composer who was accused now of once again 'soaking the populace in hopeless sentimentality and decadence'. In general, Hibari's repertoire seemed to reflect America's desire to prise Japan apart from its neighbours. She continued to sing a little boogie-woogie and mambo, a nod to the new Pacific alliance, while her *yonanuki*-minor songs homed in on specifically

Japanese history and hardships, helping to shift that evocative key from suggesting 'Asia' as a cultural whole to betokening 'Japan' alone. Just when bridges to the mainland were needed more than ever after the tragedies of the war, Hibari seemed to be helping to set them alight.

*

Misora Hibari gave her debut live performance of 'Apple Folk Song' on 27 April 1952. The starting salary, that year, for a bank clerk with a university education was around 72,000 yen: Hibari's earnings for the year were in the region of 12 million yen. In 1953, she built herself a mansion, the 'Hibari Palace'. Sprawling across 3,000 square metres of prime Yokohama real estate, it boasted fifteen rooms and a swimming pool. Tour buses soon began cruising past, passengers hoping to catch a glimpse of the girl whose wildly successful film work – more than a billion cinema tickets sold every year between 1957 and 1960 – established her as the conventional, dutiful, traditional Japanese daughter.

Hibari went on to make around 160 films and 1,500 records, performing well into the 1980s as Japan's undisputed 'Queen of Enka'. Hard-working and hard-drinking, famously brash yet reliably lachrymose when a song called for tears, she became one of the great cultural icons of post-war Japan: dressed in a kimono, hair coiffed and microphone in hand, she sang about lost love, shattered dreams, *sake* and the call of home. A karaoke staple, as that technology spread in the 1970s and 1980s, Hibari remained synonymous above all with Japanese resilience during the early months and years after 1945: the formative time of her life, but regarded soon enough in Japan as *mukashi* – 'the olden days'.

The day of Hibari's first performance of 'Apple Folk Song' was also the day that the Occupation formally ended. Japan's American decade, beginning with the turning of the war in the United States' favour and the planning of an occupation, drew to a close at last. Like Hibari, the country was on course for considerable prosperity. But as with Hibari, it would be a prosperity rooted – to the point, critics would say, of stagnation – in the political decisions and cultural

THE JAPANESE

compromises made during the Occupation era. Tens of thousands of American soldiers would continue to be stationed in Japan for decades to come, notably in Okinawa, which remained completely in American hands until 1972. Japan would have little that resembled an independent foreign policy. And the country would struggle to develop a viable two-party political system, in part because the Central Intelligence Agency (CIA) worked early on to frustrate rivals to the sort of conservative, staunchly anti-Communist politics that the United States required of its primary East Asian ally.

And yet 'stagnation' would not quite be fair. The Americans arrived in the summer of 1945 intent on remaking the Japanese. They left in April 1952 with the task at best half-done. The anxieties and arguments of those seven years, which shaped Hibari's career, were far from over. The meaning, for the Japanese, of 'forward with culture' – led by whom, going where, and to what end? – would be many dynamic and remarkable years yet in the unfolding.

18
Tezuka Osamu

(手塚治虫)

1928–1989

Dream Weaver

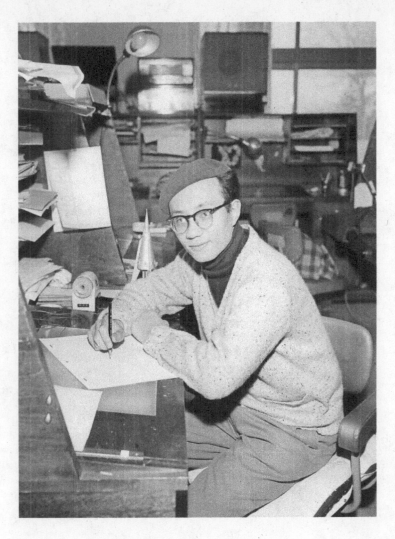

Tezuka Osamu, photographed in 1962 in Tokyo.

In April 1952, the Occupation came to an end, Misora Hibari's career stepped up a gear – and bath-time in Japan changed forever. Growing numbers of children refused to leave the tub until their parents had sculpted their shampooed hair into a new and iconic style: two great horns, one at the front of the head and another at the back. Thrusting a suds-soaked arm purposefully forward, fist clenched as though flying to the rescue, they were transformed for a few precious moments into the boy-robot 'Atom', a bestselling comic-book character introduced to the world that month by the 'god of manga', Tezuka Osamu.

One of the most potent pieces of visual imagery ever produced in Japan, Atom was drawn in the rounded contours of a Disney character, and with more than a passing resemblance to Mighty Mouse. He had large Betty Boop-like eyes and hair of shiny, plasticky black, with its two distinctive spikes based on the shape that Tezuka's own hair used to take on in the bath as a child. He wore black shorts with a green belt, and red boots on his feet. Powered by an atomic reactor in his chest and guided by a computer brain, he boasted jets built into his arms and feet, searchlight eyes, enhanced hearing, fluency in sixty languages and twin machine guns stashed discreetly in his backside.

Where American comic-book superheroes like Batman and Superman tended to be powerfully masculine, distant figures, Atom was cute, androgynous and emotional, making friends and passionately seeking peace. The latter became a clichéd notion in later decades, but many a Japanese child in the 1950s was growing up minus a father or a brother, waking up at night to memories of the sound of bombs exploding or the sight and smell of burning buildings. Born in Osaka on 3 November 1928, Tezuka himself had seen that city's Yodogawa River clogged with blackened bodies. 'Peace' was no mere piety for his generation, nor did they have many illusions about the realities of the adult world: it was a dangerous, dispiriting place, full of failure. In Tezuka that generation found a storyteller, a dream weaver, capable of responding with brilliant creativity to the maturity forced upon them by the war and helping them to navigate the uncertain world that had been opened up by defeat and the Occupation.

Across a career that saw him create around 500 distinct works, spanning more than 150,000 pages of manga, Tezuka turned a centuries-old tradition in Japan of satirical, storytelling art into a new visual language that was readily identifiable both there and around the world: cute, curvy characters with large eyes and complex personalities who engaged in fantastical adventures that closely reflected real-world concerns. Becoming the first post-war Japanese character to make it big abroad, Atom started a trend that peaked around the turn of the twenty-first century: 'forward with culture' was pushed beyond a matter of mapping Japan's own future to encompass grander reflections on humanity and modern life that resonated around the world.

*

Tezuka Osamu shared his birthday, 3 November, with the much-mourned Emperor Meiji. So his mother and father, Fumiko and Yutaka, bestowed upon him the second character of that illustrious name: 'Osamu' was an alternative reading for 'ji', meaning 'rule' or 'manage'. The Tezukas were not otherwise an especially political family, descended instead from medics, lawyers and – on Fumiko's side – the celebrated swordsman Hattori 'the Demon' Hanzō. He and his men had fought for the Tokugawa clan back in the late 1500s, guarding Edo Castle's western entrance and lending it their name. The new Imperial Palace, built in the 1880s, hung on to this little bit of history: right down to Tezuka's day and well beyond, it was accessed from the west via the Hanzōmon ('Hanzō Gate').

By day, Tezuka's father Yutaka was a manager for Sumitomo Metals. In the evenings and weekends he was a photographer, a composer of haiku and a foreign film buff. His pride and joy was a hand-cranked

9.5mm Pathé Baby film projector, courtesy of which the young Tezuka, together with his little brother Hiroshi and sister Minako, enjoyed home screenings of Charlie Chaplin, Mickey Mouse, Felix the Cat, Popeye and Betty Boop. Some of the reels, bought in local department stores, came with an audio accompaniment on a gramophone record. The trick was to start the film, count to three and then drop the needle, cranking the projector a little faster or slower if video and audio strayed too woefully out of sync.

Fumiko's great love was music. She taught her children to play the piano and made the most of living in the hot-spring resort town of Takarazuka, near Osaka, by taking them regularly to the Takarazuka Revue. Established in 1913, the revue was famous for its all-female troupes, its lavish costumes and its exotic settings: Paris and Arabia, Europe in the Middle Ages, the Chinese imperial court. Tezuka became so absorbed in what he later recalled as the 'sweet extravagance' of these lush fantasy worlds that in 1932 he mistook his own grandfather's funeral, conducted by Shintō priests partially secluded behind curtains, for a matinee performance at which the curtain had failed to rise.

Tezuka gave visual form to these sights and sounds of his young life by taking up the paper and pencils that his parents left for him by his bed in case he became anxious in the night. He was soon doodling away so furiously that his mother took to rubbing out his drawings so that he could reuse the paper. Tezuka's teachers were quick to notice an uncommon artistic and storytelling flair here, occasionally to the point of frustration when he added fantastic twists to written reports on school outings. What Tezuka's classmates noticed, unfortunately, was his egg-shaped head, his disorderly hair and his painful lack of sporting prowess.

Forced to alternate his route home from school to avoid the bullies, Tezuka took refuge in art and also in insects, collecting them in the hills around Takarazuka and then drawing and cataloguing them. He began writing his own name by adding the character for *mushi* (虫), 'insect', at the end, later including two dots in the central rectangular section to give the appearance of eyes staring out through thick-lensed glasses of the sort he wore from the age of eleven. Tezuka managed to improve his playground fortunes a little in 1937 by having his hair cut into a less easily ridiculed close-cropped style. But bigger problems were soon on the horizon. War broke out, and Tezuka found both his father and a genre of graphic art that he had come to cherish being conscripted into the national cause.

'Manga', 'whimsical pictures', had its origins in Chinese and Japanese picture scrolls (*emakimono*) on which the action, sometimes with text alongside, proceeded from right to left. One of Japan's earliest known *emakimono* artists was the Tendai Buddhist monk Toba Sōjō Kakuyū (1053–1140), credited with creating some or all of the *Chōjū Giga* (*Animal Caricatures*). The scroll featured frogs, rabbits and other animals engaged in human-like pursuits, from feasting and playing games to a funeral at which a monkey dressed in Buddhist robes officiates. Alongside satirizing his society – and indeed his own profession – Toba thrived on humour of a more straightforward sort, including men gorging on sweet potatoes, fuelling up for a 'Fart Battle'.

Where *emakimono* were hand-painted and too precious for most ordinary Japanese ever to lay eyes on, the woodblock printing boom of Ihara Saikaku's time had opened this world up for the masses. One of the first to use the term 'manga' was Katsushika Hokusai (1760–1849). Art-lovers around the world came to admire him for iconic prints like *The Great Wave off Kanagawa* in which tiny rowing boats are threatened by a towering, claw-like wall of water, while Mount Fuji sits tranquil in the background. But elsewhere in his *oeuvre*, a samurai sits on a toilet, smiling in blissful relief while three of his retainers crouch on the floor outside, clutching their noses.

Hokusai's malodorous verdict on the Tokugawa social order was still lingering in the air when the leaders of 1868 embarked on their nation-building work. They, too, soon had their satirists, this time combining Japanese with Western traditions of graphic art. Britain's *Punch* magazine and New York's *Puck* inspired *Japan Punch* and *Tokyo Puck*, the latter established in 1905 by Japan's first self-proclaimed 'manga artist', Kitazawa Rakuten (1876–1955). His path-breaking multi-frame comic strips included a series featuring two country bumpkins, Tagosaku and Mokube, wowed by life in the big modern city. Such things appeared first in newspapers and magazines, then from the 1910s and 1920s in dedicated publications aimed separately at girls, boys and younger children.

As with poetry and music, so with manga, war in the 1930s and 1940s brought a combination of censorship and the twisting of art and entertainment to new ends. Tezuka's favourite manga character, Norakuro, a black-and-white stray dog serving in a special canine army regiment, began to count Chinese 'pigs' amongst his enemies. Another popular character, Dankichi, could be found taming the natives of a 'barbarian island' by schooling them in the ways of Japanese civilization, converting them to Shintō and teaching them how to fight their white oppressors.

On the big screen, the Imperial Japanese Navy endorsed two propaganda cartoons starring an old Japanese folklore hero called Momotarō (Peach Boy). *Momotarō's Sea Eagles* (*Momotarō no Umiwashi*, 1943) told the story of a daring Pearl Harbor-style raid, carried out by an assortment of cuddly animals all armed to the teeth and wearing rising-sun bandanas. Bluto from the *Popeye* films stood for the stereotypical American: fat, drunk and panicking uselessly as his ship went down. *Momotarō's Divine Sea Warriors* (*Momotarō: Umi no Shinpei*, 1945) became Japan's first ever feature-length animation, showing a crack team of small furry parachute commandos sticking it to the British.

American cartoonists engaged in much the same activities, satirizing Japan's reversal of fortunes from 1942. In one scene from *Tokio Jokio* (Looney Tunes, 1943), a Japanese man in morning dress – drawn with buck teeth and thick, black-rimmed glasses – gets blown up trying to use an incendiary device to cook a sausage. In another, a similar-looking chef rustles up 'delicious Japanese club sandwich' – using a small stack of ration cards.

Tezuka briefly became caught up in all this, drawing – for his own and his friends' amusement – a well-known Japanese comic-strip character called Fuku-chan piloting a bomber over American cities, while Mickey Mouse attacked Osaka. The latter was not entirely fantastical, as Tezuka knew only too well. In the spring of 1945, he sat in an Osaka cinema watching *Momotarō's Divine Sea Warriors*:

> The audience for the film – children – had all been evacuated to the countryside . . . I sat in the freezing Shōchikuza movie theater, which

had somehow survived the bombings, and watched the film. I watched, and I was so impressed that I began weeping uncontrollably. The lyricism and the child-like spirit in all the reels were like a warm light illuminating my mummified spirit, depleted of both hope and dreams. I swore then: 'I will someday make my own animated films.'

Tezuka managed to avoid injury during the bombing of Osaka, but he fell victim instead to a ringworm infection so serious that it nearly cost him his arms from amputation. He was inspired to pursue a career in medicine, to which end during the dying weeks of the war he enrolled at Osaka University's medical school. He carried on drawing while he studied, and in 1947 he provided the illustrations for what became a groundbreaking manga: *New Treasure Island (Shin Takarajima)*.

Most manga up until this point were created using one frame to depict each scene. Right from its opening pages, *New Treasure Island* was different. Tezuka devoted frame after frame to a sports car zooming through a town, showing it from all sorts of angles – at one point steadily zooming in on the driver's stern, concentrating face – to give a moment-by-moment feel for the action that was exhilarating and breathless. One thirteen-year-old reader was left completely stunned:

All you see is a car running, for two pages. Why does this get me so excited? I feel as if I am driving the car, speeding towards the pier. This is a static comic, printed on paper. But this car *is* running, at full speed! It's like I'm watching a movie!

Tezuka was not the first Japanese manga artist to use cinematic techniques in his work. But no one was doing it quite like this, combining an enormous range of influences running from French and German film through live theatre to American and Japanese graphic artists old and new. Tezuka's juxtaposition of cartoonish main characters with realistic landscapes suggests the possible influence in his work of Hergé, creator of *The Adventures of Tintin*. If so, it was the latest link in a chain of influences spanning the globe. Hergé was influenced by Hokusai, as part of nineteenth-century Europe's Japonisme movement, and Hokusai's manga sketches are thought to have been introduced into Europe by Kusumoto Ine's father, Philipp Franz von Siebold. Hokusai, in turn, was influenced by French and Dutch art, which made its way into eighteenth-century Japan via Dejima.

With early post-war Japanese compelled to entertain themselves on a budget, these were boom-times for a traditional one-person story-telling genre called *rakugo*, narrated picture-card shows known as *kamishibai*, and above all manga. Books and magazines were available for rent from thousands of outlets, at a cost of around 10 yen for two days. Or else booklets could be bought – yours for around 15 or 20 yen – and then swapped with friends. Osaka had been a great centre of publishing innovation in Ihara Saikaku's time, and now became associated with the *akabon*, or 'red book'. These were economically produced on rough paper, often with garish cover pages printed in red and orange ink, for a target demographic who might well supplement their manga purchase with some sweeties. Selling an unprecedented 400,000 copies in just a few months, *Shin Takarajima* became the breakthrough title in the *akabon* genre, helping in turn to create a trend towards long and involved stories in place of comic shorts.

Word began to spread about Tezuka, until he came to the notice of an editor in Tokyo who was searching for a Japanese answer to the comics that he had seen American GIs reading: titles like *Superman* and *Batman*. Inspired by talk around this time of 'atoms', and of the promise of atomic energy in revolutionizing everyday life, Tezuka offered up a story inspired by *Pinocchio* (which he had seen performed at the Takarazuka Revue) and set in the impossibly futuristic context of 2003. A scientist mourning his dead son creates a little boy-robot to replace him. But a robot cannot grow, and so his disillusioned father ends up selling him off to the circus where he acquires his name, 'Atom'. A kindly scientist, Professor Ochanomizu, rescues him, helps him to get along in human society – even enrolling him in school – and sets him on the road to becoming a crime-fighting superhero.

The *Mighty Atom* (*Tetsuwan Atomu*) manga proved an instant hit, vindicating a decision that Tezuka had already taken with the help of his mother: to make his way in the world as a manga artist rather than as a doctor. Moving to Tokyo in the summer of 1952, he set about devising a production system for manga that would shape the industry for decades to come. Its key components were low pay, inhuman working hours, hiding from – and occasionally being locked in a room by – furious editors to whom extravagant promises had been made, and employing up-and-coming artists as sanity-saving assistants. In return for training on the job, they would complete the inking of black spaces in the pictures and fill in background details while the master moved on to the next frame. Amongst those to work with Tezuka in these early years was Motō Abiko, the teenage reader who had been 'so excited' by *New Treasure Island* a few years before, and who would go on to co-create one of Japan's greatest manga heroes: the blue, earless robotic cat Doraemon.

Tezuka's system made it possible for him to produce nearly 250 works across the 1950s, from magazine supplements through to full-length manga books. He became Japan's best-known manga artist, a rare high-earner who could afford in 1960 to build a home studio complex in north-west Tokyo for himself and his wife Etsuko. Their son Makoto was born in the house the following summer, but Tezuka saw relatively little of him at first. After a decade of mounting success for *Mighty Atom*, a new Fuji Television Network commissioned him in the autumn and winter of 1962 to make an animated version. Having set post-war manga on its path, Tezuka was about to do the same for animation.

Tezuka's hero was Walt Disney, whose studio had pioneered ways of producing animation that matched the frame-rate of live-action films – the equivalent of twenty-four drawings for every second of a cartoon. Photographing each drawing twice halved the workload at a stroke, while the use of 'cels' (sheets of clear celluloid laid over one another) meant that only new elements of movement in a scene needed to be drawn afresh. Where Disney's major challenge had been cost, Tezuka's was personnel: at this point, there weren't enough animators in the whole of Japan to produce Disney-quality animation. Tezuka's new production company, Mushi Puro ('Insect Productions'), was forced to develop its own technique of 'limited animation': lingering on the same drawing for up to five seconds; zooming in and out, even sliding an image around under the camera to create the illusion of movement from a single drawing; and animating the mouth alone in speech scenes.

In later years, Tezuka would enjoy watching intellectuals working themselves into a froth trying to interpret these simple practicalities in terms of high art – some claimed to find kabuki-influenced dramatic pauses in his work. At the time, with *Mighty Atom* slated for broadcast on New Year's Day 1963, he and his production staff found themselves under enormous pressure. Many worked seven-day weeks, sleeping under their desks and developing such raw skin from constant drawing that illustrations ended up smudged with blood. The deadline was met nonetheless, and Japanese audiences welcomed the animated *Mighty Atom* with open arms.

A deal was secured later that year with America's NBC network, bringing Atom to American screens as 'Astro Boy'. The Japanese media were delighted. After nearly two post-war decades spent debating the influence of American culture, Japan was for the first time sending a home-grown animation series back the other way. For Tezuka and Mushi Puro, the deal was a mixed blessing. One welcome outcome of television success was the huge demand generated for merchandise – Atom dolls above all else. With animation production budgets always low in relation to labour costs – something for which later generations of animators blamed Tezuka's trend-setting example – sales of merchandise did much to help to balance the books. But as Atom went global, Tezuka found his politics and philosophy of life coming under scrutiny as never before.

Ever since the first *Mighty Atom* manga, small numbers of Japanese parents had complained about the effect on impressionable young children of preposterous ideas. A talking robot – really? People travelling to the moon? Come off it. Copies were burned in the street. Tezuka's publishers argued in response that *Mighty Atom* was a serious 'science manga'. But Tezuka himself was more interested in presenting children with the varied challenges of adult life – the fear, misunderstanding and discrimination – which created the conditions for governments to 'switch people's concept of reality', as he put it, thereby dragging them into war. Too many people lived as though they were 'programmed' to obey. Tezuka was delighted to find *Mighty Atom* stimulating research in Japan on humanoid robotics. But the mad scientists and evil inventors who populated his stories revealed his ambivalence about the uses to which science and technology could be put; he even suspected the Meiji-era slogan of *bunmei kaika* ('civilization and enlightenment') of dangerous naivety.

Tezuka sometimes used scenes of graphic violence to make his point. The impact on Japanese children was blunted by their brutal experiences during the war. NBC worried that American children, on the other hand, were less equipped to handle it. A producer at the network, Fred Ladd, was charged with editing episodes of *Mighty Atom* to make them less explicit and to render them culturally more intelligible. Scripts were rewritten, character names were changed, American humour was smuggled in and the theme tune was given less martial-sounding lyrics in its English version.

Even so, six out of the first batch of around a dozen episodes sent by Mushi Puro to NBC were rejected – a financial disaster for Tezuka's company. Fred Ladd journeyed to Tokyo in the autumn of 1964 to talk to Tezuka in person and see what might be done. Sitting across a table from him at Mushi Studios, Ladd began with a simple rule for American children's television: no one dies. So in a scene where Atom stands over a person lying in the street, saying, 'He's dead!', Astro Boy would simply declare him to be 'unconscious' – adding, 'Get him to a hospital!' Another unacceptable moment was when a criminal pressed a gun barrel to someone's temple. As Ladd explained to a group of animators beginning to gather around the two men, you can show a gun being brandished, but not threatening someone directly. This episode, too, could be saved, by cutting away from the action a little early.

Three episodes remained beyond redemption. One featured vivisection. Another involved a portrait of a naked woman on a wall – a detail added as a joke, without Tezuka's knowledge, by a sleep-deprived assistant pulling yet another all-nighter. The last showed a villain hiding out in a church, leaving his comrades a secret message by etching it into one of the eyeballs of Christ on a crucifix. Religion was an absolute no-no, as were Japanese animators' rather crude portrayals of ethnic minorities. Astro Boy's machine guns, meanwhile, remained largely undeployed, saving NBC the inevitable letters and phone calls from parents.

The encounter at Mushi Puro ended amicably, thanks in no small measure to a sense that Ladd personally was on the company's side. There was considerably less warmth, however, for the NBC censors. One of Tezuka's younger members of staff pointed to the high body-count in American westerns. Others, including Tezuka himself – who still vividly recalled being beaten up, more than a decade before, by a group of drunken American GIs – had in mind the ongoing Vietnam War. 'Americans', he later wrote, 'were sensitive about scenes of violence in fantasy [but they had] little trouble going over to South East Asia and killing people.' Here, again, was Tezuka's deep aversion to war, becoming part now of a bigger divide in Japanese life that was opening up in the late 1950s and into the 1960s: between those who were generally content at the prosperity that Pax Americana had brought since the Occupation and those, on the other hand, perturbed by the price that the Japanese seemed to be paying for it.

*

From 1953 through to the early 1970s, Japan's Gross National Product (GNP) grew at a rate never before seen in history, averaging more than 10 per cent every year. At the start of what came to be called the 'high growth era', the Japanese economy lagged behind that of every major Western country. By the end, only the world's two superpowers, the United States and the Soviet Union, remained ahead of it.

What *The Economist* magazine dubbed Japan's 'economic miracle' owed much to a Meiji-style channelling of scarce resources by an interventionist state. The old triangular relationship between politicians, businessmen and bureaucrats was given Atom-style jet boosters in 1955 when Japan's two conservative parties, Yoshida Shigeru's Japan Liberal Party and the Democratic Party, came together to form the Liberal Democratic Party (LDP, abbreviated to 'Jimintō' in Japanese). They spent the best part of the next four decades in continuous power. Meanwhile, bureaucrats in the Ministry of International Trade and Industry (MITI) began in the 1950s to encourage the formation of combines called *keiretsu*: companies clustering around a single bank as a source of still-scarce capital, bargaining collectively (including with foreign companies) and pooling their technical research and intelligence on the shape of the global economy. Shibusawa Eiichi might not have approved as shareholder power was minimal and the new system effectively allowed old *zaibatsu* like Mitsubishi and Mitsui to re-form. But he could not have argued with the results.

The United States played a significant part in all this. The Occupation-era settlement absolved Japan of the need to spend on defence, while the

Marshall Plan (1948) helped to revive Western Europe as a marketplace for goods, encouraging growth in the global economy. Japanese tariffs were tolerated, alongside a dollar–yen exchange rate that favoured Japanese exporters. America even chaperoned Japan's re-entry into the international community: starting with the International Monetary Fund and World Bank in 1952, the General Agreement on Tariffs and Trade (GATT) in 1955 and the United Nations in 1956.

As pre-war capabilities and wartime technical expertise were invested in innovative and commercially successful post-war projects, Japan became home to a growing roster of internationally recognized brands. Long before most of the world had heard of manga or anime, they were familiar with Sony, founded by two former employees of the Imperial Japanese Navy and famous for producing the world's first 'pocketable' radio (albeit a boast that could only be fulfilled by adding extra-large pockets to their salesmen's shirts). Older companies, now rebranded, joined them as household names in Europe and America: Panasonic, Canon and Nissan – the last producing military vehicles during the war as Nihon Sangyō (Japan Industries) and now retooling as a maker of consumer cars.

The greatest year of all for the new Japan was 1964. A team of men who during the war had worked on the Mitsubishi Zero fighter aircraft and in navy signals intelligence, took an idea memorably described by a senior executive at Japan National Railways as 'the height of madness . . . doomed to fail' and somehow made it work. The shinkansen ('new trunk line'), better known as the 'bullet train', was unveiled in October of that year: sleekly futuristic rolling stock, guided from a space-age control centre, propelled people between Japan's major cities at unheard-of speeds. In Shibusawa's day, Osaka to Tokyo had taken sixteen hours by rail. The same journey could now be done in four.

The shinkansen's inauguration was timed to coincide with Japan's hosting of the first Summer Olympics ever to be held in Asia, staged that year in Tokyo. This, too, proved an epoch-making success, adding to Japan's emerging reputation for high technology in association with good-natured sporting patriotism. The competitive highlight, for the Japanese, came courtesy of the women's volleyball team. In yet another repurposing of wartime expertise, their coach, Daimatsu 'the Demon' Hirobumi, turned his experience as an army platoon commander into a practice regime so demanding that it was dubbed 'homicidal training', while a Russian newspaper referred to his team as the 'Witches of the Orient'. Daimatsu's team ended up pitted against the Soviet Union in the tournament final, mounting a dramatic late comeback to claim a historic Olympic gold medal.

More important, in the long term, was the rehabilitation during the 1964 Olympics of three controversial symbols of militarism and war, their status uncertain since 1945. The Constitution wasn't clear on whether the Emperor was Japan's head of state. So he opened the games as an Olympic sponsor, to much the same statesman-like effect. Japan didn't have a national flag any more. For some Americans at Pearl Harbor in 1941, the sight on fighter fuselages of the *Hinomaru* – red disc on white background – had been the first sign that the chaos around them was something other than a military exercise gone horribly wrong. *Time* magazine celebrated America's victory in 1945 by showing it crossed out with a simple, deeply felt 'X'. Now those colours were affixed to the chest of the most innocent of young Japanese: born the day of the Hiroshima bomb, Sakai Yoshinori jogged up 160 steps with the Olympic torch to light the urn and start the Games. Japan also lacked an official national anthem. So *'Kimi ga yo'* ('His Imperial Majesty's Reign'), Japan's national anthem from 1888 to 1945, was presented as a song of peace, its playing timed to coincide with the release of white doves, as the Olympics drew to a successful close.

All of this provided visitors and viewers around the world, tuning in via satellite thanks to collaboration between NHK and NASA, with an overdue update to their images of Japan. Gone were the slavers, butchers and buck-toothed buffoons of *Tokio Jokio*. Here, instead, were the residents of the cleanest city they had ever seen, giving them the warmest welcome they could remember, and investing what one commentator described as 'hard work, humility and charm' in putting on 'the most brilliantly organized spectacle ever held in international sport'.

All this came as the Japanese were starting to feel steadily wealthier. Sales of television sets had been brisk in the run-up to the televised wedding, in April 1959, of the Emperor's son Crown Prince Akihito to a commoner called Shōda Michiko. Many more made the investment now. Possessing a TV set became a symbol of success, while the

American programmes that played on it encouraged viewers to aspire to still higher standards of material comfort – including the possession of the various electronic appliances that onscreen Americans seemed to take for granted, from air-conditioning units to refrigerators.

And yet all was not well, even in 1964. Alongside the usual Olympic party-poopers, asking whether a record-breaking $2 billion might not have been better spent elsewhere, were those who worried about the far larger price-tag attached to Japan's new-found peace and prosperity. Few believed that the San Francisco Peace Treaty and associated Security Treaty had brought the country real independence. They seemed, instead, to tie Japan uncomfortably close to America's post-war rise as an imperial power – with precious little that ordinary Japanese could do about it.

A hundred thousand people took to the streets in 1960 to protest against the renewal of the Security Treaty. But though Japan's LDP Prime Minister Kishi Nobusuke was forced to resign over the unrest, the renewal took place and his successor Ikeda Hayato moved swiftly to soothe the nation's spirits with an 'income doubling plan': a pledge to double GNP in a decade, which ended up achieving its goal in just seven years. Critics saw this as an attempt to substitute prosperity for national purpose, part of a dispiriting political quietism that seemed to be settling in.

Salarymen working long hours lacked the energy to aspire to much more than a drink, some rest or a short holiday. Schoolchildren were increasingly subjected to the sort of narrowly functional education against which Tsuda Umeko and Yosano Akiko had once campaigned. It was pursued now primarily in the interests of economic nationalism. But the Ministry of Education moved swiftly in the years after the Occupation ended to regain centralized control over educational content. A version of the old moral education was restored to the curriculum, one element of a general return – in part, at least – to a more traditional educational environment. Textbooks from which education boards would be permitted to choose were first vetted by ministry bureaucrats, countering what conservatives saw as a one-sided and demoralizing American take on the events of the 1930s and early 1940s. There was a push, at the same time, to restore the pre-war Japanese *ie*, or household – an ancient and beloved Japanese institution, from which the Occupation-era authorities had tried to lure women away with voting rights, the availability of divorce, and inheritance rights. The impressive performance of female candidates in the Diet elections of 1946 was destined to go unmatched for many years.

As the creator of hugely popular manga and anime, Tezuka Osamu enjoyed the kind of reach into people's imaginations, and potential sway over their opinions, of which most intellectuals and politicians could only dream. He never became deeply involved in politics, once declaring that he considered 'anyone who is thoroughly steeped in the ideology of the left or the right to be an idiot'. But he did use his platform to create cultural space for imagery and ideas that ran counter to the dominant trends of the day.

One of his earliest *shōjo* (girls') manga was *Ribon no Kishi*. Known in English as *Princess Knight*, it began to be published in the 1950s and was turned into an anime in the late 1960s. The main character, Sapphire, is born into a female body, but after something goes awry with the soul-implanting process in heaven she is left possessing both male and female souls. Her parents, the king and queen of Silverland, are relying on her as their heir. So they raise her as a boy, allowing her to dress as a girl for just one hour early every morning. She is discovered nonetheless, and imprisoned by her enemies, escaping to embark on a series of fantastical adventures as she works to rid her kingdom of evil forces and to find romance with Prince Frantz Charming.

Princess Knight set a major visual trend in Japan. The starry-eyed Sapphire looks like Betty Boop crammed into outfits inspired by Disney, the Takarazuka Revue and an old, idealized Europe: pink leotard and Snow White dress; cutlass and ruby-red cape; silky-sleek white horse and magnificent castle. The series also helped Japan's long history of cross-dressing and gender-bending – from kabuki to the Takarazuka itself – to make it through into mainstream post-war culture, while presenting Japanese girls with a strong and adventurous role model. In the hands of female artists from the 1970s, *shōjo* manga went on to offer characters with ever richer interior lives, new takes on love and relationships, and the great manga staple of the *bishōnen*, the androgynously beautiful, sensitive, unthreatening boy.

Still, the 1960s proved a mixed decade for Tezuka. He was a popular commentator on radio and television. In 1964, he met his hero Walt Disney in New York – who turned out to be an admirer of *Astro Boy*. And Stanley Kubrick, another *Astro Boy* fan, asked him to help with the design work for *2001: A Space Odyssey*. (Tezuka was too busy to say yes, later contenting himself instead with playing the film's soundtrack while he worked.) But Tezuka's stylistic debt to Disney led Japanese critics to level at him a charge made against American missionaries nearly a century before: of being *bata kusai* ('stinking of butter') – that is, westernized to the point of snubbing Japanese culture.

Others thought Tezuka too tame for the times. With politics sewn up by the right for the time being, it fell to protesters and the culture industries to try to change the country's course. While university students engaged in radical and sometimes violent campus activism towards the end of the 1960s – protesting against the cost, content and social context of their dismally dull educations – avant-garde filmmakers, theatre directors, dancers and performance artists sought to shock audiences awake from a somnolent 'everydayness'. 'New wave' directors like Ōshima Nagisa set out to make films that would serve as 'forms of action'. *Night and Fog in Japan* (*Nihon no Yoru to Kiri*, 1960) was a prime example. Claustrophobic and politically charged, it was a million miles away from blockbusters like *Godzilla* (*Gojira*, 1954) or *Season of the Sun* (*Taiyō no Kisetsu*, 1956), a tale of adolescent violence and debauchery. Even highly regarded directors like Ozu Yasujirō came in for criticism. *Tokyo Story* (*Tōkyō Monogatari*, 1953) was greeted internationally as a masterpiece of spaciousness and serenity. For Ōshima, Ozu was too 'congenial'.

At the cutting edge of manga in the 1950s and animation in the early 1960s, Tezuka now risked looking a little old hat. Other manga artists were responding to the rising political temperature in Japan with a new genre called *gekiga* ('dramatic pictures') that was grittier and more visually realistic than Tezuka's child-like worlds. Shirato Sanpei's *Ninja Chronicles* (*Ninja Bugeichō*, 1959–62) became an early classic, meeting with approval from Ōshima who turned it into a film in 1967 by photographing the manga pages and adding music and dialogue. Shirato also helped to launch the monthly magazine *Garo* in 1964 as a forum for experimental work in the *gekiga* vein.

Tezuka responded to all this in 1967 with a new and experimental magazine of his own: *COM* – standing for 'Comics, Community and Communication'. He began producing more manga for adults, offering satires on Japan's consumerist and male-centric culture. And yet he could never resist working with the largest possible canvas. Included in the initial issue of *COM* was the first instalment of Tezuka's unfinished epic manga series *Phoenix* (*Hi no Tori*). Having grown up amidst war, firebombing raids and bodies floating along the Yodogawa River, Tezuka ended up placing his faith not in politics or even in human nature but in *seimei*: 'life' itself – real, mysterious, 'pervading everything' and symbolized here by the Phoenix. Humans participate in this life, thought Tezuka, and yet we cling to the idea of possessing it for ourselves in the form of personal immortality. This tragedy plays out in *Phoenix* across a vast expanse of time, from Queen Himiko – greedy and grasping, seeking to capture the Phoenix and drink its immortality-giving blood – through to the thirty-fifth century, when a few remaining human communities struggle on in the wake of nuclear apocalypse.

In this way, Tezuka became one of the first artists to take the particularities of Japanese history, the ancient through to the modern and contemporary, and ask what it meant not just for the Japanese but for humanity as a whole. To his critics, he was absenting himself from high-stakes social and political battles at home. To his fans, he was working above and beyond nations and peoples, having seen for himself where tribalism could lead. One of the main characters in the *Phoenix* series is Masato. He becomes the last human being left alive, tasked by the Phoenix with overseeing the regeneration of Earth after humanity has trashed it with technology. Such was the scale of Tezuka's imagination, inspiring generations of later manga and anime artists, including Studio Ghibli's Miyazaki Hayao, to produce great cosmic – sometimes apocalyptic – visions of their own.

*

In 1971, Shueisha, publishers of the manga magazine *Weekly Shōnen Jump*, set up the Tezuka Award. Here was a bittersweet moment for

Tezuka: contributions to his field were being recognized, but with disconcertingly heavy use of the past tense. As if to confirm that his glory days were over, *COM* ceased publication around the same time, while employees at the deeply indebted Mushi Puro formed a union, leading Tezuka to step down as president. The company later went bankrupt. Tezuka was meanwhile faced with increasing competition from a new generation of manga artists who were inspired by his early work but sought to move beyond it – and out of his shadow.

And yet such was Tezuka's inexhaustible originality, and the universalism of his subject matter, that rather than passing in and out of fashion as times changed he kept creating fresh characters who proved capable of setting new trends of their own. The greatest of these in the 1970s was Black Jack, a prodigiously talented surgeon with black-and-white hair, a black cape and theatrical ribbon bowtie, who after being spurned by the establishment embarks alone on a series of exciting medical adventures. This was Tezuka returning to his 1952 fork in the road, exploring in rich fantasy the sort of doctor that he might have become. Ensuring that Black Jack's escapades were not just anatomically explicit but anatomically on-the-money, he tapped into a desire amongst evermore discerning readers in Japan for well-informed themed manga in a variety of fields, from history and sport through to philosophy and cookery.

As if to emphasize the timelessness of his creations, Tezuka imagined his heroes and bit-part players alike not just as characters confined to particular stories but as 'actors' capable of being cast in a range of roles – taking on slightly different guises each time, but always recognizably themselves. This 'Star System', inspired by the way that theatrical directors of the Takarazuka Revue went about their work, saw Atom and his mentor Professor Ochanomizu showing up in *Black Jack*, while an evil character called Acetylene Lamp stalked the pages of *Black Jack*, *Phoenix* and other manga besides. Sapphire enjoyed outings beyond her own dedicated manga, as did a character who ended up rivalling Atom for his international appeal. Leo, the orphaned African lion, was the star of a much-loved manga series *Jungle Emperor* (*Janguru Taitei*), which in the mid-1960s became Japan's first colour television anime series and was soon exported to the United States as *Kimba the White Lion*.

Tezuka continued working more or less up until the day of his death in 1989. His status as 'Japan's Disney' and 'god of manga', and an instantly recognizable symbol – with his trademark beret and thick glasses – of rediscovered national pride, caused Japanese audiences to respond with a mixture of puzzlement and outrage when in 1994 they sat down to watch a Disney film about an African lion cub. It all seemed terribly familiar. Innocent little lion as cuddly main character? *Check*. 'Simba' rather than 'Kimba'. Mercurial, controlling adult lion? *Check*. A baboon, a hornbill and a bunch of hyenas anthropomorphized as sage-like, comical and evil, respectively? *Check*. Unrealistic setting – rocky landscape rather than savannah? *Check*. Around 500 Japanese manga and anime artists signed a letter of protest to the Walt Disney Company, whose subtext was that to disrespect Tezuka was to insult Japan.

Disney responded by denying any role for *Jungle Emperor* in inspiring *The Lion King* (working title: *King of the Jungle*). And Tezuka Productions, a surviving spin-off of Mushi Puro which dealt with copyright, decided to let the issue lie. They perhaps had in mind the circle of life. Disney had shaped Tezuka: *Bambi*, which he watched more than a hundred times, was said to have influenced *Jungle Emperor*. And now Tezuka appeared to have returned the favour. Here was a vivid illustration of one of two trends in the way that 'forward with culture' seemed to have worked out since the war: an early period of heavy influence for American entertainment had given way to Japanese accomplishments in literature and the visual arts that were sufficiently insightful about human life to find audiences and exert a creative impact around the world.

One of Tezuka's great contemporaries here was Kurosawa Akira, who helped to put Japanese film on the map with *Rashōmon* (1950) and *Seven Samurai* (*Shichinin no Samurai*, 1954), the latter fully acknowledged by the makers of *The Magnificent Seven* (1960) as the basis for their story. Kurosawa was also making films over these years that reflected life during and after the Occupation. *Drunken Angel*

(*Yoidore Tenshi*, 1948), about the relationship between a doctor and a gangster, showed as much of the devastation of post-war Tokyo as the American censors would allow. Kasagi Shizuko appeared in one scene, singing a song called 'Jungle Boogie'. With music by Hattori Ryōichi and lyrics by Kurosawa, it satirized the chaotic side to the freedom brought to Tokyo by the Americans – with bomb craters, ruined buildings, gangsters and prostitutes. *To Live* (*Ikiru*, 1952) homed in on the question of purpose in post-war Japan through the life of an ageing government bureaucrat whose terminal diagnosis prompts him to secure permission for the building of a children's playground as one final, meaningful act in his life.

A second deeply influential figure of Tezuka's era was the novelist and playwright – and avid Hibari fan – Mishima Yukio, whose work began to appear in English translation in the 1950s and 1960s. But Mishima also offered an unfortunate illustration of a second trend in 'forward with culture': an apparent disconnect between entertainment, high and low brow alike, and politics. In Mishima's case, this took tragic-comic form one day in 1970 at the Tokyo barracks of the 'Self-Defence Forces' – the successor institution to the National Police Reserve of 1950. Having made an appointment with the barracks' commander, Mishima tied him to a chair with the aid of a small right-ist militia and then proceeded to deliver an impassioned plea from the commander's balcony to some soldiers below. Mishima urged them to 'hurl their bodies against the Constitution' and to help fill what he saw as Japan's post-war spiritual void by returning the Emperor to power. Met with laughter and derision, this great cultural icon retired back inside the commander's office to perform ritual suicide, cutting open his stomach while a member of his militia stood behind him and took off his head.

Elsewhere, the relative failure of Japan's creative arts to exert a decisive impact on politics was less dramatic but no less real. They could satirize. They could offer alternative visions. They could present audiences with heroes of the Japanese past, as an implied rebuke to the leaders of the present. What they couldn't do, it seemed, was contribute to the dislodging from power of a broad-church conservative establishment that was happy enough to let the Japanese indulge their fantasies in any way they wished as long as the country's political and economic character remained unaffected. Tezuka never saw the Liberal Democratic Party (LDP) out of government in his lifetime. He had helped to liberate the Japanese imagination once again, in the wake of authoritarianism and war. But he could not free the Japanese from their political constraints: lingering legacies of the pre-war era's rather limited party politics, post-war American self-interest, and the extraordinary success of the LDP in shaping – and gaming – the system.

19
Tanaka Kakuei

(田中角栄)

1918–1993

Shadow Shogun

Tanaka Kakuei on the campaign trail in Niigata, 1976. Japanese politicians traditionally wear white gloves to symbolize purity and trustworthiness.

The fifth of July 1972. Tanaka Fume, getting on in years now, leans in towards her television set and wipes it with her handkerchief. There are those in her home prefecture of Niigata, on Honshū's north-western coast, who might think this – or at least wish it – an act of ultra-modern voodoo, an attempt to scrub from existence the Liberal Democratic Party politicians onscreen. They are gathered in the capital a few hundred kilometres to the south to select a new party leader – and with it, such is their continued dominance, a new prime minister.

Samurai descent; politics in the family; a law degree from Tokyo University; and a track record of high-level service in major government ministries – such is the pedigree required of a Japanese premier these days. Familiarity with, much less active concern for, Fume's chilly, remote corner of the archipelago means very little. It was ever thus. Known in centuries past as Echigo Province, Niigata is hemmed in by mountains on three sides, so that Siberian winds blowing in from across the Sea of Japan ricochet around and encase much of the local landscape and population in snow and ice from November through to March. Shinran was exiled here in 1207. Zeami followed in 1434, banished to Sado Island just off the coast. Modern Japanese know the region as *yukiguni* – 'snow country'. Ideal for a rustic getaway and romanticized first in Kawabata Yasunari's classic novel *Snow Country* (*Yukiguni*, 1948) and then in Misora Hibari's 'Echigo Lion Dance Song' (1950), Niigata can be a punishing place actually to make one's life. It has become known, in recent decades, for waves of desperate outward migration.

Tanaka Fume knows this as well as anyone. But, handkerchief in hand, she isn't trying to wipe out Japan's political class. She is tending, with great love, to the glistening brow of one of its number. Short and stocky, he is sitting with his eyes closed and arms folded as the LDP election process draws to a close and the result is announced.

This is her son, Kakuei. And against all odds, he has just become the Prime Minister.

The Japanese, it seems, are in the mood for something new. A series of rather safe, rather dull prime ministers, trained as bureaucrats and ill-suited to an age of mass communication, have failed to get to grips with the problems thrown up across the prosperous 1960s: overworked adults and children, overstuffed cities, a polluted environment and a lack of national purpose beyond steady enrichment. Perhaps Tanaka can make the difference. He is a charismatic construction magnate, a self-made man, who has risen through the ranks of the LDP and taken the rare step, earlier in 1972, of publishing a lengthy and highly philosophical manifesto for building a new Japan.

Fume watches as he rises now from his seat, raising his hand to calm the applause echoing around the hall. Japan's youngest Prime Minister since the war, unique in his lack of a university degree, Tanaka vows to tackle Japan's 'mountain of difficult problems'. His pledge is met with celebratory cries of 'Banzai!' from the LDP delegates surrounding him, beneath which lurk more mixed feelings about their new leader. There is optimism at what he might achieve; an awareness, amongst many, of the heavy political debts they already owe him; and nervousness that this supreme political operator has now bagged himself the biggest job of all.

*

Tanaka Kakuei was born on 4 May 1918, the only boy in his family alongside six girls – two older sisters, four younger. His father Kakuji was a relatively wealthy man, with around ten square kilometres of forest and rice land to his name, in the village of Futada. Managed well, it could support a comfortable living of rice cultivation and livestock farming. Kakuji, unfortunately, managed it very badly. Imagining himself to be Niigata's answer to Shibusawa Eiichi, he made a series of ambitious investments that went disastrously awry. He sold the family forests to buy three cows from the Netherlands, only for two of the Friesians to die on the long sea journey, while a third made it all the way to the Tanaka homestead before expiring on the lawn. An attempt to import racehorses from Australia fared little better, and thereafter Kakuji took to a life of drinking, gambling and general neglect of his family. Fume was left working alone in the rice paddies, carrying other people's rice up mountainsides for a little extra money and apologizing profusely to her husband's creditors.

To this unpromising start in life were added fresh misfortunes as Tanaka Kakuei grew. At two, he nearly died from diphtheria. At four, he suffered a serious head injury, inflicted by his own grandmother while she was trying to dig him out of an avalanche with a spade. Boys and girls at school bullied him for his stammer, forcing him into more than his fair share of playground fights. And with no money in the family to continue his education beyond the age of fourteen, he ended up working on government construction projects, pushing heavy carts laden with stones and mud.

In 1934, Tanaka left all this behind to seek his fortune in Tokyo. He found it a 'tough town', from an over-charging taxi driver who knew an easy rural mark when he saw one to hucksters running a board-game scam in the street, with whom Tanaka made a bet and lost his watch. Tanaka persevered nonetheless, taking on menial work to support himself through three years of night-school. He left at nineteen with enough knowledge of engineering and architecture to start his own construction company.

A burgeoning business career was briefly interrupted in 1939 when Tanaka was conscripted, sent across to Manchuria and beaten up in his barracks for having the temerity to grow a moustache – an affectation of the officer class alone, not to be seen on the upper lips of country-bumpkin cannon fodder. A fortunately timed bout of pneumonia and pleurisy got Tanaka transported back to Japan, where he was discharged from the army just weeks before the Pearl Harbor attack. He went on to win building contracts from the Riken industrial group, which specialized in developing commercial applications for the scientific findings of the Institute of Physical and Chemical Research (RIKEN) which Ikeda Kikunae had helped to found. Additional business came his way after he married Sakamoto Hana in March 1942 and inherited her father's construction company, complete with government and private clients.

On the day of Japan's surrender, Tanaka was in Korea, working on a lucrative contract to relocate factory facilities from Tokyo – at constant risk of air attack – to the comparative safety of the southern peninsula. While most Japanese spent the weeks that followed waiting in camps to be repatriated, Tanaka managed to hitch an early ride back to Honshū aboard a naval ferry. Few believed his later claim that a clerical error in his favour had opened up a berth for 'Kakuei' that had been intended for a woman named 'Kikue'. More likely, a fraction of the enormous sum for his Korea contract – some 15 million yen – had found its way into the right pockets.

Returning to Tokyo, where most of his property had somehow survived the devastating air raids, Tanaka found his wealth opening doors for him into politics. He stood unsuccessfully for the country's first post-war elections in 1946, but learned from his myriad mistakes and did better when a poll was called for 1947. The first time round, Tanaka had turned up to a campaign meeting in a morning coat, while rivals donned artfully muddied workers' boots. This time, Tanaka decked himself out as a working man – a role he knew better than most of his rivals – and hired a hundred campaign workers. It did the trick. The boy whose mother thought that he might, with luck, make a living punching railway tickets headed off to Tokyo to take his seat in the new national Diet.

Post-war Japanese politics was a close match for Tanaka's talents. Japan had no great pre-war tradition of grassroots political parties on which to build. Instead, what mattered in garnering local support was the making of deals with individuals, companies and interest groups, who wanted specific things accomplished in return for their votes and campaign contributions. In this way, personal support networks known as *kōenkai* would form around promising candidates. Tanaka built his by assuring the voters of Niigata that they would no longer be overlooked. He and his Etsuzankai ('Association for Crossing the Mountains') would put them on the map.

The *kōenkai* model of politics encouraged parties to remain broad churches, avoiding clear commitment to big ideas or issues that might play well in one district while poisoning prospects in another. The LDP succeeded early on, after its formation in 1955, by keeping its policy platform modest, focusing on the needs of key economic constituencies. Farmers received price protections and workers were offered better wages and conditions, including healthcare and subsidized holidays, in return for participating in productivity drives. Small business owners were supported with minimal taxation and the banning from their neighbourhoods of larger-scale competition from supermarkets and department stores. When challenges arose, the LDP borrowed popular policies from its rivals and worked closely with bureaucratic and business allies to find compromise solutions.

None of this seemed to earn the LDP lasting affection from the Japanese public, who were grateful for their prosperity but tended to associate it more with their own hard graft than with inspired political leadership. Successive iterations of a Socialist Party did reliable if unspectacular business at most national elections. So, too, to a lesser extent, did the Japanese Communist Party. From 1964 a new party, Kōmeitō, began to emerge as a force in Japanese politics, staking out territory in the centre-ground. Its links to a Buddhist movement called Sōka Gakkai ('Value Creation Society'), which claimed around 7 million members by the end of the 1960s, helped it to build a voter base but led to allegations of violating the post-war prohibition on church–state collaboration. Critics continued to worry even after Kōmeitō announced its formal separation from Sōka Gakkai in 1970. The LDP, meanwhile, kept winning elections but on steadily smaller portions of the vote.

It was into this party – more a constellation of competing factions than a single united organization – that Tanaka made his entrance in 1957. He presented Kishi Nobusuke, who had just become prime minister, with a small backpack whose seams were straining from the sheer bulk of the 3 million yen in cash that Tanaka had managed to cram inside. Duly rewarded with his first Cabinet role, as Minister of Posts and Telecommunications, Tanaka set to work enriching both Niigata and himself out of the public purse.

Most of the economic rewards across the 1960s went to pre-existing urban and industrial areas along the 'Pacific Belt': from Tokyo to Yokohama through Nagoya and Osaka to Kobe down to the northern

Kyūshū city of Fukuoka. Rural Japanese began flocking to these areas, until by 1970 fully half the population, or around 50 million people, was living in an urban corridor running from Tokyo through to Osaka. Amongst the few areas of rural Japan to develop with notable rapidity was Niigata. Fresh railway track was laid. Older rail services were upgraded. And new roads were built, including one that bored through the Mikuni Mountains – slashing the journey time to Tokyo, but at astronomical cost.

Tanaka was diligent in taking the credit. He cast himself as the archetypal local boy made good, speaking to the people of Niigata – who called him 'Kaku-san' – with rare power and passion, and milking his hard-graft backstory as relentlessly as he might have done the family's Friesians, had they lived. He published a bestselling autobiography in the mid-1960s and encouraged media fascination with his family: the doting rural mother and the Americanized urbanite daughter, Makiko (born 1944), returning home from school in Philadelphia to scold her father for his heavy drinking and rambling conversation – helpfully highlighting two things that for many voters were part of Tanaka's earthy charm.

Patrician colleagues in the LDP were largely immune to Tanaka's shtick. They valued him instead for his deal-making skills and his extraordinary command of Japan's electoral landscape, the fruits of long nights of research and a memory that earned him the nickname 'Computerized Bulldozer'. Tanaka was also popular with the media: a useful quality in a senior Cabinet member, but not one considered conducive to the top job – until 1972. By that point, Japan had had a run of three prime ministers all of whom had started out as ministry bureaucrats and none of them especially warm or sympathetic characters: Kishi Nobusuke (1957–60), Ikeda Hayato (1960–64) and Kishi's younger brother Satō Eisaku (1964–72). The Japanese public, or at least the press, were in the market for someone capable of providing more vigorous representation abroad and more inspiring leadership at home.

Tanaka resolved to oblige them, rooting his pitch in a timely critique of the state of the nation. In *A Plan for Remodelling the Japanese Archipelago (Nihon Rettō Kaizō Ron,* 1972), he lamented the overcrowding, car and rail carriage congestion, pollution and rising prices that seemed to be plaguing Japan's cities. The cherry blossoms bore silent witness to it all, he suggested – smaller, thinner petals appeared each year, struggling forth in sickly shades of pink and white. The countryside, meanwhile, was being hollowed out by urban migration, contributing to a regional imbalance that he personally knew only too well: Japan's Pacific coast prospering – home to politics, diplomacy and tourism; Sony and Nissan; music, manga and film – while the Sea of Japan coast fell ever further behind.

New cities and industrial bases were needed, claimed Tanaka, to take the pressure off existing ones. Rural areas must be revitalized with high-tech farming, higher incomes and the provision of social and cultural pleasures such that no rural son or daughter need run off to a city in search of company or fun. The proceeds of Japan's world-famous growth should be distributed more fairly, with a boost in welfare provision for the elderly in particular. The resulting 'spiritual affluence' at home would be complemented by greater assertion abroad, including a more generous overseas aid regime.

Plenty of Japanese sympathized with Tanaka's analysis. Some migrants to Japan's cities had ended up living the dream. They took up residence in newly built apartment complexes, stocking them with the latest consumer goods: washing machines and fridges, 'pocketable' radios and televisions. Marriages, careers and families followed, completing a middle-class identity that was claimed by up to 90 per cent of the population by around 1970. But of the 11 million new homes built in the boom years, many were cramped and poorly constructed, with sub-standard sewage systems and a thick latticework of hurriedly connected electricity and telephone cables. Cars crawled along in dense traffic, contributing to a broader pollution problem with which a company called Shin Nihon Chisso Hiryō became grimly synonymous in the late 1960s and early 1970s. It was successfully sued over Minamata disease, a severe – often fatal – neurological syndrome caused by high levels of mercury in factory effluent that Chisso had for years pumped into Minamata Bay in Kyūshū. The government was forced by this and other scandals to pass a series of anti-pollution measures in 1970, creating an Environment Agency and establishing 'polluter pays' arrangements. Bureaucrats advised businesses behind the scenes on how to reduce their emissions and thereby avoid becoming the next Chisso.

Tanaka was right about the countryside, too. Prosperity, better healthcare and the advent of mechanized farming meant that rural lives were for the most part much less harsh than they had been when Tanaka's mother Fume was raising her family. And the world of mass entertainment bound people closer to their city cousins than ever before. But village schools were closing down for lack of students. And seasonal festivals were falling by the wayside for want of participants. By 1970, less than 20 per cent of the Japanese labour force was engaged in agriculture.

Nor would a little diplomatic backbone go amiss, especially with Richard Nixon in the White House – his economic policy: 'Stick it to the Japanese.' In 1971, Nixon ramped up import taxes on Japanese products and threatened sanctions against textiles (where competition was hitting his southern voter base). That same year, he declared live on television, and without informing the Japanese ahead of time, that he would travel to Beijing in 1972 to seek a new relationship with the People's Republic of China. Japan now risked being left out in the cold: it was less urgently required by the US as a balancing force in East Asia, and had done little over the last quarter-century – on American orders – to rebuild its own relationships in the region.

Victorious in the LDP election in July 1972, Tanaka established a commission to look at ways of making a reality of 'remodelling the archipelago' while preparing to visit Beijing, following in Nixon's footsteps to normalize relations with the People's Republic. Tanaka was welcomed there in September with the flying of the Hinomaru flag and the strains of 'Kimi ga yo'. For all that the United States had sought to keep Japan and Communist China apart, many Japanese had long sought healing and the restoration of ties. China's leaders, meanwhile, hoped to secure Japanese investment and to apply a little diplomatic solvent to the bonds that America was building up in Asia – with Japan, South Korea, Taiwan, the Philippines.

Both sides had their red lines in the run-up to Tanaka's trip. For the Japanese, the US–Japan security relationship was not up for debate. For the Chinese, it was vital that Japan recognize its old colony of Taiwan as part of the People's Republic. The latter issue remained unresolved when Tanaka touched down on 25 September. Nor did Tanaka help his general cause when, at a banquet on the first evening, he apologized for the war of 1931–45 using a phrase which, particularly in the Chinese (mis)translation offered that evening, risked equating a tragedy that had cost up to 20 million Chinese lives with a trifling inconvenience. Tanaka had used the phrase '*tadai no gomeiwaku*', 'enormous trouble'. The translator opted for *mafan* in Mandarin, which means an 'annoyance' or 'bother'. Zhou Enlai and Mao Zedong both expressed extreme displeasure.

But Mao in particular found much about Tanaka to which he could relate: his rustic roots, his rheumatism, a brilliant strategic brain and an interest in traditional East Asian culture. Bonding over talk of Buddhism, Confucius and incense, the two men found they could put the Taiwan question aside for the moment. Before the world's cameras, on 29 September, Tanaka and Zhou took up Asian writing brushes and signed a normalization agreement. Sino-Japanese ties developed steadily from there, with the value of trade between the two countries rising from around $1 billion in 1972 to $4 billion in 1975. Japan became China's closest trading partner, with petroleum travelling from the mainland to a perennially resource-poor archipelago, while goods and industrial expertise flowed the other way.

Arriving back home in Japan, Tanaka enjoyed a few months of blissful popularity. His approval ratings ran above 60 per cent and the *New York Times* compared his visionary ambition with that of Franklin D. Roosevelt. Proclaiming 1973 to be the 'First Year of Welfare' in Japan, Tanaka doubled pension benefits and indexed them to the cost of living. He bestowed free healthcare on the elderly and launched a universal child allowance.

But that year the oil crisis struck, prices nearly tripling in response to unrest in the Middle East. At the same time, land prices in places earmarked for development under Tanaka's grand schemes began to rise steeply. The combined result was a spike in inflation and a hoarding of essential goods lest supplies run out. Tanaka had promised shiny new cities and a spiritually fulfilled population. Instead, people were fighting over toilet rolls. For once, Tanaka found himself out of touch with the popular mood, harping unperturbed on his plans for 'remodelling the archipelago' and frustrated by the minutiae of governance.

The aura of global statesman also seemed quickly to fade. Under the terms of the San Francisco Peace Treaty of 1952, Japan had made reparations payments to Burma, the Philippines, Indonesia and South Vietnam, largely in the form of goods and services provided by Japanese companies and subsidized by the Japanese government. Hundreds of millions of dollars in reparations were also paid to South Korea, after a Treaty on Basic Relations was signed in 1965. But the element of economic self-interest involved here, together with the harsh dealings of some Japanese companies in the years that followed, smacked of empire by other means. Relationships with South Korea remained strained, while on visits to Thailand and Indonesia in January 1974 Tanaka found himself denounced as an 'Ugly Economic Imperialist' in Bangkok and then a focal point for anti-Japanese riots in Jakarta. Tens of thousands of people protesting against Japanese economic competition and the shortcomings of their own leaders set fire to Japanese cars and burned a showroom selling Toyotas to the ground. Tanaka had to be helicoptered to the airport so that he could make an early exit.

Most damaging of all were rumours of dodgy dealing. A good amount of the wealth that Tanaka had channelled into Niigata since he was first elected seemed to have ended up in his own pocket. His construction companies helped to build some of the new infrastructure. New roads meant new routes for his bus company, along with a rise in property prices that benefited his sizeable portfolio – portions of which had been acquired under false pretences, including the use on documents of the name of a geisha whom Tanaka had made his mistress.

To these tales of personal enrichment was added, in 1974, a backlash against Tanaka's plan to encourage businesses and interest groups effectively to adopt their own pet parliamentary candidate. They would be responsible for getting that person elected, and in return the candidate would lobby in government for their interests. This had long been the basic logic of collaboration between government, business and civil society, and organizations as varied as Toyota, Hitachi, dentists and the Self-Defence Forces took up Tanaka's offer at Upper House elections that year. But so naked a display of clientelism sat poorly with the public, as did the record-breaking number of electoral law violations that resulted.

Tanaka's political and media enemies went for him as never before. Fukuda Takeo, defeated by Tanaka two years before in the leadership race, called piously for 'reform' in the LDP and for an end to money politics. A Japanese magazine called *Bungei Shunjū* meanwhile published detailed revelations about Tanaka's property dealings, his use of 'ghost companies' and his lavish lifestyle. All this at a time when ordinary Japanese were still reeling from the financial and psychological effects of the oil shock – most of all, the stark realization that Japan's economic miracle would not go on forever. Tanaka's approval ratings nosedived to just 12 per cent, his health began to deteriorate, and in November 1974 he decided to call it quits and resign.

*

What does Mejiro think? That was the question on everyone's lips whenever some new conundrum or opportunity arose in Japanese politics across the second half of the 1970s and into the 1980s. 'Mejiro' was not a person. It was a place – a neighbourhood in Tokyo, home to the Mejiro Palace: a luxurious estate featuring beautifully sculpted gardens, a tulip field, a pond filled with precious carp, and a steady stream of petitioners on their way to meet with the owner – one Tanaka Kakuei.

Tanaka's career did not end with his surrender of the premiership. It had always been a less dynamic role than in many other parts of the world. Bureaucrats tended to formulate policy. The LDP was cautious about big initiatives. And the Constitution placed executive authority with the Cabinet, rather than the Prime Minister. Senior party men tended to take turns in the job as a result, dispatched when their time was up or if a change of face promised a short-term electoral boost.

Real power was exercised behind the scenes, helping LDP members to build up their personal support networks and then bringing those members together in a faction large enough to dominate the Cabinet and important government committees. This was Tanaka's speciality, and he approached his task afresh in the years after resigning, even while fighting a new and gargantuan corruption charge. A horrified Japanese public discovered in 1976 that as Prime Minister

Tanaka had taken a bribe from the American aerospace giant Lockheed, persuading All Nippon Airways (ANA) to choose a Lockheed jumbo jet for its fleet over a rival McDonnell Douglas model, in return for a generous share of a contract worth hundreds of millions of dollars. Tanaka sent his limousine cruising around Tokyo to collect cardboard boxes full of cash from various locations as part of a process facilitated by an influential ultranationalist gangster named Kodama Yoshio.

Arrested in July 1976 and resigning from the LDP, Tanaka became the first person in Japan to be charged with criminal abuse of prime ministerial office. His trial began in January the next year and lasted for almost seven years. Every Wednesday he would arrive to give public testimony to prosecutors. And then for the rest of the week he would receive visitors at Mejiro, sometimes as many as 300 in a single day: from farmers who had travelled overnight from Niigata to beg a favour, through to senior figures in Japan's 'iron triangle' of LDP politicians, bureaucrats and businesspeople. Tanaka listened to each of them from the comfort of a chair nicknamed 'the Prime Minister's seat'. Nearby sat a small golden turtle, engraved with stars, flowers and birds. A push on its head rang a bell to summon the next petitioner from the crowd crammed into his waiting area.

A notable caller in October 1978, probably not made to wait long, was Deng Xiaoping, who had wielded national power in China since the deaths in 1976 of Zhou Enlai and Mao Zedong. A Sino-Japanese Treaty of Peace and Friendship was signed in the summer of 1978, and Deng's subsequent visit to Japan made him the first Chinese leader in history to go there while still in office. It was a diplomatic triumph. Deng lauded Japan's modernizing achievements, from the shinkansen to the use of robotics at a Nissan car plant, and happily conceded that China had much to learn. The Japanese, in turn, took him around Kyoto, highlighting just how much of its splendour was Chinese in origin and inspiration. Chatting to Tanaka at the Mejiro Palace, Deng thanked him for his efforts in bringing about peace between the two nations. 'When we drink water,' he said, 'we cannot forget those who dug the well.'

It was not long before Tanaka regained his former level of political influence. The Niigata electors never left his side; happy, it seemed, to agree with Tanaka that his legal troubles were an establishment stitch-up, they returned him as their representative time after time and continued to reap the infrastructural rewards – including two national highways, an international university and a bullet-train line said to have cost 6 billion yen per kilometre because of the difficult terrain involved. LDP members were meanwhile tempted to his side with largesse on a scale that earned Tanaka a new nickname: 'the Private Bank of Japan'. Members of his faction, current and prospective, visited him in Mejiro and took home with them thick wads of 10,000-yen notes, wrapped up in traditional Japanese cloth or stuffed into bags: electoral expenses, parcelled out in 'bullets' of 100 million yen. Aspiring parliamentary candidates received other forms of assistance besides, from senior faction members making supportive visits to their districts to campaigning tips and electoral analysis courtesy of the 'shadow shogun' himself.

By 1983, more than one in four LDP Diet members were part of Tanaka's revived faction, and he had had a hand in the rise to party leadership of three prime ministers. The last of them, Nakasone Yasuhiro (in power 1982–7), found space in his administration for no fewer than eight Tanaka faction members. The press called it the 'Tanakasone Cabinet'. Tanaka's faction also ended up in control of half of the party's policy-making sub-committees. Alongside personal support networks (*kōenkai*), policy 'tribes' (*zoku*) within the LDP became an essential component of Japan's politics from the 1970s onwards. Members collaborated with the relevant ministries and industries, and in so doing ensured that the interests of their constituents and *kōenkai* members were looked after. Amongst the most influential was the 'road tribe', with deep links to the construction industry.

A guilty verdict in October 1983 changed little for Tanaka. The chief judge declared that he had done 'irreparable damage to public trust in politics', fined him 500 million yen and sentenced him to four years in prison. Tanaka immediately appealed, putting the Prime Minister and the Diet in a bind. Nakasone could not force him to relinquish his parliamentary seat – it was Tanaka who held Nakasone's future in his hands, not the other way around. The Diet was meanwhile so divided over whether or not to censure him that the country was forced into a general election in December. Such was the miracle of *kōenkai* politics that despite national opinion polls showing that 90 per cent of the public wanted Tanaka gone, his faction lost only two seats, while Tanaka himself won more votes than ever.

Fortunately, for those Japanese inclined more than ever to despair of their leaders, national politics was not the only way to get things done. The 1960s and 1970s saw a wave of citizen activism that tackled everything from big political issues to the minutiae of everyday life.

Between 1965 and 1974, a loose-knit group called Citizens' Federation: Peace to Vietnam! (abbreviated to 'Beheiren' in Japanese) engaged millions of people in protesting against America's use of Japanese territory as a staging base for their war in South East Asia. Neighbourhood and apartment-complex associations cleaned up their streets, resisted unreasonable amenities charges and put pressure on corrupt or recalcitrant local officials. Communities tackled high-rise developers and building regulators over a person's basic 'right to sunshine' – and won. People kept an eye out for signs of environmental pollution, ensuring that measures passed by the Diet in 1970 yielded real results and helped to put Japan at the forefront, for a time, of environmentalism. Consumers deployed their spending power in new 24/7 convenience stores (*konbini*) and in covered, pedestrianized shopping districts (*shōtengai*), punishing companies touting shoddy or dangerous products. Record numbers of people became volunteers, assisting the vulnerable in daily life.

Where citizens led, politicians and civil servants often followed. The socialist politician Minobe Ryōkichi owed his lengthy governorship of Tokyo, running from the late 1960s throughout the 1970s, to a policy of listening seriously to his voters. On their advice, he set 'civil minimums': guaranteed standards of living to whose provision his staff were required to commit themselves. He offered free health insurance to those most in need. As national dissatisfaction with the LDP brought most of Japan's cities under the control of left-wing parties, LDP leaders were forced to adopt some of the latter's policies. Tanaka's blueprint for a new Japan had owed much to this process – hence the optimism which had first greeted his ascent to power, and the crushing disappointment that followed.

But while civil society activists could make up for some of the shortcomings of their politicians, it took the implosion of elite-level politics for more thoroughgoing change to become possible. That process began in 1984, when three of Tanaka's protégés – Takeshita Noboru, Kanemaru Shin and Ozawa Ichirō – started plotting against him. Each would play his own role in the ending of the system that Tanaka had gamed better than anyone else. In February 1985, Tanaka's own body rebelled. A stroke left him paralysed down his right-hand side, robbing him of clear speech. Even then it took two years for the plotters to feel confident that Tanaka was not about to mount some terrifying, retributive comeback. In July 1987, they left the Tanaka faction and started a successor. It was the beginning of the end, not just for Tanaka but for the uncontested dominance of the LDP.

The challenges of Japanese affluence were coming to a head, abroad and at home. Sino-Japanese relations continued on their upward course, Official Development Assistance was ramped up, most of it going to Asia, and in 1984 Emperor Hirohito met South Korea's visiting President and expressed his regret for the war. The following year, Prime Minister Nakasone made similar comments at the United Nations. And yet it remained all too easy in Asia to construe Japan's economic power as a besuited form of imperialism. Matters were not helped by the well-known desire of some in the LDP to be rid of what they regarded as the constraining pacifism of the 'MacArthur Constitution', or by a number of controversies to erupt on Nakasone's watch as prime minister.

In 1982, it emerged that Japan's Ministry of Education was encouraging the creators of school history textbooks to moderate their coverage of the 1930s and 1940s, avoiding the term 'invasion' for the events of 1937 in mainland Asia. The impact of Ministry advice on publishers was limited, but China and South Korea protested vehemently nonetheless, as they did three years later when Nakasone marked the fortieth anniversary of the end of the war by leading his Cabinet, in full mourning dress, to Tokyo's Yasukuni Shrine. It was dedicated to all those who had died serving in Japan's armed forces since the time of the Boshin War, and Nakasone's own brother was amongst the 2.46 million souls enshrined there. But fourteen

Class A war criminals had also called Yasukuni home since their souls were enshrined there in 1978, initially in secrecy. Nakasone at first defended his visit, but later said that he would not attend the shrine again.

Americans meanwhile had their own reasons for disliking 1980s Japan. By the middle of that decade, a country that they had first defeated and then helped back to its feet was hammering them economically. Japanese exports to the United States were fully twice the value of American exports to Japan, despite a series of deals being struck across the 1970s and 1980s to protect American industry from excessive Japanese competition – notably in cars and colour televisions. Sony's purchase of Columbia Pictures in 1989 and Mitsubishi's of a controlling stake in New York's Rockefeller Center the same year helped to pile the anxiety and antipathy still higher. And with the Soviet Union starting to collapse that year, there seemed less need than ever for behaving indulgently towards their Pacific ally.

At home, Tanaka's generosity during his time as prime minister – which saw spending on social security rising in 1975 to ten times what it had been just a decade before – left Nakasone struggling to address serious economic problems. Drawing on examples set in the West by Ronald Reagan and Margaret Thatcher, and portraying his actions as part of an international trend, Nakasone deregulated the Japanese economy and privatized key state enterprises – most notably Nippon Telephone and Telegraph (NTT) in 1985 and Japan National Railways in 1987, the latter deeply in debt thanks in no small measure to Tanaka's Niigata bullet train.

These decisive moves earned the LDP a good election result in 1986. By 1987, the annual deficit had been almost halved while productivity and middle-class life in Japan – earning, spending, travelling abroad – continued to be the envy of the world. But in 1988, Tanaka's protégé and Nakasone's successor as Prime Minister, Takeshita Noboru, took things a step too far. He introduced a 3 per cent consumption tax, designed to help tackle an approaching demographic crisis in Japan brought about by an ageing population and shrinking birth rate, threatening a smaller tax base in the future alongside expanding health and welfare costs. The unpopularity of the tax was compounded by exceptions in the legislation covering the buying and selling of assets like land and securities. These were precisely the sorts of big-money deals in which – as the public discovered during 1988 and 1989 – Takeshita and a number of his faction members had been involved, accepting cash donations and unlisted stocks (which could be sold on at considerable profit once listed) from a powerful conglomerate called Recruit. Takeshita saw his poll ratings slump below 4 per cent, a new low in Japanese politics. He resigned in June 1989.

Thanks to opposition disarray, the LDP still managed to win an election in February 1990. But a speculative bubble had been growing in the late 1980s, due in part to government efforts to placate foreign competitors like the United States by stimulating import demand at home. Stock prices had soared, the combined value of land in Tokyo was rumoured to outstrip that of the entire United States and mortgage terms now stretched across three generations. An attempt to ease some air out of the bubble by tightening up on credit caused it, instead, to collapse. By the summer of 1992, the Nikkei index had fallen 65 per cent from its peak in December 1989. Big names in the property world went bankrupt, banks struggled as multiple loans went bad, the value of assets was wiped out and ambitious new construction projects ground to a halt. More and more sectors of the economy were drawn in, until a country famed for its post-war economic miracle found itself in recession.

Just as the reputation for basic economic competence on which the LDP had traded for so long started to fall away, its reputation for corruption received the most spectacular boost. It emerged in 1992–3 that a private delivery service, Sagawa Kyūbin, had paid billions of yen to around 200 Diet members over a span of twenty years in return for assistance over government regulations – including labour laws – that threatened its profitability.

Kanemaru Shin – the second of Tanaka's protégés, nicknamed 'the Don' – was heavily implicated. Stacks of cash equivalent to 500 million yen (around $4 million) were reported to have been placed on to a trolley by Sagawa employees, who then wheeled it over to his office, the 'Palais Royal', to which he motored each day in the back of a black Bentley from his home in the exclusive Moto-Azabu neighbourhood of Tokyo. When he agreed to a fine of just 200,000 yen, and pleaded that he couldn't answer questions about most of the relevant dealings because he had been drunk at the time, public protests erupted and he was forced from the Diet and his faction. He was arrested in March 1993 on suspicion of tax evasion, leading to raids on his home and office that turned up 100 kilograms of gold bars, tens of millions of yen in cash, and a further 3 billion yen in bond certificates. His trial began later that year, and was still ongoing when he died three years later.

The final blow for the LDP came in 1993, and was dealt by the third of Tanaka's great protégés. More than twenty years before, Tanaka had made Japan's warped urbanization the focus of his appeal to the people; now Ozawa Ichirō homed in on Japanese politics' lack of open competition and true accountability. Change, he declared in A Plan for the Reform of Japan (Nihon Kaizō Keikaku, 1993), must begin with the LDP itself: the party should do its bit to help foster, at last, a genuine two-party system in Japan. He threatened to take his small personal faction out of the party if it refused. This he soon did, forming the Japan Renewal Party, selling half a million copies of his book and, in the aftermath of an election in July, helping to forge an eight-party coalition. They made for unlikely bedfellows: Socialists, Kōmeitō, Ozawa's party and another new reformist organization called the Japan New Party, led by Hosokawa Morihiro. Still, it was enough. After nearly forty years of uninterrupted power, the LDP was out in the cold.

*

Hosokawa Morihiro took the helm as Prime Minister, amidst high hopes that things might be different now. He was young, suave and telegenic, descended on his mother's side from Konoe Fumimarō and claiming ancestry through his father all the way back, via the medieval Minamoto clan, to Emperor Kanmu and beyond. He enjoyed approval ratings above 70 per cent when, on Christmas Day 1993, he joined eight former prime ministers at Aoyama Funeral Hall. They were there to say a final farewell to Tanaka Kakuei. Powerless after 1985 to save his faction or the broader LDP, he had passed away on 16 December from pneumonia. The streets around the hall were packed with thousands of mourners, many of them making the journey all the way from Niigata – more quickly and in greater comfort than a generation before, thanks to the many promises that Kaku-san had made them, and kept.

For some, 1993 felt like the end of an era. For others, that moment had come four years earlier. In January 1989, the Shōwa Emperor had passed away, followed by Tezuka Osamu in February and Misora Hibari in June. The loss of three defining figures of post-war Japan combined now with Tanaka's death and the rocky fortunes of the LDP and the national economy to create a powerful sense that Japan was entering uncharted waters.

Who would steer the ship? Hosokawa perhaps, sitting solemnly in the Aoyama Funeral Hall amidst chrysanthemums and wafts of incense. Maybe, with the LDP now humbled, politics would become more porous to outside influences such as celebrities and civil-society activists, journalists and academics, a new generation of businessmen – even the voters themselves, freshly enthused thanks to credible multi-party competition. Might it even be that Japan's oldest institution, the imperial family, still had a defining contribution to make to the life of the Japanese?

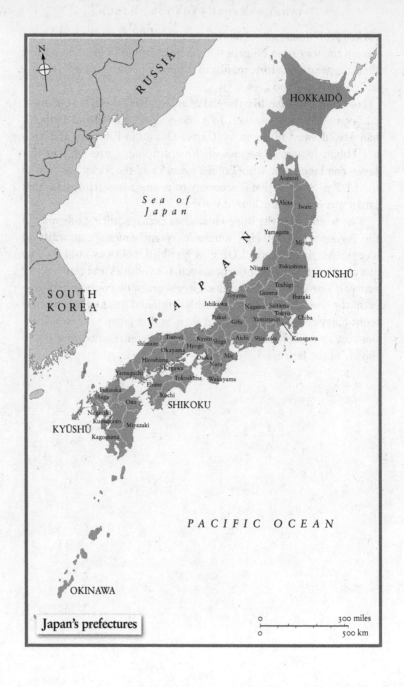

N

RUSSIA

Sea of
Japan

SOUTH
KOREA

J A P A N

HOKKAIDŌ

Aomori

Akita   Iwate

Yamagata
Miyagi

Niigata   Fukushima

HONSHŪ

Tochigi
Toyama   Gunma   Ibaraki
Ishikawa   Nagano   Saitama
Fukui   Gifu   Yamanashi   Tokyo
Shiga   Aichi   Shizuoka   Kanagawa
Tottori   Kyoto   Chiba
Shimane   Okayama   Hyogo
Hiroshima   Osaka   Mie
Kagawa   Nara
Yamaguchi   Tokushima   Wakayama
Ehime
Fukuoka   Kochi
Saga   SHIKOKU
Oita
Nagasaki
Kumamoto   Miyazaki
KYŪSHŪ
Kagoshima

PACIFIC OCEAN

OKINAWA

Japan's prefectures

0   300 miles
0   500 km

20

Owada Masako

（小和田雅子）

1963–

Uncertain Symbol

Empress Masako at the Ise Shrine (Mie Prefecture), November 2019, completing a set of rites for her husband's enthronement as Emperor.

Tanaka Kakuei's high-profile send-off in December 1993 was the second time in a year that the Japanese establishment had gathered together in sombre ceremonial. The first occasion was on 9 June 1993, when around 800 guests crammed themselves into a purpose-built stand not far from a simple cedarwood shrine, secluded amongst trees made misty that morning by a light rain. Located within the grounds of the Imperial Palace in central Tokyo, the Imperial Sanctuary (Kashikodokoro) was one of the most sacred structures in Japan, dedicated to the Sun Goddess Amaterasu.

Crown Prince Naruhito entered the shrine at 10 a.m., dressed in an orange-red silk robe and holding a flat ceremonial sceptre. He offered up a branch of the sacred *sakaki* tree to the gods, bowed four times and recited a solemn pledge to cherish forever the woman seated nearby. Fresh from a purifying bath, she was dressed in clothes that Murasaki Shikibu, a thousand years before, would readily have recognized: a twelve-layered garment, weighing around fourteen kilograms, its outermost layer made from green and gold silk. Handmaidens had taken two and a half hours to dress her, oiling her hair and sweeping it back into the centuries-old courtly *osuberakashi* style, pinning it all in place with a golden comb. Her face whitened, her lipstick a stark red, only one word was required from the bride during a fifteen-minute ceremony that was sealed with cups of sacred *sake*. She gave her name: Masako.

In offering up these three syllables, Owada Masako was parting with a great deal: a promising career in Japan's Ministry of Foreign Affairs, with aspirations one day to become an ambassador; business suits and a Toyota coupé, plus her passport, driving licence and her right to vote. Even the opportunity to see relatives and friends as and when she pleased was relinquished. Her name would soon be physically inked out of the Owada family register, and added instead to an imperial line stretching back to the Yamato clan's claiming of the Sun Goddess Amaterasu for their own in the sixth century.

It was a lot to lose. But this was a gamble rather than a sacrifice. As Crown Princess, and one day Empress, Masako might be able to turn the role of 'symbol of the state', mandated for the monarchy by the post-war Constitution, into a form of diplomatic heft all her own. There was much that she might accomplish at home, too. Like their counterparts on that other rainy island, slightly adrift of the Eurasian continent at its far western edge, Japan's royals were under constant pressure to 'modernize'. A high-flying commoner, educated at Oxford, Harvard and Tokyo universities, Masako might be able to lend the imperial family a little colour and credibility, helping it to reconnect with the public. She might be able to persuade Japan's men to think differently about women's role in society, and Japan's women to think differently about themselves. For a nation in need, with its economy stagnating and its political class struggling to respond, Masako might even be able to help an ancient institution provide contemporary guidance.

*

Owada Masako was born in Tokyo in December 1963. Her mother Yumiko was a literature graduate from Keio University and her father Hisashi a diplomat with Japan's Ministry of Foreign Affairs (MOFA). The demands of Hisashi's job meant that Masako spent much of her childhood away from Japan. The family moved first to Moscow, in 1965, joined by their maid, and then in 1966 by two new siblings for Masako: twin girls, Setsuko and Reiko. Masako had the chance to pick up a little Russian in a state-run nursery near the Kremlin, before the family moved to Riverdale, New York, in 1968. Speaking no English at this point she remained almost completely silent for her first four months of nursery, until one day her teacher phoned home to announce, with great excitement, that Masako had asked to go to the toilet.

Knowledge of English soon turned out to be a mixed blessing. Much like Tsuda Umeko a century before, Masako found herself bullied by some of her young American hosts. At New York's Public School number 81, she was told by one boy that Japanese people were 'disgusting' because they ate with their hands – Masako had been enjoying a sushi roll from her packed lunch at the time. Someone else called her a 'yellow monkey'. When Hisashi's work took the family home to Tokyo in 1971, Masako got the chance to be bullied in Japanese instead. Boys in her primary school called her *Amerika-gaeri*, literally 'back from America', but also carrying the connotation of a cultural sell-out. Masako was forced, one day in the playground, to deny ever having eaten a hamburger. 'No!' she replied. 'Because I'm *Japanese*!' Girls, meanwhile, envied her foreign clothes and stationery.

Life improved in 1973 when Masako entered the highly competitive Denenchōfu Futaba Elementary School. Established by French Catholic nuns at the beginning of the twentieth century, it was located in Tokyo's leafy, upscale Denenchōfu neighbourhood – a Japanese take on the British and American 'garden city' ideal, developed with the help of Shibusawa Eiichi. As in Tsuda's day, Christian schooling in Japan often had a distinctly internationalist flavour. Some of Masako's teachers were Westerners, and many of her classmates were recent returnees from abroad. Masako flourished there, enjoying maths, science, dodge-ball and the care of the school's pets – earning herself the nickname 'Animal Professor' along the way. At Futaba Junior High, her attention turned to baseball. Tokyo's Yomiuri Giants were her team. She watched games on television with her father, became an avid reader of sports-themed manga and went, when she could, to the banks of the Tama River to watch the Giants train. Having lobbied her school, unsuccessfully, for the establishment of a baseball club, Masako made do with softball instead. She wore the number eight shirt when she played, in honour of her favourite Giants player, Takada Shigeru.

Never in one place for very long, Masako moved back to the United States in 1979, when her father landed a visiting professorship at Harvard University. She went to high school in Boston, studying French and German and playing for the school's softball team, before accepting a scholarship to study at Harvard University's Department of Economics. Graduating in 1985, Masako turned down offers of work on Wall Street in favour of studying for a short time at the University of Tokyo's law faculty as she prepared to enter one of Japan's most competitive selection processes the following year. Around 800 candidates sat the entrance examination for the Ministry of Foreign Affairs in the summer of 1986. Only twenty-eight passed. Just three of those were women: and one was Masako.

Success marked her out. Masako was invited to do press interviews when the results were announced, and not long afterwards her name was hastily added by hand to a computer print-out of invitees to an imperial tea party scheduled for October 1986. Held in honour of the Infanta Elena of Spain, it would double as a chance for the Shōwa Emperor's twenty-six-year-old grandson Prince Naruhito to exchange a few words with potential brides, picked out for him by the Imperial Household Agency (IHA, or 'Kunaichō' in Japanese). It was a necessary but painfully transparent ruse, devised by an institution with roots in the seventh-century Sinification of Japanese court life, but which had acquired its modern form during the Occupation. Japan's aristocracy had been abolished after the war, the imperial family trimmed in size and the IHA established as an external agency within a new Prime Minister's Office. Its role included overseeing imperial properties and mausolea, and setting the day-to-day schedules of Japan's remaining royals. While their British counterparts enjoyed independent wealth, alongside an extended network of relations with whom holidays and pastimes could be enjoyed, the Japanese imperial family found itself financially dependent on the state, tightly bound to it constitutionally and, by all accounts, rather lonely.

The IHA's search for a match for Naruhito proceeded according to strict criteria. The successful candidate must be younger than her Prince, and shorter. She must be well educated and in sound physical health. She must not come from a political family or one with a criminal record – two categories that increasingly overlapped in Japan by this point. Girls with tattoos could not be considered, signifiers as these often were of *yakuza* gangland connections. No foreigners need apply, nor adherents of religions other than Shintō, since as Empress the successful candidate would one day enter sacred spaces and perform sacred rites. Finally, a team of private detectives would have to satisfy themselves of a skeleton-free cupboard and as limited as possible a romantic track record.

The IHA's bride-hunters had not thus far had an easy time of it. The difficulty was not Naruhito, a kind and intelligent man who enjoyed music and mountain-climbing. If a lady could look past his rather niche interest in the history of transportation systems, she might do very much worse for herself. The issue was his mother, or rather what had happened to her after she had married the Emperor's son, Crown Prince Akihito, in 1959. Shōda Michiko, from a Catholic family and educated at Futaba Elementary School in central Tokyo (a sister school to Masako's), became the first commoner to marry into the world's oldest monarchy. People at the time hailed a 'fairy-tale couple'; a 'love match' rather than an arranged marriage, ideally suited to a newly egalitarian country on the economic up and up. Some, however, were opposed from the outset to such an unconventional union. Mishima Yukio worried about damage to the institution's mystique. Akihito's own mother appears to have been hostile, too, and was later accused of contributing to Michiko's widely publicized struggles with stress and depression across the 1960s.

Masako and her father would have been well aware of all this. Still, on Saturday, 18 October 1986, they set out together for Naruhito's residence: the Tōgū Palace, a few kilometres west of the Imperial Palace. There they discovered a demographic that leaned suspiciously towards young Japanese women of about Masako's age. There were around forty in total, with the Prince steadily doing the rounds. When Masako's turn came, he congratulated her on her exam success, asked her what sort of diplomat she'd like to be, offered the standard Japanese words of encouragement – ganbatte kudasai (Good luck, do your best!) – and moved swiftly on. It was the briefest of exchanges, but Naruhito was smitten. A series of further meetings was arranged, and Masako was eventually 'outed' in the Japanese media as a contender for Crown Princess. Amidst the ensuing storm of attention, her father begged the IHA for 'time to think' – as close as one could diplomatically go to declining further contact. Masako herself decided to take a sabbatical from the Ministry of Foreign Affairs, and from Japan, heading to Oxford University in 1988 to study for a Masters.

Masako's time at Balliol College, Oxford, was at first blissfully free of the press. But by autumn 1989, rumours had begun doing the rounds that the Naruhito–Masako match might be back on. The long-reigning Shōwa Emperor had died in January, turning that year from 'Shōwa 64' into 'Heisei 1' as Crown Prince Akihito became Emperor. Then, in September, Naruhito's younger brother, Prince Akishino, had become engaged: an unusual move while his elder brother and heir presumptive remained unwed. Now, Crown Prince Naruhito was scheduled to travel to Brussels – not so very far from Oxford. Parts of that latter city soon appeared to be under attack. The Japanese were invading, helicopters hovering overhead while a handful of operatives crept through Balliol's Front Quad. A second detachment was deployed to leafy Bardwell Road, a little way to the north of Balliol, munching miserable English sandwiches in a windowless van as they lay in wait for their target: a second-year postgrad studying international relations.

Masako at last emerged, pausing briefly to refute the new rumours before pushing her way as best she could through a chaos of reporters, TV cameras and bulb-flashes to seek refuge in a library. But her denials were reported back home without much conviction, and with plenty of disdainful attention paid to her studenty beige trench coat and fashionable bob. In June 1990, Masako found herself suddenly recalled by MOFA before she had the chance to complete her degree. She had been sick with stress after the media assault, but some were convinced that there was more to it than that. Members of the imperial family were strictly confined to anodyne interests and pursuits. For the Shōwa Emperor, it had been marine biology, as it was, too, for Emperor Akihito, a published ichthyologist (fish scientist). With Crown Prince Naruhito insisting that he would marry only Masako, rumour had it that someone in the IHA had vetoed Masako's thesis topic – Japan's recent purchase of warplanes from the United States – in order to preserve her as a future Crown Princess.

Back in Japan, Masako began working at MOFA's North American Affairs Bureau: a prestigious, high-stakes role, in which she soon made a name for herself with long hours of overtime, forensic attention to the minutiae of trade deals and service as an English language interpreter for some of the country's top politicians on trips to the

United States. All the while, renewed pressure was being placed on her father to get her to agree to fresh meetings with Naruhito. Masako eventually acquiesced, but when the Crown Prince finally proposed to her in October 1992, at the Imperial Wild Duck Preserve just east of Tokyo, she asked politely whether she was allowed to decline.

Naruhito had come prepared for a response like that. The imperial family, he offered, is no less in the business of diplomacy than MOFA. Mindful of his mother's suffering as an incoming member of the family, he added at a later meeting that he would protect Masako 'with all my power'. In December 1992, Masako relented. Some said that she had negotiated herself a deal, guaranteeing herself a little more freedom than the all-seeing IHA would usually permit. Friends claimed a simple change of heart.

Whatever the reasons, Naruhito at last received the answer for which he had waited six years. His contribution on 1 January 1993 to the Utakai Hajime (First Poetry Reading) ceremony, held at the Imperial Palace each New Year, was described by the IHA as a reference to a particularly pleasant sightseeing trip he had taken recently to Hokkaidō. Others suspected inspiration closer to home:

> I gaze with delight
> As the flock of cranes take flight
> Into the blue skies.
> The dream cherished in my heart
> Since my boyhood has come true.

Masako looked forward to 1993 with more mixed feelings. Her eventual acceptance of Naruhito's proposal had seemed to blend modesty with reticence: 'Would I . . .' she had said, 'really be the best choice?' Her Christmas card to her family that year continued in a similar vein:

> After much thought, I have decided to take the first step in a new life. This may be the last time that we can all celebrate Christmas together. Thank you for bringing me up in a warm and happy household. I am sure things will become more difficult now. I wish you much happiness.

*

Masako experienced little difficulty with the 'Princess Education' given to all new royal consorts. This covered the history of Japan and the imperial court; calligraphy and *waka* poetry; and the laws, rites and ceremonies pertaining to the modern monarchy. The media, however, was another matter. Members of the imperial family were heavily restricted in the opinions they might offer, and yet they were expected to submit themselves to the democratic rigours of a press conference now and again. They were required to maintain the mystique so prized by Mishima Yukio, and yet they risked irrelevance, particularly to younger Japanese, if they came across as entirely free of bonhomie. Their perceived success in managing these conflicting demands hinged largely on how Japan's army of cultural commentators – in the press, on TV, in universities and elsewhere – decided to interpret their words and deeds.

Masako discovered all this to her cost at her first official press conference, held with Naruhito in January 1993 to announce their engagement. She sat beside her betrothed, snappy business suit exchanged for a Jackie Kennedy-style plain yellow dress, pillbox hat and matching yellow purse. Neither her clothes nor her comments were entirely her own choice. Both proved controversial.

The writer Hayashi Mariko, watching on television, was stunned. She took in Masako's 'downcast eyes and stiff expression', heard her declare her wish to 'be of some use' to the monarchy – and began to cry. A new wave of feminists in the 1970s had urged Japanese women to move on from post-war activism rooted in roles as housewives and mothers, and instead to tackle head-on a system that denied them equality with men. A victory of sorts had been won in 1985, with the passage of an Equal Employment Opportunity Law for men and women. Masako's press interviews after the MOFA exam in 1986 had been arranged for her by the Ministry itself, keen to burnish its credentials in light of the new law. Understanding what they were up to, Masako had gently chided the media over their breathless interest in her success. Few at Harvard, she said, regarded the idea of women in the workforce as revolutionary. 'It is a shame', she added, 'that in Japan I'm seen as special, and receive remarks based on my looks.'

Legislative progress and exceptional cases aside, by 1993 most women in Japan's workforce were still 'office ladies', or 'OLs': poorly paid clerical workers, expected to quit when they married. Hayashi was one of those hoping that Masako might prove a catalyst for change. Some called her 'Japan's Hillary Clinton': she was educated, progressive and cosmopolitan, surely destined to open up the monarchy to the modern world. And yet here she was now, wearing what she was told, cowering before the cameras and trying her best to field insulting questions about her cooking and how many children she'd like to have – quipping gently in reply that though her husband liked music he was hopefully not expecting to raise his own orchestra.

The press conference also revealed long-standing cultural faultlines with the United States, tinged in recent years with resentment at Japan's rise as an economic competitor. American commentators talked about a smart and 'sassy' career woman, made in America, now captured, caged and encased in pastels by a woefully anachronistic institution, forced to carry 'one of those silly little purses that the Queen of England favours'. They seemed almost to thrill at the tragedy of it all. Masako faced a life cloistered in a palace, hectored in antiquated Japanese by antiquated Japanese courtiers, and forced on public outings to walk three steps behind her Prince. *Vanity Fair* titled their piece 'Masako's Sacrifice'. *Newsweek* went with 'The Reluctant Princess'.

Commentary like this set off Japan's conservatives in turn. From Commodore Matthew C. Perry's threats back in 1853 through to the cultural vandalism of the Occupation, the story had been one, they claimed, of Westerners – and the United States in particular – seeking to push Japan around, hoping to recreate it in their own image and for their own reassurance: as proof of the universal worth and applicability of modern Western values. Some conservatives, including staff at the Imperial Household Agency, regarded Masako as a kind of fifth columnist in this project: here she was in a distinctly American-looking outfit, speaking to the media, one noted, for a total of nine minutes and thirty-seven seconds – an immodest twenty-eight seconds longer, they observed, than the future Emperor.

Out in the country, there existed a wide range of opinion where the imperial family was concerned. Some felt angry that tax money was being used to prop up an unwanted institution with a shady past. Others expressed pride, tinged with sympathy given the obvious difficulties of the role. Amongst businesses, there was excited anticipation of Japan's flagging economy receiving a royal wedding boost to rival the nuptials of Akihito and Michiko back in 1959 or even those of Charles and Diana in 1981. They set to work producing special coins, stamps, cigarettes, tea, train tickets and beer labels. A 'Princess Cocktail' was created, alongside 'Princess Ramen'. Interest in Masako's old life spurred sales of Hermès scarves, pearl necklaces, Paloma Picasso leather bags and even Yorkshire terriers – after the Owada family's long-suffering Chocolat, whose outdoor toilet time had come to be ruined by helicopter noise and camera flashes.

By the time the big day arrived, on 9 June 1993, telephone boxes along the planned parade route from the Imperial Palace to the Tōgū Palace had been painted gold. Drink vending machines were removed, lest some outraged republican seek to improvise a projectile. And 30,000 police officers were placed on duty. In expectation of tens of millions of viewers tuning in, television stations prepared computer simulations of the Kashikodokoro ceremony and decked their studios out with wedding cakes. There was a life-size re-creation of Masako's dormitory room at Harvard. One foreign observer spotted a trained monkey called Tsurusuke amongst studio guests, gazing into a crystal ball and predicting that the couple would have three children.

A crowd of around 200,000 supporters lined the rain-soaked motorcade route that afternoon, brandishing umbrellas and *Hinomaru* flags as the newly-weds' black open-topped Rolls-Royce went by, its number plate replaced with an imperial chrysanthemum. Masako and Naruhito ate their first formal meal together that evening at the Tōgū Palace, before ending the day with a fertility ceremony at 9 p.m. The couple placed twenty-nine marble-sized *mochi* rice-cakes – one for each year of Masako's life – on to four silver trays, inside a rosewood box. They then kept the box by their bedside for three nights, praying for the birth of a prince, before the box was buried in an auspicious spot in the palace gardens.

Babies were, for the IHA at least, the most pressing business of this marriage. Over the days to come, Masako and Naruhito would attend six official banquets in their honour, meeting nearly 3,000 dignitaries from Japan and around the world. They would make visits to the sources of the imperial tradition into which Masako had just been initiated: the ancient city of Nara and the Grand Shrine at Ise. But with no male child born into the imperial family for almost thirty years, Masako would find her diplomatic ambitions placed firmly on the back-burner. This became brutally clear after a banquet held in July 1993 to welcome leaders of the G7 countries to Japan. Masako sat with Bill Clinton on one side of her and Boris Yeltsin (present as a guest of the G7) on the other. Well travelled, fluent in English and with the rare distinction of having been pre-schooled at both ends of the old ideological spectrum, she kept both leaders engaged for much of the evening. But it was later reported that she had been reprimanded by the Imperial Household Agency. The Emperor had been hosting that banquet, not her. She had embarrassed His Majesty, and would need to watch herself in future.

As Masako began to get used to her new life, Emperor Akihito was settling into his. The first Emperor to have his era-name chosen by democratically elected politicians – Heisei meant 'peace everywhere' – he had made a promising, personable start to his duties. In 1992, he became the first Japanese emperor to visit China, using the opportunity to express his 'deep sorrow' at the 'severe suffering inflicted by my country' on the Chinese people during the war.

The timing was important. The 1980s and 1990s saw a vocal minority in Japan denying or downplaying wartime tragedies such as the Nanjing Massacre and the biological warfare research of Unit 731 in Manchuria, which had included human vivisection. Opponents in Japan of this sort of revisionism backed three former Korean 'comfort women' in 1991 when they took their case for compensation to court. While revisionists claimed that such women had been paid volunteers, and that the Imperial Japanese Army had not been involved in the establishment of so-called 'comfort stations', the court found that the evidence suggested otherwise. In 1992, the Japanese government formally apologized.

These so-called 'history wars', which stretched on well into the twenty-first century, were only partly about history. With the Cold War at an end, there was uncertainty over how Japan's role in world affairs might shift over the decades to come. In north-east Asia, the new Russian Federation recognized a Soviet–Japanese Joint

Declaration of 1956, which had restored basic diplomatic contact. But a full peace treaty had yet to be signed: Russo-Japanese relations continued to founder over the Kuril island chain which had been disputed between the two sides since the end of the Second World War. Relations with North Korea were far frostier, thanks to a combination of Japan's colonial past on the peninsula, the North's missile programme and the abduction in the late 1970s and 1980s of an unknown number of Japanese from coastal areas of Japan to North Korea, some for the purpose of training North Korean agents.

Relations with China and South Korea were the most difficult and consequential of all in the region. Both countries looked on as the Japanese slowly began to flex some long-underused diplomatic and foreign policy muscles across the 1990s. In Ogata Sadako, Japan discovered the sort of trailblazing diplomat that Masako might have been. As the first female head of the UN refugee agency across the 1990s, Ogata flew to northern Iraq, Turkey and Iran to help broker solutions for Kurdish refugees fleeing Saddam Hussein in the wake of the 1991 Gulf War. She later tended to refugee crises in the Balkans and Rwanda. At home, Japan's political leaders, having contributed $13 billion to the cost of the Gulf War only to be overlooked by the Kuwaitis when they took out an advert in the New York Times to thank their rescuers, set out to do more than throw money at global problems. The Self-Defence Forces began to be deployed to non-military roles in United Nations peace-keeping operations, taking up postings in Africa and Latin America. Alongside nervousness at where all this might be leading, a Chinese Communist leadership still reeling from the Tiananmen Square protests of 1989 was busy making historic Chinese suffering at Japanese and European hands the focus of a new 'patriotic education'. South Korean politicians were similarly motivated in their stance towards Japan by a blend of real historical grievance, anger at revisionist interpretations, concern over Japanese strategic intentions and a shrewd sense of when some well-timed Japan-bashing might bear useful domestic fruit.

Prone to the occasional diplomatic gaffe when talking about the war, Japan's politicians continued to underwhelm at home, too. Economic growth limped along at around 1 per cent or worse during the 1990s, while the hoped-for new broom, Prime Minister Hosokawa

Morihiro, lasted all of eight months in his job. His fate held important lessons for future anti-LDP insurgents. Make sure your coalition shares more in common than dislike of the LDP. Don't demonize ministry bureaucrats while out on the stump, because you will need their support if you get elected. And don't preach clean politics if at any point your own hands have been in the till. Hosokawa's resignation in April 1994 was prompted by questions over a large loan that he had received from Sagawa Kyūbin, the private delivery service involved in the corruption scandal for which 'the Don', Kanemaru Shin, was currently on trial.

The LDP returned to power in 1994, in an unlikely coalition that gave Japan its first Socialist Prime Minister in almost half a century. Murayama Tomiichi marked the fiftieth anniversary of the end of the war by offering a 'heartfelt apology' for the 'tremendous damage and suffering' caused by Japanese 'colonial rule and aggression'. But several senior politicians followed up with rather less conciliatory comments, and a few years later Tokyo's Yasukuni Shrine once again found itself at the centre of a diplomatic row. The cause this time was a charismatic LDP politician with long, wavy grey hair, a deep appreciation for Elvis Presley and a gift for the catchy political soundbite. Koizumi Junichirō enjoyed an unusually long stint as prime minister, from 2001 through to 2006, but insisted on visiting Yasukuni no fewer than six times across that period.

Koizumi did better in domestic politics, where his imperviousness to criticism was more of an advantage. He rescued Japan's banks from bad debt, forced through a controversial privatization of the country's postal savings and insurance systems, cut back on public spending and deregulated the labour market – encouraging the use of short-term contract workers who enjoyed comparatively weak employment rights. Unlike some of his forebears, Koizumi seemed willing, too, to confront Japan's powerful construction industry, which had been blamed for corrupting the country's politics while concreting over large swathes of its beautiful natural landscape in ruinously expensive and largely pointless pork-barrel projects.

The economy was just starting to grow again when the global financial crisis of 2007–8 came along and exposed the downsides of Koizumi's quest for greater market efficiency. Struggling companies laid off contract workers in large numbers, rendering those who had been living in company housing instantly homeless. As the media descended on a 'New Year's Village for Contract Workers', established in January 2009 in Tokyo's Hibiya Park and consisting of tents and soup kitchens, a fresh blow was dealt to the post-war image of Japan as a place of stable if rather staid lifetime employment. Three and a half million people were now unemployed. Publicity for the New Year's Village embarrassed political and business leaders into backtracking on welfare payments, housing allocations and job losses. And later that year the LDP was again thrown out of power, this time by a centrist Democratic Party of Japan (DPJ) pledging to reject neo-liberal economics, improve relations with China and temper Japan's rather slavish attachment to the United States.

Public enthusiasm for politics, however, remained at a low ebb. Politicians had failed in their stewardship of the economy: one 'lost decade', the 1990s, had now become two. Meanwhile, twin disasters back in 1995 had caused long-lasting damage to people's faith in government even to achieve its basic task of keeping them safe. When an earthquake measuring 7.2 on the Richter scale hit Kobe in January 1995 – killing more than 6,000 people and destroying hundreds of thousands of buildings – ordinary Japanese rushed to the rescue, while the government was revealed as woefully ill-prepared. A few weeks later, on 20 March, five members of a doomsday cult called Aum Shinrikyō (Aum Supreme Truth) released sarin gas on to five underground trains near the Kasumigaseki district just south of the Imperial Palace, home since the Meiji era to Japan's central government ministries. With the police closing in on the cult's activities, and with an array of imaginary enemies to boot – from the Vatican to the CIA – its leader, Asahara Shōkō, intended to wipe out the government and replace it with his own. Twelve people ended up dead, gassed on their way to work. Thousands more were injured. And alongside the police failures implied in the rise of so dangerous an organization came the shock of discovering that many of the cult's members were promising young students and white-collar professionals – decent and intelligent people, profoundly disillusioned with life in Japan.

Away from politics, there were two points of light. The first was that the majority of Japanese continued to live the comfortable, middle-class urban lives they had known since the 1960s, in a country where crime rates remained enviably low. The second was the country's steady emergence as a cultural superpower.

Cultural diplomacy was not new to Japan. Since the 1960s, efforts had been made to promote a civilized, sophisticated image of the country abroad, drawing on centuries-old achievements in painting, poetry, flower-arranging, kabuki and Nō theatre, martial arts, kimono-making and the tea ceremony. Masako had done her bit while at Harvard, helping to establish a 'Japan Culture Club', performing the folk song 'Cherry Blossoms, Cherry Blossoms' ('*Sakura, Sakura*') on the piano at concerts and making fresh *tempura* and *sōmen* (wheat-flour noodles). But international images of 'the Japanese' were now increasingly informed by the work of Miyazaki Hayao's Studio Ghibli, video games giants including Nintendo and writers like Murakami Haruki and Ōe Kenzaburō (the latter becoming, in 1994, Japan's second Nobel Laureate in Literature, after Kawabata Yasunari in 1968). Japanese food, pop music and consumer fads circled the globe as never before, joined by a colourful roster of manga and anime characters.

Japan's leaders were quick to spot the potential of what came to be known across the noughties as 'Cool Japan'. In 2008, the Ministry of Foreign Affairs went as far as recruiting the blue robotic cat Doraemon as Japan's 'Anime Ambassador'. The question now, as in Tezuka's day, was whether culture and politics might meaningfully connect. Was the former capable of challenging and invigorating the latter, or was it destined merely to temper its disappointments?

Amongst those with a strong vested interest in knowing, perhaps even shaping the answer to that question was Crown Princess Masako. She had turned her back on a career with MOFA, in part at least, on a promise from the man who was now her husband that the imperial family was a diplomatic corps all of its own – albeit of a soft, symbolic sort. Crown Prince Naruhito spent the nineties and noughties making good on his other promise to Masako, that of protecting her as an incoming member of the family. Amidst hectoring from the Imperial Household Agency and hounding by the press over their fertility as a couple, his press conference contributions began steadily to push the boundaries of protocol. In February 1994, he lamented the 'great influence' of the press on society and the 'objectionable' way that 'blatant untruths take on a life of their own' – not least the interminable rumours of a pregnancy, based on close scrutiny of Masako's body contours during her performance of public duties.

Two years later, Naruhito offered pointed remarks about 'the stork' preferring a 'quiet environment': a rebuke directed towards both the press and the IHA, where scepticism in some quarters about Masako's suitability as Crown Princess was intensified by off-the-record remarks that she made to journalists in 1996, and which somehow ended up in print. Asked what she was reading at the moment, Masako had mentioned the novelist Ōe Kenzaburō, who had recently declined the offer of Japan's highest artistic award, the Order of Culture, because it was bestowed by the Emperor. 'I do not recognize,' he had said, 'any authority, any value, higher than democracy.' His refusal, and his comments, had earned him death threats from Japan's extreme right. For the Crown Princess to be revealed as a fan was highly embarrassing.

Masako herself, in a birthday press conference in 1996, gave hints of the sort of symbol that she might become for the Japanese, given half a chance. Choosing her words carefully, she noted that Japanese society was currently in flux and there were 'a variety of ways of thinking about the role of women'. She was still learning how to 'harmonize the traditional way of life of a Crown Princess with my own self', she said. It had, she added, 'been a struggle':

> I am [neither] extremely modern, nor conservative . . . rather – and I
> feel this is the same for many others – there is within me both a trad-
> itional and a 'new' part, and it is a question of how to live out the
> characteristics of each, depending on the situation.

Here was – or might be – a brand of leadership quite distinct from everyday politics, rooted not in making promises or issuing commands but in offering sympathy and in holding up a mirror to society now and again. For now, though, fertility came first. Masako at last gave birth, in December 2001, to Princess Aiko. And yet despite having had Empresses Regnant in the past, under Meiji-era rules that were affirmed during the Occupation only men could now ascend the Chrysanthemum Throne. Aiko would never rule, and Masako could not yet relax. As the IHA chief explained to the press, as though discussing an endangered species being cajoled into breeding in captivity (which is perhaps how he saw the matter), 'One more is needed.'

One more did indeed appear, but in the family of Naruhito's brother, Prince Akishino. In September 2006, his wife Princess Kiko gave birth to a son, Prince Hisahito: the first male to be born into the imperial family for more than forty years. For a few short years, debate had raged over whether Imperial House law should be changed to allow Princess Aiko one day to become Empress Regnant. The Japanese public had been overwhelmingly in favour. All that now subsided, as the future of the Chrysanthemum Throne looked reasonably secure under the current rules. Emperor Akihito would be succeeded by Naruhito, with Prince Akishino and then Hisahito waiting in line.

By this time, Masako had entered a lost decade of her own, making few public appearances across the noughties and suffering with what the IHA insisted on calling an 'adjustment disorder'; to the vast majority of royal-watchers it was depression. Naruhito's spirited defence of his wife never flagged. At one point, he took the unprecedented step of publicly accusing the IHA of denying Masako's diplomatic aspirations, clamping down on the 'personality' behind them and contributing to her 'complete exhaustion'. Ordinary Japanese were sympathetic, hundreds of them writing to the IHA to express disapproval of the way they were treating the Crown Princess.

Though she had little chance, and perhaps little inclination, to discuss her situation publicly, Masako came to symbolize a dimension of Japanese life that was only just beginning to be openly discussed: psychological distress. Cultural ideals had long persisted, in Japan, of romanticizing sadness, reverencing stoicism and understanding suicide, in some cases at least, as a dignified assuming of responsibility – the so-called 'suicide of resolve', seen most graphically in *seppuku* (ritual suicide by disembowelment). Psychiatry had come to be associated, as in many parts of the world, with social stigma and lengthy, potentially traumatic hospital stays. If people sought medical treatment for distress, it was often for what they and their doctors insisted was a 'sleep disorder' of some kind. Others turned variously to literature, drink, friends, travel, hypnosis, special diets, Chinese medicine, shrine and temple cures, and new forms of psychotherapy inspired by Japan's Buddhist inheritance.

That situation had been changing of late. After the 1995 earthquake, volunteers and the media had begun talking about survivors' need of *kokoro no kea*, 'care of the heart' – a clever turn of phrase that exploited to reassuring effect the multiple meanings of *kokoro*: self, soul, emotional centre and aspect of the physical body. A sharp jump in Japan's suicide rate in 1998, to more than 30,000 people that year, focused minds on the links between suicide and despair – much of the latter connected with the end of Japan's economic good times and the social stability that had come with them. The first SSRI antidepressants reached Japan the next year, marketed by imagining depression as a 'cold of the soul' (*kokoro no kaze*); in other words, as common, innocent and treatable.

As celebrities began sharing their own experiences of depression, Masako found herself deployed in her absence as a case study by Japanese cultural commentators arguing over what all this said about the state of the nation. Some saw Japan sliding towards the abyss, from 'compensated dating' – teenage girls, some still at school, offering sexual services to middle-aged men in exchange for money and luxury goods – to 'parasite singles': young women shirking their procreational responsibilities while funding a devotion to brands like Louis Vuitton by living rent-free at home. This latter category sometimes overlapped with 'freeters': young women and men willing to accept only casual employment, lest anything more committed get in the way of their hobbies or their social lives. Elsewhere in this lexicon of alleged social breakdown were 'herbivorous men', sacrificing work and serious relationships to much-loved hobbies, and '*hikikomori*': young men, for the most part, who shut themselves away in their bedrooms, often in the parental home and sometimes for years on end. Most familiar of all to foreigners interested in Japan were *otaku*: fans of manga, anime, games or pop idols, whose obsessive tendencies were – depending on your point of view – tragic and dangerous or lovable and cuddly.

Critics spotted in all this a disastrous retreat from the public-spiritedness and civic engagement that had built modern Japan during the Meiji era and again after the war. It is no use blaming politicians for the country's woes, they argued, if ordinary people are unwilling to put their shoulders to the wheel. Opponents of this view accused the media of exaggerating the nature and scale of these social problems, while failing to show much interest in how young Japanese really lived. This was a harsher world, now, than the one in which their parents had grown up. Rather than selfishly opting out of society, perhaps they were being squeezed out by declining prospects. 'Freeters' was increasingly used to describe youngsters who wanted permanent jobs but simply couldn't find them. In the same way, many of those accused of being too selfish to have children – apparently insensitive to the country's plummeting birth rate – felt that a family was beyond their financial reach.

Those in Japan who were ill-disposed towards Masako pictured her as a delinquent of sorts; a symbol of the era's destructive self-absorption. Having failed to solve the imperial family's own demographic crisis (Princess Kiko and her husband were enjoying a wave of popularity, having taken care of it themselves), Masako appeared to be using a rather vaguely defined ailment to avoid the punishing schedule of public engagements kept by the Emperor, Empress and her own husband. She was spotted playing tennis with her daughter, taking her to Tokyo Disneyland in 2006 and jetting off for a holiday in the Netherlands the same year at the invitation of Queen Beatrix. Two years later, as the global financial crisis battered Japan, Masako was criticized for eating out in upscale Chinese, French and Mexican restaurants and shopping in Tokyo's fashionable Aoyama and Ginza districts.

Naruhito, along with Masako's psychiatrist, kept insisting that recovery from depression hinges not just on medication or therapy (both of which Masako was believed to be receiving) but on the chance to enjoy some peace and pleasure now and again. Husband and psychiatrist alike had joined Masako on her trip to the Netherlands, intended as it was to help her recovery – Queen Beatrix's husband had himself suffered with severe depression. Still, the IHA was forced to deny media rumours that Masako had been upbraided by her mother-in-law, the Empress, about her work ethic. Such treatment by the media foreshadowed the claims soon faced by salarymen who were signed off work with depression of 'faking' their condition to get time off, while colleagues became genuinely ill from taking on their burdens.

*

The hope was often expressed in Japan throughout the difficult decades of the nineties and noughties that a strong, visionary leader would emerge to provide the population with fresh purpose: a new Itō Hirobumi, or Yoshida Shigeru. What the country got, in the end, was not a great character but a great catastrophe. On 11 March 2011, a magnitude 9.0 earthquake struck off the north-eastern coast of Honshū, shifting the island about two and a half metres eastwards. Television crews focused first of all on a tsunami that went racing inland: forty metres high in places, it took cars and buildings with it and submerged large swathes of the north-eastern Tōhoku region under water. There followed a battle – quickly lost – to prevent three reactors at the Fukushima No. 1 nuclear power plant from melting down.

Nearly 20,000 people died, and many more were rendered homeless. Profound anxiety set in across the country, amidst conflicting claims about the implications for agriculture and human health of a radiation leak of uncertain proportions. One of the earliest to help bring the nation together was Emperor Akihito, making a televised address whose desperate context and sombre tone were reminiscent of his father's radio broadcast back in August 1945. The Emperor urged his fellow Japanese to treat one another with compassion, and to cooperate in helping to 'overcome difficult times'. He was later captured on camera with Empress Michiko, dressed in plain clothes and kneeling down in evacuation shelters to console the newly homeless. Naruhito and Masako followed suit in the months that followed, travelling around some of the worst-affected areas. They offered silent prayers before the sea in Miyagi prefecture, its now calm waters the source of terrifying devastation back in March. Public approval for the imperial family's response ran sky-high, as it did for the Self-Defence Forces, 100,000 of whose personnel worked alongside 24,000 American troops in transporting emergency supplies, clearing roads and runways and establishing temporary facilities. Many wore uniform patches or helmet stickers bearing the words *Ganbare Tōhoku* – 'Be Strong, Tōhoku'.

The contrast could hardly have been starker with the 6 per cent approval rating given to Japan's political class for their handling of the crisis. Since taking power in 2009, the Democratic Party of Japan (DJP) had yet to impress as a viable alternative to the LDP. Prime Minister Hatoyama Yukio failed to heed the warnings of his anti-LDP predecessor, Hosokawa Morihiro. Disliked by powerful senior bureaucrats, he became embroiled in a financial scandal, accused of receiving hundreds of millions of yen in improperly reported campaign contributions. Much of the money was said to have come from his own mother, marking him out as soiled *and* spoiled. His successor in 2010, as DJP leader and prime minister, was Kan Naoto, to whom fell the task of dealing with an unprecedented disaster in March 2011. Turned down by the LDP when he suggested a coalition of national unity, Kan and his party struggled to respond in a way that engendered national or international trust, not least because of a lack of transparency over radiation risks. Kan resigned in September 2011, and in December 2012 his party was removed from power by an LDP–Kōmeitō coalition led by Abe Shinzō.

As a child, Abe had been briefly but vigorously opposed to the US–Japan security relationship. His grandfather was Prime Minister Kishi Nobusuke, who was responsible for renegotiating the US–Japan Security Treaty – its name abbreviated to 'Anpo' in Japanese – and selling it to a sceptical public in 1960. Kishi had enjoyed rare moments of respite, crawling around at home on all fours while little Shinzō rode on his back shouting the opposition war cry of the day, which he had seen on TV: *'Anpo hantai! Anpo hantai!'* ('No to Anpo! No to Anpo!'). The adult Abe was very much more in line with his grandfather's thinking. He valued Japan's American ties but hoped, in the name of conservative values and meaningful sovereignty, to unpick parts of the Occupation-era settlement. The constitutional status of the Emperor must be clarified: was he, or was he not, the head of state? And the Constitution's so-called 'peace clause' required attention, relic as it was of a bygone era.

For now, the Japanese public simply wanted competent government. The rest of the 2010s duly came to be defined, in political terms, by 'Abenomics', with 'womenomics' a significant dimension. The former aimed to reboot Japan's economy via government stimulus spending, quantitative easing and further neo-liberal reform. The latter was Abe's plan to tackle Japan's demographic as well as its economic problems. The country's fertility rate had been in decline since Tanaka Kakuei had been prime minister in the early 1970s. The result was that Japan's population was predicted to decline from a peak of 128 million in 2010 to just 83 million in 2100. By 2040, a full third of this shrinking population would be over the age of sixty-five, requiring costly and labour-intensive care. Abe's hope was that by making it easier for women to balance family with a successful working life, he could shore up today's labour force while guaranteeing tomorrow's.

Abe's supporters praised the return of strong government, led by so reliable an election-winner that by the time of his resignation on health grounds in the summer of 2020 he had become the longest-serving prime minister in Japanese history. Diplomatic relations with China, Japan's largest trading partner and since 2010 the world's second-largest economy, seemed at last to be on the up. At the same time, ambitious new trading relationships were being pursued with India and throughout South East Asia. Abe's critics, meanwhile, vigorously opposed a new stance of 'collective self-defence', whereby the Self-Defence Forces would come to the aid of an ally if Japan itself was ultimately in danger, alongside Abe's euphemistic-sounding talk of making 'proactive contributions to peace' in the world. Abe faced charges, too, of political cronyism, and there was disappointment as the 2010s drew to a close that his policies had delivered no more than anaemic levels of economic growth. This in return for a national debt approaching 240 per cent of GDP, the largest in the industrialized world, and an International Monetary Fund forecast that GDP would shrink by as much as 25 per cent over the next forty years.

It was amidst these lingering uncertainties over Japan's future that the Reiwa era – 'beautiful harmony' – began on 1 May 2019. Emperor Akihito abdicated the throne, citing the impact of advancing years on his ability to perform his duties, and Naruhito ascended in his place. Masako had, in recent years, been seen more and more in public. In 2015, she attended her first imperial garden party in twelve years. In 2018, she began to take over some of Empress Michiko's duties, including the keeping of silkworms – a role associated with the

Japanese Empress since the Meiji era. In May 2019, she performed her first solo public duties as Empress, attending a meeting of the Japanese Red Cross after succeeding Michiko as its honorary president. Then, in late October 2019, she sat on a purple-canopied throne at the Imperial Palace, dressed in a multi-layered kimono, while next to her, on his own throne and dressed in orange-brown robes, sat Naruhito. He pledged to fulfil his constitutional responsibility 'as the symbol of the state and of the unity of the people of Japan . . . turning my thoughts to the people and standing by them'.

Empress and Emperor: after years of struggles with the media and the IHA, might this moment of formal enthronement be the point at which Masako's gamble, long ago, began at last to pay off? Her mother-in-law, now 'Empress Emerita', had found more freedom and influence as Empress than as Crown Princess. Masako and Naruhito had some added advantages besides. Children of the 1960s and '70s, they were the first imperial couple to be born after the war and to receive a university education – partly abroad in both cases: Naruhito studied at Merton College, Oxford, once declaring it amongst the happiest periods of his life. They shared with many couples of their age the experience of marrying late, and of dividing between them the parental duties of nappy-changing and bath-time. Those inclined to take familiarity with new technology as a portent could point to Naruhito's use of a smartphone to take selfies with members of the public. The imperial couple spoke fluent English too, ignoring protocol for a while to converse without official interpreters when President Donald Trump became the first statesman to meet the new Emperor and Empress. They did the same again a few weeks later during a visit by President Emmanuel Macron of France and his wife Brigitte, Masako conversing with Brigitte in a mixture of English and French.

Much would depend on how Naruhito and Masako chose – and were permitted, by Japan's politicians, the IHA and the media – to fulfil the role they effectively shared as 'symbol of the state and of the unity of the people of Japan'. Or, rather, what Naruhito and Masako might seek to make those words mean. All too easy to interpret as a limitation on a person's power, the role of 'symbol' carried active responsibilities too. To succeed as a symbol of national unity required keeping up with and supporting the changing expectations and self-perceptions of the Japanese. A diplomat by nature and by profession, who knew from personal experience what it was to be treated as an outsider and who well understood how Japan looked in international eyes, Empress Masako might contribute much as an active symbol of national unity.

The time had undoubtedly come for the Japanese to explore a more expansive definition of leadership, and perhaps of national community too. The last thirty years had revealed the limits of what Japan's fabled 'iron triangle' of politicians, bureaucrats and businesspeople could accomplish by themselves. Shibusawa Eiichi had been part of a Meiji-era golden age, when a handful of powerful men, fresh from revolution in 1868, bound these three groups together in imposing from above a national vision of 'Japan'. The Occupation era was characterized by authority enjoyed and deployed in a similar way. These basic power structures remained, but their reputation for effectiveness had been lost.

Pop culture helped Japan to make new friends abroad. But plenty of young Chinese and South Koreans found it possible to love J-pop and anime while still harbouring their parents' hostility towards Japan over past actions in Asia. Doraemon's tenure as Anime Ambassador, meanwhile, had failed to bear fruit where long-running disputes with China were concerned over ownership of the Senkaku/Diaoyu islands in the East China sea, and with South Korea over Takeshima/Dokdo in the Sea of Japan.

After the triple disasters of March 2011, some in Japan had hoped to see a renaissance of local government and a boost for non-profit organizations (NPOs), balancing out a central government in Tokyo that seemed unhelpfully to combine micro-management with a lack of good ideas. Japan was home to tens of thousands of small NPOs, involved in social welfare, disability and LGBT rights, rural regeneration, boosting local economies and encouraging lifelong education. Large numbers of young people had travelled to the Tōhoku region from March 2011 onwards, setting up social enterprises ranging across food, crafts, housing, independent radiation monitoring and sustainable energy generation and distribution – at a time when all of Japan's nuclear reactors had been taken offline for safety testing and some anti-nuclear protesters hoped never to see them return to service. And yet, like pop culture, civil society had its limitations. Now, as in the 1970s, the worry was that government bureaucrats seeking to save money or to wield some easy influence would co-opt NPOs as auxiliaries, draining their energy, harming their independence and ceding little real influence along the way.

If there was no single, stand-out source of answers to Japan's uncertain direction of travel, this was perhaps becoming an age instead, as elsewhere in the world, in which leadership took the form of persuasion, consensus-building and the setting of examples by a broad constellation of actors, many given voices for the first time by social media. A piece of well-chosen symbolism had the potential to succeed as never before in a landscape like this, if the new Empress and Emperor, along with a faction-ridden IHA, could find the right opportunities.

Nowhere was the need for this more acute, or the potential so great, as with the question of national identity. Three basic solutions existed to Japan's enormous demographic challenges: more babies, more immigrants or more robots. There was little sign, yet, of progress on the first solution. On the third, Japanese firms were racing to develop 'care-bot' technology: robots capable of serving as companions and care-givers for the elderly, freeing up flesh-and-blood human beings to join an ever-tighter labour market. Immigration was the most controversial of all, and there was little by way of national consensus. And yet matters would soon reach the point where the survival of the Japanese depended on the definition of 'the Japanese'.

Abe Shinzō was amongst those to champion, in his writing and rhetoric at least, a civic nationalism over an ethnic one for Japan. Back in 1986, Abe's mentor, Prime Minister Nakasone, had claimed that 'Japan has one ethnicity, one state, and one language'. But since then, a Meiji-era law attempting to assimilate the Ainu of Hokkaidō had been reversed, with an Ainu Cultural Promotion Law (1997) aimed at recovering and reviving old place names, alongside remnants of Ainu oral literature and craftwork. Ainu delegates had joined Okinawan representatives at a United Nations-backed World Conference on Indigenous Peoples in 2014. Two years later a Hate Speech Law had been passed, aimed at protecting Japan's half a million 'Zainichi Koreans' – people of Korean descent living in Japan – and in general tackling hostility to the idea, as the text of the law put it, that 'foreign residents and their children [ought to be excluded] from the community'. The same year saw a law passed to eliminate discrimination against Japan's former outcasts, whose living conditions had been improved through government intervention since the 1960s but against whom old prejudices still lingered.

The challenge, for those who sought to imagine 'the Japanese' now in civic rather than narrowly ethnic terms, was to turn law into culture. In Japan, as elsewhere in the world, this was easier said than done. Gender equality legislation had been on the books for a while, but despite some important exceptions – including Ogata Sadako at UNHCR, Tanaka Makiko (daughter of the former PM) as Japan's first female foreign minister, and Koike Yuriko as the first female defence minister and later the first female Governor of Tokyo – Japan had yet to see many women filling senior roles in politics or business. In 2019, the country was ranked 121st out of 153 in the World Economic Forum's Global Gender Gap Index. Paternity leave was generous: up to a year off work, on nearly 60 per cent of full salary. And yet very few new fathers made use of it, fearful of what it might mean for their professional reputations and promotion prospects. Meanwhile, plenty of ethnic minority workers remained subject to abuse, stuck in so-called '3k' work – jobs that no one else wanted to do because they were *kitsui* (physically demanding), *kitanai* (dirty) or *kiken* (dangerous).

There was no guarantee that Japan's imperial institution any longer possessed the clout, or would be given the opportunity, to help address any of this. But Emperor Akihito had set a promising example: moving away from the personal style of his father to reach out to the public, to help mend fences abroad, and even to make an unexpected contribution to broadening the notion of 'the Japanese' when at his birthday press conference in 2001 he spoke of the kinship he felt with Korea, descended as he was via Emperor Kanmu from a Korean king.

Now it was Empress Masako's time to find her voice, backed by a quietly determined Emperor and working within an institution well used, across the past fifteen centuries or so, to squeezing the symbolic potential out of an existence marked by tight political constraints. Her recovery from illness had continued apace during her first year as Empress. She attended every scheduled event, latterly in a face mask during the COVID-19 pandemic. She and Naruhito received official briefings on the virus and its impact on children, offered encouragement for those working on the frontline and donated tens of millions of yen to a child poverty charity and to an NPO involved with assisting in disaster relief.

Hopes were high, for a time, that the delayed Tokyo Olympics and Paralympics might mark a crowning moment of return in front of a global public: for Empress Masako after years of ill-health, and for Japan as a whole from the privations of a pandemic. It was not to be. Imperial symbolism and diplomacy instead took an unexpected turn. Emperor Naruhito opened the Games in a shadowy, sombre, near-empty stadium, into which Tokyo's humid summer air carried the voices of protestors outside. Amidst public disquiet at the decision to go ahead with the Olympics, the Emperor chose to speak not of 'celebrating' the Games – as the rubric required – but of 'commemorating' them. Empress Masako stayed away. The official reason was that numbers at the ceremony had to be kept to a minimum. Some wondered, however, whether by her absence the Empress might be sending a message, intended to complement her husband's – and whether, beyond the immediate upheaval of COVID-19, Japan's oldest institution might once again be setting itself on a new course.

*

The place of those who came before Masako, helping Japan to question itself and to move itself along, was by this point secure. Himiko was everywhere: in manga, anime and computer games she served alternately as an icon of female power, a symbol of a primordial Japanese spirituality, a cute, child-like character and a sexy sorceress. Foodies celebrated her too, from a restaurant offering 'Himiko cooked rice' (served with an earthy combination of seaweed, onions and sauce) to advocates of a 'Himiko Diet', shorn of processed food and other modern corruptions. A handful of cities claiming a connection to her life even held Himiko contests, complete with home-made costumes.

Few children left school without knowing the name of Prince Shōtoku. Many had been on school trips to Hōryū-ji temple, dating back to his era and long a focus of his veneration. Such trips often incorporated the ancient sites of Nara not far to the north, including the great temple of Tōdai-ji – home to the world's largest bronze statue of the Buddha Vairocana, whose great eye-opening ceremony had been conducted while Emperor Kanmu was still a boy. The Prince's face was also well known – from 5,000 yen and 10,000 yen banknotes. For a time, his name in Japanese – 'Shōtoku Taishi' – served as slang for 'cash'.

Emperor Kanmu received a recognition boost from Emperor Akihito's mention of his Korean mother in 2001. He was celebrated, too, as the founder of Kyoto: a great centre of Japanese history and culture, and in the early twenty-first century so central to Japan's burgeoning tourist industry that some Kyotoites started to resent the attention, producing 'mind your manners' campaigns for the benefit of boorish incomers.

The personality and writings of Murasaki Shikibu meanwhile remained a byword for Heian-era high culture: a proud period for Japan, when few of its modern problems could yet have been imagined. Meanwhile any Japanese whose history education skipped past Hōjō Masako was sure to encounter her later in life, alongside heroines inspired by her deeds in books, films or television dramas: strong martial women, stepping in when drunken, emotional, strategically incapable or otherwise feckless men threatened ruination for some proud samurai family or other.

Shinran's legacy thrived in Buddhist communities across Japan and around the world, offering a model of egalitarianism to the politically minded and providing consolation for those tempted to pressure themselves over the state of their souls. His message, translated into modern parlance, was that no one can pull themselves up by their own bootstraps: progress in the religious life is the preserve of *tariki* ('other-power') and a work of grace. Nor would 'grace' be a bad way of summing up Zeami's ongoing contribution to the life of the Japanese. Few, now, might possess the literary education required to pick up on all the allusions in his Nō plays. And yet audiences had little trouble appreciating the subtlety of feeling that characterized his craft, of a piece with a broader traditional culture – painting, calligraphy, gardens, the tea ceremony – that ran happily alongside its pop counterpart of recent years.

Oda Nobunaga reigned supreme as the most popular figure in Japanese history: a heroic if blood-soaked unifier. The island of Tanegashima, synonymous in his era with the first Portuguese travellers and the firearms they brought, now played host to fiery, combustive miracles of another kind altogether: it was Japan's primary spaceport, home to a Space Centre where rockets were assembled, tested, launched and tracked. The great voyages of Hasekura Tsunenaga were memorialized in statues spread across north-eastern Japan, Mexico, Cuba and also Coria del Río in Spain, where hundreds of inhabitants still bore the name 'Japón', marking them out as descended from members of that pioneering delegation.

The merchant-poet Ihara Saikaku weathered centuries of controversy – literary pioneer, soft-pornographer, prophet of capitalism? – to become a beloved symbol of the era of the 'floating world', rivalling Heian for people's favourite epoch. Sakamoto Ryōma and Kusumoto Ine offered invigorating examples, each in their own way, of how to deal robustly and profitably with foreign cultural incursions. Shibusawa Eiichi and Tsuda Umeko were slated for celebration on new yen banknotes in 2024. And though *umami* – MSG – ended up encountering more criticism from nutritionists than Ikeda Kikunae might have expected, inventiveness and internationalism like his were crucial to the self-image of a Japanese scientific establishment that was becoming ever more accustomed to receiving Nobel prizes, in subjects from astrophysics to stem cells.

Her later-life politics and poetry notwithstanding, Yosano Akiko remained an inspiring feminist figure and one of her country's greatest modern poets. Misora Hibari lived on in karaoke bars, nostalgic TV documentaries and latterly as a 4K, 3D hologram, endowed thanks to artificial intelligence with the ability to sing new songs in that old, instantly recognizable voice. Tezuka Osamu continued to inspire new generations of visual artists in Japan and around the world, revered at home as the father of his country's cultural superpower status. There was room in people's hearts even for Tanaka Kakuei, naturally in Niigata, but also amongst those who remembered a charismatic leader who helped to bring Sino-Japanese rapprochement one precious step closer.

Masako's own place in Japan's history was still being written. She remained, for now, a hopeful yet still uncertain symbol for the

Japanese, finding her way back – much like her country – from difficult decades. In her New Year's poem for 2020, she managed to
speak, at one and the same time, for herself and for the Japanese:

> The power of youth
> Brings hope
> To those who strive
> To rise up from the calamity they suffer.

Chronology

Note: the dating of periods and events prior to *c*.700 CE in Japan relies heavily upon ongoing archaeological investigations, alongside texts where the dating of key events may be unreliable. Currently accepted estimates and ranges are given below, and used throughout the book. 'Circa' should be assumed unless otherwise stated.

JAPANESE PALAEOLITHIC (35,000–14,500 BCE)

35,000–30,000 BCE Earliest reliable evidence of human settlements in Japan.

JŌMON PERIOD (14,500–500 BCE)

14,500 BCE Early evidence of people storing and boiling food in clay pots.

YAYOI PERIOD (500 BCE–250 CE)

500 BCE Short-grain rice cultivation along with iron and bronze objects (and the techniques required to produce them) begin to enter Japan from mainland Asia.
c.170 CE Birth of Queen Himiko.
190 Beginning of Himiko's rule in Yamatai.
238 Himiko sends envoys to China.
248 Death of Queen Himiko.

YAMATO PERIOD (250–710)

300s and 400s A clan based in the Yamato basin, south-central Honshū, steadily consolidates its hegemony over surrounding chiefdoms.

Mid-400s Construction of the Daisen Kofun (in present-day Osaka), traditionally regarded as the resting place of a Yamato leader, the great sovereign Nintoku.

552 An envoy from the Korean kingdom of Paekche brings a Buddhist statue and sutras to Japan.

573 Birth of the semi-legendary Prince Shōtoku.

608 Prince Shōtoku, serving as regent at the Yamato court, drafts a letter to the Chinese Emperor, referring to Japan as the 'land where the sun rises' and to his sovereign as 'Child of Heaven'.

621 Death of Prince Shōtoku.

NARA PERIOD (710–794)

710 A new imperial capital is established at Nara.

712 Completion of the *Record of Ancient Matters* (*Kojiki*).

720 Completion of the *Chronicles of Japan* (*Nihon Shoki*).

737 Birth of Emperor Kanmu.

752 Grand dedication ceremony for the newly built Tōdai-ji Buddhist temple in Nara.

767 Birth of Saichō, founder of the Tendai Buddhist sect.

774 Birth of Kūkai, founder of the Shingon Buddhist sect.

781 Emperor Kanmu ascends the throne.

HEIAN PERIOD (794–1185)

794 Emperor Kanmu establishes a new imperial capital: Heian-kyō (modern-day Kyoto).

806 Death of Emperor Kanmu.

*c.*973 Birth of Murasaki Shikibu.

*c.*1001 Sei Shōnagon's *Pillow Book* (*Makura no sōshi*).

*c.*1001 Murasaki Shikibu begins work on *The Tale of Genji* (*Genji monogatari*).

1005/6 Murasaki Shikibu enters the service of Empress Shōshi, at the Heian court.

1014? 1020s? Death of Murasaki Shikibu.

1157 Birth of Hōjō Masako.

1173 Birth of Shinran, founder of the Jōdo Shinshū Buddhist sect.

1180–85 Genpei War.

KAMAKURA PERIOD (1185–1336)

1185 Minamoto no Yoritomo is victorious in the Genpei War.

1192 Yoritomo becomes the first shogun of the Kamakura *bakufu.*

1199 Death of Yoritomo; Hōjō Masako's influence in the Kamakura *bakufu* grows.

1221 The Jōkyū Incident.

1225 Death of Hōjō Masako.

1262 Death of Shinran.

1274 and 1281 Attempted invasions of Japan by Mongol forces.

1333 Ashikaga Takauji defeats the Kamakura *bakufu*, handing power in Japan to Emperor Go-Daigo.

1333–6 Kenmu Restoration.

MUROMACHI PERIOD (1336–1573)

1336 Ashikaga Takauji wrests power from Emperor Go-Daigo and founds the Ashikaga *bakufu*, based in the Muromachi suburb of Kyoto.

1363 Birth of Zeami Motokiyo.

1408 Death of Ashikaga Yoshimitsu, celebrated shogun and Zeami's major sponsor.

1443 Death of Zeami.

1467–77 Ōnin War.

1534 Birth of Oda Nobunaga.

1543 The first known Europeans to set foot in Japan are a small group of Portuguese landing on the island of Tanegashima.

1568 Oda Nobunaga enters Kyoto in triumph.

1571 Birth of Hasekura Tsunenaga.

AZUCHI-MOMOYAMA PERIOD (1573–1600)

1573 Oda Nobunaga forces Ashikaga Yoshiaki out of Kyoto, bringing the Ashikaga *bakufu* to an end and solidifying his own position as overlord.

1579 Completion of Nobunaga's Azuchi Castle.

1582 Assassination of Oda Nobunaga.

1590 Toyotomi Hideyoshi confirms his position as Nobunaga's successor with victory at Odawara.

1592–8 Hideyoshi's invasions of Korea.

1594 Completion of Hideyoshi's Fushimi-Momoyama Castle in Kyoto (which together with Azuchi Castle gives the era its name).

1597 Hideyoshi orders the execution of twenty-six Christians at Nagasaki: the 'Twenty-Six Martyrs of Japan'.

1598 Death of Toyotomi Hideyoshi.

EDO (TOKUGAWA) PERIOD (1600–1868)

1600 Tokugawa Ieyasu wins an epoch-making victory at the Battle of Sekigahara, against supporters of Toyotomi Hideyoshi's son, Hideyori.

1603 Ieyasu accepts the title of shogun; the new *bakufu* bases itself in the Tokugawa stronghold of Edo.

1613 Hasekura Tsunenaga's embassy departs Japan.

1616 Death of Tokugawa Ieyasu.

1620 Hasekura returns to Japan.

1622? Death of Hasekura.

1630s *Sakoku* – 'closed country' – edicts issued.

1642 Birth of Ihara Saikaku.

1682 Publication of Ihara Saikaku's *Life of an Amorous Man* (*Kōshoku ichidai otoko*).

1693 Death of Ihara Saikaku.

1720 The reforming shogun Tokugawa Yoshimune eases restrictions on the importing of foreign books.

1827 Birth of Kusumoto Ine.

1835 Birth of Sakamoto Ryōma.

1840 Birth of Shibusawa Eiichi.

1853 Commodore Matthew C. Perry arrives in Edo Bay, seeking diplomatic relations between the United States and Japan.

1854 'Treaty of Peace and Amity' signed between the United States and Japan; other Western powers quickly follow suit, signing peace and trade treaties with Japan – the so-called 'unequal treaties'.

1864 Birth of Tsuda Umeko and Ikeda Kikunae.

1866 Sakamoto Ryōma helps to broker an anti-*bakufu* alliance between Satsuma and Chōshū domains.

1867 Assassination of Sakamoto Ryōma.

MODERN JAPAN (1868–1945)

1868 Meiji Restoration: return of imperial rule.

1868–9 Boshin War, ending with the defeat of the Tokugawa *bakufu* and its allies by pro-imperial forces.

1871–3 The Iwakura Mission; at home, a flurry of far-reaching new laws covering economics, education, property, conscription and social status.

1878 Birth of Yosano Akiko.

1885 Establishment of Cabinet government in Japan; Itō Hirobumi becomes the country's first Prime Minister.

1889 Promulgation of the 'Constitution of the Empire of Japan'.

1890 Japan's first general elections; the Diet meets for the first time; Imperial Rescript on Education.

1891 Tsuda Umeko co-authors *Japanese Girls and Women*.

1894–5 The First Sino-Japanese War.

1901 Yosano Akiko publishes *Tangled Hair* (*Midaregami*).

1902 Anglo-Japanese Alliance.

1903 Death of Kusumoto Ine.

1904–5 The Russo-Japanese War.

1910 Japan annexes Korea.

1912 Death of the Meiji Emperor; the Meiji era gives way to the Taishō era.

1914 First World War begins; Japan declares war on Germany.

1915 Japan's 'Twenty-One Demands' on China.

1918 Birth of Tanaka Kakuei.

1923 The Great Kantō Earthquake destroys much of the Tokyo–Yokohama area and gives rise to anti-Korean violence.

1925 Universal male suffrage; a draconian new Peace Preservation Law.

1926 Death of the Taishō Emperor; beginning of the Shōwa era.

1928 Birth of Tezuka Osamu.

1929 Death of Tsuda Umeko.

1931 Death of Shibusawa Eiichi; Manchurian Incident.

1932 Declaration of 'Manchukuo'; assassinations at home in Japan by ultranationalist extremists.

1936 Death of Ikeda Kikunae; attempted military coup in Tokyo.

1937 The Second Sino-Japanese War begins; birth of Misora Hibari.

1940 Japanese plans are announced to build a 'Greater East Asia Co-Prosperity Sphere'; Tripartite Pact signed with Mussolini's Italy and Hitler's Germany.

1941 Attack on Pearl Harbor; Japanese declaration of war against the United States and the British Empire.

1942 Death of Yosano Akiko; Battle of Midway; the tide of war begins to turn against Japan.

1944–5 Allied firebombing of Japanese cities.

1945 Atomic bombing of Hiroshima; the Soviet Union declares war on Japan; atomic bombing of Nagasaki; Japan surrenders.

POST-WAR AND CONTEMPORARY JAPAN (1945 TO THE PRESENT)

1945 Allied Occupation of Japan begins.

1946 First post-war elections; women eligible to vote and serve in the Diet.

1947 The Constitution of Japan comes into effect.

1949 Misora Hibari's breakthrough film is released: *Mournful Whistle (Kanashiki Kuchibue)*; the Occupation's 'reverse course' begins.

1950 Outbreak of the Korean War.

1952 The San Francisco Peace Treaty and the US–Japan Security Treaty come into effect; the Occupation ends; the first instalment of Tezuka Osamu's *Mighty Atom (Tetsuwan Atomu)* is published.

1955 Formation of the Liberal Democratic Party (LDP; 'Jimintō' in Japanese).

1960 Large-scale demonstrations fail to stop the renewal of the US–Japan Security Treaty.

1963 *Mighty Atom* premieres on Japanese television and later that year on American television (as *Astro Boy*) – the first Japanese animation to be broadcast in the United States; birth of Owada Masako.

1964 Tokyo becomes the first Asian city to host the Summer Olympics; launch of the shinkansen (bullet train).

1970 Around half the population now lives in an urban corridor running between Tokyo and Osaka; 90 per cent of Japanese regard themselves as 'middle class'.

1972 Tanaka Kakuei becomes Prime Minister; rapprochement with China.

1974 Tanaka resigns as Prime Minister, but retains significant political influence.

1985 Equal Employment Opportunity Law.

1989 Death of the Shōwa Emperor, Misora Hibari and Tezuka Osamu; the Heisei era begins.

1990 Sharp stock-market fall in Japan; beginning of serious economic troubles.

1993 Marriage of Owada Masako to Crown Prince Naruhito; the LDP find themselves out of power for the first time since 1955; death of Tanaka Kakuei.

1995 Kobe hit by a major earthquake; sarin gas attack on the Tokyo underground.

2010 China overtakes Japan as the world's second-largest economy.

2011 Japan suffers triple disasters: earthquake, tsunami and nuclear meltdown.

2019 Emperor Akihito abdicates; Naruhito becomes Emperor and Masako becomes Empress; the Reiwa era begins; Abe Shinzō becomes Japan's longest-serving Prime Minister.

2020 Worldwide spread of the COVID-19 virus threatens Japan's still-fragile economy.

Bibliographic Notes

INTRODUCTION

Epigraphs: adapted from Isabella L. Bird, *Unbeaten Tracks in Japan: An Account of Travels in the Interior, Including Visits to the Aborigines of Yezo and the Shrines of Nikko and Ise* (John Murray, 1880); adapted from Christopher Dresser, *Japan: Its Architecture, Art, and Art Manufactures* (Longmans, Green, and Co., 1882).

I HIMIKO – SHAMAN QUEEN

On Himiko's life and times, see Walter Edwards, 'In Pursuit of Himiko: Postwar Archaeology and the Location of Yamatai', *Monumenta Nipponica* 51/1 (1996); Laura Miller, 'Searching for Charisma Queen Himiko', in Laura Miller and Rebecca Copeland (eds), *Diva Nation: Female Icons from Japanese Cultural History* (University of California Press, 2018), and 'Rebranding Himiko, the Shaman Queen of Ancient History', in *Mechademia* 9 (2014); William E. Deal, 'Religion in Archaic Japan', in Karl F. Friday (ed.), *Routledge Handbook of Premodern Japanese History* (Routledge, 2017); Conrad Totman, *A History of Japan,* second edition (Blackwell Publishing, 2004); J. Edward Kidder, 'The Earliest Societies in Japan', Matsumae Takeshi and Janet Goodwin, 'Early Kami Worship', and Okazaki Takashi and Janet Goodwin, 'Japan and the Continent', in Delmer M. Brown (ed.), *The Cambridge History of Japan, Volume 1: Ancient Japan* (Cambridge, 1993); Helen Hardacre, *Shintō: A History* (Oxford University Press, 2017). On earlier periods in Japan, see Junko Habu, *Ancient Jomon of Japan* (Cambridge University Press, 2010); Kōji Mizoguchi, *An Archaeological History of Japan, 30,000 BC to AD 700* (University of Pennsylvania Press, 2002).

'The people agreed' and 'They select' are from the *Wei Chih* (*Records of Wei*), known in Japanese as *Wajinden* (*An Account of the People of Wa*), c.297

AD. These English translations, along with the other excerpts from the *Wei Chih* used in this chapter, are adapted from Ryūsaku Tsunoda (trans.) and L. Carrington Goodrich (ed.), *Japan in the Chinese Dynastic Histories: Later Han through Ming Dynasties* (P. D. and Ione Perkins, 1951).

2 PRINCE SHŌTOKU – FOUNDING FATHER

The question of Prince Shōtoku's historicity remains a topic of lively debate in Japan. Prominent contributors include Ōyama Seiichi ('*Shōtoku Taishi*' *no tanjō* [Yoshikawa Kōbunkan, 1999]) and Morita Tei (*Suiko-chō to Shōtoku Taishi* [Iwata shoin, 2005]). On the Prince in English, see Michael I. Como, *Shōtoku: Ethnicity, Ritual, and Violence in the Japanese Buddhist Tradition* (Oxford University Press, 2008), alongside a review of Como's book by W. J. Boot in *Monumenta Nipponica* 65/2 (2010); Akiko Walley, *Constructing the Dharma King: The Hōryūji Shaka Triad and the Birth of the Prince Shōtoku Cult* (Brill, 2015); Sey Nishimura, 'The Prince and the Pauper: the Dynamics of a Shōtoku Legend', *Monumenta Nipponica* 40/3 (1985). On the broader historical context: Matsumae Takeshi and Janet Goodwin, 'Early Kami Worship', Sonoda Kōyū and Delmer M. Brown, 'Early Buddha Worship', Inoue Mitsusada and Delmer M. Brown, 'The Century of Reform', Edwin A. Cranston, 'Asuka and Nara Culture', Naoki Kōjirō and Felicia G. Bock, 'The Nara State', and Okazaki Takashi and Janet Goodwin, 'Japan and the Continent', in Delmer M. Brown (ed.), *The Cambridge History of Japan, Volume 1: Ancient Japan* (Cambridge, 1993); Helen Hardacre, *Shintō: A History* (Oxford University Press, 2017); Toby Slade, *Japanese Fashion: A Cultural History* (Bloomsbury, 2009); Charlotte von Verschuer, 'Japan's Foreign Relations, 600 to 1200 AD: A Translation from Zenrin Kokuhōki', *Monumenta Nipponica* 54/1 (1999); June Teufel Dreyer, *Middle Kingdom and Empire of the Rising Sun: Sino-Japanese Relations, Past and Present* (Oxford University Press, 2016); Ezra F. Vogel, *China and Japan: Facing History* (Harvard University Press, 2019) and Karl F. Friday (ed.), *Japan Emerging: Premodern History* to 1850 (Routledge, 2018). On Hōryū-ji, see Walley, *Constructing the Dharma King*, and Kenneth Doo Lee, *The Prince and the Monk: Shōtoku Worship in Shinran's Buddhism* (SUNY Press, 2012).

'Delivered of him without effort', 'If we are now made to gain', 'Alas! for / The wayfarer' and 'In the middle of the night' are adapted from W. G. Aston (trans.), *Nihongi: Chronicles of Japan from the Earliest Times to A.D. 697*, translated by W. G. Aston (Kegan Paul, Trench, Trübner and Co, 1896). (NB. *Nihongi* is another name for the *Nihon Shoki*). 'The Child of Heaven' appears in English translation in D. S. Fuqua, 'Classical Japan and the Continent', in Karl F. Friday (ed.), *Routledge Handbook of Premodern Japanese History* (Routledge, 2017). 'This letter from the barbarians' appears in English translation in Dreyer, *Middle Kingdom and Empire of the Rising Sun*. For the textual complexities surrounding the story of Prince Shōtoku's celebrated letter(s) to the Chinese Emperor, see von Verschuer, 'Japan's Foreign Relations, 600 to 1200 AD'.

3 EMPEROR KANMU – BOUNDARY PUSHER

On the military debacle of 789, and the warfare of this period, see Karl F. Friday, 'Pushing beyond the Pale: The Yamato Conquest of the Emishi and Northern Japan', *The Journal of Japanese Studies* 23/1 (1997). On Kanmu's times in general, see Donald H. Shively and William H. McCullough, 'Introduction', William H. McCullough, 'The Heian Court, 794–1070,' and Takeuchi Rizō, 'The Rise of the Warriors', in Donald H. Shively and William H. McCullough (eds), *The Cambridge History of Japan, Volume 2: Heian Japan* (Cambridge University Press, 1999). For an accessible introduction to Kyoto's history and culture, see John Dougill, *Kyoto: A Cultural History* (Oxford University Press, 2005). See also Ivan Morris, *The World of the Shining Prince: Court Life in Ancient Japan (Alfred A. Knopf, 1964)*; Nicolas Fieve and Paul Waley (eds), *Japanese Capitals in Historical Perspective: Place, Power and Memory in Kyoto, Edo and Tokyo* (Routledge, 2013); Joan R. Piggott, 'From Royal Centre to Metropole', in Karl F. Friday (ed.), *Routledge Handbook of Premodern Japanese History* (Routledge, 2017); William H. McCullough, 'The Capital and Its Society', in Shively and McCullough (eds), *The Cambridge History of Japan, Volume 2*. The 'large area of water to the south' of Heian/Kyoto was Lake Ogura, since disappeared. On the Kamo Festival, see Helen Hardacre, *Shintō: A History* (Oxford University Press, 2017). On Buddhism, see H. Gene Blocker and Christopher L. Starling, *Japanese Philosophy* (State University of New York Press, 2001); Jikō Hazama, 'The Characteristics of Japanese Tendai', in *Japanese Journal of Religious Studies* 14/2–3 (1987); Paul Groner, *Ryōgen and Mount Hiei: Japanese Tendai in the Tenth Century* (University of Hawaii Press, 2002); Naoki Kōjirō and Felicia G. Bock, 'The Nara State', and Sonoda Kōyū and Delmer M. Brown, 'Early Buddha Worship', in Delmer M. Brown (ed.), *The Cambridge History of Japan, Volume 1: Ancient Japan* (Cambridge University Press, 1993); Stanley Weinstein, 'Aristocratic Buddhism', in Shively and McCullough (eds), *The Cambridge History of Japan, Volume 2*. A classic work in Japanese, on Buddhist thought, is Ienaga Saburō, *Nihon Bukkyō shisō no tenkai* (Heiraku-ji shoten, 1956).

'To advance' and 'Government losses' come from the *Shoku Nihongi* (a Japanese chronicle, completed in 797), adapted from the English translation in Friday, 'Pushing beyond the Pale'. 'Amongst these savages' adapted from W. G. Aston (trans.), *Nihongi: Chronicles of Japan from the Earliest Times to A.D. 697*, translated by W. G. Aston (Kegan Paul, Trench, Trübner & Co, 1896). The phrase 'sacred centre' comes from Kōjirō and Bock, 'The Nara State' in Brown (ed.), *The Cambridge History of Japan, Volume 1*. 'Light green they shine' appears in English translation in Morris, *The World of the Shining Prince*. 'Black magic' comes from a series of decrees issued by Emperor Kanmu, appearing in English translation in Weinstein, 'Aristocratic Buddhism'. 'There is room' is reproduced in Hazama, 'The Characteristics of Japanese Tendai'.

4 MURASAKI SHIKIBU – COURT REPORTER

On Murasaki Shikibu's life and times, see Richard Bowring, 'Introduction', in Murasaki Shikibu and Richard Bowring (trans.), *The Diary of Lady Murasaki* (Penguin, 1996); Murasaki Shikibu and Edward Seidensticker (trans.), *The Tale of Genji* (Everyman, 1992); Felice Fischer, 'Murasaki Shikibu: The Court Lady', in Chieko Irie Mulhern (ed.), *Heroic with Grace: Legendary Women of Japan* (Routledge, 1991); Donald Keene (ed.), *Anthology of Japanese Literature, from the Earliest Era to the Mid-Nineteenth Century* (Grove Press, 1955), and *Seeds in the Heart: Japanese Literature from Earliest Times to the Late Sixteenth Century* (Columbia University Press, 1999); Robert Borgen and Joseph T. Sorenson, 'The Canons of Courtly Taste', in Karl F. Friday (ed.), *Japan Emerging: Premodern History to 1850* (Routledge, 2018); R. H. P. Mason and J. G. Caiger, *A History of Japan* (Tuttle Publishing, 1997); Helen Craig McCullough, 'Aristocratic Culture', and William H. McCullough, 'The Capital and Its Society', in Donald H. Shively and William H. McCullough (eds), *The Cambridge History of Japan, Volume 2: Heian Japan* (Cambridge University Press, 1999).

Except where otherwise indicated, quotations from Murasaki's diary are adapted from Murasaki and Bowring (trans.), *The Diary of Lady Murasaki*. 'Sad am I' appears in English translation in Edward Seidensticker (trans.) (1964), *The Gossamer Years: The Diary of a Noblewoman of Heian Japan* (Tuttle Publishing, 2011). See also Fischer, 'Murasaki Shikibu: The Court Lady'. The translation of Murasaki's and Michinaga's poetic exchange comes from Ivan Morris, *The World of the Shining Prince: Court Life in Ancient Japan* (Alfred A. Knopf, 1964).

5 HŌJŌ MASAKO – THE NUN SHOGUN

The sad fate of Heian-kyō and its rulers is traced in William H. McCullough, 'The Capital and Its Society', and G. Cameron Hurst III, 'Insei', in Donald H. Shively and William H. McCullough (eds), *The Cambridge History of Japan, Volume 2: Heian Japan* (Cambridge University Press, 1999); Ivan Morris, *The World of the Shining Prince: Court Life in Ancient Japan* (Alfred A. Knopf, 1964); Helen Craig McCullough, 'Introduction', in Helen Craig McCullough (trans.), *The Tale of the Heike* (Stanford University Press, 1988), and Conrad Totman, *A History of Japan*, second edition (Blackwell Publishing, 2004). The major source on Hōjō Masako's life is the chronicle *Azuma Kagami* (*Mirror of the East*; late thirteenth century), available in English online via the Japanese Historical Text Initiative (University of California, Berkeley). See also Margaret Fukazawa Benton, 'Hōjō Masako: the Dowager Shogun', in Chieko Irie Mulhern (ed.), *Heroic with Grace: Legendary Women of Japan* (Routledge, 1991); Kimberly Ordel, 'Three Perspectives on the Hōjō: A Warrior Family in Early Medieval Japan', MA Thesis, University of Southern California, 2016; Marcia Yonemoto, *The Problem of Women in Early Modern Japan* (University of California Press, 2016); R. H. P. Mason and J. G. Caiger, *A History of Japan* (Tuttle Publishing, 1997); William McCullough, 'The Azuma Kagami Account of the Shōkyū War', *Monumenta Nipponica* 23/1–2 (1968); Jeffrey P. Mass, 'The Kamakura bakufu', in Kozo Yamamura (ed.), *The Cambridge History of Japan, Volume 3: Medieval Japan* (Cambridge University Press, 1990); John Brownlee, 'Crisis as Reinforcement of the Imperial Institution: The Case of the Jōkyū Incident, 1221', *Monumenta Nipponica* 30/2 (1975). On acts of revenge in Japanese entertainment culture, see Steven T. Brown, *Theatricalities of Power: The Cultural Politics of Noh* (Stanford University Press, 2002). For the Genpei War and warrior culture, see Thomas Conlan, 'Medieval Warfare', in Karl F. Friday (ed.) *Japan Emerging: Premodern History to 1850* (Routledge, 2018); Takeuchi Rizō, 'The Rise of the Warriors', and Stanley Weinstein, 'Aristocratic Buddhism', in Shively and McCullough (eds), *The Cambridge History of Japan, Volume 2: Heian Japan*; Stephen R. Turnbull, *The Book of the Samurai* (Simon and Schuster, 1985), and *The Samurai Sourcebook*, new edition (Orion, 2000).

'What is wrong?' comes from the chronicle *Gempei jōsui ki*, adapted from the English translation in Royall Tyler, 'Tomoe: The Woman Warrior', in Mulhern (ed.), *Heroic with Grace*. A 'warrior worth a thousand', 'Take a look, easterners!' and the abbreviated and adapted quotation beginning 'The

Nun of Second [court] Rank' are from McCullough (trans.), *The Tale of the Heike*. 'It was most praiseworthy' comes from *Azuma Kagami*, via the Japanese Historical Text Initiative (University of California, Berkeley). 'Since the days' and 'No tidings' are from *Azuma Kagami*, appearing in English translation in McCullough, 'The Azuma Kagami Account of the Shōkyū War'.

6 SHINRAN – POWER TO THE PEOPLE

On Shinran's life and his religious movement, see Shinran, *Tannishō* ('Notes Lamenting Deviations'), available online in English as Taitetsu Unno (trans.), *Tannishō: A Shin Buddhist Classic* (Buddhist Study Center Press, 1984); James C. Dobbins, *Shin Buddhism in Medieval Japan* (Indiana University Press, 1989); Alfred Bloom, 'The Life of Shinran Shōnin: The Journey to Self-Acceptance', *Numen* 15/1 (1968), and *Shinran's Gospel of Pure Grace* (University of Arizona Press, 1965); Carol Richmond Tsang, *War and Faith: Ikkō Ikki in Late Muromachi Japan* (Harvard University Press, 2007); Amos Yong, 'Ignorance, Knowledge and Omniscience: At and Beyond the Limits of Faith and Reason after Shinran', *Buddhist-Christian Studies* 31 (2011); Dennis Hirota, 'The Awareness of the Natural World in *Shinjin*: Shinran's Concept of *Jinen*', *Buddhist-Christian Studies* 31 (2011), and 'Shinran and Heidegger on Dwelling: Reading Shinran as a Phenomenology of Shinjin', *Contemporary Buddhism* 15/2 (2014); Galen Amstutz, *Interpreting Amida: History and Orientalism in the Study of Pure Land Buddhism* (State University of New York Press, 1997). For the broader religious and philosophical context, see Stanley Weinstein, 'Aristocratic Buddhism', in Donald H. Shively and William H. McCullough (eds), *The Cambridge History of Japan, Volume 2: Heian Japan* (Cambridge University Press, 1999); Mimi Hall Yiengpruksawan, *Hiraizumi: Buddhist Art and Regional Politics in Twelfth-Century Japan* (Harvard University Press, 1999). Fujiwara no Michinaga's death is recounted in the chronicle *Eiga monogatari* ('Story of Splendour'; completed around 1107), available in English online via the Japanese Historical Text Initiative (University of California, Berkeley). See also Elizabeth Ten Grotenhuis, *Japanese Mandalas: Representations of Sacred Geography* (University of Hawaii Press, 1999); G. Cameron Hurst III, 'Michinaga's Maladies: A Medical Report on Fujiwara no Michinaga', *Monumenta Nipponica* 34/1 (1979).

'Foodless monks of Hiei' comes from Weinstein, 'Aristocratic Buddhism'. 'A priest who gives' and 'I must say' are adapted from Sei Shōnagon and Meredith McKinney (trans.), *The Pillow Book* (Penguin, 2006). The account of Hōjō-ji comes from William H. McCullough, 'The Capital and Its Society', in Shively and McCullough (eds), *The Cambridge History of Japan, Volume 2: Heian Japan*. 'Grasped', 'the *nembutsu* is beyond description' and 'knowledge is essential . . .' are Shinran, *Tannishō*: see Unno (trans.), *Tannishōd: A Shin Buddhist Classic*.

7 ZEAMI – MASTER OF ARTS

On Zeami and Nō, see Thomas Blenman Hare, *Zeami's Style: The Noh Plays of Zeami Motokiyo* (Stanford University Press, 1996); Zeami and William Scott Wilson (introduction and trans.), *The Flowering Spirit: Classic Teachings on the Art of Nō: A New Translation of the Fūshikaden* (Tokyo: Kodansha International, 2006); Royall Tyler (trans. and ed.), *Japanese Nō Dramas* (Penguin, 1992); Kunio Konparu, *The Noh Theatre: Principles and Perspectives* (Floating World Editions, 2005). On Zeami's era, see Ishii Susumu, 'The Decline of the Kamakura bakufu', and Martin Collcutt, 'Zen and the *gozan*', in Kozo Yamamura (ed.), *The Cambridge History of Japan, Volume 3: Medieval Japan* (Cambridge University Press, 1990); Stephen R. Turnbull, *The Samurai Sourcebook*, new edition (Orion, 2000); John Whitney Hall, *Japan in the Muromachi Age* (University of California Press, 1977). On Japan's performing arts traditions, see Edwin A. Cranston, 'Asuka and Nara Culture', in Delmer M. Brown (ed.), *The Cambridge History of Japan, Volume 1: Ancient Japan* (Cambridge University Press, 1993); Benito Ortolani, *The Japanese Theatre: From Shamanistic Ritual to Contemporary Pluralism*, revised edition (Princeton University Press, 1995); Donald Keene, *Seeds in the Heart: Japanese Literature from Earliest Times to the Late Sixteenth Century* (Columbia University Press, 1999); Noel J. Pinnington, *A New History of Medieval Japanese Theatre* (Palgrave Macmillan, 2019); H. Paul Varley, 'Cultural Life in Medieval Japan', in Yamamura (ed.), *The Cambridge History of Japan, Volume 3: Medieval Japan*. On the Palace of Flowers, see Matthew Stavros and Norika Kurioka, 'Imperial Progress to the Muromachi Palace, 1381: A Study and Annotated Translation of Sakayuku hana', *Japan Review* 28 (2015); Hall, *Japan in the Muromachi Age*.

Quotations from *The Well-Cradle* are adapted from the English translation given in Tyler, *Japanese Nō Dramas*. 'The origin of the art of Nō' is Zeami, in the *Fūshikaden*, reproduced in Wilson, *The Flowering Spirit*. 'We, the Great Mongolian Empire' appears in English translation in Ishii, 'The Decline of the Kamakura bakufu'. 'Specks of dust' is translated in Pinnington, *A New History of Medieval Japanese Theatre*. 'I quite lost my heart' and 'The shogun has shown' (adapted) appear in English translation in Hare, *Zeami's Style*. 'Can perform without criticism' and 'The actor himself' is reproduced in Wilson, *The Flowering Spirit*. Quotations from *Wind Through the Pines* (*Matsukaze*) are adapted from Tyler, *Japanese Nō Dramas*.

8 ODA NOBUNAGA – UNITY OR ELSE

On Oda and his times see Jeroen Lamers, *Japonius Tyrannus: The Japanese Warlord Oda Nobunaga Reconsidered* (Hotei Publishing, 2000); N. McMullin, *Buddhism and the State in Sixteenth-Century Japan* (Princeton University Press, 1985); Mary Elizabeth Berry, *Hideyoshi* (Harvard University Press, 1982); Stephen Turnbull, *War in Japan, 1467–1615* (Osprey Publishing, 2002), and *The Book of the Samurai* (Simon and Schuster, 1985); R. H. P. Mason and J. G. Caiger, *A History of Japan* (Tuttle Publishing, 1997); Andrew Rankin, *Seppuku: A History of Samurai Suicide* (Kodansha International, 2012); John Whitney Hall, 'The Muromachi bakufu', Kozo Yamamura, 'The Growth of Commerce', and Nagahara Keiji, 'The Medieval Peasant', in Kozo Yamamura (ed.), *The Cambridge History of Japan, Volume 3: Medieval Japan* (Cambridge University Press, 1990); Kristen L. Chiem and Lara C. W. Blanchard, *Gender, Continuity, and the Shaping of Modernity in the Arts of East Asia, 16th–20th Centuries* (Brill, 2017); Wakita Osamu, 'The Social and Economic Consequences of Unification', and Asao Naohiro and Bernard Susser (trans.), 'The Sixteenth-Century Unification', in John Whitney Hall (ed.), *The Cambridge History of Japan, Volume 4: Early Modern Japan* (Cambridge, 1991); Carol Richmond Tsang, *War and Faith: Ikkō Ikki in Late Muromachi Japan* (Harvard University Press, 2007); Peter D. Shapinsky, *Lords of the Sea: Pirates, Violence, and Commerce in Late Medieval Japan* (University of Michigan Press, 2014). On Kyoto during these years, see Matthew Stavros, *Kyoto: An Urban History of Japan's Pre-Modern Capital* (University of Hawaii Press, 2014); John Dougill, *Kyoto: A Cultural History* (Oxford University Press, 2005). Rumours surrounding Oda's behaviour at his father's funeral can be found in the Edo-era chronicle of Oda's life, *Shinchō-kōki*, cited in Lamers, *Japonius Tyrannus*.

'He wore a short-sleeved shirt' and 'When we consider' appear in English translation in McMullin, *Buddhism and the State in Sixteenth-Century Japan*.

9 HASEKURA TSUNENAGA – VOYAGER

On Hasekura's times, see Mary Elizabeth Berry, *Hideyoshi* (Harvard University Press, 1982); Asao Naohiro and Bernard Susser (trans.), 'The

Sixteenth-Century Unification', in John Whitney Hall (ed.), *The Cambridge History of Japan, Volume 4: Early Modern Japan* (Cambridge University Press, 1991); Matthew P. McKelway, *Capitalscapes: Folding Screens and Political Imagination in Late Medieval Kyoto* (University of Hawaii Press, 2006); Jurgis Elisonas, 'Christianity and the Daimyō', and 'The Inseparable Trinity: Japan's Relations with China and Korea', in Hall (ed.), *The Cambridge History of Japan, Volume 4: Early Modern Japan*; Yoshimi Orii, 'The Dispersion of Jesuit Books Published in Japan: Trends in Bibliographical Research and in Intellectual History', *Journal of Jesuit Studies* 2/2 (2015); James Murdoch (1903), *A History of Japan, Volume 2* (TheClassics.us, 2013); Kitajima Manki, 'The Imjin Waeran: Contrasting the First and the Second Invasions of Korea', in James B. Lewis (ed.), *The East Asian War, 1592–98: International Relations, Violence and Memory* (Routledge, 2014); Marius Jansen, *The Making of Modern Japan* (Harvard University Press, paperback edition 2002); A. L. Sadler, *Shogun: The Life of Tokugawa Ieyasu* (Tuttle Publishing, 2009); Michael Cooper, *The Japanese Mission to Europe, 1582–1590: The Journey of Four Samurai Boys through Portugal, Spain and Italy* (Global Oriental, 2005); Reinier H. Hesselink, *The Dream of Christian Nagasaki: World Trade and the Clash of Cultures, 1560–1640* (McFarland, 2015). On the broader global context: Kenneth M. Swope, *A Dragon's Head and a Serpent's Tail: Ming China and the First Great East Asian War, 1592–1598* (University of Oklahoma Press, 2013); James Kai-sing Kung and Chicheng Ma, 'Autarky and the Rise and Fall of Piracy in Ming China', *Journal of Economic History* 74/2 (2014); Marco Polo and Nigel Cliff (trans.), *The Travels* (Penguin, 2015); James B. Lewis, '*The Japan That Does Not Exist* and *The Ugly Korean*', in James B. Lewis and Amadu Sesay (eds), *Korea and Globalization: Politics, Economics and Culture* (RoutledgeCurzon, 2002); Jefferson Dillman, *Colonizing Paradise: Landscape and Empire in the British West Indies* (University of Alabama Press, 2015); Geoffrey Gunn, *World Trade Systems of the East and West: Nagasaki and the Asian Bullion Trade Networks* (Brill, 2017); M. Antoni and S. J. J. Ucerler, 'The Christian Missions in Japan in the Early Modern Period', in Ronnie Po-Chia Hsia (ed.), *A Companion to Early Modern Catholic Global Missions* (Brill, 2015); Ron P. Toby, *Engaging the Other: 'Japan' and Its Alter-Egos, 1550–1850* (Brill, 2019); Ronnie Po-Chia Hsia, *The World of Catholic Renewal, 1540–1770* (Cambridge University Press, 2001); Christina H. Lee, *Western Visions of the Far East in a Transpacific Age, 1522–1657* (Routledge, 2016); Donald F. Lach, *Asia in the Making of Europe, Volume 1: The Century of*

Discovery, Book Two (University of Chicago Press, 1965); Cornelius Conover and Cory Conover, 'Saintly Biography and the Cult of San Felipe de Jesús in Mexico City, 1597–1697', *The Americas* 67/4 (2011); Simon Barton, *A History of Spain*, second edition (Red Globe Press, 2009); Cornelius Conover, *Pious Imperialism: Spanish Rule and the Cult of Saints in Mexico City* (University of New Mexico Press, 2019); Grant K. Goodman, *Japan and the Dutch, 1600–1853* (Psychology Press, 2000). On art and globalization in this era: David Bindman and Henry Louis Gates, *The Image of the Black in Western Art, Volume 3: From the 'Age of Discovery' to the Age of Abolition, Part 1: Artists of the Renaissance and Baroque* (Harvard University Press, 2010); Hugh Honour and John Fleming (eds), *A World History of Art* (Laurence King Publishing, 2005); Rie Arimura, 'Nanban Art and Its Globality: A Case Study of the New Spanish Mural *The Great Martyrdom of Japan in 1597*', *Historia y Sociedad* 36 (2019); Opher Mansour, 'Picturing Global Conversion: Art and Diplomacy at the Court of Paul V', *Journal of Early Modern History* 17 (2013). On Hasekura's travels, see Gonoi Takashi, *Hasekura Tsunenaga* (Yoshikawa Kōbunkan, 2003) [in Japanese]; Nobuko Adachi, *Japanese and Nikkei at Home and Abroad* (Cambria Press, 2010); Ed Gutierrez, 'Samurai in Spain', *Japan Quarterly* (March 2000); James Lockhart, Susan Schroeder and Doris Namala (eds and trans.), *Annals of His Times: Don Domingo de San Antón Muñón Chimalpahin Quauhtlehuanitzin* (Stanford University Press, 2006); Robert Richmond Ellis, *They Need Nothing: Hispanic-Asian Encounters of the Colonial Period* (University of Toronto Press, 2012); Colyer Meriwether, 'Date Masamune', *Transactions of the Asiatic Society of Japan* 21/22 (1892); Ikuko Torimoto, *Okina Kyūin and the Politics of Early Japanese Immigration to the United States, 1868–1924* (McFarland, 2017); Gopal Kshetry, *Foreigners in Japan: A Historical Perspective* (Xlibris Corporation, 2008); Adriana Boscaro, Franco Gatti and Massimo Raveri, *Rethinking Japan: Social Sciences, Ideology and Thought* (Psychology Press, 1990).

'The 4th of the month of March' is from Lockhart, Schroeder and Namala (eds and trans.), *Annals of His Times: Don Domingo de San Antón Muñón Chimalpahin Quauhtlehuanitzin*. 'I have learned of the afterlife' is the author's translation from a document reproduced in Gonoi, *Hasekura Tsunenaga*.

10 IHARA SAIKAKU – AMOROUS MAN

On early modern Japan in general: Elizabeth Lillehoj, *Art and Palace Politics in Early Modern Japan, 1580s–1680s* (Brill, 2011); Asao Naohiro and

Bernard Susser (trans.), 'The Sixteenth-Century Unification', Susan B. Hanley, 'Tokugawa Society: Material Culture, Standard of Living, and Life-Styles', Donald H. Shively, 'Popular Culture', and John Whitney Hall, 'The *bakuhan* System', in John Whitney Hall (ed.), *The Cambridge History of Japan, Volume 4: Early Modern Japan* (Cambridge University Press, 1991); James McClain, *Japan: A Modern History* (W. W. Norton & Company, 2002); Marius Jansen, *The Making of Modern Japan* (Harvard University Press, paperback edition 2002); Akira Hayami, *Population, Family and Society in Pre-Modern Japan* (Global Oriental, 2010); William E. Deal, *Handbook to Life in Medieval and Early Modern Japan* (Oxford University Press, 2007); Ning Ma, *The Age of Silver: The Rise of the Novel East and West* (Oxford University Press, 2016); Mary Elizabeth Berry, *Hideyoshi* (Harvard University Press, 1982). On Ihara Saikaku's life and his era's literary scene, see Ivan Morris, 'Introduction', in Ihara Saikaku and Ivan Morris (trans.), *The Life of an Amorous Woman and Other Writings* (New Directions, 1969); Herbert H. Jonsson, *Reading Japanese Haikai Poetry* (Brill, 2016); Christopher Drake, 'Saikaku's Haikai Requiem: A Thousand Haikai Alone in a Single Day, The First Hundred Verses', *Harvard Journal of Asiatic Studies* 52/2 (1992); Mary Elizabeth Berry, *Japan in Print: Information and Nation in the Early Modern Period* (University of California Press, 2007); Adolphe Clarence Scott (1955), *The Kabuki Theatre of Japan* (Dover Publications, 1999); James R. Brandon and Samuel L. Leiter, *Kabuki Plays on Stage* (University of Hawaii Press, 2002); H. Paul Varley, *Japanese Culture* (University of Hawaii Press, 2000); Howard Hibbett (1959), *The Floating World in Japanese Fiction*, new edition (Tuttle Publishing, 2002); Ihara Saikaku and Paul Gordon Schalow (trans., Introduction), *The Great Mirror of Male Love* (Stanford University Press, 1990).

'The waitress', 'Blow out the light', 'With his winning, cajoling ways', 'Dead leaves pile up' and 'What they saw' are adapted from Ihara Saikaku and Kenji Hamada (trans.), *The Life of an Amorous Man* (Tuttle Publishing, 1963). 'While you lived' appears in English translation in Drake, 'Saikaku's Haikai Requiem'. 'The men wear women's clothing' is from Shively, 'Popular Culture'. 'Which is to be preferred' is reproduced in Saikaku and Schalow (trans.), *The Great Mirror of Male Love*. 'I have gazed at it now' comes from Saikaku and Morris (trans.), *The Life of an Amorous Woman*.

11 SAKAMOTO RYŌMA – REVOLUTIONARY

On Sakamoto's life and times, see Marius B. Jansen, *Sakamoto Ryōma and the Meiji Restoration* (Princeton University Press, 1961); William E. Deal,

Handbook to Life in Medieval and Early Modern Japan (Oxford University Press, 2007); James McClain, *Japan: A Modern History* (W. W. Norton & Company, 2002); Marius B. Jansen, 'Japan in the Early Nineteenth Century', in Marius B. Jansen (ed.), *The Cambridge History of Japan, Volume 5: The Nineteenth Century* (Cambridge, 1989); Helen Hardacre, *Shintō: A History* (Oxford University Press, 2017); Romulus Hillsborough, *Samurai Tales* (Tuttle Publishing, 2011); Jesse C. Newman, *History of Kyudo and Iaido in Early Japan* (AuthorHouse, 2015); Marius Jansen, *The Making of Modern Japan* (Harvard University Press, paperback edition 2002); Eiko Maruko Siniawer, *Ruffians, Yakuza, Nationalists: The Violent Politics of Modern Japan, 1860–1960* (Cornell University Press, 2008); D. Colin Jaundrill, *Samurai to Soldier: Remaking Military Service in Nineteenth-Century Japan* (Cornell University Press, 2016); Donald Keene, *Emperor of Japan: Meiji and His World, 1852–1912* (Columbia University Press, 2005).

'I must say', 'spending your time', 'I think there will be a war', 'It is my firm desire', 'Loyalty to what is called' and 'I don't expect' appear in English translation in Jansen, *Sakamoto Ryōma*. 'Only silver' is reproduced in Ihara Saikaku and Ivan Morris (trans.), *The Life of an Amorous Woman and Other Writings* (New Directions, 1969).

12 KUSUMOTO INE – BUILDING THE BODY

On Kusumoto Ine, see Yi Soo-kyung, 'Kusumoto Ine: Nihon hatsu no josei sanka senmoni', in Ueki Takeshi (ed.), *Kokusai shakai de katsuyaku shita nihonjin Meiji-Showa 13 nin no kosumoporitan* (Kōbundō, 2009) [in Japanese]; Ugami Yukio, *Bakumatsu no jyoi Kusumoto Ine: Shiiboruto no musume to kazoku no shōzō* (Gendai Shokan, 2018) [in Japanese]; Herbert Plutschow, *Philipp Franz von Siebold and the Opening of Japan* (Global Oriental 2007); Grant K. Goodman, *Japan and the Dutch, 1600–1853* (Psychology Press, 2000); Ellen Nakamura, 'Working the Siebold Network: Kusumoto Ine and Western Learning in Nineteenth-Century Japan', *Japanese Studies* 28/2 (2008). On the Dutch in Japan, see Donald Keene, *The Japanese Discovery of Europe, 1720–1830* (Stanford University Press, 1969); Arnulf Thiede et al., 'The Life and Times of Philipp Franz von Siebold', *Surgery Today* 39/4 (2009); Grant K. Goodman, *Japan and the Dutch*, and *Japan: the Dutch Experience* (Bloomsbury, 2013); Marius B. Jansen, 'Rangaku and Westernization', *Modern Asian Studies* 18/4 (1984); Marcia Yonemoto, *The Problem of Women in Early Modern Japan* (University of California Press, 2016); Gary P. Leupp, *Interracial Intimacy in Japan: West-*

ern Men and Japanese Women, 1543–1900 (Continuum, 2002); Edwin Palmer Hoyt, *America's Wars and Military Encounters* (Da Capo Press, 1988). On medicine, see Jansen, 'Rangaku and Westernization'; Margaret Lock, *East Asian Medicine in Urban Japan* (University of California Press, 1984); Yuki Terazawa, *Knowledge, Power, and Women's Reproductive Health in Japan, 1690–1945* (Palgrave Macmillan, 2018); Donald Keene, 'Hirata Atsutane and Western Learning', *T'oung Pao*, Second Series, 42/5 (1954); Aya Homei, 'Birth Attendants in Meiji Japan: The Rise of the Biomedical Birth Model and a New Division of Labour', *Social History of Medicine* 19/3 (2006). On the early Meiji era, see Ian Inkster, *Japanese Industrialisation: Historical and Cultural Perspectives* (Psychology Press, 2001); E. Patricia Tsurumi, 'The State, Education, and Two Generations of Women in Meiji Japan, 1868–1912', *U.S.–Japan Women's Journal: English Supplement* 18 (2000); Ayako Hotta-Lister, *The Japan–British Exhibition of 1910: Gateway to the Island Empire of the East* (Psychology Press, 1999); James McClain, *Japan: A Modern History* (W. W. Norton & Company, 2002); Marius Jansen, *The Making of Modern Japan* (Harvard University Press, paperback edition 2002); Christopher Harding, *Japan Story: In Search of a Nation, 1850 to the Present* (Allen Lane, 2018); Andrew Gordon, *A Modern History of Japan* (Oxford University Press, 2013).

'[Do not] scorn' and the story of the two sisters appear in English translation in Yonemoto, *The Problem of Women in Early Modern Japan*. Kusumoto's letters to her father are reproduced in Ugami, *Bakumatsu no jyoi Kusumoto Ine* (author translation). See also Plutschow, *Philipp Franz von Siebold and the Opening of Japan*.

13 SHIBUSAWA EIICHI – ENTREPRENEUR

On Shibusawa Eiichi, see Shibusawa Eiichi and Teruko Craig (trans.), *The Autobiography of Shibusawa Eiichi* (University of Tokyo Press, 1994), and Shibusawa Eiichi and Teruko Craig (trans.), 'A Journal of a Voyage to the West', included in Shibusawa and Craig, *Autobiography of Shibusawa Eiichi*; John H. Sagers, *Confucian Capitalism: Shibusawa Eiichi, Business Ethics, and Economic Development in Meiji Japan* (Palgrave Macmillan, 2018); Donald Keene (ed.) and trans.), *Modern Japanese Diaries* (Columbia University Press, 1999); Patrick Fridenson and Kikkawa Takeo, *Ethical Capitalism: Shibusawa Eiichi and Business Leadership in Global Perspective* (University of Toronto Press, 2017); Shimada Masakazu and Paul Narum (trans.), *The Entrepreneur Who Built Modern Japan: Shibusawa Eiichi* (Japan Publishing Industry Foundation for Culture, 2017); Kuo-Hui

Tai, 'Confucianism and Japanese Modernization: A Study of Shibusawa Eiichi', in Subhash Durlabhji, Norton E. Marks and Scott Roach (eds), *Japanese Business: Cultural Perspectives* (SUNY Press, 1993). On Shibusawa's times, see André Sorenson, *The Making of Urban Japan* (Routledge, 2004); Edward Seidensticker, *A History of Tokyo, 1867–1989* (Tuttle Publishing, 2019); Paul Waley, 'Japan', in Peter Clark (ed.), *The Oxford Handbook of Cities in World History* (Oxford University Press, 2013); Ayako Hotta-Lister, *The Japan–British Exhibition of 1910: Gateway to the Island Empire of the East* (Psychology Press, 1999); David G. Wittner, *Technology and the Culture of Progress in Meiji Japan* (Routledge, 2007); Mikiso Hane, *Peasants, Rebels, Women and Outcastes: The Underside of Modern Japan* (Rowman & Littlefield, 2003); James McClain, *Japan: A Modern History* (W. W. Norton & Company, 2002); Marius Jansen, *The Making of Modern Japan*, (Harvard University Press, paperback edition, 2002); Christopher Harding, *Japan Story: In Search of a Nation, 1850 to the Present* (Allen Lane, 2018); Andrew Gordon, *A Modern History of Japan* (Oxford University Press, 2013); Ian Inkster, *Japanese Industrialisation: Historical and Cultural Perspectives* (Psychology Press, 2001); E. Sydney Crawcour, 'Economic Change in the Nineteenth Century', and 'Industrialization and Technological Change, 1885–1920', in Kozo Yamamura (ed.), *The Economic Emergence of Modern Japan* (Cambridge University Press, 1997); David Flath, *The Japanese Economy*, third edition (Oxford University Press, 2014); Louise Young, *Japan's Total Empire: Manchuria and the Culture of Wartime Imperialism* (University of California Press, 1999).

'Tonight, in keeping with my promise' is from Shibusawa and Craig (trans.), *The Autobiography of Shibusawa Eiichi*. 'If one learns the Way at dawn', 'Besides relations with women', and 'Lucky he was a Confucian' are reproduced in Sagers, *Confucian Capitalism*. 'Still clinging to their old system' is reproduced in Keene, *Modern Japanese Diaries*. 'A single wealthy individual' is reproduced in Fridenson and Kikkawa, *Ethical Capitalism*.

14 TSUDA UMEKO – CULTURE SHOCK

On Tsuda Umeko's life, see Barbara Rose, *Tsuda Umeko and Women's Education in Japan* (Yale University Press, 1992); Yoshiko Furuki, *The White Plum: A Biography of Ume Tsuda, Pioneer in the Higher Education of Japanese Women* (Shambhala Publications, 1991); Yoshiko Furuki et al. (eds), *The Attic Letters: Ume Tsuda's Correspondence to Her American Mother* (Shambhala Publications, 1991); Linda L. Johnson, 'Tsuda Umeko and a Transnational Network Supporting Women's Higher Education in Japan during the Victorian Era', *American Educational History Journal* 37/2 (2010). On 'culture shock', discontent with Meiji-era reforms and the lives of women in this era, see Sharon L. Sievers, *Flowers in Salt: The Beginnings of Feminist Consciousness in Modern Japan* (Stanford University Press, 1983); Hiroko Tomida, *Hiratsuka Raichō and Early Japanese Feminism* (Brill, 2004); Mikiso Hane (trans. and ed.), *Reflections on the Way to the Gallows: Rebel Women in Prewar Japan* (University of California Press, 1993); Stephen Vlastos, 'Opposition Movements in Early Meiji, 1868–1885', in Marius B. Jansen (ed.), *The Cambridge History of Japan, Volume 5: The Nineteenth Century* (Cambridge University Press,1989). On Saigō Takamori and the Satsuma Rebellion, see C. L. Yates, 'Saigō Takamori in the Emergence of Meiji Japan', *Modern Asian Studies* 28/3 (1994); Jordan Sand, *House and Home in Modern Japan: Architecture, Domestic Space, and Bourgeois Culture, 1880–1930* (Harvard University Press, 2005); Christopher Harding, *Japan Story: In Search of a Nation, 1850 to the Present* (Allen Lane, 2018); James McClain, *Japan: A Modern History* (W. W. Norton & Company, 2002); E. Sydney Crawcour, 'Industrialization and Technological Change, 1885–1920', in Kozo Yamamura (ed.), *The Economic Emergence of Modern Japan* (Cambridge University Press, 1997); Andrew Gordon, *A Modern History of Japan* (Oxford University Press, 2013). On Christianity, see James M. Hommes, 'Baptized Bushidō: Christian Converts and the Use of Bushidō in Meiji Japan', *Journal of the Southwest Conference on Asian Studies* 7 (2011); Emily Anderson, *Christianity and Imperialism in Modern Japan: Empire for God* (Bloomsbury, 2014); Harding, *Japan Story*.

Tsuda's letters to Mrs Lanman from Japan come from Yoshiko Furuki et al. (eds), *The Attic Letters*. 'I am very happy' is reproduced in Rose, *Tsuda Umeko and Women's Education in Japan*. 'In the beginning' is the author's translation from Hiratsuka Raichō, 'Genshi, josei wa taiyo de atta' ['In the Beginning, Woman was the Sun', *Seitō* (September 1911). See also Hiratsuka Raichō and Teruko Craig (trans. and notes), *In the Beginning, Woman Was the Sun: The Autobiography of a Japanese Feminist* (Columbia University Press, 2006). 'Although I feel sorry for him personally', comes from Hane (trans. and ed.), *Reflections on the Way to the Gallows*.

15 IKEDA KIKUNAE – TASTE-MAKER

On Ikeda's life, see Ikeda Kikunae, 'New Seasonings' (1909), English translation published by Yoko Ogiwara and Yuzo Ninomiya in *Chemical Senses* 27 (2002); Eiichi Nakamura, 'One Hundred Years Since the Discovery of the "Umami" Taste from Seaweed Broth by Ikeda Kikunae, Who Transcended His Time', *Chemistry: An Asian Journal* 6 (2011); Bruce P. Halpern, 'What's in a Name? Are MSG and Umami the Same?', *Chemical Senses* 27 (2002); Chiaki Sano, 'History of Glutamate Production', in *American Journal of Clinical Nutrition* 90 (2009); Bernd Lindemann, Yoko Ogiwara and Yuzo Ninomiya, 'The Discovery of Umami', *Chemical Senses* 27 (2002); Shinichi Hashimoto, 'Discovery and History of Amino Acid Fermentation', *Advances in Biochemical Engineering/Biotechnology* 159 (2017); Jordan Sand, 'A Short History of MSG: Good Science, Bad Science, and Taste Cultures', *Gastronomica: The Journal of Critical Food Studies* 5/4 (2005); Louisa Daria Rubinfien, 'Commodity to National Brand: Manufacturers, Merchants and the Development of the Consumer Market in Interwar Japan', PhD dissertation, Harvard University, 1995. On industry, science and culture in Ikeda's era, see E. Sydney Crawcour, 'Industrialization and Technological Change, 1885–1920', in Kozo Yamamura (ed.), *The Economic Emergence of Modern Japan* (Cambridge University Press, 1997); John H. Sagers, *Confucian Capitalism: Shibusawa Eiichi, Business Ethics, and Economic Development in Meiji Japan* (Palgrave Macmillan, 2018); James McClain, *Japan: A Modern History* (W. W. Norton & Company, 2002); Morris Low (ed.), *Building a Modern Japan: Science, Technology, and Medicine in the Meiji Era and Beyond* (Palgrave Macmillan, 2005); James R. Bartholomew, 'Modern Science in Japan: Comparative Perspectives', *Journal of World History* 4/1 (1993); Naomichi Ishige, 'Food Culture', in Yoshio Sugimoto (ed.), *The Cambridge Companion to Modern Japanese Culture* (Cambridge University Press, 2009); Katarzyna Joanna Cwiertka, *Modern Japanese Cuisine: Food, Power and National Identity* (Reaktion Books, 2006); Christine Yano, 'Defining the Modern Nation in Popular Song, 1914–32', in Sharon Minichiello (ed.), *Japan's Competing Modernities: Issues in Culture and Democracy, 1900–1930* (University of Hawaii Press, 1998); E. Taylor Atkins, *A History of Popular Culture in Japan: From the Seventeenth Century to the Present* (Bloomsbury, 2017), and *Blue Nippon: Authenticating Jazz in Japan* (Duke University Press, 2011); Christopher Harding, *Japan Story: In Search of a Nation, 1850 to the Present* (Allen Lane, 2018); Marie Højlund Roesgaard, *Moral Education in Japan: Values in a Global Context* (Taylor & Francis, 2016); Susan Eyrich Lederer, 'Hideyo Noguchi's Luetin Experiment and the Antivivisectionists', *Isis* 76/1 (1985); Paul Franklin Clark, 'Hideyo Noguchi, 1876–1928', *Bulletin of the History of Medicine* 33/1 (1959). On violence against Koreans in the wake of the 1923 earthquake, see Sonia Ryang, 'The Great Kanto Earthquake and the Massacre of Koreans in 1923: Notes on Japan's Modern National Sovereignty', *Anthropological Quarterly* 76/4

(2003). On America's early planning for a potential war with Japan, see Louis Morton, 'War Plan Orange: Evolution of a Strategy', *World Politics* 11/2 (1959). On Justus von Liebig, see William H. Brock, *Justus von Liebig: The Chemical Gatekeeper* (Cambridge University Press, 2002); Kathy Martin, *Famous Brand Names and Their Origins* (Pen and Sword, 2017). 'Be it known' comes from United States Patent Office, Specification of Letters Patent, No. 1,035,591 (13 August 1912). 'If you only even learn' from Marie Højlund Roesgaard, *Moral Education in Japan: Values in a Global Context* (Taylor and Francis, 2016). 'The national taste essence!' appears in English translation in Sand, 'A Short History of MSG'.

16 YOSANO AKIKO – POET OF PEACE AND WAR

On Yosano's life, see 'Introduction' in Akiko Yosano, Sanford Goldstein (trans.) and Seishi Shinoda (trans.), *Tangled Hair: Selected Tanka from Midaregami* (Tuttle Publishing, 1987); Yosano Akiko, *Man-mō yūki* [*Travelogue of Manchuria and Mongolia*], available in English translation in Yosano Akiko and Joshua A. Fogel (trans.), *Travels in Manchuria and Mongolia: A Feminist Poet from Japan Encounters Prewar China* (Columbia University Press, 2001); Janine Beichman, *Embracing the Firebird: Yosano Akiko and the Rebirth of the Female Voice in Modern Japanese Poetry* (University of Hawaii Press, 2001); Steve Rabson, 'Yosano Akiko on War: To Give One's Life or Not: A Question of Which War', *The Journal of the Association of Teachers of Japanese* 25/1 (1991), and *Righteous Cause or Tragic Folly: Changing Views of War in Modern Japanese Poetry* (University of Michigan Press, 1997); Laurel Rasplica Rodd, 'Yosano Akiko and the Taisho Debate Over the "New Woman"', in Gail Lee Bernstein (ed.), *Recreating Japanese Women, 1600–1945* (University of California Press, 1991); Laurel Rasplica Rodd, 'Yosano Akiko and the Bunkagakuin: "Educating Free Individuals"', *The Journal of the Association of Teachers of Japanese* 25/1 (1991). On Japanese artists and intellectuals in China, see Joshua A. Fogel, *The Literature of Travel in the Japanese Rediscovery of China, 1862–1945* (Stanford University Press, 1996); E. Taylor Atkins, *Blue Nippon: Authenticating Jazz in Japan* (Duke University Press, 2011); Paul D. Scott, 'Introduction', *Chinese Studies in History* 30/4 (1997); Akutagawa Ryūnosuke, Joshua A. Fogel (trans.) and Kiyoko Morita (trans.), 'Travels in China', *Chinese Studies in History* 30/4 (1997); Christopher Harding, *Japan Story: In Search of a Nation, 1850 to the Present* (Allen Lane, 2018); James McClain, *Japan: A Modern History* (W. W. Norton & Company, 2002). On Japan and the Japanese empire in the 1930s, see Louise Young, *Japan's Total*

Empire: Manchuria and the Culture of Wartime Imperialism (University of California Press, 1999); Mark Peattie, *Ishiwara Kanji and Japan's Confrontation with the West* (Princeton University Press, 1975); Harding, *Japan Story*; Joshua A. Fogel, ' "Shanghai-Japan": The Japanese Residents' Association of Shanghai', *Journal of Asian Studies* 59/4 (2000); Peter Harmsen, *Shanghai 1937: Stalingrad on the Yangtze* (Casemate Publishers, 2013); Yang Tianshi, 'Chiang Kai-Shek and the Battles of Shanghai and Nanjing', in Mark Peattie et al. (eds), *The Battle for China: Essays on the Military History of the Sino-Japanese War of 1937–1945* (Stanford University Press, 2010).

Statistics for the Pearl Harbor attack come from the factsheet 'Remembering Pearl Harbor', published by the National WWII Museum in New Orleans (www.nationalww2museum.org). 'Murasaki has been my teacher', 'From one room over', 'Casually I left', 'Aren't you nice, Genji and Narihira', 'From the mouth of a whore' and 'Precocious prattle' appear in English translation in Beichman, *Embracing the Firebird*. Verses from *Midaregami* come from Yosano, Goldstein and Shinoda (trans.), *Tangled Hair*. 'Oh, my brother', 'To the west of the river', 'Ah, the augustness' and 'It is a time for falling tears' appear in English translation in Rabson, 'Yosano Akiko on War'. 'Making students useful' and 'Breathing the air of the *Genji*' are reproduced in Rodd, 'Yosano Akiko and the Bunkagakuin'. 'Sick old man' is reproduced in Fogel, *The Literature of Travel in the Japanese Rediscovery of China*. 'What a horror' is from '*Watakushi no Kojinshugi*' ['My Individualism'] (1914), reproduced in Jay Rubin and Natsume Sōseki, 'Sōseki on Individualism: "Watakushi no Kojinshugi"', *Monumenta Nipponica* 34/1 (1979). 'Decrepit tea-house' is reproduced in Akutagawa, Fogel (trans.) and Morita (trans.), 'Travels in China'. Excerpts from Yosano's travel diary in Manchuria come from Yosano and Fogel (trans.), *Travels in Manchuria and Mongolia*. 'Political parties are blind' appears in English translation in *Mainichi Daily News: Fifty Years of Light and Dark: The Hirohito Era* (Mainichi Newspapers, 1975).

17 MISORA HIBARI – STARLET/HARLOT

On the war, see Paul H. Kratoska (ed.), *The Thailand-Burma Railway, 1942–1946: Voluntary Accounts* (Taylor & Francis, 2006); Arthur Cotterell, *A History of South East Asia* (Marshall Cavendish International (Asia), 2014); Thomas Havens, *Valley of Darkness: The Japanese People and World War Two* (University Press of America, 1986); Thomas R. Searle, ' "It Made a Lot of Sense to Kill Skilled Workers": The Firebombing of

Tokyo in March 1945', *Journal of Military History*, 66/1 (2002); Edwin P. Hoyt, *Inferno: The Fire Bombing of Japan* (Madison Books, 2000); James McClain, *Japan: A Modern History* (W. W. Norton & Company, 2002); David Flath, *The Japanese Economy*, third edition (Oxford University Press, 2014); Mark Peattie, *Ishiwara Kanji and the Japanese Army* (Princeton University Press, 1972). On the Allied Occupation, see John Dower, *Embracing Defeat: Japan in the Aftermath of World War II*, new edition (Penguin, 2000); Ian Inkster, *Japanese Industrialisation: Historical and Cultural Perspectives* (Psychology Press, 2001); McClain, *Japan*; Christopher Harding, *Japan Story: In Search of a Nation, 1850 to the Present* (Allen Lane, 2018); Alisa Gaunder (ed.), *The Routledge Handbook of Japanese Politics* (Routledge, 2011); Vera Mackie, *Feminism in Modern Japan: Citizenship, Embodiment and Sexuality* (Cambridge University Press, 2003). On Misora Hibari's life and Japan's early post-war music culture, see Takeshima Shigaku, '*Misora Hibari Gaku' nyūmon kōza: karizumasei no miryoku to wa nani ka* (Nisshin-Hōdō, 1997) [in Japanese]; Saitō Mitsuru, *Eiga de shiru Misora Hibari to sono jidai: ginmaku no joō ga tsutaeru Showa no ongaku bunka* (Stylenote, 2013) [in Japanese]; Deborah Shamoon, 'Misora Hibari and the Girl Star in Postwar Japanese Cinema', *Signs* 35/1 (2009) and 'Recreating Traditional Music in Postwar Japan: A Prehistory of Enka', *Japan Forum* 26/1 (2014); Christine R. Yano, 'From Child Star to Diva: Misora Hibari as Postwar Japan', in Laura Miller and Rebecca Copeland (eds), *Diva Nation: Female Icons from Japanese Cultural History* (University of California Press, 2018); E. Taylor Atkins, *A History of Popular Culture in Japan: From the Seventeenth Century to the Present* (Bloomsbury, 2017), and *Blue Nippon: Authenticating Jazz in Japan* (Duke University Press, 2011); Christine Yano, *Tears of Longing: Nostalgia and the Nation in Japanese Popular Song* (Harvard University Press, 2002); Joanne Izbicki, 'Singing the Orphan Blues: Misora Hibari and the Rehabilitation of Post-Surrender Japan', *Intersections: Gender & Sexuality in Asia and the Pacific* 16 (2008); Michael K. Bourdaghs, *Sayonara Amerika, Sayonara Nippon: A Geopolitical Pre-History of J- Pop* (Columbia University Press, 2012). On film, see Donald Richie, *A Hundred Years of Japanese Film*, revised and updated edition (Kodansha America, 2012). A post-war study of Yosano Akiko's anti-war poem is cited in Steve Rabson, 'Yosano Akiko on War: To Give One's Life or Not: A Question of Which War', *The Journal of the Association of Teachers of Japanese* 25/1 (1991). For Graham Greene's comments on Shirley Temple, see Gaylyn Studlar, *Precocious Charms: Stars Performing Girlhood in Classical Hollywood Cinema* (University of California Press, 2013), and David

Finkelstein, 'The Dangerous Third Martini: Graham Greene, Libel and Literary Journalism in 1930s Britain', in Richard Keeble and Sharon Wheeler (eds), *The Journalistic Imagination: Literary Journalists from Defoe to Capote and Carter* (Routledge, 2007).

'If the British sucked our blood' is reproduced in Cotterell, *A History of South East Asia*. 'In the flow of the stars' is the author's translation from lyrics reproduced in Takeshima, *'Misora Hibari Gaku' nyūmon kōza*. 'More than the *sake*' and 'Over the mountain peak' are the author's translations from the Japanese originals. 'Soaking the populace in hopeless sentimentality' is reproduced in Saitō, *Eiga de shiru Misora Hibari to sono jidai*.

18 TEZUKA OSAMU – DREAM WEAVER

On Tezuka and his connections with Japan's visual art tradition, see Frederik L. Schodt, *The Astro Boy Essays* (Stone Bridge Press, 2007), and *Dreamland Japan: Writings on Modern Manga* (Stone Bridge Press, 2014); Helen McCarthy, *The Art of Osamu Tezuka* (Harry N. Abrams, 2009); Brigitte Koyama-Richard, *One Thousand Years of Manga* (Flammarion-Pere Castor, 2014); G. Clinton Godart, 'Tezuka Osamu's Circle of Life: Vitalism, Evolution and Buddhism', *Mechademia* 8 (2013); Natsu Onoda Power, *God of Comics: Osamu Tezuka and the Creation of Post World War II Manga* (University of Mississippi Press, 2009); Martin Repp, 'Socio-Economic Impacts of Hōnen's Pure Land Doctrines: An Inquiry into the Interplay Between Buddhist Teachings and Institutions', in Ugo Dessi (ed.), *The Social Dimension of Shin Buddhism* (Brill, 2010); E. Taylor Atkins, *A History of Popular Culture in Japan: From the Seventeenth Century to the Present* (Bloomsbury, 2017); Michael Wert, *Samurai: A Concise History* (Oxford University Press, 2019); Thomas Lamarre, 'The Biopolitics of Companion Species: Wartime Animation and Multi-Ethnic Nationalism', in Richard Calichman and John Namjun Kim (eds), *The Politics of Culture: Around the Work of Naoki Sakai* (Routledge, 2010); Kawamura Minato, Kota Inoue (trans.) and Helen J. S. Lee (trans.), 'Popular Orientalism and Japanese Views of Asia', in Michele M. Mason and Helen J. S. Lee (eds), *Reading Colonial Japan: Text, Context and Critique* (Stanford University Press, 2012); Kenneth L. Bartolotta, *Anime: Japanese Animation Comes to America* (Greenhaven Publishing, 2017); John E. Ingulsrud and Kate Allen, *Reading Japan Cool: Patterns of Manga Literacy and Discourse* (Lexington Books, 2010); Craig Norris, 'Manga, Anime and Visual Art Culture', in Yoshio Sugimoto (ed.), *The Cambridge Companion to Modern Japanese Culture* (Cambridge University Press,

2009); Fred Ladd with Harvey Deneroff, *Astro Boy and Anime Come to the Americas* (McFarland, 2014); Rachael Hutchinson, 'Sabotaging the Rising Sun: Representing History in Tezuka Osamu's *Phoenix*', in Roman Rosenbaum (ed.), *Manga and the Representation of Japanese History* (Routledge, 2012); Laura Miller, 'Rebranding Himiko, the Shaman Queen of Ancient History', in *Mechademia* 9 (2014); Yasue Kuwahara, 'Japanese Culture and Popular Consciousness: Disney's *The Lion King* vs. Tezuka's *Jungle Emperor*', *Journal of Popular Culture* 31/1 (1997); Gina O'Melia, *Japanese Influence on American Children's Television* (Springer, 2019). On Japan in the 1950s and 1960s, see Andrew Gordon, *A Modern History of Japan* (Oxford University Press, 2013); Christopher Harding, *Japan Story: In Search of a Nation, 1850 to the Present* (Allen Lane, 2018); Ian Inkster, *Japanese Industrialisation: Historical and Cultural Perspectives* (Psychology Press, 2001). On Sony, see Morita Akio with Edwin M. Reingold and Mitsuko Shimomura, *Made in Japan* (E. P. Dutton, 1986); John Nathan, *Sony: the Private Life* (HarperCollins, 1999). On the women's volleyball team in the 1964 Olympics, see Helen Macnaughtan, 'The Oriental Witches: Women, Volleyball and the 1964 Tokyo Olympics', *Sport in History* 34/1 (2014). On the politics of the Olympics, see Christian Tagsold, 'The Tokyo Olympics as a Token of Renationalization', in Andreas Niehaus and Max Seinsch (eds), *Olympic Japan: Ideals and Realities of (Inter)Nationalism* (Ergon Verlag, 2007). The possible influence of Hergé on Tezuka is mooted in Adam L. Kern, 'East Asian Comix: Intermingling Japanese', in Frank Bramlett et al. (eds), *The Routledge Companion to Comics* (Routledge, 2016).

'The audience for the film', 'switch people's concept of reality', 'Americans were sensitive' and 'anyone who is thoroughly steeped' are reproduced in Schodt, *The Astro Boy Essays*. 'All you see is a car running' is adapted from Power, *God of Comics: Osamu Tezuka and the Creation of Post World War II Manga*. 'The most brilliantly organized spectacle' was Christopher Brasher. See Christopher Brasher, *Tokyo 1964: A Diary of the XVIIIth Olympiad* (Stanley Paul, 1964).

19 TANAKA KAKUEI – SHADOW SHOGUN

On Tanaka Kakuei, see the English translation of his 1972 manifesto, published in the US as Tanaka Kakuei, *Building a New Japan: A Plan for Remodeling the Japanese Archipelago* (Simul Press, 1973); Jacob M. Schlesinger, *Shadow Shoguns: The Rise and Fall of Japan's Postwar Political Machine* (Stanford University Press, 1999); Janis Mimura, *Planning for*

Empire: Reform Bureaucrats and the Japanese Wartime State (Cornell University Press, 2011); Kent E. Calder, *Crisis and Compensation: Public Policy and Political Stability in Japan, 1949–1986* (Princeton University Press, 1988). On Japan across the 1960s, 1970s and 1980s, at home and abroad, see Ian Neary, *The State and Politics in Japan*, revised edition (Polity Press, 2019); Steven R. Reed, 'The Liberal Democratic Party: An Explanation of Its Successes and Failures', in Alisa Gaunder (ed.), *The Routledge Handbook of Japanese Politics* (Routledge, 2011); André Sorenson, *The Making of Urban Japan* (Routledge, 2004); Ezra F. Vogel, *China and Japan: Facing History* (Harvard University Press, 2019); Glen Hook et al., *Japan's International Relations: Politics, Economics and Security* (Routledge, 2011); Terence Lee, *Defect or Defend: Military Responses to Popular Protests in Authoritarian Asia* (Johns Hopkins University Press, 2015); Elizabeth Fuller Collins, *Indonesia Betrayed: How Development Fails* (University of Hawaii Press, 2007); Harold Crouch, *The Army and Politics in Indonesia* (Equinox Publishing, 2007); David E. Kaplan and Alec Dubro, *Yakuza: Japan's Criminal Underworld* (University of California Press, 2003); Simon Andrew Avenell, *Making Japanese Citizens: Civil Society and the Mythology of the Shimin in Postwar Japan* (University of California Press, 2010); Mong Cheung, *Political Survival and Yasukuni in Japan's Relations with China* (Routledge, 2016); Ito Peng, 'Welfare Policy Reforms in Japan and Korea: Cultural and Institutional Factors', in Wim van Oorschot et al. (eds), *Culture and Welfare State: Values and Social Policy in Comparative Perspective* (Edward Elgar Publishing, 2008); James McClain, *Japan: A Modern History* (W. W. Norton & Company, 2002); Andrew Gordon, *A Modern History of Japan* (Oxford University Press, 2013); Christopher Harding, *Japan Story: In Search of a Nation, 1850 to the Present* (Allen Lane, 2018). On Minamata disease and the environment, see Timothy S. George, *Minamata: Pollution and the Struggle for Democracy in Postwar Japan*, paperback edition (Harvard University Press, 2002); Jeffrey Broadbent, *Environmental Politics in Japan: Networks of Power and Protest* (Cambridge University Press, 1998).

'When we drink water' is reproduced in Vogel, *China and Japan.*

20 OWADA MASAKO – UNCERTAIN SYMBOL

On Owada Masako, see Tomonō Naoko, *Kōgō Masako-sama monogatari* (Bungeishunjū, 2019) [in Japanese]; Jan Bardsley, 'Japanese Feminism, Nationalism and the Royal Wedding of Summer '93', *Journal of Popular Culture* 31/2 (1997); Ben Hills, *Princess Masako: Prisoner of the Chrysanthemum Throne* (Jeremy P. Tarcher, 2007); Richard Lloyd Parry, 'A Royal

Crisis, Japanese Style', *The Independent*, 6 March 1996, and 'The Depression of a Princess', *The Times*, 21 May 2004; 'Princess Masako's "High Life" Shocks Japan', *The Telegraph*, 5 February 2008. Translations of poems and press conference comments by Empress Masako (and by Emperor Naruhito, along with other members of the imperial family) can be found at the official website of the Imperial Household Agency: www.kunaicho.go.jp/e-about. On Denenchōfu, see K. T. Oshima, 'Denenchōfu: Building the Garden City in Japan', *Journal of the Society of Architectural Historians* 55/ 2 (1996). On media attention while Masako was studying at Oxford University, see Hirai Fumio and Nippon.com (trans.), 'A Change of Heart: The Courtship of Princess Masako', Nippon.com, 8 March 2019; Hills, *Princess Masako*; Tomonō, *Kōgō Masako-sama monogatari*. For coverage in English of Masako's and Naruhito's wedding, see the various pieces featured in *The Japan Times* on 9 and 10 June 1993, and the Imperial Wedding Supplement; David E. Sanger, 'Royal Wedding in Japan Merges the Old and New', *New York Times*, 9 June 1993; 'The Reluctant Princess', *Newsweek*, 23 May 1993; Edward Klein, 'Masako's Sacrifice', *Vanity Fair* (June 1993); Bardsley, 'Japanese Feminism, Nationalism and the Royal Wedding of Summer '93'; Brian J. McVeigh, *Interpreting Japan* (Routledge, 2014). On comparisons with the British royal family, see Jeff Kingston, *Contemporary Japan: History, Politics, and Social Change Since the 1980s* (John Wiley, 2012). On Japanese politics and society from the 1990s through to the present, see Peter J. Katzenstein, *Cultural Norms and National Security: Police and Military in Postwar Japan* (Cornell University Press, 1998); Arthur Stockwin, 'Japanese Politics: Mainstream or Exotic?', and Akihiro Ogawa, 'Civil Society: Past, Present, and Future', in Jeff Kingston (ed.), *Critical Issues in Contemporary Japan* (Routledge, 2014); Ian Neary, *The State and Politics in Japan*, revised edition (Polity Press, 2019); Kingston, *Contemporary Japan: History, Politics, and Social Change Since the 1980s*; Ian Reader, *Religious Violence in Contemporary Japan: The Case of Aum Shinrikyō* (Curzon Press, 2000); David Pilling, *Bending Adversity: Japan and the Art of Survival* (Allen Lane, 2014); Andrew Gordon, *A Modern History of Japan* (Oxford University Press, 2013); James McClain, *Japan: A Modern History* (W. W. Norton & Company, 2002); Christopher Harding, *Japan Story: In Search of a Nation, 1850 to the Present* (Allen Lane, 2018). On the role of pop culture in Japanese diplomacy, see Koichi Iwabuchi, 'Pop-Culture Diplomacy in Japan: Soft Power, Nation Branding and the Question of "International Cultural Exchange"', *International Journal of Cultural Policy* 21/4 (2015). On death threats directed at Ōe Kenzaburō, see Robert Jay Lifton, *Witness to an Extreme Century: A Memoir* (Simon and Schuster, 2011). On depression in Japan, see Junko Kitanaka, *Depression in Japan: Psychiatric Cures for a Society in Distress* (Princeton University Press, 2011); Hiroshi Ihara, 'A Cold of the Soul: A Japanese Case of Disease Mongering in Psychiatry', *International Journal of Risk and Safety in Medicine* 24 (2012); Ethan Watters, *Crazy Like Us: The Globalization of the Western Mind* (Hachette, 2011). On 'compensated dating', see Sharon Kinsella, 'From Compensating Comfort Women to Compensated Dating', *US–Japan Women's Journal* 41 (2011). On 11 March 2011 and its aftermath, see Richard J. Samuels, 'Japan's Rhetoric of Crisis: Prospects for Change After 3.11', *The Journal of Japanese Studies* 39/1 (2013); Susan Carpenter, *Japan's Nuclear Crisis: The Routes to Responsibility*, new edition (Palgrave Macmillan, 2012); Gordon, *A Modern History of Japan*; Harding, *Japan Story*. On nationalism and Japan's minorities, see Kevin Doak, 'Japan Chair Platform: Shinzo Abe's Civic Nationalism', *Center for Strategic and International Studies Newsletter*, 15 May 2013; John Lie, *Multiethnic Japan* (Harvard University Press, 2004); Sonia Ryang and John Lie (eds), *Diaspora Without Homeland: Being Korean in Japan* (Global, Area, and International Archive, University of California Press, 2009); Christopher Bondy, *Voice, Silence, and Self: Negotiations of Buraku Identity in Contemporary Japan* (Harvard University Press, 2015); Ian Neary, 'Burakumin in Contemporary Japan', Richard M. Siddle, 'The Ainu: Indigenous People of Japan', and in Michael Weiner (ed.), *Japan's Minorities: The Illusion of Homogeneity* (Routledge, 1997); Brett L. Walker, *The Conquest of Ainu Lands: Ecology and Culture in Japanese Expansion, 1590–1800* (University of California Press, 2001); Katarina Sjöberg, *The Return of the Ainu: Cultural Mobilization and the Practice of Ethnicity in Japan* (Psychology Press, 1993); Glenn D. Hook and Richard Siddle (eds), *Japan and Okinawa: Structure and Subjectivity* (Routledge, 2002); Davinder L. Bhowmik and Steve Rabson (eds), *Islands of Protest: Japanese Literature from Okinawa* (University of Hawaii Press, 2016). On Himiko's afterlife in Japan, see Laura Miller, 'Searching for Charisma Queen Himiko', in Laura Miller and Rebecca Copeland (eds), *Diva Nation: Female Icons from Japanese Cultural History* (University of California Press, 2018).

'Time to think', 'After much thought', 'It is a shame' and 'I am [neither] extremely modern, nor conservative' are the author's translations from Tomonō, *Kōgō Masako-sama monogatari*. 'I gaze with delight' and 'The power of youth' is reproduced on the official website of the Imperial Household Agency. 'One of those silly little purses' is in Anna Quindlen, 'Public & Private; Happily Ever', *New York Times*, 23 May 1993. 'Japan has one ethnicity' is reproduced in Lie, *Multiethnic Japan*.

Acknowledgements

The Japanese forms a pair with a previous book: *Japan Story: In Search of a Nation, 1850 to the Present* (Allen Lane, 2018). My debts have duly doubled as a result, to many of the same people and organizations. Simon Winder and his colleagues at Penguin have been wonderful once again, transforming a few kilobytes-worth of files from my computer into a handsome finished product that I hope people will enjoy having in their hands. Martin Redfern and the team at Northbank Talent Management have been doing their utmost to convert those same files into an honest living for me. Leo Howard scouted out source materials in Tokyo when I couldn't get there myself. And my students at the University of Edinburgh have allowed me to prattle at them, as I test out my ideas. Thank you, one and all. I am grateful, too, to Jane Robertson for her careful copy-editing, to Rachel Thorne for securing permissions for the fabulous poetry and prose that appear in these pages, and to Cecilia Mackay for arranging the images.

I hope this book, together with *Japan Story*, does some justice to the many decades worth of extraordinary and engrossing scholarship on which they draw. My wife Kae and our children – Shoji, Yocchan and Hana – will attest to my fascination with it, or at least to my tendency to combine lengthy absences with tedious excuse-making. Thank you for putting up with me. I don't know how you do it.

Finally, to my Mum and Dad. Having primary school teachers for parents did occasionally make it feel as though the school day never ended. But all that precious time reading together gave words and stories a comforting power that has never faded. Thank you.

Permissions

University Press, www.sup.org; an extract from *Hasekura Tsunenaga* by Takashi Gonoi, Yoshikawa Kōbunkan, 2003. Translated by Chris Harding with permission of the author and Yoshikawa Kobunkan Co. Ltd; extracts from *The Life of An Amorous Man* by Saikaku Ihara, translated by Kenji Hamada, Tuttle, copyright © 1963 Charles E. Tuttle. Reproduced by permission of Tuttle Publishing; a Haikai from *The Life of an Amorous Woman* by Ihara Saikaku, translated by Ivan Morris, copyright © 1963 by New Directions Publishing Corp. Reprinted by permission of New Directions Publishing Corp; extracts from *Sakamoto Ryōma and the Meiji Restoration,* translated by Marius B. Jansen, Columbia University Press, 1995, pp. 118, 166, copyright © 1994 Columbia University. Reprinted with permission of the publisher; an extract from *The Attic Letters: Ume Tsuda's Correspondence to Her American Mother* by Yoshiko Furuki et al., Weatherhill, 1991, p. 14. Reproduced by permission of Tankosha Publishing Co., Ltd; three poems from *Embracing the Firebird: Yosano Akiko and the Rebirth of the Female Voice in Modern Japanese Poetry,* translated by Janine Beichman, University of Hawaii Press, pp. 141,143, 170, copyright © 2002 University of Hawaii. Reproduced with permission; four poems from 'Yosano Akiko on War: To Give One's Life or Not: A Question of Which War', by Steve Rabson in *The Journal of the Association of Teachers of Japanese,* 25/1, 1991, pp. 45–74. Reproduced by permission of AATJ, American Association of Teachers of Japanese; two poems by His Imperial Highness the Crown Prince and Her Majesty the Empress, The Imperial Household Agency website, https://www.kunaicho.go.jp/e-culture/utakai-ho5.html and www.kunaicho.go.jp/e-about. Reproduced with permission; and extracts from *Kōgō Masako-sama monogatari* by Tomonō Naoko, translated by Chris Harding, Bungeishunjū, 2019. Reproduced by permission of the publisher.

In some instances we have been unable to trace the owners of copyright material, and we would appreciate any information that would enable us to do so.

Index

Page references in *italic* indicate illustrations.

Ihara Saikaku (*cont.*)
  The Eternal Storehouse of Japan
    (*Nippon Eitaigura*) 189
  Five Women Who Chose Love
    (*Kōshoku gonin onna*) 188
  The Great Mirror of Male Love
    (*Nanshoku ōkagami*)
    188–9
  and *haikai* 178–80, 189
  The Life of an Amorous Man
    (*Kōshoku ichidai otoko*)
    173–4, 180–83, 184, 187,
    189–90
  The Life of an Amorous Woman
    (*Kōshoku ichidai onna*) 188
Ii Naosuke 203
Ikeda Hayato 364, 380
Ikeda Kikunae 281–2, 285–6, 288,
    291–2, 295–6
  and RIKEN 291, 377
  as *ryūgakusei* 286, 295
  and *umami* 280, 281, 286–7,
    292, 295–6, 425 see also
    umami (MSG)
ikki 137
ikkō ikki 138–9
Imagawa Yoshimoto 132
immigration
  to Japan 421 *see also* Korean
    migrants
  US Immigration Act (1924)
    294–5
Imperial Household Agency (IHA)
    400–401, 402, 403, 406,
    407, 411, 412, 413, 421
Imperial Rescripts 232, 271,
    318, 331
Imperial Way faction (*Kōdōha*) 310
Inada 97
Inari (fox deity) 204

India 152, 294, 418
  and Buddhism 48, 49, 113
indigo 242
individualism 306, 316
Indochina 294, 317, 327
Indonesia 384
industrial relations *see* labour
    relations
industrialization 230, 252
inequality 16, 283
  unequal marriage 275
  'unequal treaties' 252
'In the Flow of the Stars' ('*Hoshi no
    nagare ni*') 338
Inland Sea 43, 137, 206
  pirates 139
Innochō (Retired Emperor's
    Office) 75
Inoue Kaoru 207, 216
Inoue Tetsujirō 273
Institute of Physical and Chemical
    Research (RIKEN)
    291, 377
International Military Tribunal for
    the Far East 333
International Monetary Fund
    362, 418
internationalism 292, 293–4,
    295, 425
  in schooling 399
Inukai Tsuyoshi 314
Inuō 117
iron 15
  ore 327
'iron triangle' 386, 420
Ise Shrine 46, 55–6, 82,
    86, 202, 396, 406–7
Ishii Sōken 224–5
Ishiwara Kanji 296, 309, 310–11,
    317, 318, 333

rice (*cont.*)
  price hike in 1918 283
  seeds planted in deer's blood 19
  storage structures 18
  tax paid in 176, 178, 228
RIKEN *see* Institute of Physical and
    Chemical Research
Riken industrial group 377
'*Ringo no Uta*' ('Apple Song') 337
'*Ringo oiwake*' ('Apple Folk Song')
  344, 347
Ritthausen, Karl 287
rituals
  Buddhist 27, 29, 50, 268
  fertility ceremony 406
  and integration of the foreign and
    the domestic 31
  Jōmon era 18–19
  and *kami* 25, 27
  and the Mononobe 27
  mourning 19
  ritual dances 112–13
  ritual suicide 129–30, 151, 158,
    161, 370, 413
  shamanic 18–19
  tea ceremony 110, 140, 151, 424
  temples and ritual worship 29
  washing 63
robotics 386
  'care-bots' 421
  Doraemon 358, 411
Roches, Léon 209
Rockefeller Center, New York 390
Rockefeller Institute for Medical
    Research 291
Rokkakudō temple 95
Rome 164–7, 168
Roosevelt, Edith 274
Roosevelt, Franklin D. 317
Roosevelt, Theodore 255, 274

rubber 327
Russia 202, 252, 254
  and Anglo-Japanese Alliance 254
  Baltic Fleet 254
  Japanese agreement over Kuril
    Islands and Sakhalin 251
  Kuril Islands dispute and Russo-
    Japanese relations 408
  and Manchuria 253
  Russo-Japanese War 254–5, 256,
    273, 304–5
  Siebold accused of
    spying for 219
  Soviet–Japanese Joint Declaration
    of 1956 and new Russian
    Federation 407
  and Triple Intervention 253
  see also Soviet Union
ryūgakusei 285, 286, 295
ryūkōka ('popular song') 336
Ryūkyū islands 155, 251, 294
  see also Okinawa
Ryūmonsha ('Dragon Gate
    Society') 248

Sado Island 103, 121–2
Sagawa Kyūbin 391–2, 409
Saichō 48–9, 50, 91
Saigō Takamori 207, 216, 266
Saigon 244
St Hilda's College, Oxford 271, 272
St Tropez 164
Saipan, Battle of 328–9
Sakai (city) 300, 303
Sakai Yoshinori 363
Sakamoto family 193, 198
  Gompei 198
  Hana 377–8
  Otome 193, 198, 204, 205, 212
  Ryōma *see* Sakamoto Ryōma

zaibatsu (family-controlled
    conglomerates) 249,
    333–4, 361
Zeami Motokiyo *106*, 107–24,
    129, 424
  adaptation of play by his father,
    Kan'ami 122–4
  and Ashikaga Yoshimitsu
    113–14, 115, 116–17
  and Ashikaga Yoshinori
    121, 129
  Atsumori 119, 132, 189
  cultural and historical back-
    ground to work of
    109–16
  exiled to Sado Island 121–2, 375
  mugen nō 119
  Tadanori 119
  *The Transmission of Style and
    the Flower (Fūshikaden)*
    118, 121

warrior plays 118–19
The Well-Cradle (Izutsu)
    107–9, 119
*Wind Through the Pines (Matsu-
    kaze)* 281
'woman' plays 119
and Zen 120–21
Zeami Motomasa 121
Zeami Motoyoshi 121
Zen 102, 116
  monks 116
  'no-mind' *(mushin)* 120–21
  Rinzai 102, 115–16
  and samurai 116
  Sōtō 102
  and Zeami Motokiyo 120–21
Zenchiku 121
Zenran 100
Zhang Zuolin 309
Zhou Enlai 383
zoku (policy 'tribes') 387